In this landmark volume, Walter Kintsch presents a theory of human text comprehension that he has refined and developed over the past 20 years. Characterizing the comprehension process as one of constraint satisfaction, this comprehensive theory is concerned with mental processes – not primarily with the analysis of materials to be understood. The author describes comprehension as a two-stage process: first, approximate, inaccurate representations are constructed via context insensitive construction rules, which are then integrated via a process of spreading activation.

In Part I, the general theory is presented and an attempt is made to situate it within the current theoretical landscape in cognitive science. In the second part, many of the topics are discussed that are typically found in a cognitive psychology text. How are word meanings identified in a discourse context? How are words combined to form representations of texts, both at the local and global level? How do texts and the mental models readers construct from them represent situations? What is the role of working memory in comprehension? The book addresses how relevant knowledge is activated during reading and how readers recognize and recall texts. It then draws implications of these findings for how people solve word problems, how they act out verbal instructions, and how they make decisions based on verbal information.

Comprehension is impressive in its scope, bringing in relevant ideas from all of cognitive science. It presents a unified, sophisticated theory backed by a wealth of empirical data.

D1598504

Comprehension

Comprehension

A paradigm for cognition

Walter Kintsch
University of Colorado, Boulder

CAMBRIDGE
UNIVERSITY PRESS

CAMBRIDGE UNIVERSITY PRESS
Cambridge, New York, Melbourne, Madrid, Cape Town, Singapore, São Paulo

Cambridge University Press
32 Avenue of the Americas, New York, NY 10013-2473, USA

www.cambridge.org
Information on this title: www.cambridge.org/9780521583602

First published 1998
Reprinted 2000, 2003, 2007

Printed in the United States of America

A catalog record for this publication is available from the British Library.

Library of Congress Cataloging in Publication Data

Kintsch, Walter, 1932–
Comprehension : a paradigm for cognition / Walter Kintsch.
    p.   cm.
Includes bibliographical references and index.
ISBN 0-521-58360-8 (alk. paper). – ISBN 0-521-62986-1 (pbk.: alk. paper)
1. Comprehension.   I. Title.
BF325.K56   1997
153 – dc21   97-26406
                                                                    CIP

ISBN   978-0-521-58360-2 hardback
ISBN   978-0-521-62986-7 paperback

For Eileen

Contents

Preface   *page* xiii
Acknowledgments   xv

1. Introduction   1
    1.1.   Understanding and comprehension   2
    1.2.   A paradigm for cognition   3
    1.3.   The architecture of cognition   5
    1.4.   The goals and scope of the book   7

I. **The theory**   11

2. Cognition and representation   13
    2.1.   Multiple representations: How the mind
           represents the world   13
           2.1.1.   Types of mental representation   15
           2.1.2.   The evidence for levels of
                    representations   19
           2.1.3.   Implications   30
    2.2.   Propositional representations: How science
           represents the mind   32
           2.2.1.   Features, semantic nets, and schemas   34
           2.2.2.   The predicate–argument schema:
                    Networks of propositions   37
           2.2.3.   Encapsulated meaning   42
           2.2.4.   Imagery   44
3. Propositional representations   49
    3.1.   The propositional representation of text   49
           3.1.1.   The microstructure   50

	3.1.2.	The macrostructure	64
	3.1.3.	The psychological reality of propositions	69
3.2.		The propositional representation of knowledge	73
	3.2.1.	The construction of meaning: Concepts	74
	3.2.2.	Emergent structures	82
3.3.		Latent semantic analysis: A vector representation	86
4.		Modeling comprehension processes: The construction–integration model	93
4.1.		Construction and integration	96
4.2.		Processing cycles in text comprehension	101
4.3.		Textbase and situation model	103
	4.3.1.	Imagery as a situation model	108
	4.3.2.	A script-based situation model	111
4.4.		Earlier versions of the model	118

II. Models of comprehension — 121

5.		Word identification in discourse	123
5.1.		The construction of word meanings	123
	5.1.1.	From the retina to working memory	124
	5.1.2.	Homographs	128
	5.1.3.	Local and global priming in discourse: What words mean	130
	5.1.4.	A simulation of priming effects in discourse	136
5.2.		Anaphora	144
	5.2.1.	The psycholinguistics of anaphora resolution	144
	5.2.2.	Anaphora resolution in the CI model	149
5.3.		Metaphor	157
6.		Textbases and situation models	167
6.1.		Parsing	168
6.2.		Macrostructure formation	174
	6.2.1.	Signaling the macrostructure	177
	6.2.2.	Dominance of the macrostructure: Contradictions in the text	181

Contents

6.2.3. Macrostructures as vectors in the
LSA space 184
6.3. Inferences 188
6.3.1. Classification of inferences 189
6.3.2. Inference generation during
discourse comprehension 193
6.3.3. Time course for constructing
knowledge-based inferences 198
6.3.4. The construction of situation
models 198
6.4. Spatial situation models 199
6.5. Literary texts 204
6.5.1. Versification as a source of
constraints 206
6.5.2. Multilevel situation models 209
6.5.3. Comprehension strategies for
literary language 211
7. The role of working memory in comprehension 215
7.1. Working memory and skilled memory 217
7.2. Long-term working memory in text
comprehension 221
7.3. Retrieval structures in the CI model 224
7.3.1. Episodic text memory during
comprehension 224
7.3.2. The activation of knowledge
during comprehension 227
7.3.3. The short-term memory buffer 234
7.4. An LSA model of retrieval structures 235
7.5. Capacity differences in working memory? 238
8. Memory for text 247
8.1. Recognition memory 247
8.1.1. List-learning data and theory 247
8.1.2. Sentence recognition 251
8.2. Recall and summarization 264
8.2.1. Simulations of story recall 268
8.2.2. Evaluation of summaries 277
9. Learning from text 282
9.1. What makes for a good reader? 282
9.1.1. Decoding skills 282

	9.1.2.	Language skills	284
	9.1.3.	Domain knowledge	287
9.2.		Learning and memory	290
	9.2.1.	Textbase and situation model	291
	9.2.2.	Learning	293
9.3.		The measurement of learning	295
9.4.		A simulation of learning with the CI model	302
9.5.		Using coherent text to improve learning	307
9.6.		Improving learning by stimulating active processing	313
9.7.		Matching students with instructional texts	323
9.8.		Educational implications	327
10.		Word problems	332
10.1.		Word arithmetic problems	333
	10.1.1.	Schemas for solving word arithmetic problems	334
	10.1.2.	Error simulation	339
	10.1.3.	Situation models	345
	10.1.4.	The CI model for word problem solving	347
	10.1.5.	The emergence of schemas	354
10.2.		Word algebra problems	358
	10.2.1.	Algebraic schemas	359
	10.2.2.	A model for word algebra problems	360
	10.2.3.	The ANIMATE tutor for solving word algebra problems	364
11.		Beyond text	371
11.1.		Action planning	372
	11.1.1.	Routine actions	372
	11.1.2.	Novices and experts	381
	11.1.3.	Simulation of errors	387
11.2.		Problem solving, decision, and judgment	394
	11.2.1.	The role of comprehension in problem solving and decision making	394
	11.2.2.	Impression formation	402

Contents

11.3. The representation of the self in working
memory   409
    11.3.1. Evaluative and motivational
    functions of self representation   413
    11.3.2. Cognition and emotion   419
11.4. Outlook   421

References   425
Name Index   449
Subject Index   459

Preface

A few years ago some of my friends, colleagues, and former students put together a book entitled *Discourse Comprehension,* with chapters that relate in some way to work that I have done in this area. They are excellent chapters and illustrate how far research on discourse processes has advanced in the last few decades. Building on and incorporating earlier work in linguistics and philosophy, cognitive scientists have gained new insights about how language is understood and have refined their experimental methods and elaborated their theories. Indeed, although the contributors to that book did not represent a single or uniform theoretical viewpoint, it seemed to me that the current research on discourse comprehension in cognitive science, at least in the section represented there, could be brought under a unifying, overarching theoretical framework. In fact, I thought I knew what that framework could be – the construction–integration (CI) model of comprehension that I had been developing. More than that, I believed that that framework was broad and powerful enough to include related areas in cognitive psychology beyond discourse comprehension proper.

The only problem was that this framework was nowhere stated explicitly and in detail. I had published the basic ideas, and several applications of the model had also appeared in the last few years, but a complete and coherent treatment was lacking. Although it seemed that the CI model could provide an account for many interesting findings in the study of cognition, in many cases the actual work of developing and testing a detailed simulation of the phenomena in question had not yet been done. So I, could not even be sure that the model was really as powerful as I surmised. Worse, the applications that had been done were often published in inaccessible places, making it difficult for a reader to gain an understanding of the scope of the model and to evaluate its effectiveness. Furthermore, even if a reader studied all the available publications, it would not have been easy to arrive at a coherent picture, because in the published papers each application of the model stood by itself, and the all-important links between them were rarely made explicit.

Therefore, this book was written to present to my colleagues and students interested in discourse comprehension a coherent and broad theoretical framework to better investigate its effectiveness. In so doing I had to explore for myself just how adequate this framework was: Could it really do all the things claimed for it? Readers are entitled to their own answers, but I became more and more convinced of the power of CI architecture as I continued to explore new issues in discourse comprehension within that framework. In fact, I came to realize that the framework I proposed applies not only to discourse comprehension but also to a broader range of issues in the study of cognition in general.

Thus, my own goals changed as I engaged more deeply with the research for this book. I realized that not only discourse comprehension but also other cognitive processes may be viewed from the vantage point of the CI model. I became interested in just how far the domain of the comprehension paradigm extends. Comprehension is modeled as a constraint satisfaction process in the CI model. It is apparent now that some other cognitive processes, such as action planning and decision making, can be modeled in the same way. Hence, the title of this book, which suggests that comprehension can serve as a theoretical paradigm for a wider range of cognitive processes. It does not encompass all of cognition – there are truly analytic thinking processes that are beyond the range of the CI model. Such is the case even in the discourse area itself. For instance, certain kinds of inference processes require conscious, active problem solving rather than mere constraint satisfaction. But on the other hand, I was able to show that most of what goes under the label of inference in discourse comprehension can in fact be accounted for within the proposed framework.

Writing this book thus became a quest to determine the limits of the comprehension paradigm. I am still not quite sure where these limits lie, except that they are farther out than most psychologists had assumed. Further study will be required to explore in depth some of the suggestions made here, but I think that the usefulness of the comprehension paradigm for the study of cognitive processes has been established.

Acknowledgments

The research reported here could not have been performed without the long-term support afforded by a Merit Award from the National Institute of Mental Health, grant MH-15872. Additional support has been received in the past ten years for various special projects: from the National Science Foundation (with James G. Greeno) for the work on word arithmetic problems, from the National Science Foundation (with Gerhard Fischer, Clayton Lewis, and Peter G. Polson) and the Army Research Institute (with Fischer) for the research on action planning, from the Mellon Foundation (with Eileen Kintsch) for the research on learning from texts, and from the McDonnell Foundation (with Fischer and Thomas K. Landauer), and from DARPA (with Landauer) for the exploration of the Latent Semantic Analysis technique. I am deeply grateful to these institutions for permitting us to develop and evaluate the ideas about discourse comprehension that eventually led to this book.

The University of Colorado has been blessed with an exceptional group of graduate students, several generations of whom participated in this endeavor. Their dedication and enthusiasm, experimental and modeling skills, but above all their fresh ideas and infectious inquisitiveness, have profoundly shaped this research program. It is one the great pleasures of being a professor to be able to collaborate with an ever changing but eternally young team of the brightest and the best. Among the students and post-docs who were associated most closely with the work described here are, in roughly chronological order: Randy Fletcher, Chuck Weaver, Ernie Mross, Susan Zimny, Suzanne Mannes, Walter Perrig, Denise Cummins, Kurt Reusser, Franz Schmalhofer, Stephanie Doane, Jose Otero, Isabelle Tapiero, Mitch Nathan, Danielle McNamara,

Evelyn Ferstl, Marita Franzke, Julia Moravcsik, Mike Wolfe, Dave Stein-hart, and Missy Schreiner.

The Institute of Cognitive Science and the Department of Psychology at the University of Colorado has provided an ideal environment for my work. I am deeply indebted to my colleagues for many stimulating discussions and arguments. I could not have worked without their feedback, whether critical or encouraging. Over the years, Peter Polson has been a most valuable partner in this respect. I also want to mention two specific collaborations that had a significant influence on the work presented in this book. My former colleague Anders Ericsson and I became intrigued with the functioning of working memory, which resulted in the theory of long-term working memory – ideas that put a whole new twist on our understanding of discourse comprehension. Last, I gratefully acknowledge my debt to Tom Landauer who introduced me to latent semantic analysis (LSA) and who has been my companion in exploring this exciting new technique.

My intellectual debts are owed not only to my collaborators at Colorado but also to a much broader group of researchers in psychology, cognitive science, and education. I shall not try to list them here, but I want to express my appreciation and my hope that in the pages that follow I always have given credit where credit is due.

Special thanks, however, go to those who read and criticized one or more of the chapters of this book: Anders Ericsson, Tom Landauer, Akira Miyake, Peter Polson, Paul van den Broek, and Sashank Varma. I also thank Julia Hough of Cambridge University Press for her interest and support.

This book is dedicated to my wife and co-worker, Eileen Kintsch. She has been my supporter, research collaborator, discussion partner, critic, and editor – not only on this project but throughout many wonderful joint years. This book would certainly not exist without her. I only hope that she and the many others who helped me with this book will be happy with what it has become.

Walter Kintsch

1

Introduction

The study of thinking has been characterized by a multitude of different approaches, first in philosophy and the arts, later in science. Many scientific disciplines today are concerned in one way or another with the study of thinking, or higher-level cognition, the somewhat fuzzy term currently preferred in cognitive science and cognitive psychology.

If one looks at books on thinking in those areas, they are most frequently compendiums of observations that people have made about the phenomena of thinking, both anecdotal observations and laboratory investigations, descriptive as well as prescriptive, interspersed with some more or less formal and more or less speculative theories focused on particular phenomena. During the last 100 years, scientists have mostly left global theorizing about human cognition to philosophers. On the whole that has proved to be a wise choice, in that this focus on the specific has helped us to acquire much solid information about cognition in that time, unhampered by too many false theoretical starts. Nevertheless, even good data are not totally satisfying if they are not tied together within some theoretical framework, and in recent years interest in global frameworks for cognition – architectures of cognition – has resurfaced.

Indeed, Newell (1990) has argued that we might miss something essential if we focus too much on the facts and unrelated minitheories. Explanations of complex cognitive processes have too many degrees of freedom. That is, there are too many ways to explain a local phenomenon, so that it is not possible to tell which one is right or best. One way out of this dilemma is to develop a single theory that explains many different local phenomena, preferably all the phenomena of cognition, in the same way. That is, we look for a general architecture that would allow us to develop principled models of particular phenomena in such a way that the individual models constrain and support one another. Newell's own work and the research program of J. R. Anderson are stellar examples of this approach to cognitive science (Anderson, 1983, 1993; Newell, 1990).

Comprehension may be another paradigm for cognition, providing us with a fairly general though perhaps not all-encompassing framework within which cognitive phenomena can be explained. Since Newell and Simon's groundbreaking book, *Human Problem Solving* (1972), problem solving has been the paradigm for the higher cognitive processes, in particular these authors' conceptualization of problem solving as search in a problem space. The task of the problem solver is conceived of as finding a solution path in a large, complex problem space full of dead ends. This has been an extremely successful way of thinking about human cognition. But it may be that for at least some cognitive processes there are alternative conceptualizations that could be fruitfully explored. For instance, one can look at cognition, at least certain forms of cognition, as a constraint–satisfaction, or comprehension, process instead. In this book, I work out a constraint–satisfaction theory of comprehension and show how this kind of cognitive architecture can serve as a paradigm for much of cognition.

1.1 Understanding and comprehension

The terms *understanding* and *comprehension* are not scientific terms but are commonsense expressions. As with other such expressions, their meaning is fuzzy and imprecise. To use them in a scientific discourse, we need to specify them more precisely without, however, doing undue violence to common usage. First, understanding and comprehension are used as synonyms here. The choice of one or the other term is thus purely a matter of linguistic variation.

But just what do we mean by either *understanding* or *comprehension?* What seems most helpful here is to contrast understanding with perception on the one hand and with problem solving on the other. In ordinary usage, *perceive* is used for simple or isolated instances of perception, especially when no specific action is involved. *Understand* is used when the relationship between some object and its context is at issue or when action is required. The boundaries between the two terms are certainly fuzzy, however. *Understanding* is clearly the preferred term when a perception involves language.

Both perception and understanding can each be described as a process of constraint satisfaction. Given a certain environmental configuration and a particular state of an organism, including its knowledge and goals, the organism responds with either an overt action in the environment or a mental event that in turn may be related to an action. The features of the environment and relevant organismic factors are processed in parallel in an automatic way, with relatively little demand on resources. Although the end result is conscious, the processes themselves are not. Problem solving, or thinking, in contrast, is typically under conscious control and is resource demanding and sequential. Constraint satisfaction is still a requirement, but the constraints are not directly given in the environment and by the organism; they must first be generated through possibly complex procedures. Perception and understanding are the processes people normally use; when an impasse develops in perception or understanding, they resort to problem solving as a repair process.

We see this process occurring in concurrent verbal reports during reading. The reports yield little information beyond the actual content of the text being read, as long as reading proceeds normally. When it breaks down, however, because a reader does not understand something, rich verbal reports are obtained about the problem-solving processes needed to repair the impasse (Ericsson & Simon, 1993).

1.2 A paradigm for cognition

We have thus defined comprehension by pointing to phenomena that people commonly label as such. It makes little difference that some people use the term *comprehension* in slightly different ways than others do. Indeed, by the end of this book, the reader might be even less certain just where comprehension starts and where it ends, for I argue that comprehension provides a good paradigm for areas of cognition that have not traditionally been viewed from this vantage point (e.g., in chapter 11, action planning, which is usually treated as problem solving). The paradigm I am speaking of is not the fuzzy commonsense notion of comprehension but the theory of comprehension that is developed in the following pages.

What are the distinctive features of this theory? First, it is a psychological process theory. That is, it is concerned with the mental processes involved in acts of comprehension – not primarily with the analysis of the material that is to be comprehended. Applied to text comprehension, this means that it is not a theory of text structure, or a text analysis. The text structure is only indirectly important, in that it is one determinant of the comprehension process and therefore of the product of this process: the mental representation of the text and actions based on this construction.

Second, at the most general level the theory characterizes the comprehension process as one of constraint satisfaction. Comprehension occurs when and if the elements that enter into the process achieve a stable state in which the majority of elements are meaningfully related to one another and other elements that do not fit the pattern of the majority are suppressed. The theory thus must specify what these elements are and how they reach a stable configuration.

All kinds of elements enter into the comprehension process. In commonsense terms, these may be perceptions, concepts, ideas, images, or emotions. We need a way to deal with all these in the theory. A propositional representation will be described that provides a common notation for these elementary units of the comprehension process and for the description of the relations among them.

A crucial consideration is where these elements come from: from the world via the perceptual system, as well as from the organism in the form of memories, knowledge, beliefs, body states, or goals. At the heart of the theory is a specific mechanism that describes how elements from these two sources are combined into a stable mental product in the process of comprehension.

Roughly, the story goes like this. We start with a comprehender who has specific goals, a given background of knowledge and experience, and a given perceptual situation. The perceptual situation may, for instance, be the printed words on a page of text. We mostly skip the question of how the reader forms basic idea units from these words (though we deal extensively with word identification in a discourse context and, at least tangentially, with the question of how sentences are parsed into their constituents). Given these idea units in the form of propositions as well as the reader's goals, associated elements from the reader's long-term memory (knowledge, experience) are retrieved to form an interrelated network together with the already existing perceptual elements. Because this retrieval is entirely a bottom-up process, unguided by the larger discourse context, the nascent network will contain both relevant and irrelevant items. Spreading activation around this network until the pattern of activation stabilizes works as a constraint–satisfaction process, selectively activating those elements that fit together or are somehow related and deactivating the rest. Hence, the name of the theory, the construction–integration (CI) theory: A context-insensitive construction process is followed by a constraint–satisfaction, or integration, process that yields if all goes well, an orderly mental structure out of initial chaos.

1.3 The architecture of cognition

The theory presented here is a proposal for an architecture of cognition. That is, it is a collection of specific models, all employing the same general architectural framework. Thus, it is quite possible to develop alternative models within that framework, that is, models that differ in their specific implementations but that share a common architecture. Hence, a model may be inadequate not because of its basic architecture but for the way it has been realized within that architecture, for every model involves assumptions that are situation-specific and not dictated by the basic cognitive architecture. On the other hand, the architecture itself is not directly testable. Only cumulative experience with many different models involving a broad range of psychological phenomena allows us to determine the usefulness of a cognitive architecture.

The features that are most characteristic of the architecture that is proposed and explored here are (1) assumptions about the mental representation of texts and knowledge and (2) processing assumptions about comprehension. Both texts and knowledge are represented as networks of propositions (or, loosely equivalent, semantic vectors). Such associative networks are relatively unstructured and hence differ considerably from assumptions about the representation of meaning in logic or in frameworks based on formal semantics. The mind in this view is not a well-structured, orderly system but is a little chaotic, being based on perception and experience rather than on logic, being Aristotelian rather than Cartesian. The assumptions made about cognitive processes are similar: The construction of mental representations does not involve the application of precise, sophisticated, and context-sensitive rules; instead, construction rules may be crude and relatively context-free and may yield only approximate solutions full of irrelevancies and redundancies that need to be cleared up by constraint satisfaction – specifically, a spreading activation mechanism.

In recent years, since the pioneering work of Marr (1982), we have learned a great deal about the different levels at which information-processing theories can be developed (Anderson, 1990; Newell, 1990; Pylyshyn, 1981). Marr and his followers, always using a new and different terminology, distinguished three levels of psychological theory, the middle level being once more subdivided into two sublevels. The most general level of analysis is at the rational level (I follow Anderson's terminology). An information-processing theory at the rational level must ask what the goals of the computation are and must analyze how these goals can be carried out. The lowest level of analysis is the biological level, which consists of an account of cognition in terms of the organism's underlying brain processes. In between these two extremes is the more typical psychological information-processing theory that is concerned with the nature of mental representations and the computations that are performed on these representations. At this level, the theorist is concerned with cognitive algorithms and their implementation. A cognitive algorithm is a specification of all the steps in a cognitive process, the states of the system at each point in time, and their transformations. The implementation is a particular mechanism that achieves these transformations. A cognitive architecture can be described as a recipe for constructing implementations of a cognitive algorithm. In the case of the CI architecture, it requires the theorist to use simple, bottom-up rules to construct a preliminary but incoherent propositional network, followed by a spreading activation process that integrates this network into a coherent mental representation.

The problem for information-processing theories has been and continues to be the identifiability of the mechanisms postulated. There are many ways to achieve a goal, and more to implement them. How can we be sure the one we happen to think of is the right one? It may explain the data, but so might many other mechanisms. As Anderson (1990) points out, this is a particular problem at the implementation level. At the algorithm level, there are at least behavioral data that can be directly compared to the proposed steps of the algorithm, but the implementational mechanisms of our theories can be inferred only from the behavioral observations at the algorithm level. For instance, we may be able to determine that a given model correctly predicts whether readers make a certain type of inference on line, but the mechanism that produced the inference may be only partially constrained by our observations.

Psychologists have tried various ways to deal with this dilemma, including ignoring it. An obvious solution is to look to the biological level for the constraints that would disambiguate information-processing theories. Indeed, in some areas such as mental imagery and attention, something like this is already happening. Perhaps the rapidly improving methods of cognitive neuroscience will soon also yield information about such complex processes as reading comprehension and language understanding. However, it is not obvious that such primarily culturally determined processes are sufficiently distinct at the biological level to warrant their study at this level.

The rational level of analysis provides another set of constraints that are very important for information-processing theories, as both Newell and Anderson have argued and demonstrated in their work. Thus, the logical requirements of information retrieval can serve to constrain theories of memory retrieval. Certainly, information-processing theories need to find help wherever they can get it. But one need not give up hope of solving the identifiability problem at the architecture level. Although a particular model may not be identifiable, it may be possible to design a cognitive architecture capable of accounting for a wide variety of behavioral data over the whole range of cognitive psychology. If the same architecture explains many different phenomena, both simple and complex, it becomes much harder to think of plausible alternatives. Or at least there may be only a few architectures that are reasonable candidates. Newell (1990) has most convincingly made this argument in his call for unified theories of cognition. Information-processing theories of isolated cognitive phenomena, whether simple or complex, are of much less importance, however elegant and successful they may be empirically, than theories that are able to account for a broad range of phenomena with the same set of principles.

I see cognitive architectures as languages that scientists develop to talk about (describe, predict, postdict) cognitive phenomena. Some theorists may aspire to a loftier epistemological status for their theories than just a useful and convenient language. It is not a goal to be despised, however, and it is perhaps all we can do for the time being.

1.4 The goals and scope of the book

The research reported in this book focuses on text comprehension. Although I do not neglect comprehension processes in general, most of the empirical work and modeling have been done in the area of text comprehension. Furthermore, the theory of comprehension presented here is a computational theory. It describes a sequence of steps that, given certain initial conditions, yields outcomes comparable to human comprehension. Because computation presupposes a representation on which computations can be performed, the concept of mental representation and the role that mental representations play in cognition is discussed in the second chapter. Parts of this chapter are highly speculative, and a wiser author may have refrained from touching on these issues. It is important, however, that we attempt to place our work within a broader framework.

In the third chapter, propositional representations are introduced and justified. The fourth chapter discusses the computations performed on these propositional representations that form the basis of text comprehension. This first section of the book concludes with a discussion of the processing theory, the construction–integration model.

The second part of the book consists of seven chapters touching on many of the topics that are typically discussed in a cognitive psychology text. How are word meanings identified in a discourse context, including anaphora and metaphors? How are words combined to form coherent representations of texts, at both the local and global level? How do texts and the mental models readers construct from them represent situations? What is the role of working memory in comprehension? How is relevant knowledge activated during reading, and how is the information provided by a text integrated with a reader's knowledge? How do readers recognize and recall texts? What is the distinction between remembering a text and learning from a text, and what principles govern remembering and learning? What are the implications of these findings for how people solve word problems, how they execute verbal instructions, and how they make decisions based on verbal information? Thus, the book is concerned with attention and pattern recognition, knowledge representations, working memory, recognition and recall, learning, problem solving, and judgment – almost the complete range of topics in cognitive psychology. I have tried to discover for myself and to show others how comprehension theory can be applied to these phenomena. Some of this work has been published in scholarly journals or book chapters before; much of it is presented here for the first time. But even when I describe previously published work, it is set here into a general framework that did not exist earlier or that could not be as fully explicated as I have done here.

Some of the work reported in these chapters consists of large-scale, carefully executed, and well-documented experimental studies and theoretical simulations. But I have not resisted the temptation to include preliminary results and simple examples illustrating how the theory could be applied. Such illustrations are like *Gedankenexperiments* exploring the implications of the comprehension theory. They are no substitute for systematic experimentation, theoretical proof, or large-scale simulation. Yet we cannot do without them if we wish to explore the full scope of a theory, and although the reader may not want to take them as ultimate evidence, they may seduce the reader with their promise. Thus, many results are presented on the following pages, some with more assurance than others. If these pages convince the reader that comprehension is a useful paradigm for cognition, a conceptual framework will have been provided for use in following up on the issues that have been treated here only superficially, as well as for exploring the even more numerous issues that have not even been considered here at all.

Part I

The theory

2

Cognition and representation

Cognitive science and cognitive psychology focus on cognition and perforce neglect other aspects of human behavior. Nevertheless, we must ask where cognitive research is situated in the study of the human mind and human behavior. I argue here, and also in the last chapter of this book where I return to these arguments in a somewhat different way, that an all too narrow focus on cognition places intolerable restrictions on cognitive science and that progress beyond a certain point depends on our ability to redintegrate the cognitive and emotional-motivational aspects of human behavior. It is imperative to begin with a clear idea of the range of psychological phenomena that must be considered and an understanding of how they fit together.

Thinking, comprehending, and perceiving presuppose representation – of some kind. The theory of text comprehension that is the primary concern of this book mostly assumes that these representations are propositional (a related vector representation is also used on some occasions). In the first section of this chapter, I discuss the variety of mental representations that appear to play a role in psychology in general and cognition in particular. In the second section, I argue that in spite of the significance of multiple forms of representations, a theory of text comprehension that relies primarily on propositional representations is nevertheless feasible.

2.1 Multiple representations:
How the mind represents the world

Geometry was one thing and algebra was quite another before Descartes discovered the isomorphism between these two fields:

Algebraic expressions can be represented as geometric figures and vice versa. For instance, a circle that is centered at the origin with radius r = 2 can be represented algebraically by the equation $x^2 + y^2 = 2^2$.

What is gained by this transformation? For some purposes, it does not matter much. We can see in Figure 2.1 that the circle has been displaced from the origin (0,0) to a point in the upper right quadrant (4,2): We can express this change of location by the equation $(x + 4)^2 + (y + 2)^2 = 4$, but the algebraic representation is not obviously superior to the geometric. The picture is as good as or better than the equation in this case. But consider a different scenario. Suppose we want to find a square centered at the origin that has the same area as the circle. This is notoriously difficult to do in the picture domain but quite trivial in the algebraic representation: The area of the circle is $r^2 * \pi$; therefore, the side of a square with the same area must be $(2^2 * \pi)^{1/2}$. Once we have calculated this value, we can translate it back into the picture domain and draw the square as was done in Figure 2.1

Some computations are easy to perform in one domain but difficult or impossible in another. Mathematics has been enormously enriched by the possibility of representing an object from one domain in another domain and operating on it with procedures peculiar to that domain. Cognition employs the same trick.

Objects and events in the environment are characterized by certain properties and relations. Perception, comprehension, and problem solving generate mental models of the environmental objects and events, and operate on these models. The cognitive system transforms the original structures, merging the current environment with the organism's previous experience of it. The mental models generated in this way are isomorphic to the environmental structures and hence provide a basis for the interaction of an organism with the environment.

What is achieved by these representations that could not be achieved otherwise? Much as the possibility of writing an equation instead of drawing a circle permits the mathematician to use operations that could otherwise not be used (the operations of algebra), representing the human environment in a mental model allows us to make mental compu-

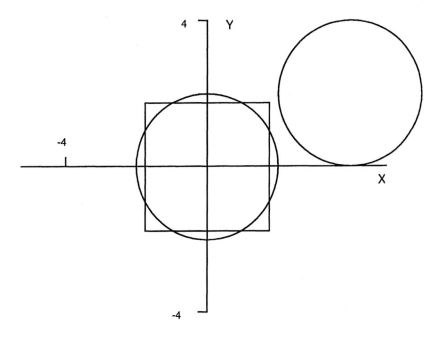

Figure 2.1

tations that are not possible in the actual environment. The environment rarely provides all the information necessary for an action. It is usually the case that human knowledge and experience are required in coordination with the environment to guide action. The knowledge representation makes this possible. At a minimum, it supplements information in the environment by filling in gaps that are unspecified. Often, however, the environmental input must be transformed in complex ways to ensure an optimal action.

2.1.1 Types of mental representation

A definitive account of mental representations does not yet exist, nor is one offered here. Instead, I briefly indicate my own views on this issue, and then discuss related or complementary positions in cognitive science and describe some of the empirical evidence for these positions, emphasizing the diversity of mental representations and their interrelations.

One can think of mental representations as forming a hierarchy of abstractness and increasing independence from the environment. The most basic forms of mental representations are procedural and perceptual representations that are tied directly to the environment. Episodic memory representations are at the next higher level. Intentional but nonverbal representations, including forms of imagery, make up the next layer of mental representations. The final two layers achieve the most independence from the environment and are both verbal: the verbal narrative level and the verbal abstract level. The hierarchy is not one of complexity, however: There are highly complex perceptual representations and very simple abstract representations. The defining feature of the hierarchy is that it changes from direct representations of the environment to ever more indirect, flexible ones that permit more and more arbitrary, unconstrained computations. The layers of the hierarchy are ordered in terms of their appearance on the mental stage, both phylogenetically and ontogenetically. As new forms of mental representations arise, the older forms do not disappear but remain embedded within the newer layer. Thus, the picture is one of gradual unfolding of the full capacity of the human mind. It is a picture the details of which are still quite vague, and as these details become better understood, some of the picture's features may have to be corrected. But the implications of the framework suggested here for cognitive theory remain relevant, even if the framework is altered in detail.

As one moves from the bottom to the top layers of mental representation, the general character of the representations changes in the following ways.

- Most significantly, the degree of environmental control weakens; stories and mathematical theories liberate man from the web of environmental dependencies.
- Representations change from sensorimotor and analog in the lower layers to symbolic and arbitrary in the upper layers.[1] In between, an image or a gesture may be used in a symbolic but nonarbitrary way.
- At the same time, the degree of consciousness increases. Similarly, the

---

1   The term *symbol* has at least two senses: (1) a symbol is defined by its referent, and (2) a symbol is abstracted from its referent and defined by its conceptual role. I am using the term here in its second sense.

degree of intentionality increases. Thus, we have at the one extreme procedural representations that are acquired through incidental, unconscious learning, and at the other extreme formal school learning that requires intentional and conscious acts.

Direct procedural and perceptual representations. These forms of representations involve largely innate systems. Many different types of affordances, abilities, and actions exist, as well as different biological mechanisms. These forms of representation can be modified through experience. Responses to environmental affordances can be modified by perceptual or procedural learning. Such learning is tightly coupled to the environment (e.g., how to tie a shoelace). Repetition and reinforcement determine the learning process within constraints imposed by the abilities of the organism and the affordances of the environment. This capacity is shared by all animals.

Episodic representations. Cognition at this level is based on episodic memory representations, that is, generalized event representations of experience that are created to guide action and anticipate changes in the environment. Event memory, unlike procedural memory, is accessible to recall and reflection, because it is a form of declarative memory. Out of event memory emerges the recollection of particular experiences, involving a certain level of consciousness and self-awareness. It permits the analysis and breakdown of perceptual events. Event memory is shared with higher animals. What is remembered and represented in memory are concrete events and scriptlike sequences of events. Learning occurs through experience and is incidental, unintentional, and goal-directed.

Organisms, such as apes, that must rely on event memory because they do not have higher forms of cognition, use signs and have a repertoire of social skills that depends on a rich episodic memory, but their actions are directly linked to the environment. Thus, cognition at this level is analytic and reflective but still environmentally bound. Human event memory is different from the "pure" event memory of apes, because humans can code their memories linguistically. Human event memory is embedded in other forms of representations. As a consequence, human event memory is tied in with higher cognition, that is, with linguistic and symbolic thought.

Nonverbal, imagery, and action representations.   These representations are sensorimotor in character but are used intentionally, often but not necessarily for the purpose of communication, especially the communication of emotions (e.g., body language). An established social community is a prerequisite for representations of this type.

Narrative oral representations.   These representations are one of two types of linguistic representation. They are verbal but not abstract. Their structure is linear, and information processing at this level is analytic and rule-governed, as in semantic memory, propositional memory, discourse comprehension, analytic thought, induction, and verification.

Much of what we know and what we learn is in the form of stories – for example, our cultural and historical knowledge. Stories are narrative mental models that allow us to learn about the world. The world becomes more comprehensible to us when we are able to tell a coherent story about it. There is again a social component to narrative learning because stories are told by someone to someone (including to oneself). Socially elaborated and sanctioned stories are the cognitive structures that hold a culture together.

Abstract representations.   Abstract representations are required for categories, logical thought, formal argument, deduction, quantification, and formal measurement. Abstract symbols are dependent on visuographic invention: written language, maps, calendars, clocks, artistic and scientific graphing, and other forms of external memory storage. Knowledge is primarily stored in the world, not in the individual brain. Biological memory carries around the code for the use of external memory, whereas the specifics are found in external symbolic storage systems. Pedagogy has always been directed at this abstract level. This is where learning problems arise and where most special instructional efforts are needed. This is what school learning is about.

To illustrate these distinctions with an example, consider the way people assign meaning to one object by transferring to it aspects of meaning from another. At the nonverbal level, an example is children's pretense play: A banana becomes a "telephone" by the child's talking into it, as adults do with a telephone. An example at the narrative linguistic level is metaphor: One concept assumes certain semantic features from another.

For example, sermons assume some properties of sleeping pills. Analogy is the corresponding example at the abstract linguistic level: Objects are no longer directly compared, but the meaning transfer depends on an abstract categorical system (the analogy between electricity and water flowing through pipes requires a precise mapping of categories).

The neat classification presented here is complicated by the fact that, in the adult human, lower forms of cognition are encapsulated by the higher forms. The types of cognition we have discussed are found in pure form in the phylogenetic development of man or in the ontogenetic development of cognition, but not in the adult human mind. Thus, people have incidental event memory, as a dog might have, but they also have explicit, language-coded event memory that is uniquely human. Even procedural memory may be language-coded, though not very well, as is testified by the inefficiency of verbally describing a tennis stroke or a skiing turn. Action representations, too, are coded with language. Thus, a modern apprenticeship situation is not purely imitational but supplemented by oral language and symbolic thought, as, for example, a graduate student doing work in some laboratory learns skills.

Conversely, the higher layers of representation that characterize the modern adult human mind do not exist in a symbolic vacuum but are based on the sensorimotor substratum that humans share with other forms of animal life. Hence, language cannot be understood only as an arbitrary disembodied linguistic system and cannot be separated from its nonlinguistic substratum.

2.1.2 The evidence for levels of representation

To keep it brief and focused, no references have been provided in the foregoing discussion, but there actually exists considerable evidence supporting a scheme like the one suggested. Indeed, that scheme is culled quite directly from the existing literature. One problem with that literature is that everyone employs a different terminology, which creates a great deal of confusion, and which is why I choose to disregard so far the literature in this discussion.

Despite differences in terminology, there exists agreement among widely varying sources for distinguishing two basic types of representation: a habit system and a cognitive system. The evidence comes from behaviorism, animal learning, perception, situated cognition, and cognitive neuroscience. I do not claim that all these people talk about exactly the same things, and if they do, they certainly do so with very different words, but there are some commonalities worth considering.

Behaviorism: S–R connections and mediated responses.   The behaviorists originally had no use for mental representations, but soon the mind crept back into behavioral theories in the form of *mediating responses.* Whereas orthodox behaviorism (Skinner, 1938) was interested in only the functional relationships that hold between various stimulus classes, S, and responses, R, most of the great theorists of behaviorism in the 1930s and '40s acknowledged the necessity of inserting a mediating representational level between the S and the R, the mediating response, r. Thus, the behaviorist paradigm changed from $S \rightarrow R$ to $S \rightarrow r \rightarrow R$ (Hull, 1943; Spence, 1956; Tolman, 1932; for a modem account, see Kimble, 1996). *Little-r* is clearly a kind of mental representation, but it is far from a full-fledged symbolic representation. For Hull and Spence little-r was still a response, at least potentially observable. A great deal of research effort was in fact devoted to measuring and observing little-r. For instance, Witte and I (Kintsch & Witte, 1962) spent many months observing how conditioned salivary responses develop in dogs that are learning an instrumental response – bar pressing for a food reward. We were able to show a lawful relationship between the act of bar pressing (R) and the mediating salivary response (r), depending on the schedule of reinforcement. It is not too strong to say that our dogs "thought" with their salivary glands! I argue later that similar concrete representations play a role in human cognition as well.

   The main limitation of the mediating response concept is its simplicity. The kinds of computations people perform with their mental representations are much more complex than the mediating response concept allows for. Unlike dogs, people have language and symbolic thought, requiring mental representations at a different level of complexity.

Animal learning: Direct and indirect representations.   Gallistel (1990) brings an ecological and biological view to the study of animal learning. A basic distinction in his approach is that between direct and indirect representations. Gallistel uses the term *direct representation* when others would say that no representation is involved at all. This is because he wants to emphasize that even in the simplest cases of learning, some change in the organism is occurring, that is, some representation of the environment is formed in the organism's neural system. Originally, a stimulus S elicits a response R_1, but as a consequence of learning the organism is changed (has formed a "direct" representation), so that S now elicits R_2. The direct representation does not involve a mediating level – it cannot be used for computational purposes. It is still direct action, tied to the environment. Only indirect representations break up the S–R link, providing the power to plan and prepare and to control the environment.

Gallistel's approach is explicitly representational. He is concerned with the "formal structure of the *represented* system and the formal structure of the *representing* system that enables one to predict results in the represented system on the basis of operations conducted within the representing system" (Gallistel, 1990, p. 582, italics in original). Among the learning processes he has analyzed, some can be described as the acquisition of direct isomorphisms between the environment and the organism's representation thereof, whereas others require indirect representations. Classical conditioning, for instance, involves the formation of indirect mental representations, according to Gallistel. It is not a direct associative process but reflects the operation of higher-order processes and involves the computation of temporal intervals, rates, and statistical uncertainties.

Perception.   Gibson's pioneering work on direct perception (Gibson, 1977) has recently been extended by Neisser to include both direct and representation-based perception. Neisser (1994, p. 228) has elaborated his position to include three perceptual modules. Two modules are direct systems and one is representational, as follows:

1. *Direct perception/action,* which enables us to perceive and act effectively on the local environment.
2. *Interpersonal perception/reactivity,* which underlies our immediate social interactions with other human beings.
3. *Representation/recognition,* by which we identify and respond appropriately to familiar objects and situations.

Module 1 is the field first defined by J. J. Gibson (1977); module 2 has been the domain of social and developmental psychologists; and module

3 is what information–processing psychology and cognitive science have focused on.

Direct perception (module 1) links the organism to the surrounding optic array. The full optic array includes movement–produced information and is highly redundant, forming a single, mathematically tightly constrained complex. Any part of that complex allows the reconstruction of the whole. The perceiver's location and movement are a central component of that complex. The organism perceives not only what *is* but what *might* be done: "Every purposive action begins with perceiving an affordance" (Neisser, 1994, p. 235). The knowledge obtained by direct perception is immediate, bottom–up, and cognitively impenetrable; it does not have to be constructed.

Interpersonal perception (module 2) is similar in these respects, but its object is not the relationship between self and the environment but the relationship between self and another person. It is highly interactive. Neisser cites an experiment by Murray and Trevarthen (1985) in which babies were observed to interact successfully with their mothers over closed–circuit television, as long as the mother directly responded to the baby. In a noninteractive condition, where the baby was shown the rewound tape of its mother, the babies quickly became distressed. What they had enjoyed before apparently was the coordinated interaction between themselves and their mother, not the mother herself.

Interpersonal perception always engages emotion. Mother and baby, or for that matter any human partners, form a dynamic, finely attuned affective system. The continuous flow of emotions in interpersonal interactions, but undoubtedly also in less direct interactions, such as occur in reading a story, functions as a modulator and motivator of cognition.

The representation/recognition system is the third module of perception described by Neisser. It ranges from classical conditioning to pattern recognition, language understanding, expertise, and problem solving. Neisser points out that recognition is always dependent on past experience, whereas direct perception and interpersonal perception are based on currently existing situations. Recognition depends on individual details and can be dissociated from direct perception. Neisser illustrates this point with the famous Kohler studies of adaptation to inverting prisms (Kohler, 1962): After 18 days of wearing left–right reversing prisms, Kohler could ride his bicycle through town, but all letters and number still looked backward to him. At that point, the direct perception system had returned to normal, allowing him to act normally in his environment, but the recognition system had not yet adapted.

Situativity: Direct action and symbolic representations. Another extension of the Gibsonian system has been suggested by Greeno (1994), who combines Gibsonian ideas on direct action with the situated cognition research coming from anthropology (Lave, 1988; Suchman, 1987).

Properties of both the environment and the organism are relevant for the analysis of the interaction between an organism and its environment. Mental representations are needed to keep track of and compute the implications of the constraints between environmental situations that an organism has experienced.

Properties of the environment that determine the organism–environment interaction are called *affordances*, after Gibson. Properties of the organism that allow it to be attuned to the environmental affordances are called *abilities*. The interaction between an organism and its environment can be described in terms of affordances and abilities that reflect the constraints existing in the environment. Affordances and abilities are therefore inherently relational terms, one being defined in terms of the other. Affordances and abilities yield smooth, efficient performance in a well-attuned interactive system.

Consider, for example, a professor who has just finished his lecture. The students are leaving. The professor gathers his notes that are dispersed on the table, closes and unplugs the overhead projector, grabs the notes and the projector, and walks out the door, all the time conversing with a student who had asked for the clarification of a point that had not been presented well in the lecture. The notes on the table, the projector, and the open classroom door provide affordances to which the professor responds without thinking. He directly understands the environment and interacts with it, cleanly picking up the notes and projector and leaving the room, without needing to recognize his notes, projector, or the door as the objects they are. He is certainly conscious of what he is doing, but he is not thinking about it, he is just doing it. He perceives the door and the floor, not as door or floor but simply as something to walk on or walk through. It is of course possible for him to stop and say, "Aha, this is a floor," but normally he just walks, which leaves him with plenty of resources to carry on his conversation with his student. This is direct action. On the other hand, the conversation itself involves symbolic representations. The professor must access his own memory of his lecture, realize just what confused the student, and reformulate his explanation in a more judicious manner. This is no longer a direct response to the environment based on some well-established ability – but neither does it require a deliberate act of problem solving. The professor "understands" what the student is saying and why, and responds appropriately.

Greeno emphasizes the social origin of mental representations. People do not think and act alone but as part of a social and cultural community. Concepts evolve out of the discourse of communities of practitioners in some particular domain. For instance, the concept of the turning radius of a car was constructed in response to certain constraints experienced by drivers and automotive engineers. It may be used quite differently by different groups of people. It may be an implicit concept – affordance plus ability of an experienced driver. Or it may be an explicit symbolic concept – for example, for the driving instructor who must explain it to students, or for the engineer who describes it with a mathematical formula. And if the engineer also drives a car, it may be an implicit and an explicit concept at the same time.

Cognitive neuroscience: Habit and cognition systems.   The idea that there are two distinct psychological systems involved in cognition and learning, direct action and representation, has attracted a great deal of attention within cognitive neuroscience. Many patients with damage to certain areas of the brain have been studied who are unable to recognize objects but behave appropriately with respect to these objects (e.g., the *blindsight* phenomenon first reported by Weisskratz, Warrington, Sanders, & Marshall, 1974). Leibowitz and Post (1982) provide a succinct summary of this research that supports a distinction between visual processes devoted to object recognition on the one hand and orientation on the other. They demonstrate this distinction by the ease with which it is possible to walk while simultaneously reading. Attention is focused on the reading material, but locomotion in most environments is smooth and troublefree. Focal vision is primarily involved in reading, whereas orientation engages peripheral vision. Recognition is conscious, whereas the ambient functions usually operate without awareness. Evidence that supports these common observations from both anatomical studies involving ablations and perceptual experiments is reviewed by Leibowitz and Post.

Mishkin and Petri (1984) and other neuropsychologists (Squire, Knowlton, & Musen, 1993) distinguish between two learning systems: a cognitive memory system and a habit system. The cognitive memory system stores information from past experience in locations where it can be reactivated by new sensory inputs. The brain areas involved are the rhinal cortex, connecting to the thalamus and mamillary bodies, and from there to the prefrontal cortex. The habit system is activated by sensory input from the sensory processing systems to the caudate nucleus and to the putamen, where the probabilities of particular stimulus–response connections are stored and updated as a result of new experiences. Habit-regulated behavior is obtained through the sequential activation of further structures in the brainstem that project to the ventral portions of the thalamus and eventually to motor portions of the frontal cortex. The content of this habit store are not neural representations of objects or events but merely response tendencies varying in strength. Thus, the two systems have fundamentally different learning and retention properties, use different circuits in the brain, and store different aspects of experience. Closely related dual-learning models have been proposed by Squire (1992), who uses the terms *declarative* and *nondeclarative,* and by Graf and Schacter (1985), who talk about *explicit* and *implicit memory.* Thus, there are many observations in the field of neuroscience that point to the same dichotomy between processes based on direct representations and those based on symbolic representations.

The literature referred to is much too rich and complex to be discussed here in detail. Instead I describe a prototypical study by Squire and Knowlton (1995), which nicely makes the main points of interest. Squire and Knowlton gave normal and amnesic subjects a probability learning task. Subjects saw on each trial several cards with unusual designs and had to predict the "weather" – sun or rain – on the basis of these cards. Each card was associated in an arbitrary, probabilistic way with a prediction; for example, a double X on top of a card might predict "sun" 70% of the time. The subjects looked at each display, made a prediction, and then were told whether they were right or wrong. After a large number of trials, they reached a performance level that was well above chance, as is typical in such experiments. There were three interesting results in this study. First, although the subjects responded well above chance, they insisted that they were merely guessing and that they did not know what they were doing; this is also typical for studies of this kind. Second, and more surprisingly, normal and amnesic subjects performed about equally well. This is a striking result, because Squire and Knowlton's amnesic subjects had severe memory deficits. In the extreme case, such subjects could remember nothing at all; even after many experimental sessions, they did not remember ever having performed the experimental task – although they had learned the reinforcement contingencies quite well, as well as normal subjects. Third, once subjects reached their performance asymptote on the prediction task, amnesic subjects remained at this level, but normal subjects showed a small further improvement with continued training. This improvement was correlated with verbalizations such as "Now I understand that the double X on top is more likely to predict sun than rain."

The probability learning task did not involve the formation of mediating mental representations. Learning was slow, based on reinforcement, and understanding played no role. The brain areas that perform this function were unaffected by the brain damage that destroyed the event memory of the amnesic patients. Thus, although the amnesic patients could not remember events such as having participated in this experiment before, their acquisition of a direct isomorphism (implicit learning, habit formation) was unimpaired. The superior representational facilities of normal subjects were of no use in this task – the experimenters cleverly manipulated the environment in such a way that there was nothing to learn except rote stimulus–response contingencies, thus depriving the normal subjects of a chance to use their superior abilities. Only with prolonged training did normal subjects start to reflect on the habit they had acquired and to verbalize their experiences and formulate rules, which the amnesics could not do. The task was rigged in such a way that reflection and rule formulation were of little help, however. Nevertheless, it is of great interest theoretically. It demonstrates that the lower habit system is encapsulated within the higher cognitive system. Our habits are not merely habits, as in a dog or an amnesic patient; we can reflect on them, talk about them, mathematize them, and so on. In Squire and Knowlton's experiment, this ability was of little consequence, but in everyday life this ability to link habits with language and symbolic thought can have profound consequences. It permits the higher cognitive systems a certain amount of control over the lower ones. If one asks a tennis player to analyze a certain stroke, he will be at a loss and ask to be allowed to demonstrate what he does; the tennis coach, however, has learned how to talk about the player's stroke, and the kinesiologist may be able to provide a scientific analysis of it.

The fact that so many investigators in such different areas have found it useful to distinguish two broad categories of mental representations suggests that we are on fairly solid ground in differentiating a *habit* and a *cognitive* system. In addition, there seems to be fairly general agreement about the need to separate *procedural representations* from *episodic memory*. The best evidence comes from studies of child development (Karmiloff-Smith, 1992; Nelson, 1996). Procedural learning tends to be unconscious and is fully under environmental control. Episodic memory may involve different degrees of consciousness and provides an organism with the earliest opportunities to weaken the direct link between action and environment.

The distinctions within the cognitive system that have been made here are based partly on Bruner (1986), who argued for a distinction between what he termed the narrative and paradigmatic forms of language use, and partly on studies of cognitive development, both its ontogeny and philogeny. In particular, it is the work of Donald (1991) on the evolution of human cognition and the related work of Nelson (1996) on child development that have strongly influenced my thinking in these matters. I briefly discuss their ideas, both as justification for the types of representations assumed here and to further elaborate them.

Cognitive development: Phylogeny and ontogeny. Donald (1991) argues that the kind of mental model of the world that an organism can construct depends on its representational facilities. He describes a sequence of four cultures, or ways of modeling the world, in the evolution of the modern mind: episodic culture, mimetic culture, narrative culture, and theoretic culture.

1. *Episodic culture.* All animals learn and have procedural memories. At some point in evolution, certainly at the level of primates but perhaps earlier, animals reach a level of awareness that makes possible declarative memory and certain limited mental representations. Episodic memory is an event memory (rather than an object memory). Nelson (1996) calls this the general event memory and shows that it is ontogenetically prior to both specific episodic memory and semantic memory. Mental models

in the episodic culture are representations that are generalized records of past experience. Such models suffice to guide actions in the present and to plan for the future, although specific memory episodes are not differentiated in this model. The organism acquires a habit to react in a certain situation in a certain way, which summarizes its past experience with that situation, but the past experiences are not separately retrievable and no abstract semantic categories are formed. As biological evolution continues, a new representational system emerges allowing for the development of:

2. *Mimetic culture.* Intentional imitation is the characteristic achievement of this stage of development of the earliest humans. This imitation is for an audience, that is, social communication is the driving force behind it. Speech appears at this stage; its function is not representation but social communication. The representation is through action, including speech action. Cultural achievements of this period are trades and crafts, as well as games, ritual, and art. Individuals are self-aware (something very rare in apes) and have a high degree of social intelligence, but the representation-through-action limits the kind of mental representations they can achieve.

At this point in human evolution, language begins to be the decisive factor in the further evolution of mankind. Biological evolution is replaced by cultural evolution. The sensorimotor apparatus of humans is not very different from that of the other primates, but the possibility of sharing knowledge, first by imitation then by the representational use of language, makes humans unique.

3. *Narrative culture.* Narrative culture is an oral narrative culture, the characteristic product of which is myth. Myth, in Donald's catalogue, is a kind of mental model that is fundamentally linguistic. As a story about the world, this kind of representation is removed from the actual world and hence is less dependent on it. More flexible computations can be performed with models of this kind. The human mind can be dissociated from its environmental context to achieve symbolic control over the world. Words and thoughts are like two sides of a coin and are inseparable. Most human cultural achievements are within the purview of narrative mental models.

4. *Theoretic culture.* This final stage is characterized by formal thought,

abstract analyses and taxonomies, formal measurement, formal science, and logic. Whereas the source of mythic culture is the oral narrative, the source of theoretic culture lies in written language and external memory devices. Thus, evolution has reached a technology-driven stage. Books, records, maps, the establishment of libraries, all have made possible formal models of the world. The human mind expands; in addition to the *engrams* of memory, there are now the *exograms* procured by our technology (though both of them are dependent on the human mind, Schönpflug & Esser, 1995). With external symbolic storage comes the need for formal education; it is no longer enough to imitate the master at work, or to listen to the stories of the elders; instead, formal schooling becomes an individual's admission ticket to the culture.

Cultural needs drive the unfolding of mental representations. One cannot have symbolic thought in an individual mind, only in a mind that is part of a certain culture. We think the way we think only because generations before us have invented the ways of thinking we now use and have accumulated much of what constitutes the specific contents of our thought. Greeno (1994; 1995) has pointed out that people more typically think and solve problem in teams than individually, but even when we think as individuals, our thought processes are shaped by our cultural environment and traditions. Bartlett (1932), one of the direct ancestors of modern research on memory, was well aware of these social aspects of cognition. He pointed out that memory is a constructive process and as such, a social act.

There exists, thus, almost a consensus about multiple levels of mental representation. The few serious attempts to argue for a single representation have lost favor among the majority of today's cognitive scientists. Skinner's behaviorism is no longer an intellectual force today. Newell and Simon (1976) once proposed as a working hypothesis that all cognitive representations are symbolic, the "Physical Symbol System Hypothesis," but Simon (1995) readily accepts the reality of multiple representations. Only some of Gibson's followers (though not Greeno or Neisser) and some of the more radical members of the situated cognition camp seem to cling to a unitary, direct action position. On the other hand, there is much less agreement among cognitive scientists about the specific types of mental models that have been distinguished here.

2.1.3 Implications

Embedding is a fact of cognition at every level. Thus, event memory is not basically linguistic, but frequently it is linguistically encapsulated. It is not the event itself that is remembered but the story told about it (Barsalou, 1993). For example, in walking through an unfamiliar hotel lobby, I notice a telephone booth and say to myself, "Good to know, I might need that tomorrow," as well as a softdrink machine, which I pass by without awareness. Later, when I need to make a phone call and am thirsty, I may remember both the telephone booth (intentional, goal-directed learning – event memory plus linguistic code) and the drink machine (incidental, non-goal-directed learning – pure event memory).

Karmiloff-Smith (1992) makes another important point: that mental representations are not only embedded but that they are subject to representational redescription. Experiences that are encoded at a lower level of representation can be intentionally redescribed at a higher level. Representational redescriptions of episodic memory at the narrative–language level is probably quite automatic and, for the adult, requires few or no resources. However, redescription at the abstract level may be difficult and resource demanding, something we learn laboriously in school, not something that comes naturally.

A number of other familiar distinctions between types of representations that are made in cognitive psychology can also be mapped into this framework. For example, the procedural declarative distinction. Perceptual memory can be considered as the most elementary form of representation. All the other representations described are forms of declarative memory. However, it must be remembered that lower forms of representations are encapsulated within higher forms, so that in adult humans, procedures may be represented at multiple levels (the example of the turning radius of cars discussed earlier).

The semantic episodic memory distinction can also be captured: Episodic memory is memory for events. All other declarative knowledge representations are semantic.

How can we distinguish between propositional and imagery representations? Event memory as well as concrete, nonlinguistic mimetic representations may involve imagery in the broad sense, that is, not restricted to visuospatial imagery. Propositions are the basic representational units at the narrative–language level, to which I shall turn in the next section.

Just as we need to broaden our concerns beyond the individual mind to the social group and culture, we must explicitly include in our analysis the environment with which the individual is interacting. This is by no means a novel observation. Simon in the *Sciences of the Artificial* (1969) has made this point very clearly with his image of the ant on the beach: If we want to understand why the ant takes a particular path along the beach, we need to know something about the ant (its motor and perceptual abilities), but mostly we need to study the sand, where the big grains are that force a detour and where there is smooth going. It is the structure of the environment, the affordances the sand provides, that determine the behavior of the wandering ant. Simon has analyzed the Tower of Hanoi problem in this way, and others have provided similar analyses (e.g., how to use a coffee pot, Larkin, 1983; see also chap. 11 of this book). Donald (1991) extends Simon's image by adding culture to it: As generations of ants move along the beach, they leave a scent trace that tells other ants where to go.

However, the typology of mental representations has even stronger implications. If symbolic thought, for instance, is indeed made possible by external devices, such as written language, then these external devices must be part of any analysis of cognition. The boundaries between the internal and external become obscured in such an analysis, as Bateson (1972) argued with his example of the blind man and his stick: The cognitive process must be ascribed to the system, not to the blind man alone or the stick by itself. This point has been elaborated effectively by Hutchins (1995), who provides a wealth of examples and detailed scientific analyses of the cognitive processes involved in ship navigation. It is simply not possible to understand navigation as an individual cognitive process. It involves team performance, and it includes the use of tools and instruments. Navigation is the product of a system that consists of a team of people, their instruments, and their social organization.

The representational system discussed here thus has the virtue of providing a framework within which some of the current limitations of cognitive science may be overcome. That, of course, is more a program for a future cognitive science than a current achievement, but it is a goal worth keeping in mind in discussing what we have achieved so far in the study of cognition and comprehension.

2.2 Propositional representations:
How science represents the mind

Les langues sont le meilleur miroir de l'esprit humain.
(Languages are the best mirror of the human mind.)

Gottfried Wilhelm (Leibniz, 1765/1949)

Der Mensch lebt mit den Gegenständen hauptsächlich, ja, da
Empfinden und Handeln in ihm von seinen Vorstellungen abhän-
gen, sogar ausschliesslich so, wie die Sprache sie ihm zuführt.

(We interact with objects mainly as they are represented by
language; indeed exclusively so, since perception and action
depend on memory images.)

Wilhelm von Humboldt (1792)[2]

We can take for granted that several different types of mental representation play a role in behavior and cognition and that some representations are embedded in others. How are we as scientists to represent these
layers of embedded representations in our theories? It is not easy to
envisage a theory of complex cognition that provides an optimal formalism for each type of representation and that adequately describes their
interactions, though for some purposes that may be required. However,
for a theory of comprehension, especially one that focuses on text comprehension, a simpler solution is available: Find one form of representation that fits everything. Obviously, a single format cannot fit everything
precisely, or we would not need to talk about different types of representation in the first place. However, there may be a form of representation that allows us to adequately approximate the various types of representation. One does not have to look far to find a candidate for such a
superrepresentation: language. Language has evolved to enable us to talk
about all the world and all human affairs and is as suitable a tool for our
purposes as we have. Not that expressing everything through language
does not sometimes distort things. It simply means that on the whole
language is the best tool we have available.

What are the difficulties that arise when we represent the complexity

2   Both quotes are from *Cartesian Linguistics* (Chomsky, 1966).

of the human mind by using language? There is the inevitable problem of distortion. Text comprehension involves primarily language representations at the narrative level. Therefore, if we find a good formalism for the narrative level, we ought to be able to deal quite well with text comprehension. However, even at the level of text comprehension, we often must deal with nonnarrative representations, especially imagery and emotion. I argue later that there are language-based representations of imagery that are serviceable, that allow us at least to deal with visuospatial imagery in text comprehension, not perfectly, but sufficiently for some purposes (section 2.2.4). Emotion is harder to deal with, in part due to the dearth of research in that area. I return to this topic only in the final chapter of this book with some very tentative suggestions.

There exists, however, a second potential problem that is more subtle. I have emphasized in the previous section the embeddedness of mental representations. Thus, the narrative–language level that I suggest here as the common format for all forms of mental representation does not stand on its own but is constructed from nonlinguistic, episodic, and procedural building blocks. A formalism suited for narrative–language representations does not by itself reflect this somatic, experiential basis of language.

Choosing the narrative–language level as the theory language is not what is commonly done in philosophy and linguistics. Instead, some form of logical system, that is, the abstract language level, is usually the choice for a formalism to describe cognition. However, to squeeze all human cognition into a logical formalism greatly compounds the distortion problem noted earlier: Compared with narrative language, logic (and comparable, abstract mathematical formalisms) is a very inflexible system, not notably suited for the representation of natural language, and even less so for lower levels of mental representation.

What form do narrative-level representations take? Natural language itself is not an adequate medium for our theory of language. What we need is a format suitable for the expression of meaning, of the semantic relations that are also expressed in natural language. Natural language serves many other functions besides the expression of semantic relations – for example, communicative and social functions. It has long been recognized in psychological research on language that it would be desirable to have a formalism for the representation of meaning that is at least to some extent independent from the way this meaning is expressed in natural language on a particular occasion and in a particular context.[3] The problem is that the same meaning can be expressed in words in many different ways. Of course, just which way is chosen in a specific context is by no means arbitrary and, indeed, is an important subject for study, but for other purposes researchers must be able to abstract from the particular words and phrases and to deal with meaning relations directly. For most of the research described in this book, it is not the words themselves that matter but the meaning they convey.

2.2.1 Features, semantic nets, and schemas

The representation system that we need must fulfill multiple functions: It must serve for the mental representation of texts but also for other memory structures, such as general knowledge, concepts and word meanings, and personal experiences (episodic memory traces). Because the mental representations of text are in part derived from knowledge and experience, it is desirable that both can be described in the same format. Four kinds of systems have been widely used for the representation of meaning: feature systems, networks, schemas, and propositions.

Feature systems were developed in philosophy and linguistics but have become enormously popular in psychology. The original goal of feature analysis was to find a finite set of basic semantic features that then could be combined by semantic composition rules to form complex semantic concepts, much as the 100-plus chemical elements are combined to yield all the substances in this world. Thus, Katz and Fodor (1963) defined "bachelor" as +HUMAN, +MALE, and +HAS-NEVER-MARRIED. Apart from the obvious objection that there is more to the meaning of "bachelor" than what is captured by these features, this program failed because it proved impossible to come up with a list of basic semantic features corresponding to the chemical elements. However, psychologists were satisfied with a weaker version of feature systems, allowing in addition to *defining features* ad hoc *characteristic features* as needed (Smith, Shoben, & Rips, 1974). In a similar vein, Smith & Medin (1981) have suggested a probabilistic feature representation.

3   Among others, Kintsch (1974), pp. 244ff.

Almost all psychological models of categorization (e.g., Estes, 1986; Rosch & Mervis, 1975; Smith & Medin, 1981) assume a feature representation, as do the dominant models of episodic memory (Gillund & Shiffrin, 1984; Hintzman, 1988; Murdock, 1982). Connectionist models typically rely on a feature coding of their input (Rumelhart & McClelland, 1986).

Feature representations are popular because they are so simple. But they are deceptively simple because they do not explicitly represent conceptual relations. People and even animals are, however, highly sensitive to relations. It not sufficient to assign to "rose" the features RED and FRAGRANT; these features are the values of the attributes COLOR and SMELL and hence stand in a particular kind of relationship to the concept that must be represented. Similarly, "break" is not defined by features such as BOY, VASE, and HAMMER, for this neglects the fact that BOY is the agent, VASE the object, and HAMMER the instrument of the action. The features MOUNTAIN, SKI, and BINDING do not define "skiing," no matter how many additional features are added to the list, because their relationship to the to-be-defined concept as well as their relationships among each other are neglected. It is true that feature representations capture some aspects of the meaning of concepts, as their successful use in so many psychological theories attests. For purposes that require more than a rudimentary representation of meaning, however, feature representations are inadequate.

The use of feature representations may be questionable on additional grounds. Features are often thought of as something out there in the real world – namely, the feature – that can be attended to, selected, and used for various psychological purposes. This seems not to be the case, however. Wisniewski (1995) has argued convincingly that features are psychological constructions and that what is constructed to be a feature depends on context, goals, and experience. Thus, a line starting from the neck of a crudely drawn human figure may be constructed as a "tie" by a subject trying to differentiate city and farm dress, but as a "row of buttons" by someone attending to the presence or absence of detail in the drawings. Theories of categorization ought to explain how people construct features; they should not start with features as representational primitives.

Associative networks have concepts as nodes and unlabeled links. They are the oldest form of knowledge representation, going back to Aristotle. In an associative net, knowledge is represented as a net of concepts linked by associations of varying strength. For Aristotle, these associations were based on temporal and causal contiguity. Later associationists elaborated on these ideas. A wide variety of experimental data support the psychological reality of such structures. For example, associative strength is commonly estimated by the frequencies of responses in free-association experiments. When people are asked in a lexical decision experiment to say whether a particular letter string is an English word or not, they are 85 ms faster when they have just seen a strongly associated word rather than an unrelated control word (Meyer & Schvaneveldt, 1971), which suggests that these associative links play a role in lexical access. On the other hand, associative nets are clearly limited in scope, beause not all knowledge can be represented by unlabeled links between simple concepts.

Semantic networks have concepts as nodes and labeled links. Links are formed by relations such as class inclusion (*IS-A*) or *PART-OF*. In the simplest case, well-ordered hierarchies are obtained in this way. The great advantage of semantic nets lies in their ability to account for the inheritance of properties and hence for economy of storage. The classic data supporting the psychological reality of semantic nets were reported by Collins and Quillian (1969), who showed that sentence verification times for sentences like *A canary has skin* were longer than for sentences like *A canary can fly*, which in turn were longer than for sentences like *A canary can sing*. These results were interpreted to mean that the verification time for statements that were derived by chains of arguments such as *Canaries are birds – birds are animals – animals have skin* is proportional to the number of steps in the hierarchy that have to be traversed (two for *skin*, one for *fly*, none for *sing*). Later results modified and qualified this interpretation in several ways. The number of steps in the hierarchy seems to be only one factor determining verification times, and it is often overridden by saliency, typicality, and frequency (e.g., Conrad, 1972). In particular, very frequent properties of an object appear to be stored directly, even when they could be derived through property inheritance in a semantic net. Various forms of semantic nets are widely used in Artificial Intelligence (AI) (Barr & Feigenbaum, 1982).

Schemas, frames, and *scripts* are structures used to coordinate concepts that are part of the same superstructure, or event. Well-known examples are the room frame of Minsky (1975) and the restaurant script of Schank and Abelson (1977). Scripts, frames, and schemas have proved to be powerful computational devices in AI. Their psychological status has been investigated in such studies as Bower, Black, and Turner (1979), which showed that readers given parts of a schema readily infer the missing components. Indeed, they often believe that they have actually read what they infer.

Schemas in one form or another seem to be indispensable theoretical constructs for cognitive theory. There has been an important change, however, in the way schemas are conceived of. For Schank and Abelson (1977), a schema was a fixed, complex mental structure that was retrieved from memory when needed and used to organize some experienced event. This concept proved to be difficult because a fixed schematic structure had to be imposed on the contextually variable, fluid events that humans actually experience. Therefore, schemas came to be thought of, not as fixed structures to be pulled from memory upon demand, but as recipes for generating organizational structures in a particular task context (Kintsch & Mannes, 1987; Schank, 1982; Whitney, Budd, Bramuci, & Crane, 1995). Context-sensitive generation ensures that the structure that is generated is always adapted to the particular context of use.

2.2.2 The predicate–argument schema: Networks of propositions

The various knowledge representations discussed above all have their strengths and all have their uses, but none of them is sufficient for our purposes by itself, for the reasons mentioned. Networks of propositions provide an alternative that combines and extends their advantages and avoids some of their limitations.

The predicate–argument schema can be regarded as a basic unit of language. It is commonly referred to as a *proposition,* a term borrowed from logic but used here in a different sense.[4] For the purpose of text representation, a proposition is simply a predicate–argument schema.

Atomic propositions (e.g., Kintsch, 1974) consist of a relational term, the predicate, and one or more arguments, written as PREDICATE [ARGUMENT, ARGUMENT, . . .]. The predicate determines the number and kinds of arguments that may fill argument slots, that is, the seman-

---

4   Some of the borrowers did not intend originally to stray beyond the boundaries of the field of logic (e.g., Bierwisch, 1969; van Dijk, 1972), but others (including Kintsch, 1974) extended the meaning of the term, in spite of the possibility of confusion with its original logical meaning.

tic role of the participants. For example, the predicate GIVE may have three argument slots, as in GIVE[agent:MARY, object:BOOK, goal: FRED]. Atomic propositions may be modified by embedding one proposition within another, as in GIVE[agent:MARY, object:OLD [BOOK], goal:FRED]], or INADVERTENTLY [GIVE[agent:MARY, object: OLD[BOOK], goal:FRED]].

Complex propositions (van Dijk & Kintsch, 1983) are compounds composed of several atomic propositions that are subordinated to a core propositional meaning. The general schema for complex propositions is given by

> Category (action, event or state):
> ├ Predicate:
> └ Arguments (agent, object, source, goal, . . .);
>
>   └ Modifiers:
>
> Circumstance:
> ├ Time:
> └ Place:

Thus, the sentence *Yesterday, Mary gave Fred the old book in the library* would be represented as:

> Action:
> ├ Predicate: GIVE
> └ Arguments:
>   ├ Agent: MARY
>   ├ Object: BOOK
>   Modifier: OLD
>   └ Goal: FRED
>
> Circumstance:
> ├ Time: YESTERDAY
> └ Place: LIBRARY

Not all expressions in the surface structure are represented in this notation (e.g., tense is not, nor is the definite article, which is a discourse signal that identifies that that *book* is known to the hearer). In general, surface structure may express pragmatic, rhetorical, stylistic, cognitive, or interactional properties, as well as additional syntactic and semantic properties that are neglected by this notation. The choice of which sentence properties to represent in the propositional notation is pragmatic: Whatever seems of little importance for a given theoretical or experimental purpose is omitted. Hence, significant differences may be found in the explicitness and completeness of propositional representations constructed for different uses.

The van Dijk and Kintsch (1983) notation in terms of complex propositions has several advantages over the earlier notation of Kintsch (1974) in terms of atomic propositions. In the earlier notation, the sentence would have been represented as follows (using [.] as an abbreviation for a list of arguments when it is clear what these arguments are):

```
GIVE[MARY,BOOK,FRED]
INADVERTENTLY[GIVE[.]]
OLD[BOOK]
YESTERDAY[GIVE[.]]
IN-LIBRARY[GIVE[.]]
```

or, equivalently,

```
P1   GIVE[MARY,P3,FRED]
P2   INADVERTENTLY[P1]
P3   OLD[BOOK]
P4   YESTERDAY[P1]
P5   IN-LIBRARY[P1]
```

Complex schemas preserve more of the actual structure of the sentence and hence some of the discourse signals the speaker wanted to convey. For example, the speaker's choice of sentence subject determines the subordination relations within a complex proposition. They also are generally easier to use for such psychological purposes as scoring recall protocols.

Texts consist of more than one complex proposition that may be related in different ways. Three levels of relationship among propositions have been distinguished by van Dijk and Kintsch (1983). By definition, unrelated meaning units do not form a text or discourse. The three levels are the following:

1. *Indirect coherence.* The meaning units are part of the same episode. That is, they share a time, place, or argument.
2. *Direct coherence.* The same as indirect coherence, but in addition the

coherence is specifically marked by separate clauses or sentences. Sentence adverbials such as *therefore, then, so, as a result,* and so on, compound sentences, or explicit coordinating connectives may be used when the meaning units are linearly ordered or when pairs or *n*-tuples are formed (e.g., cause–consequence pairs).

    3. Subordination. Various devices indicate that one meaning unit is subordinated to another. When one predicate–argument schema is taken as a specification of another (e.g., a condition), a complex sentence with a full embedded clause is typically used, represented propositionally as two underlying complex propositions. When only one aspect of a schema is specified rather than a whole clause, such as a specification of the manner of action or the property of a participant, restrictive relative clauses are used. Adjectivization signals an even stronger degree of subordination. The latter kinds of subordination are considered part of the same meaning unit, or complex proposition.

    Consider the following minitext:

(1)   The snow was deep on the mountain. The skiers were lost, so they dug a snow cave, which provided them shelter.

The propositional representation would be as follows:

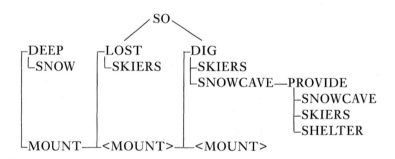

The coherence between the first two meaning units is indirect, through the shared place, because the skiers presumably were lost on *the mountain.* The coherence between the second and third proposition is direct, expressed by *so,* but in addition coherence is provided by argument overlap via agent and place, for the skiers presumably are still on the mountain. The fourth meaning unit, PROVIDE[SNOWCAVE, SKIERS,

SHELTER], is embedded into the third as a specification for one of its argument. (Propositionalizing is discussed in detail in section 3.1.1.) The predicate–argument representation of meaning has advantages over the alternative forms of representation discussed in the previous section because it is flexible enough to subsume these systems. Predicate–argument schemata are a more general form of representation within which all the alternative meaning representations described can be expressed, as follows:

1. Features can be expressed in a predicate–argument schema as in the following example: RED[ROSE,COLOR] is a meaning unit that expresses a value–object–attribute relation. (To simplify things, the redundant attribute is often omitted in practice.) We could even add a modifier, like .6-PROBABILITY.

2. Associations, of course, are basic to the kind of networks advocated here. Meaning units may be linked by unlabeled links varying in strength. That is, a propositional network is an associative network, the nodes of which consist of predicate–argument units.

3. Semantic networks are networks with labeled links. Such networks can be constructed by creating units that label the relation between two nodes. For instance, the IS–A relation between BIRD and ROBIN in a semantic net can be mimicked by a predicate–argument unit IS–A [ROBIN,BIRD], linking the nodes BIRD and ROBIN in a network.

4. Frames, scripts, and schemas can also be expressed in this notation. Thus, a concept like ROBIN can be a node in the network that is linked to all kinds of other nodes that specify our knowledge of "robin."

Writing the restaurant schema as a predicate–argument unit with embedded arguments that are themselves schemas is quite straightforward:

```
RESTAURANT
    props[OBJECTS[. . .],ROLES[. . .], . . .]
    event-sequence[ENTER[. . .],ORDER[. . .],
    EAT[. . .],LEAVE[. . .]]
```

where the ellipsis dots indicate information that has been omitted for the sake of brevity. A complex proposition like this does the same work as a conventional schema: It specifies relevant attributes and lists their default values.

5. It is also worth noting that production rules, which are the preferred representational system for procedural knowledge (Anderson, 1983; 1993; Newell, 1990), can also be written as schemas with two slots IF[. . .] and THEN[. . .].

The predicate–argument notation, therefore, is sufficiently flexible to serve as a notational variant for other forms of representation, such as features, frames, and productions. Important aspects of other forms of knowledge representations, such as the notion of defaults in schemas or the executability of productions, can be imported into this notation. The advantage that is gained by this rewriting is that all these variants can be brought together in the same format – a propositional network. Good psychological reasons can be advanced for the use of every one of these alternatives for representing meaning, but none of them is adequate by itself. By using a uniform format, one can take advantage of what all these systems have to offer without having to accept the limitations of any one.

2.2.3 Encapsulated meaning

For all its advantages, the propositional representation proposed here also has some limitations, even when it is used primarily to represent the meaning of texts. One problem arises from the fact that higher levels of representation encapsulate lower levels. Hence, separating propositional representations from the layers of representation that are embedded within them introduces some distortion. The kind of mental models people construct changes with the level of their phylogenetic and ontogenetic development. The adult human mind is a hybrid system that relies on all types of mental models simultaneously. Abstract thought does not displace storytelling or generalized event memory. Rather, they exist side by side, each with its own function. A cognitive representation of meaning should capture relevant aspects of meaning at all these different levels.

How people understand a proposition, therefore, also depends on the meaning that the proposition encapsulates. Consider the meaning of a simple statement like *red rose*. It originates from a perceptual experience of certain flowers of a certain color range. The verbal expression originally acquired meaning by the procedure of looking at a certain object and experiencing a certain color sensation. Looking at many objects of the same color, a generalized perceptual procedure red(X) is generated. Once the procedure red(X) has been acquired, it can be applied to other words, even without the actual sensory experience: *red bird* is meaningful even though I may have never seen such a bird, because I can apply the perceptual procedure *red* to the object in question. The perceptual procedure *red* has become extended, so that we now have a linguistic procedure *red*. Assigning *red* to light of a certain wavelength creates an abstract procedure that gives meaning to *red* in the symbolic system of physics. Similarly, there is a perceptual–motor procedure that is the basis for my understanding of *flying bird* and an perceptual–emotional experience that is the basis for my understanding of *angry dog,* and the extension to *flying dragon* and *angry dragon,* which I need not actually experience in reality. The point is that meaning is rooted in perception, action, and emotion. But it does not stay there, words become meaningful because of their relation to other words, abstract concepts become meaningful because of their relation to words, and so on. Lakoff (1987), among others, provides many illustrations of how abstract concepts are embodied in the pattern of bodily interactions with the world. He is concerned with the origins of abstractions, because their origins explain how we understand and use abstractions. But although words as well as abstract concepts are perceptually based and embodied, one must not forget that as words and abstractions they take on a new role and function within higher-order mental models, which have properties of their own that are not expressible by and reducible to the models at a lesser level of the cognitive hierarchy. Cognition is not all symbolic thought, but neither is it all direct action.

The cognitive-meaning representations in different types of models are not independent, however. The units remain the same at each level, or at least highly interdependent. What changes are the procedures used to give these units their meaning, varying from perceptual–motor procedures to relations among words, to abstract relations. *Red* has a procedural interpretation at the level of perceptual experience, but the linguistic *red* or the *red* of the physical model has emergent properties that are not present in the basic perceptual experience. *Red Guards* derives its meaning from a linguistic, metaphorical extension; *red shift* depends for its meaning on a complex, abstract argument.

Propositional representations of meaning are designed to capture salient semantic relations at the narrative–linguistic level of encoding, but they do not necessarily express some of the encapsulated, lower-level meaning relations. However, one should not forget that language did not evolve in a vacuum but that it is a tool humans invented in the service of action. Thus, from the very beginning, language was attuned to the world in which we live and act. Language developed to reflect the constraints of human action and human perception, probably as well as they can be reflected in any medium. Barsalou (1993) and Glenberg (1997) argue for cognitive representations that are closely tied to human perception and action – perceptual symbols in Barsalou's case and a spatial-functional medium in the case of Glenberg. However, their arguments do not speak as much against the use of propositional units for mental representations as for the need to interpret these units in terms of perceptual and spatial-functional considerations, not purely in terms of a linguistic or abstract level. One should be wary of potential distortions introduced by the linguistic medium, but we talk successfully all the time about what we do and perceive – we ought to be able to do science in a similar way.

2.2.4 Imagery

Predicate–argument schemas impose a propositional format on all meaning units. Although this format is not very limiting and capable of expressing a wide variety of structures, predicate–argument schemata are clearly most suitable for the representation of propositional information, and human knowledge and cognitive processes are not restricted in this way. Both observation and experiment have yielded incontrovertible evidence for the importance of nonpropositional representations in cognition. For instance, the well-known mental rotation experiments of Shepard and Metzler (1971) and the various studies of Kosslyn (1980) clearly show that spatial imagery is used to represent certain perceptual information. In addition, Santa (1977) provided evidence that shows that nonpropositional representations may be either spatial or linear. Anderson (1983) claims that we must deal with at least three forms of mental representations in cognition – linear, spatial, and propositional.

Whether nonpropositional representations are really needed or whether they can and should be translated into propositional representations (Anderson, 1978; Kosslyn, 1980; Pylyshyn, 1981) has been the subject of a long-standing debate. No definitive conclusions have been reached in this debate on the basis of either logical argument or behavioral data. However, Kosslyn (1994) has tried to resolve the imagery debate by considering the evidence from brain studies. The processes underlying mental imagery in the brain appear to be closely related to perceptual processes and can be clearly differentiated from verbal and symbolic processes.

Nevertheless, for many purposes – including modeling text comprehension with the construction–integration model – it is desirable to work with a uniform medium, that is, the predicate–argument schema. Therefore, imagery and linear strings will be translated into this format – not because all information is by nature propositional but because of practical considerations. We know how to work with predicate–argument units, and it is not clear how to interface linear or spatial analog representations with such units. On the other hand, the translation from the linear or spatial analog to propositional form should be done in such a way that the unique properties of the analog representations are maintained in the propositional form. That is, correspondences must be established between direct forms of reasoning that are possible in these analog systems in the propositional domain (e.g., Furnas, 1990). Thus, ideally, representational properties that are characteristic of imagery but not of verbal or propositional information (some such properties are the existence of a canonical view, symmetry biases, the hierarchical structure of space, framing effects, alignment, and perspective) should be representable in the propositional format. This is not an easily achieved ideal, however.

The best-known approach to relating propositional and imagery representations is that of Kosslyn (1980). Kosslyn distinguishes a deep, nonpictorial level of representation (names and lists of spatial coordinates) and a surface, quasi-pictorial representation in a spatial medium. Spatial information can thus be translated into propositional form through the use of spatial predicates. This procedure does not necessarily satisfy the criterion stated above that the properties of spatial reasoning be preserved in the transformation. It is not entirely satisfactory, therefore, and can only be considered as a stopgap solution in the absence of a more adequate procedure.

To illustrate this treatment of spatial imagery, a brief example from

Kintsch (1994a) will be described. Consider the sentence *John traveled by car from the bridge to the house on the hill.* This sentence involves the concepts JOHN, CAR, BRIDGE, HOUSE, and HILL and expresses the proposition TRAVEL[agent:JOHN, instrument:CAR, source:BRIDGE, goal:HOUSE, modifier:ON[HOUSE,HILL]. The visual image associated with this sentence contains somewhat different information. In particular, *John's car* might be *on a road,* and a *river* might be *under the bridge.* Thus, the representation that contains both the verbal, propositional information derived from the sentence, and the propositional translation of the image that was generated by that sentence, might look like Figure 2.2.

The spatial predicates are shown above the arguments of the propositions, and the verbal predicates below. There is no claim made that every reader will form just such an image, just as we cannot be certain that every reader will interpret a sentence in exactly the same way. The point to be illustrated here is merely that (some) spatial information can be translated into a propositional format by using spatial predicates and thus becomes an integral part of the text representation. Furthermore, the verbal and imagery information are in part redundant (*the house is on the hill*) but not entirely so. In some cases the verbal information is richer (*John travels*); in other respects the image is richer (the inclusion of the *road* and the *river*).

Thus, although we are unable to deal with imagery representations in a fully satisfactory manner, there is at least some way to deal with

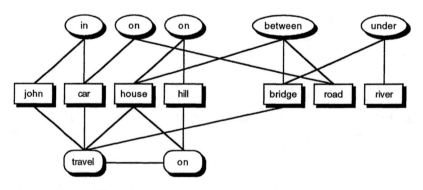

Figure 2.2

imagery in modeling comprehension processes. The problem is by no means restricted to the present model but afflicts much of cognitive science today. It is to be hoped that the results that are beginning to become available from researchers focusing on this question (e.g., Chandrasekaran & Narayanan, 1990) will provide better solutions in the near future.

Among the building blocks of cognition are perceptual symbols, imagery, and actions. The predicate–argument schema that we use for the representation of cognitive structures, on the other hand, stems from the linguistic domain. By extending it from the linguistic domain to all of cognition, from abstract thought to concrete action, we have created a unitary representational format for all of cognition. This has some obvious advantages, but it also carries some risks: The predicate–argument schema does not necessarily highlight relations that are significant in the realm of action and perception in a direct, analogous manner. The theorist has to be more careful to make sure that salient perceptual information is indeed represented. The representation format invites a verbal bias, which the theorist must try to compensate for. Nevertheless, the predicate–argument schema is not only the best we have, it is also reasonably satisfactory on an absolute scale; it is quite satisfactory, indeed, for work on text comprehension, which has a strong verbal component; and it provides an at least feasible approach for research more directly related to perception and action.

The study of cognition entails the need for some way of representing mental structures. The difficulty is that there are many different kinds of mental structures and that a good format for the representation of mental structures should be suitable for all kinds of structures. The basic linguistic meaning unit is the predicate–argument schema, and this schema can be used to represent other types of structures as well. It is a very general format that subsumes feature representations, semantic nets, production systems, and frame systems. However, predicate–argument units must not only represent abstract units of meaning but must also represent meaning at multiple levels, including the perceptual, action, linguistic, and abstract–symbolic levels. Although predicate–argument units are more suitable for the representation of

meaning at some levels than at others (simply put, it is more natural to represent a sentence that way than as an image), they can
be used generally with proper care, and they appear to be the best
format available for representing mental structures in a general
theory of cognition.

3

Propositional representations

3.1 The propositional representation of text

Psychologists studying language processing need a better representation of meaning than is provided by the words and sentences of the language itself, that is, a representation that more directly reflects the semantic relations that are crucial for how people understand, remember, and think with language. Language itself serves too many other goals, so that a representation focused on meaning is often needed for the empirical study of language processing. Propositional representations of text serve that purpose. They make explicit those aspects of the meaning of a text that are most directly relevant to how people understand a text. Such representations fall short of a complete formal analysis, but then, that is not what we need for our purposes. A cruder, but robust representational system is sufficient.

As in previous work (van Dijk & Kintsch, 1983), we distinguish on the one hand between the microstructure and the macrostructure of a text, and on the other between the textbase and the situation model. The textbase–situation model distinction refers to the origin of the propositions in the mental representation of the text. Those propositions that are directly derived from the text constitute the *textbase*. However, only in rare cases is the result of comprehension a pure textbase; usually in order to understand a text, comprehenders supplement the information provided by a text from their knowledge and experience (long-term memory) to achieve a personal interpretation of the text that is related to other information held in long-term memory. The complete structure that is composed of both text-derived propositions (the textbase) and propositions (this includes imagery and action, which we also represent as propositions) contributed from long-term memory is called the *situation model*.

The micro- and macrostructure distinction is orthogonal to the textbase–situation model distinction. The *microstructure* is the local structure of the text, the sentence-by-sentence information, as supplemented by and integrated with long-term memory information. The *macrostructure* (van Dijk, 1980) is a hierarchically ordered set of propositions representing the global structure of the text that is derived from the microstructure. It is sometimes directly signaled in a text, but often it must be inferred by the comprehender. An ideal summary is (or should be) a text expressing the macrostructure. Because summaries can vary in their level of generality, the macrostructure is also hierarchical, so that one may have macropropositions at different levels of generality (e.g., corresponding to major headings and subheadings in a text).

Thus, the textbase, with its micro- and macrostructure, is obtained from a semantic analysis of a text and its rhetorical structure, as the author of the text intended it. It is the sort of analysis linguists and semanticists perform. The mental representation of a text a reader constructs includes the textbase (not necessarily complete or veridical) plus varying amounts of knowledge elaborations and knowledge-based interpretations of the text – the situation model. Neither the micro- nor the macrostructure of the situation model is necessarily the same as the micro- and macrostructure of the textbase, for the reader may deviate from the author's design and restructure a text both locally and globally according to his or her own knowledge and beliefs.

An example may help illustrate these distinctions (after E. Kintsch, 1990). Suppose we have a text of four paragraphs, each comparing the geography, agriculture, industry, and population of two countries, Argentina and Brazil. And suppose we have a reader who knows a lot about and is much interested in Argentina but neither knows anything nor cares much about Brazil. The textbase formed by such a reader would consist of a microstructure derived from the sentences and phrases of the text, in the order they were presented in the text. It is the translation of the verbal text into a corresponding propositional structure. The top-level macrostructure would have four major subdivisions corresponding to the four topics discussed in the text. At a lower level there would be two macropropositions generalizing the information presented on each topic for both countries. The microstructure propositions would be directly subordinated to these second-level macropropositions, yielding a hierar-

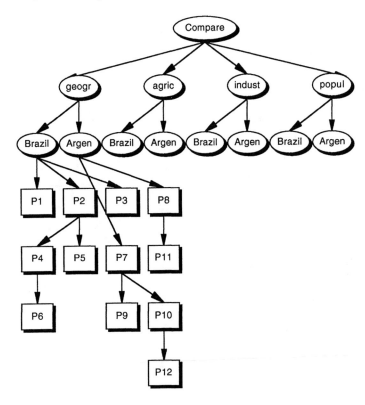

Figure 3.1

chical structure, as in Figure 3.1 (hypothetical text propositions are denoted as P_j; only a single branch of the text hierarchy is filled in). What sort of situation model might be constructed by our hypothetical reader? Because our reader knows nothing about Brazil and does not care much about it, textbase and situation model would be the same in this part of the text. However, the reader might add information from his own knowledge to the Argentina part of the text, elaborating it as in Figure 3.2, where S1–S4 are the knowledge elaborations added to the textbase. In Figure 3.2, textbase and situation model are not much different, and the macrostructure remains unaffected by the Argentina elaborations we have added. However, a knowledgeable and interested reader may reorganize his mental representation much more thoroughly. For instance, the

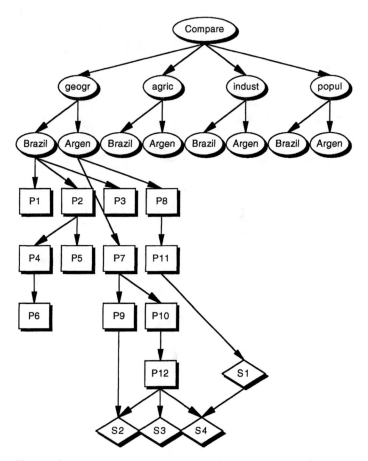

Figure 3.2

reader may structure his situation model according to countries, rather than topics as was done in the text, arriving at something like Figure 3.3.

In addition to the new macrostructure, the microstructure in Figure 3.3 has also been reorganized. Although the Brazil portion of the text remains unchanged, the Argentina part has been restructured: The propositions the reader has added from his knowledge about the country are not just added elaborations but are integrated with the text and impose a different structure from the one suggested by the text.

Which of these structures, or innumerable other variants, will readers

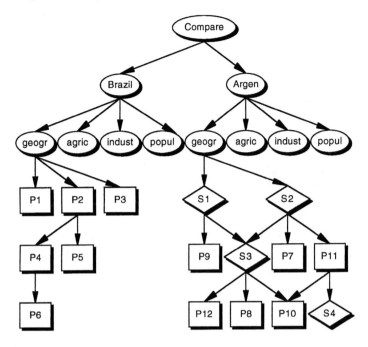

Figure 3.3

actually generate? If readers have all this freedom to reorganize and distort a text according to their ideas and beliefs, how can we ever hope to
predict what they will do? Actually the situation in text comprehension is
not that bad, and better than in some other areas of cognitive science,
notably problem solving. When we give a subject a reasonably complex
problem to solve, we really have no way of telling how the problem will be
approached. In text comprehension, on the other hand, the subjects in
our experiments tend to follow the text we present more or less faithfully.
Many texts are designed so that the subject's situation model will not differ much from the textbase and hence is fairly well predictable. When we
do studies in which prior knowledge and beliefs play a larger role, we usually have some idea what these are and are able to formulate hypotheses
about the way they should affect text processing. Thus, although we do
not have total control over our experimental subjects, we can constrain
their behavior reasonably well in our experiments. Real-life comprehension episodes are much less constrained, and instead of prediction we

often must be satisfied with postdiction based on the principles of comprehension derived from studies that are better controlled.

3.1.1 The microstructure

Even though the propositional representations of the meaning of a text that are used here fall short of the requirements of a full formal semantic analysis, or even a more informal linguistic analysis, they pose a major unsolved problem. No fully automatic parser has yet been constructed that is capable of deriving a propositional microstructure from arbitrary English text. It is fairly simple to do that for limited domains (e.g., first-grade word–arithmetic problems, as in Cummins, Kintsch, Reusser, & Weimer, 1988), but the task is formidable if no restrictions are placed on the nature of the text.

An escape route from this dilemma that I have used since my original work in this area (Kintsch, 1972, 1974) is to ignore the parsing problem. This provides no solution and hardly does justice to a highly important problem, but it allows us to go on with research that would be impossible unless we find some way to finesse the parsing problem. I am by no means the only researcher in psychology, linguistics, or AI who has taken this approach. Others have made the parsing problem the focus of their work, and much progress has been reported in recent years. Nevertheless, my hope that I could just pick a parser developed in some other laboratory from the shelf and adapt it as a front end for my comprehension models has so far not been realized.

Even if one decides to do without a formal parser, research of the kind reported later in this book requires a reliable and objective system of deriving propositions from any given text. Hand coding is slow and cumbersome, but it serves its purpose as long as it is objective. A brief guide for propositionalizing texts is given in the section that follows ("A Brief Guide to Propositionalizing Texts"). This guide is then followed by a sample analysis of a few sentences from a biology text.

A brief guide to propositionalizing texts. The meaning of a simple sentence can be represented by a *complex proposition* (section 2.2.2) consisting of a predicate with several arguments, time and place circumstances and optional modifiers. *Predicates* are relational terms, frequently expressed in language as verbs, adjectives, or adverbs. Each predicate is characterized by a predicate *frame* that specifies how many and which *arguments* that a predicate takes. A verb frame, for instance, may specify that a particular verb must have an agent, an object, and an optional goal, with restrictions on these categories, such as that the agent must be human, or the goal must be a location, Not only can concepts be arguments, but a proposition may have as an argument another embedded atomic proposition. Sentence connectives, for instance, are predicates that require propositions as arguments. *Circumstances* refer to the whole propositional frame, specifying place and time. All propositional elements may be *modified* by additional atomic propositions.

Thus, to repeat the example discussed in section 2.2.2, the sentence *Yesterday, Mary inadvertently gave Fred the book in the library* is represented as a complex proposition structured around the predicate GIVE. The arguments of this predicate are an agent MARY, an object BOOK, and a goal FRED. *Inadvertently* modifies GIVE, and *old* modifies BOOK. Time and place are specified by *yesterday* and *in the library*.

A brief list of frequently encountered propositional constructions follows. This list parallels the one provided by Bovair and Kieras (1985) to facilitate comparison. In each case, only a simple text example and its propositional form are given without much comment. When more than one version is given, these are notational variants of varying explicitness to be used as convenient.

1. *Verbs as predicates.* Verb frames specify the arguments that can go with each verb and are thus building blocks for propositions. It is usually not necessary to indicate the case role of an argument:

    The hemoglobin carries oxygen.

CARRY[HEMOGLOBIN, OXYGEN]

Prepositions indicate the case role of arguments and may be included in a proposition for clarification:

    The blood from the body arrives at the atrium through the veins.

ARRIVE[BLOOD,FROM-BODY,AT-ATRIUM,
THROUGH-VEINS]

or, abbreviated

ARRIVE[BLOOD,BODY,ATRIUM,VEINS]

2. *Propositions as arguments.* Propositions can be embedded as arguments in other propositions. For instance, an argument may be specified by a modifier:

The blood arrives at the right atrium.

ARRIVE[BLOOD,RIGHT[ATRIUM]]

The first chamber is the right atrium.

IS[FIRST[CHAMBER],RIGHT[ATRIUM]]

A sentence complement can be expressed as the argument of a superordinate proposition:

Purplish blood tends to lack oxygen.

```
TEND
 ├BLOOD
 │  └ PURPLISH
 └LACK
    ├ BLOOD
    │  └ PURPLISH
    └ OXYGEN
```

or more compactly:

TEND[PURPLISH[BLOOD],LACK[PURPLISH[BLOOD],
    OXYGEN]]

or, once again, using a different notation:

P1   TEND[P2,P3]
P2   PURPLISH[BLOOD]
P3   LACK[P2,OXYGEN]

Which of these alternative notations is employed is a matter of convenience and preference.

The doctor discovered that the defect was congenital.

DISCOVER[DOCTOR,CONGENITAL[DEFECT]]

Relative clauses are expressed as separate atomic propositions that are assigned to a modifier slot in a complex proposition:

Blood that has been drained of oxygen arrives at the right atrium.

ARRIVE[BLOOD],RIGHT[ATRIUM]]
        └─ DRAIN[BLOOD,OF-OXYGEN]

Modals are also expressed as modifiers in a complex proposition:

Heart attacks may be fatal.

FATAL[HEARTATTACK]
└─ POSSIBLE

or

POSSIBLE[FATAL[HEARTATTACK]]

3. *Modification.* Adjectives and adverbs are treated as the predicates of atomic propositions:

septal defect

SEPTAL[DEFECT]

which is abbreviated in the context of a complex proposition as

DEFECT
  └── SEPTAL

The blood returns to the heart quickly.

QUICK[RETURN[BLOOD,HEART]]

or

RETURN[BLOOD, HEART]
  └─ QUICK

Predicate nominals are treated similarly:

The doctor was a cardiologist.

CARDIOLOGIST[DOCTOR]

Multiple embeddings indicate the scope of modifiers:

the two major chambers of the heart

POSSESS[HEART,TWO[MAJOR[CHAMBERS]]]

Negated propositions are treated as special predicates. This use of negation is nonstandard but avoids some complications that arise when negated propositions become part of a network that is integrated in the comprehension process.

The heart rate is not constant.

NOT-CONSTANT[HEART RATE]

Paul did not expect Mary to come.

NOT-EXPECT[PAUL,COME[MARY]]

Superlatives, comparatives, and questions are treated in as simple a manner as possible:

The left ventricle is the largest chamber of the heart.

IS[LEFT[VENTRICLE],LARGEST[CHAMBER]]
                 └── OF-HEART

OF-HEART is used here as an abbreviation for a POSSESS (or HAVE)-proposition:

POSSESS[HEART,CHAMBER]

The right ventricle is smaller than the left ventricle.

MORE-THAN[SMALL[RIGHT[VENTRIC]],SMALL
[LEFT[VENTRIC]]]

or, simplifying some more,

SMALLER-THAN[RIGHT[VENTRIC]],
[LEFT[VENTRIC]]

How does the heart pump blood?

HOW[PUMP[HEART,BLOOD],?]

4. *Problems and issues.* Cognitive states (*hope to, decide to, expect to, fail to, be afraid to, begin to, hesitate to*), causal verbs (*cause, bring about, result in*), and verbs of saying, thinking and believing are treated as modifiers of the sentence complement:

Paul hoped Mary would come.

COME
 └MARY
 └ HOPE[PAUL]

Paul said Mary would come.

COME
 └MARY
 └ SAY[PAUL]

John left early. This shocked everyone.

LEAVE
 ├── JOHN
 └EARLY
 └ SHOCK
   └EVERYONE

or simply

P1 LEAVE[JOHN]
P2 EARLY[P1]
P3 SHOCK[P2, EVERYONE]

Sentence connectives take complex propositions as arguments:

CON[P1,P2]

Examples of connectives include causal connectives (*because, so, thus, therefore*), condition (*if-then*), purpose (*to, in order to*), contrast (*on the one hand, in contrast*), concession (*but, however*), conjunction (*and, comma, also*), and temporal connectives (*then, next, second, following*).

Note that *Mary ran quickly* and *Mary might have run* are represented in the same way here, as a proposition RUN[MARY] modified by either QUICKLY or POSSIBLY. This (and many similar "problems" one could come up with) is not a weakness of the system but a source of its strength. *Quickly* modifies *ran*, whereas *might have* applies to the whole proposition, which is a valid distinction and crucial when we are concerned with the truth value of sentences. But we are not; we want to model comprehension, to count elements in working memory, to score recall protocols, and so on – for which purposes we do not need a logically consistent system or a detailed semantics. We need a way to represent the meaning of a text sufficiently independently of the words used that preserves those aspects of meaning that are important for our purposes and glosses over those that are not. Propositions as defined here best fulfill that need.

Although the foregoing examples do not cover every case encountered in the propositional analysis of text, they should enable researchers to construct simple but consistent propositional representations for many texts. It should also be remembered that for many experimental purposes particularly troublesome constructions can be avoided.

A sample analysis. In this section the following three sentences from a junior-high biology textbook dealing with the functioning of the heart are analyzed using the foregoing method. This is a detailed theoretical analysis that would be the output of an automatic parser if we had one, but for most research purposes, a shorthand version can be used, as illustrated at the end of this section.[1]

---

1   This section is based on Kintsch (1985). An excellent discussion of the general issues involved in such an analysis is provided by Perfetti and Britt (1995).

(1) The first of the heart's four chambers, the right atrium, receives purplish blood, short of oxygen and laden with carbon dioxide. This used blood arrives through the body's two major veins, the superior and inferior venae cavae, and from the many minute blood vessels that drain blood from the walls of the chamber itself.

Each sentence is divided into text elements, labeled E_i, composed of a content word together with preceding function words. Thus, *The first/of the heart's/* . . . yields the first two text elements E1 and E2. Each text element is then annotated as to its function: For example, *first* modifies text element E4, and is also the subject for the predicate E7; *chambers* becomes the patient of the proposition to be formed from the verb phrase E4; *atrium* is linked to E1 as a specification, and so on. We do this by our intuitions; a parser would infer these annotations automatically. The annotated text elements are then used to construct propositions.

As each text element is read, either a new proposition is constructed (possibly incomplete, with the missing parts here indicated by the still to be processed text element or simply by an X – an automatic parser would have to be somewhat more precise), or an already existing proposition is modified. For instance, when the text element E3, *four,* is encountered, a new proposition is constructed with FOUR as the predicate and an unknown argument to be derived from E4. When E4 is processed, the incomplete proposition is filled in with the appropriate argument, obtaining FOUR[CHAMBER]. When E7, *receives,* is read, a new proposition with the predicate RECEIVE is constructed that has the argument FIRST[CHAMBER], a proposition already constructed for this purpose at step E4. However, RECEIVE needs at least one more argument, which we indicate by an X. It is filled in at step E9 with PURPLE[BLOOD].

In order to construct propositions in this way, a parser must have access to a considerable amount of lexical knowledge. For instance, it must know that the predicate FOUR can be used with count nouns only and that the verb frame for RECEIVE requires an object. It must also have optional slots for a source ("from the body"), a goal ("the heart"), and a medium ("through the veins"). The knowledge sources needed to construct the propositions shown in Figure 3.4 are not shown explicitly here, however (but see Kintsch, 1985).

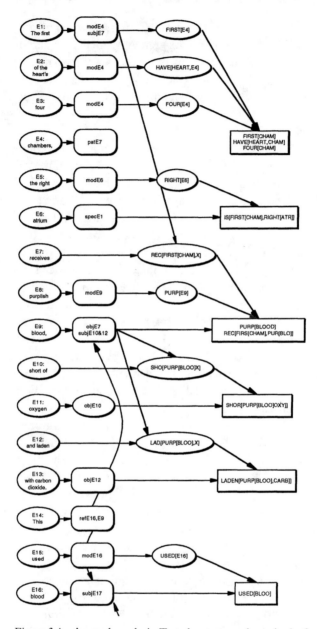

Figure 3.4   A sample analysis. Text elements are shown in the first column; the second column shows the syntactic tags required for building propositions; propositions under construction but still incomplete are shown in the third column; the completed propositions are shown in the fourth column.

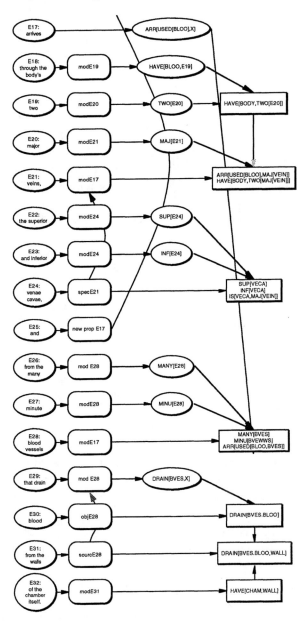

Figure 3.4   *(cont.)*

In the analysis given in Figure 3.4, Column 1 presents the complete text decomposed into individual text elements. The semantic and syntactic roles of these elements are shown in column 2. Column 3 shows the atomic propositions that are constructed as the reader processes the text. For example, a reader processing E3 knows only the predicate of a proposition, but the argument is still unspecified; only when the reader reads E4 can the proposition be completed. Completed atomic propositions are shown in column 4. Additional arguments may be added to these propositions as the reader acquires more information.

From the atomic propositions that have been formed (column 4), complex propositions can now be constructed by assigning modifiers to their proper places in the propositional schema (the Circumstance slots are empty for all the complex propositions shown in Figure 3.5).

The first two complex propositions constructed in this example are linked by an indirect coherence relation. It is marked in the surface structure by *this* (E14), which indicates that the *used blood* in P2 is identical with the *purplish blood* in P1. The relation between the P2 and P3 is one of direct coherence via the sentence connective *and* (E25). Another link is established by the elliptic subject (*used blood*) of the phrase upon which P3 is based.

Thus, the propositional representation P1–P3 could be constructed in an objective and straightforward manner by considering the syntactic relations among the various text elements as well as generally available lexical knowledge. What was done here by hand is, more or less, what a parser would have to do. Having such a parser would be most desirable, but not having one need not stop our research efforts.

In practice there is no need to go through this detailed step-by-step analysis. The step-by-step, real-time construction of the textbase is often not of interest. All we need to know (for instance, in studies of text recall) is the final product, the representation in terms of complex propositions. Hence, it is sufficient for most research purposes to construct the final propositional representation, and its genesis can be neglected.

3.1.2 The macrostructure

Texts have a global structure as well as a local structure. The microstructure of a text consists of the complex propositions that comprise the text

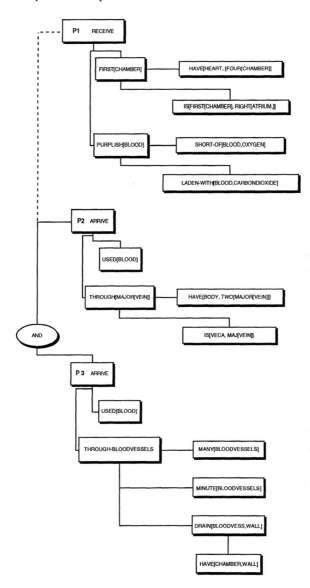

Figure 3.5   The three complex propositions constructed from the analysis in
Figure 3.4.

and their interrelationships, for example, the three propositions P1–P3 in the example analyzed earlier. The macrostructure organizes the propositions of the microstructure hierarchically. It consists of macropropositions and their hierarchical relations. Macropropositions may or may not be expressed explicitly in the text. They are related to the microstructure by three rules, called *macrorules* by van Dijk (1980):

- Selection: Given a sequence of propositions, propositions that are not an interpretation condition for another proposition may be deleted.
- Generalization: A proposition that is entailed by each of a sequence of propositions may be substituted for that sequence.
- Construction: A proposition that is entailed by the joint set of a sequence of propositions may be substituted for that sequence.

An example for the operation of selection may be obtained from the analysis in section 3.1.1. The macroproposition of the text fragment analyzed there may be obtained by deleting P2 and P3 as well as inessential elements of P1, as follows:

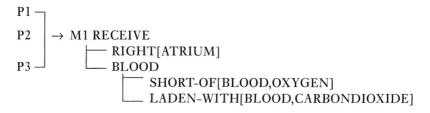

An example for the operation of generalization would be

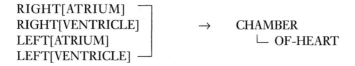

An example for a construction would be

```
EXPAND[MUSCLE]
            ┗━━━ OF-HEART  →   PUMP[HEART]
            ┏━━━
CONTRACT[MUSCLE]
```

The macrooperations may be performed recursively on macropropositions as well as on micropropositions, resulting in a hierarchical structure, such as is shown in Figure 3.6.

Macrostructures thus represent the global organization of a text. As such, they are linguistic structures, like the phrase structure of a sentence. For the psychologist, the important questions concern the psychological reality of such structures, as well as how they are formed during comprehension (for the macrorules operate on linguistic descriptions and are not in themselves a psychological process model).

As to the psychological reality of macrostructures, there exists overwhelming evidence of their significance (e.g., van Dijk & Kintsch, 1983). Indeed, for comprehension and memory, the gist of a text – expressed formally by the macrostructure – is usually what matters most. As has been described by van Dijk and Kintsch (1983), a number of interacting factors are crucial for the formation of macrostructures. These include general cultural knowledge, including the sociocultural context of the comprehension episode – its situation type (e.g., a party conversation vs. a court trial vs. reading a chapter in a textbook), the participant categories (e.g., a teacher, a friend, their interests, gender, social status, and so on), the type of interaction (e.g., a tutorial dialogue vs. a chat in the grocery

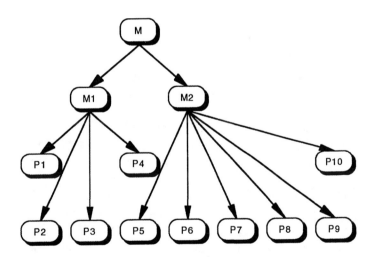

Figure 3.6

store), conventions, and habits. There are, however, also rich signals in the texts themselves that enable the formation of macrostructures. These may be structural signals, such as titles, initial topic sentences, summary statements, and the like, as well as a great variety of syntactic and semantic signals that are mainly used to indicate local importance in a discourse but that may achieve macrorelevance through cumulative inference. Text elements that have been repeatedly signaled to be of local importance become important for the macrostructure, too. Syntactic signals for discourse relevance include phonetic stress, cleft sentences, passives, the clause structure of sentences, and other foregrounding and topicalization devices. Semantic signals in a text include topic change markers (such as change in time or place, introduction of new participants, change of perspective, and so on) and various cues that indicate local coherence or a break thereof that subjects can use either to maintain or to change their current macrohypothesis (Givón, 1995; van Dijk & Kintsch, 1983).

Textual schemas, what van Dijk and Kintsch (1983) have called the rhetorical superstructures, also play an important role in the formation of macrostructures. Readers know that particular text types tend to be organized in certain ways and employ this knowledge to construct schema-based macrostructures. Thus, narratives in our culture have a basic exposition–complication–resolution structure, with the possibility of embedding. By assigning macropropositions to these schematic categories, readers can simplify for themselves the task of deriving the overall organization of a story. Indeed, as Poulsen, Kintsch, Kintsch, and Premack (1979) have shown, even four-year-olds make good use of this schematic knowledge in story understanding. Conversely, when the schema is misapplied because the narrative is constructed according to some other cultural schema, comprehension may be distorted accordingly (Bartlett, 1932; Kintsch & Greene, 1978).

Rhetorical schemas play a role in understanding descriptive texts that is as important as their role in understanding stories. If familiar schemas are present, comprehension is facilitated but only at the macrolevel, not locally. For instance, Kintsch and Yarborough (1982) wrote brief essays according to four familiar rhetorical schemas: classification, illustration, compare-and-contrast, and procedural description. The texts conformed as closely as possible to these schemas. The texts were then rewritten, and although their schematic structure was destroyed their content remained unchanged. This was done by a partial reordering of sentences and the deletion of explicit rhetorical signals from the original texts. Subjects performed much better on topic and main idea questions, which require good understanding at the macrolevel, when they read the rhetorically well-structured texts (.62 and .43 correct in one experimental condition) than when they read the same texts without the rhetorical cues (.23 and .05 correct, respectively). On the other hand, on a test that evaluated their local understanding (a cloze test), there was no significant difference between the rhetorically good and poor text versions (.33 and .39 correct, respectively, for the good and poor versions).

3.1.3 The psychological reality of propositions

Why do we need propositions at all for our theorizing, what is wrong with just plain natural language? In doing research on text understanding it is frequently the case that propositional representations of the texts are more readily related to the behavioral data than are the texts themselves. Presumably this is the case in those situations in which meaning matters most; propositions are designed to capture those semantic relations that are most salient in text comprehension, whereas natural language serves many purposes other than the expression of meaning and hence is often less suited for our purposes than a representation that is focused on meaning. Propositions appear to be the semantic processing units of the mind and hence the most useful form of representation for our studies.

What is the empirical evidence that propositions are in fact effective units in text comprehension? Because complex propositions are defined in such a way that they (generally) correspond to sentences, all the evidence that shows that sentences are psychological units also supports the notion of complex propositions. But sentences are structured according to the rules of syntax, whereas the internal structure of complex propositions is quite different and only indirectly related to syntax. Complex propositions have a central proposition and various associated elements – modifiers of various sorts and/or circumstantials. The question then becomes whether these smaller propositional elements, or atomic propositions, can be shown to function as psychological processing units. What is the evidence that atomic propositions are the functional processing units of text comprehension?

A discussion of the psychological reality of propositions can be found in most contemporary cognitive psychology textbooks as well as in van

Dijk and Kintsch (1983, chap. 2). Hence, no more than a brief summary is presented here. In a sense, every experimental study that successfully employs a propositional analysis either to design the experimental materials or to analyze the data provides evidence for the usefulness of propositional analyses. However, one would like more direct evidence as to the psychological reality of propositions. Such evidence comes from three sources: recall experiments, reading times, and priming studies.

Cued and free recall. If subjects study sentences that are based on more than one proposition and then are given a word from the sentence as a recall cue, words from the sentence that belong to the same atomic proposition as the cue word are recalled better than words from the sentence that do not come from the same atomic proposition. This result has been obtained in several studies, (e.g., Wanner, 1975). Thus, consider the two-element sentence that consists of a main proposition and a propositional modifier

(2)   The mausoleum that enshrined the tzar overlooked the square.

OVERLOOK[MAUSOLEUM, SQUARE]
    └── ENSHRINE[MAUSOLEUM, TZAR]

Subjects who are given the word *overlooked* as a recall cue will more often recall *square* than *tzar,* which are arguments of the same atomic proposition, in spite of the fact that *tzar* is closer in the surface structure to the recall cue than *square.*

Barshi (1997) studied how people were able to execute verbal instructions that differed in the number of propositions and/or words. His subject listened to messages that instructed them to move in a simulated three-dimensional space on a computer screen. They repeated these instructions orally and then attempted to follow them – as airline pilots do when receiving real air traffic control instructions. The instructions were given either in complete English sentences ("move two squares to the left") or in abbreviated form ("two left" – an unambiguous command in the context of Barshi's experiment). The number of propositions a subject had to remember and respond to mattered greatly: Doubling the number of propositions from two to four caused an increase in errors from 3% to 52%. The number of words used to express these propositions, on the other hand, had no effect at all in Barshi's experiment: A two-proposition instruction was as hard to remember and execute whether it was expressed with four words or with eight words. But there was a striking difference in difficulty whether eight words expressed two propositions or four.

There are also a number of studies that demonstrate that when recalling sentences based on complex propositions, subjects tend to recall the various elements of the complex proposition as units. That is, they either recall the whole element or omit it entirely. The most extensive of these studies is one by Goetz, Anderson, and Schallert (1981). In this study subjects read eight sentences and then recalled them. The sentences were either based on a single propositional element, such as

(3)   The customer wrote the company a complaint.

WRITE[CUSTOMER, COMANY, COMPLAINT]

or a proposition with two additional elements, such as

LECTURE[PROFESSOR]
  | └─ FAMOUS
  └─ LOC:CLASSROOM

(4)   The famous professor lectured in the classroom.

Almost all the free recall of these sentences, 94%, consisted of complete propositional elements. That is, if a subject recalled anything at all from sentences like (3), the whole sentence was recalled. In contrast, sentences like (4) were often recalled partially, that is, subjects may recall *The professor lectured, The professor was famous* or *The famous professor was in the classroom,* for instance. However, Goetz et al. argued that the holistic recall they observed may not have been owing to the fact that subjects represent the meaning of sentences in memory propositionally, but that they may be a consequence of the familiarity, concreteness, and high imagery value of these units. Therefore, they constructed similar sentences in which unlikely elements were combined and that would be much harder to image, such as

(5)   The comedian supplied glassware to the convicts.
(6)   The bedraggled, intelligent model sang.

Their results, however, remained the same. As before, the overwhelming majority of recall, 84% this time, consisted of whole propositional elements. Thus, the unfamiliar, low-imagery sentences (type 5) were recalled in an all-or-none fashion, much like type (2) sentences, whereas, sentences of type (6) broke down into their propositional elements on recall.

Reading times and recall. In a number of early studies, sentence recall was found to be a function of the number of propositional elements in the sentence when reading time was controlled. Thus, Forster (1970) presented six-word sentences at a constant rate. All sentences were six words long but contained either one or two propositional elements:

(7)   The kitten climbed over the fence.
(8)   The truck Susan was driving crashed.

The average number of words recalled for sentences of types (7) and (8) were 4.41 and 3.09, respectively.

Conversely, if reading time is subject controlled, subjects take longer to read propositionally complex sentences, even when the number of words is the same. Kintsch and Keenan (1973) constructed sentences that were all of approximately the same length (14–16 words) but that contained anywhere from four to eight propositional elements. Of course, the mere fact that a sentence contains many propositional elements does not guarantee that a reader constructs an equally complex representation. A fast reader may simply skip over some propositional elements. Hence, it is inappropriate to plot reading times against sentence complexity. However, if one plots reading time against the number of propositional elements that subjects recall on a free recall test, a rather striking approximately linear relationship results. For each additional propositional element recalled, reading times increased by 1.5 s in the Kintsch and Keenan study.

One needs to be cautious about generalizing this finding, however. Kintsch and Keenan examined only a very limited range – between four and eight propositional elements. It is not really possible to extend this range, because as sentences or texts get longer, retrieval and forgetting problems complicate the interpretation of the data. Even more critically, when sentences are constructed that vary in propositional complexity but not in length, these sentences necessarily also vary in many other ways – lexical items, syntax, familiarity, the number of repeated concepts, and so on.

Since these early studies, reading times have been analyzed repeatedly using multiple regression analyses in the attempt to untangle these confoundings. In these studies, propositions in the text, not propositions in the head (as reflected by subjects' recall) have invariably been used as the variable of interest. Hence, these studies are not entirely relevant for the question at hand – whether or not propositions are meaningful psychological units of comprehension. Nevertheless, considerable support for the usefulness of this notion can be derived from these studies (which are reviewed in section 9.1.2).

Priming studies. Additional support for the psychological reality of propositions comes from an experiment on recognition priming reported by Ratcliff and McKoon (1978). These authors showed their subjects four sentences for 7 s each. The sentences contained either one or two propositional elements, such as sentence (2) above. After reading a set of sentences, the subject was given a recognition test with single words from the sentences and unrelated distractor words. Subjects were required to answer "yes" or "no" whether a word had appeared in one of the study sentences or not. Priming effects are commonly observed on such a task: When two words from the same sentence are tested one after the other, recognition time for the second word is lower. In the Ratcliff and McKoon experiment, this priming effect amounted to 111 ms when the two words were both from the same sentence and the same atomic proposition (*square* and *mausoleum*), but to only 91 ms when the two words were from the same sentence but from different atomic propositions (e.g., *square* and *tzar*). The difference is small but statistically significant. It indicates that not only sentences (and complex propositions) are psychological units but that this is also true for the elements of complex propositions (atomic propositions).

Atomic propositions, therefore, appear to be the proper building blocks for comprehension structures. They have proven their usefulness in numerous studies, and they will do so again in the experiments and analyses reported here.

3.2 The propositional representation of knowledge

Propositional text representations are helpful for describing the semantic characteristics of experimental texts, and they are useful for scoring recall and other data from experimental subjects. Furthermore, they are widely used for modeling purposes. Although they may not be ideal for every purpose, they have proven to be a reliable workhorse. In contrast, propositional knowledge representations remain largely untried. As I have argued in chapter 2, propositional knowledge nets seem quite appropriate for the purpose of simulating knowledge use in the comprehension model, but the simulations that have been done to date employ fairly small-scale, ad hoc knowledge bases. No large-scale, general knowledge base using the knowledge net format has been constructed yet, and it is impossible to know beforehand how adequate the proposed format would turn out to be. Given the problems that seem to be encountered universally in the construction of large-scale knowledge representations, it would not be surprising to find knowledge nets as envisaged here to have some shortcomings, too. For our present, more modest purposes of simulating knowledge use in comprehension in special cases, knowledge nets appear to be quite satisfactory, however. I discuss in this section how two of the central problems in knowledge representation might be dealt with within such a framework. Of course, this discussion cannot substitute for an actual simulation of a large knowledge net, in which the processes I can only speculate about are realized computationally.

3.2.1 The construction of meaning: Concepts

In the model proposed here, knowledge is represented as a network of propositions. Such a network is called a *knowledge net*. The nodes of the net are propositions, schemas, frames, scripts, production rules – which can all be written in a formalism based on the predicate–argument schema, as argued in chapter 2. The links are unlabeled and vary in strength, that is, a knowledge net is a type of associative net.

The meaning of a node is given by its position in the net, that is, by the strengths with which it is linked to its neighbors, immediate ones as well as neighbors many steps apart. This definition of meaning is an abstract, linguistic one, not a psychological one. Psychologically, only those nodes that are actually active (that is, are held in working memory) contribute to the meaning of a node. Because the capacity of working memory is severely limited, any node at any point in time has only a few neighbors; its meaning is sparse, therefore. However, it can be readily elaborated, almost without limit, in many different directions, as the situation demands, because most nodes in a knowledge network are connected with powerful, stable links – retrieval structures – to other nodes in the net that can be brought into working memory. Thus, very complex meanings can be generated automatically and effortlessly, although at any particular time only a few nodes can be active in working memory.

Concepts do not have a fixed and permanent meaning. Rather, each time a concept is used, its meaning is constructed in working memory by activating a certain subset of the propositions in the neighborhood of a concept node. The context of use determines which nodes linked to a concept are activated when a concept is used. Goals, prior experience, emotional state, situational as well as semantic context all influence which nodes are activated and hence what the meaning of the concept will be on this particular occasion.

In constructing the meaning of a concept, the concept node and any other currently active proposition in working memory serve as the retrieval cues, both individually and as parts of a compound cue. Hence, what will be retrieved in the process of elaborating the meaning of a node will depend not only on the node itself but on the state of working memory as a whole.

The substructure from which the meaning of a concept is constructed – the knowledge net – is relatively permanent (experience and learning create and continually modify this structure). The meaning – that is, the portion of the knowledge net that is activated – is flexible, changeable, and temporary, however. Because meaning construction is based on the same substructure, there will be a certain amount of consistency in the meaning of concepts on different occasions. The likelihood that certain meaning elements will be sampled will always be greater than for other elements, but the context in which this sampling occurs will ensure a great deal of variability in the outcome.

Knowledge nets have some advantages over alternative forms of knowledge representation. First, there are good psychological data that argue for the psychological validity of each one of the knowledge structures mentioned, from associative nets to production systems, as was described in chapter 2. But at the same time, there are equally good data that show that neither of these systems is sufficient by itself for the representation of knowledge. For instance, one can show, as Collins and Quillian (1969) did, that certain psychological predictions that can be derived from semantic nets can be verified experimentally, but as an army of their detractors have demonstrated and as we can read in every cognitive psychology textbook, these predictions are wrong in many ways because there is much more to human knowledge than a semantic net. A knowledge system must account for the inheritance of (some) properties, but it also must include schema-like structures with default slots and procedural knowledge that link cognition and action, and so on. In such a net one can make distinctions between episodic and semantic memory, or procedural and declarative knowledge, but it is not always necessary to do so. These are merely different types of nodes in the same network, interacting with each other. Knowledge nets, therefore, freely combine features from other knowledge representation systems that have been shown to be useful for computational purposes in AI research or to be valid in psychological experiments.

Consider a particular node, P, in such a net. It may be linked to a set of nodes, P_1; the P_1 nodes in turn are linked to another sent of nodes, P_2; and so on in ever increasing concentric circles until the whole network is included. To say that the meaning of P is the relation between P and these concentric sets of nodes is true in some abstract sense but beside the point psychologically. At any given moment, in any given knowledge net, only those nodes contribute to the psychological meaning of P that are actually activated in working memory and linked to it. Thus, typically, instead of a very large set of nodes, only a limited number of nodes constitute the effective meaning of P at any time, perhaps only five or six nodes in the case when the meaning of P is only superficially elaborated. However, because P is embedded in a network of strong stable relationships with other nodes in the knowledge net, further elaboration via retrieval structures is readily achieved should there be a need for it. I may think of a few things concerning P and you may think of a few things, and there may be a little overlap and a miscommunication may result. However, if there is some context to guide us, we are more likely to construct similar meanings for P and communicate effectively.

Knowledge nets thus imply a commitment to a radical constructionist position in the controversy about the mental representation of word meanings. In a mental lexicon, one looks up the meaning of a word. In a knowledge net, there is nothing to look up. Meaning has to be constructed by activating nodes in the neighborhood of a word. This activation process is probabilistic, with activation probabilities being proportional to the strengths of connections among the nodes, and it may continue for a variable amount of time, spreading outward into the knowledge net from the source node. The meaning of the source word is, then, the set of activated nodes in the knowledge net.

The knowledge net serves as a retrieval structure in the sense of Ericsson and Kintsch (1995; also chap. 7). If any element of a knowledge net is in working memory (focus of attention, consciousness), other elements directly connected with it can be retrieved with a single 400 ms retrieval operation. These directly retrievable elements make up what Ericsson and Kintsch called long-term working memory. Once a particular element from long-term working memory has actually been instated in the focus of attention, it, too, will provide access to its neighbors in the knowledge net, thereby further increasing the size of long-term working memory. In addition, the pair of nodes will function as a compound cue, markedly changing the retrieval probabilities in long-term working memory.

Words, in this view, have a potential meaning given by concentric shells of ever expanding neighborhoods in the knowledge net. The most restrictive potential meaning of a concept would be given by its immediate neighbors, the most complete by the total net. There is no sense in asking how many steps away from a concept the expansion has to go to give us "the meaning" of a concept. Meaning may be more or less elaborate. And, most important, this expansion process provides only a potential meaning. The real, actual meaning of a word is not the set of all nodes that might be activated in long-term working memory but rather the nodes that have actually been activated in the particular context of use. Thus, meanings are not nearly as elaborate as they could be, because normally only an insignificant fraction of a concept's neighboring nodes in a knowledge net enters consciousness (though many more are readily available in long-term working memory). A linguist, semanticist, or psychologist studying the meaning of a concept will come up with a very rich and complex structure. That is not, however, what is actually operative when that word is used on specific occasions in a specific context, where meaning is much more sketchy and incomplete.

Contextual word meanings are not only shallow but are dynamic and fluctuating. Somewhat different word meanings are constructed on different occasions, even if the knowledge net and discourse context remain the same, simply because of the probabilistic nature of the sampling process that determines which of the many possible knowledge elements actually enter consciousness. But the discourse context is in continuous flux, and different persons operate with different knowledge nets. Hence, there must be considerable variability in effective word meanings.

Before continuing this discussion on the construction of meaning, it seems only proper to ask whether there is any psychological evidence that would support such a theory. Indeed, there is. In fact, the psychological evidence overwhelmingly favors the view that concepts are temporary constructions in working memory, generated in response to task demand

and subject to the constraints exercised by the underlying knowledge base and the situational context. Cognitive scientists might as well discard the traditional notion that concepts are stable entities to be retrieved from long-term memory – a view that we have inherited from philosophy and linguistics.

Barclay, Bransford, Franks, McCarrell, and Nitsch (1974) were the first to point out the role of encoding variability in memory retrieval. They gave to subjects words like "piano" to study in the context of playing music or moving furniture. On a later memory test, they gave either "loud" or "heavy" as a retrieval cue. The former was a better retrieval cue when "piano" had been presented in the music context, but the latter was the better cue when "piano" had been studied in the furniture context, suggesting that a context-specific concept of "piano" was encoded.

In several studies that demonstrate the flexibility and context-dependency of concepts, a sentence verification paradigm was used. A representative experiment is that of McKoon and Ratcliff (1988). They argued that two equally known properties of *tomatoes* are that they are *round* and *red*. Nevertheless, the actual availability of these properties strongly depends on the context in which *tomato* was used. Following a brief paragraph about painting a still life containing a tomato, *Tomatoes are red* was verified faster than *Tomatoes are round*. But after a paragraph describing a child rolling tomatoes around the floor, *Tomatoes are round* was verified faster. The average difference between matching and nonmatching sentences was 120 ms. In a neutral context that emphasized neither color nor shape (about *eating tomatoes*), both target sentences were responded to equally fast.

Kintsch and Welsch (1991) have shown that these results follow directly from the assumptions about meaning construction that have been discussed. They simulated the results of the McKoon and Ratcliff experiment using the construction–integration model to be descrtibed in the next chapter. Memory strength in this model is a function of the amount of activation a node attains. In Figure 3.7 the results of the simulation are shown: a fragement of the network representing the texts, as well as the two test items, *Tomatoes are round* and *Tomatoes are red,* with their activation values. For the "playing-with-tomatoes" text, more activation flows to *Tomatoes are red* than to *Tomatoes are round*. On the other hand, in the context of the "painting-tomatoes" the opposite will be true. In the context of the "eating-tomatoes" text, the activation values for the two test sentences turn out to be equal.

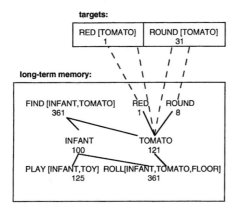

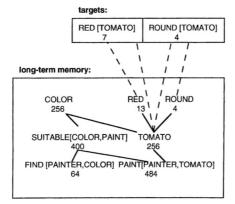

Figure 3.7   Part of the long-term memory network after reading the play-ing-with-tomatoes (top) and painting-tomatoes (bottom) paragraph and two target sentences. The numbers below the nodes in the network are long-term memory strengths; the numbers below the targets are the activation values they receive from the net.

A number of other studies demonstrating the context dependency of concepts have been reviewed by Barsalou (1993), who advocates a view related to the present one. Of particular significance is one of his own studies that he discusses. In this experiment, subjects were asked to write down features that define common categories. Only 44% of the features in one subject's description existed in another subject's description, indi-cating that the definitions subjects provided were highly idiosyncratic. Indeed, when subjects were asked to provide definitions for the same con-cepts on two successive occasions, their own overlap was merely 66%.

Thus, not only are concepts idiosyncratic, but they are also highly unstable. However, Barsalou was able to show that only the concepts that subjects constructed in this underconstrained experimental situation were so unpredictable. If subjects were given all the features generated by everyone in the experiment, they agreed very well that these were indeed features characteristic of the concept in question (97% agreement between subjects, 98% within subjects). Everyone had more or less the same knowledge base when it came to these familiar everyday concepts. Furthermore, in a more constraining context, different subjects tended to agree much better on the features that characterize a concept. Thus, in the experiment reported by Barsalou, intersubject agreement was 45% when subjects defined concepts like *vehicle* in isolation, but rose to 70% with even a minimally constraining context (*"Taking a vacation in the rugged mountains of Mexico"*).

Barsalou's data nicely illustrate the fact that, although concepts are fleeting and flexible, not all is chaos, because the knowledge bases from which these concepts are constructed are more stable and predictable, and most of the time the context itself will be sufficiently constraining to ensure that the concepts different people form will be similar. Nevertheless, concepts are never quite the same – surely a limiting factor in communication.

The theory of meaning advocated here is not only constructivist but also minimalist. Clearly, readers can study a text over and over again and construct very elaborate meanings for its propositions and concepts. Linguists, philosophers, and literary critics do this all the time, and most people do so at least some of the time. But most of the time, in reading or conversation, the process of meaning construction remains shallow, not just because comprehenders are inherently lazy but mostly because no more is required. A slight knowledge elaboration of a text is usually quite sufficient for whatever action is intended. Most of the time texts do not need much elaboration and interpretation to arrive at stable interpretations upon which appropriate responses can be based. Long-term working memory allows the comprehender easy elaborations and inferences whenever they are required. It is enough for the well-informed reader to feel that the potential for the elaboration of meaning is there – there is no need to realize it. It is of course possible to do so, and we often do so, sometimes readily, sometimes with the expenditure of considerable effort. Indeed, the deliberate construction of meaning may extend over long periods and may be a socially shared activity, as is obvious, for instance, in the case of texts that have special cultural significance, such as the Bible.

This is not a conception of meaning that will make logicians happy. What is true, what is a contradiction, if meaning is subjectively constructed in specific contexts? Logicians found it necessary to invent their own sense of meaning. They had to invent logic precisely because the everyday sense of meaning is useless for precise reasoning. Logic in its various forms is an extremely successful, well-developed, and useful system. But it is a system that was invented to make precise reasoning possible, not to describe or simulate human cognition. For that we need a very different kind of system, one that is useless for the logician or formal semanticist but that meets the needs of the researcher who is interested in describing how humans think, comprehend, decide, and act.

If the meaning of words must be constructed in their context, the difference between literal and metaphorical, or idiomatic, word meanings is minimized. Both involve constructive processes, and there is no reason to suppose that one kind of construction is necessarily prior or more difficult than the other. Consider the following examples (from Kintsch, 1989):

(9) The cat sat on the mat.
(10) He let the cat out of the bag.

Out of context, there is not much to the understanding of (9): A proposition SIT[CAT,ON-MAT] must be formed, and some more or less dysfunctional associations will be activated, such as *cats purr, my cat is black*, or *philosophical argument*. To understand (10) literally, a proposition LET[HE,CAT,OUT-OF-BAG] must be formed, and once again, some random associations having to do with carrying cats around in bags may be activated. To understand (10) as an idiom, the same proposition is formed, but this time it is embedded in a different set of associations having to do with betraying secrets and surprising revelations of some sort or another. Just how the right set of associates is selected in each case – that is, how the meaning of the phrase is actually constructed in a discourse context – is within the purview of the construction–integration model to be described in the following chapter. Out of context, all three constructions are quite trivial and (except in a linguistic or philosophical discussion) remain superficial. In context, they may be optionally elaborated, depending on the particular context. However, there are no distinct literal or nonliteral processing modes, and it takes people about equally long to come up with a literal or nonliteral interpretation for such sentences (Glucksberg, Gildea, & Bookian, 1982).

3.2.2 Emergent structures

One of the most salient differences between knowledge nets and most other forms of knowledge representation is that knowledge nets are associative, hence based on perception and experience, and therefore relatively unorganized and chaotic. Semantic nets, scripts, frames, and the like are all attempts to make knowledge organization more orderly, more logical. Clearly, knowledge can be organized logically; there is abundant evidence for the psychological reality of higher-order schematic structures such as scripts and frames. Why, then, has an associative net been chosen as the basis for representing knowledge? And how can one account for the obvious fact that people operate with schematic structures all the time if such structures are not components of the basic knowledge representation?

When psychologists and AI researchers began to use scripts and frames as knowledge units, they viewed them as preexisting structures in memory that are retrieved upon demand and used for a wide variety of purposes. This view soon came into conflict with the available psychological evidence as well as the computational demands of AI systems. Computationally, scripts and frames proved to be too inflexible to serve the purposes for which they were originally designed (Schank, 1982). Scripts have to be applied in ever changing contexts, and various ways of fine-tuning scripts proved to be inadequate to provide the flexibility that was needed. For instance, attempts to fine-tune the restaurant script by distinguishing various tracks (fancy restaurant, Chinese restaurant, fast-food restaurant) only led to an endless proliferation of subscripts. Empirically, too, there were problems. Although certain aspects of scripts (differences in the centrality of items in a script – Bower, Black, & Turner, 1979; the directionality of scripts – Haberlandt & Bingham, 1984) could be substantiated by psychological experiment, others could not. Primarily, the distance between events in a script did not behave as it should if scripts were fixed linear structures: The time it takes to retrieve an event given another script event as a cue does not vary proportionally to the distance between the events (Bower et al., 1979; Haberlandt & Bingham, 1984.)

Schank (1982) therefore modified the original script notion by introducing smaller units called Memory Organization Packets (MOPs), out of which scripts can be constructed in contextually more appropriate ways. A different but related proposal was made by Kintsch and Mannes (1987), who showed that scripts and related structures can be constructed out of associative nets. Scripts are not fixed, fully elaborated, preexisting knowledge structures that merely need to be retrieved for use. Instead, only the raw material for constructing a script is part of the knowledge net: a script–proposition that can function as a frame for other, contextually appropriate, associated information in the knowledge network. Scripts and other types of schemas are emergent structures, and because they always are constructed in the context of their use, they are well attuned to that context.

Kintsch and Mannes (1987) start from the observation that the retrieval of the items of a script occurs in quite a different way from the retrieval of the items of a conceptual category. If subjects retrieve instances of some conceptual category, such as *cars,* a plot of the number of items retrieved against time yields a scalloped, negatively accelerated curve as in Figure 3.8 (Bousfield & Sedgwick, 1944; Walker & Kintsch, 1985).

Typically, a subject produces a burst of category items in response to a retrieval cue that he or she is using, pauses, and then produces another burst. Such retrieval cues may be "Japanese cars," "cars in my dormitory parking lot," "cars my parents owned," "cars I have wrecked," and the like. Each retrieval cue works for a while, rapidly retrieving some number of items that are closely associated with it, but then dries up. What happens during the pause is that the subject is searching for a new retrieval cue when the old one has become ineffective. Finally, the subject is unable to generate new, effective retrieval cues and quits. The results of this process are the scalloped curves, steep at first and then flattening out, as shown in Figure 3.8.

If a subject retrieves the items of a script, such as *going to a grocery store,* a smooth function increasing at a constant rate is obtained, as in Figure 3.9 (Kintsch & Mannes, 1987). This pattern of retrieval might be explained by assuming that a script is retrieved and the items are read off from it at a more or less constant rate until the end is reached. However, the protocol data analyzed by Kintsch and Mannes suggest a different interpretation. The retrieval of items is associative and occurs in bursts, very much as in category retrieval. The difference is that the subject does not have to engage in the time-consuming task of generating a new retrieval cue when an old one becomes ineffective, because the next retrieval cue is readily available. It is provided by a script proposition that is part of the knowledge net. Such a proposition is not a full script but

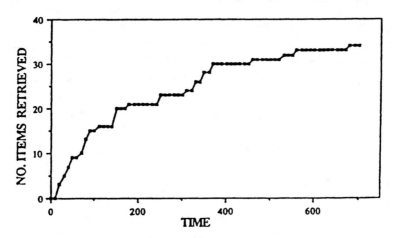

Figure 3.8   A representative retrieval function for one subject in a category retrieval task. Time is plotted in seconds. From Kintsch and Mannes (1987).

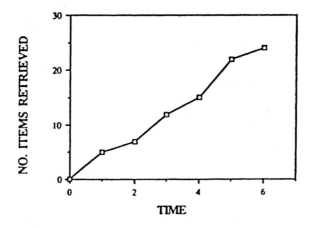

Figure 3.9   Number of grocery store items retrieved by a single subject as a function of time. Time is plotted in 30 sec. intervals. From Kintsch and Mannes (1987).

merely a skeleton script – an ordered list of episode names. For the GRO-CERY-SHOPPING script this would be as shown in Figure 3.10. Each episode name can serve as a retrieval cue. Retrieval of items associated with the retrieval cue occurs associatively, just as in the case of category retrieval, except that the associations among the elements that comprise a script are often unidirectional. *Going through the aisles* is associated with

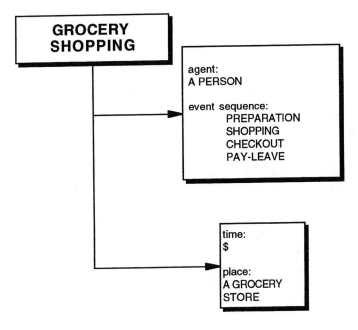

```
┌─────────────────┐
│    GROCERY      │
│    SHOPPING     │
└─────────────────┘
```

agent:
A PERSON

event sequence:
PREPARATION
SHOPPING
CHECKOUT
PAY-LEAVE

time:
$

place:
A GROCERY
STORE

Figure 3.10

going to the checkout counter, but there is no link in the reverse direction. Hence, the retrieval process will continue to move through the script without backtracking. The particular items that will be retrieved in each retrieval episode will vary in this probabilistic process and will be strongly influenced by whatever other retrieval cues are operative in the situation. But there will be no scallops as in category retrieval, for there is no need to pause to search for a new retrieval cue. The next retrieval cue is provided by the script proposition, and it is just as effective as the previous one, so that there is no general slowing down as in Figure 3.8.

Kintsch and Mannes (1987) have described a simulation that shows how scripts can emerge in this way from an associative knowledge base, given basic information about the temporal sequence of the scriptural episodes. For this purpose, they combined the model of memory retrieval proposed by Raajmakers and Shiffrin (1981) with the processes for category and script retrieval that have been discussed here. They obtained the scalloped, negatively accelerated retrieval functions typical for category retrieval and the smooth, constant-rate functions typical for script generation from the same associative net. Thus, they have demonstrated that global structures such as schemata need not be in the mind but may emerge from the action of certain types of control processes on a globally unstructured, only locally linked knowledge base.

3.3 Latent semantic analysis: a vector representation

Propositional representations of *text* have proven their usefulness in research for more than 20 years. Propositional representations of *knowledge*, as explored earlier in this chapter, may prove to be equally useful. However, both have a weakness that is even more serious in practical applications than in research: We cannot construct them automatically and must rely on hand coding (even though such coding can be reasonably reliable and objective). Hence, they are difficult or impossible to use in really large applications. It is fine to analyze propositionally a brief text for an experiment or a simulation or to construct an illustrative knowledge net to test some empirical implication of a simulation. But one cannot propositionalize a whole textbook or all the knowledge of the student studying it. There is, however, another way to represent meaning that is related conceptually to propositional representations and that is not subject to these limitations. It involves a switch in thinking about propositions not as nodes in a network but as vectors in a high-dimensional semantic space.

The meaning of a proposition or concept in the abstract is given by its place in a knowledge net. The meaning of a proposition or concept in a discourse context is given by its position in the network representing that discourse, enriched with information retrieved from the knowledge net. Thus, CAT as well as CHASE[DOG, CAT] are defined by the nodes to which they are linked in a person's knowledge net. There will be some overlap between these nodes but also some differences. For example, SCARED[CAT] will be linked only weakly to CAT but strongly to CHASE[DOG,CAT].

In fact, the labels CAT and CHASE[DOG,CAT] are superfluous; we could equally well denote the two nodes in the network as P_x and P_y. We do not do so because we would get confused rapidly if we were to use such a denotational system. English language labels are much easier to remember. But what is important is the pattern of link strengths to neighboring nodes in the network.

Furthermore, the graphical notation of a node linked to surrounding nodes in a network is not essential either. It is equivalent to a vector representation in which each row and column corresponds to the nodes of the network and the entry in the *i*th row and *j*th column is the strength of the link between nodes *i* and *j*.

A concept or proposition can thus be thought of as a vector of numbers, each number indicating the strength with which the concept or proposition is linked to another concept or proposition.

What determines these numbers? Presumably; they are the end product of lifelong experience, of interacting with the world we live in. We learn – by observation, by talking to others, by reading stories – that cats are not scared normally but that they are when chased by a dog. The values in our vectors, therefore, are the fine-tuned products of numerous and diverse experiences that we as humans have.

There appears to be no way one could provide an artificial system with these numbers by some sort of hand coding. The system is too complex and too huge and too subtle, and unavailable to reliable introspection. The only way to acquire these numbers is to live a normal human life, learning through interaction with the human environment. A machine has no chance to learn all these numbers perfectly, because it cannot live and act like a human – an obvious point, much belabored by philosophers.

Does that mean that we cannot build a machine that will simulate human cognition adequately? Are we forever restricted to hand coding of propositions, as is being done in most of the research described in this book? Not, perhaps, if we shift our criteria somewhat. Machines cannot act and live as humans can and hence they cannot learn from experience as we do, but they can read. Therefore, they can learn from reading. A machine that knows about the world only from reading surely is a far cry from a human with real red blood and surging hormones, but there is a lot to be learned from the written word. It is only the second-best choice, but suppose we teach a machine what the strength values in all these concept and proposition vectors are by experience with the written word only.

Latent Semantic Analysis (LSA) is a technique that allows us to do something like that (Landauer & Dumais, 1997; Landauer, Foltz, & Laham, in press). This technique uses singular value decomposition, a mathematical generalization of factor analysis. It was originally developed as an information retrieval technique by Deerwester, Dumais, Furnas, Landauer, and Harshman (1990) and extended to discourse analysis and general problems concerning learning and language by Foltz (1996) and Landauer and Dumais (1997). The reader will have to refer to these sources for an adequate description of the technique and technical details. Here, I try to give only a general impression of what LSA does and then discuss later some specific uses of LSA in the investigation of discourse comprehension.

In LSA the learning process is started by recording which words occur in the same textual contexts. It reads texts in digital from and counts the times that words appear in each segment of a text. For example, suppose LSA reads about 4 million words from an encyclopedia. It counts for each section of the encyclopedia which words appear and how often. It makes no inferences about the words it reads, so that *tree* and *trees* for LSA are different words. For 30,000 encyclopedia paragraphs containing 35,000 different words, we end up with a huge paragraph by words matrix, with many empty cells, because each paragraph contains only a small subset of the words. In the examples we discuss, the results are based on an analysis of this kind provided by Susan Dumais of Bellcore and described in Landauer and Dumais (1997) and Landauer, Foltz, and Laham (in press).

If words were the appropriate units of cognition, we could stop here and define each word as a very long vector, the entries of the vector being the number of times the word has appeared in each paragraph or document. But we know that will not be a workable solution, for the very reason for introducing propositional representations in the first place was that words are not satisfactory units for cognition. Thus, instead of defining words directly in terms of documents (and documents in term of words), LSA substitutes a semantic approximation. It uses the well-known mathematical technique of singular value decomposition to radically reduce the dimensionality of the space. A theorem of matrix algebra states that any square matrix, M, can be decomposed into the product of three matrices:

$$M = A * D * A'$$

where A and A' are matrices composed of the eigenvectors of the matrix and D is a diagonal matrix of the eigenvalues (or singular values) of the matrix. The theorem generalizes to the nonsquare matrices used by LSA. The eigenvalues are ordered in terms of their magnitude or importance. Multiplying the three matrices yields back the original matrix, M. What is done in LSA is to throw away most of the eigenvalues (and their associated eigenvectors), keeping only the largest ones, say, the 300 largest ones. Multiplying the three matrices thus reduced does not reproduce M precisely but only approximates the original M. That turns out to be a considerable advantage. The original matrix contains too much information – all the details and accidents of word use. By discarding all this detail, we keep only the essence of each word meaning, its pure semantic structure, abstracted from particular situations. This constructs a semantic space of, in the encyclopedia case, 300 dimensions in which each word and document from the original matrix can be expressed as a vector. Furthermore, new words and documents can be inserted into this space and compared with one another and with any of the vectors originally computed. Of the various ways to compare vectors, the only one I discuss here is closely related to correlation: A measure of relatedness between vectors is the cosine between the vectors in the 300-dimensional space. Identical vectors have a cosine of 1, orthogonal vectors have a cosine of 0, and opposite vectors have a cosine of -1. For instance, *tree* and *trees* have a cos $= .85$; *tree* and *cat* are essentially independent, cos $= -01$; *cat* and *The dog chased the cat* yield a cos $= .36$.

What is to be gained by this vector representation? Unlike propositional analysis, it is fully automatic and objective. It is computationally not very demanding (once an original semantic space has been constructed). The cosine measure of semantic relatedness is readily interpretable. Thus, it is not necessary to assign links between nodes in a network arbitrarily or by collecting empirical association data. The cosines between words, sentences, or paragraphs are easily computed and provide objective, empirically based measures. We need no longer guess what the neighboring nodes of a word (or sentence) are in semantic space – we can look it up in the LSA space. Furthermore, words and documents are treated in exactly the same way. "Documents" for LSA are akin to experiences or episodes for a human learner. For us the meaning of a word or proposition is determined as much by the episodes in our memory to which it is related as by the other words to which it is related; that is, meaning involves both semantic and episodic memory. LSA computes relationships both between words and between documents qua episodes. Thus, it allows us to explore this important aspect of meaning, which is not easily done within conventional approaches.

The initial results that the developers of LSA (Landauer, Dumais, Foltz, and their co-workers) obtained with this method impressively demonstrate its promise: LSA appears indeed capable of capturing much of word meanings. More specifically, Landauer and Dumais (1997) found that the vectors for words derived from the encyclopedia analysis predicted the correct answers to standardized vocabulary tests in which students are asked to judge similarity of meaning. Latent semantic analysis simulations matched the performance of moderately competent students: successful foreign applicants to U.S. colleges on tests of English language competence (the TOEFL). Landauer and Dumais also demonstrated that LSA learns word meanings from reading at about the same rate as late primary school children do. Both of these LSA predictions crucially depended on reducing the dimensionality of the semantic space to about 300 dimensions. That is, the words themselves do not matter, but the semantic dimensions derived from their co-occurrences do. In more recent unpublished work by Foltz, Landauer, and Laham, LSA has been trained on introductory psychology textbooks. Its concept representations were then tested with the same multiple choice tests that students took. Latent semantic analysis usually scored about 60% correct (the chance level is 22%), somewhere near the tenth percentile of the real students. These results illustrate both LSA's impressive ability to approximate human meaning but also the substantial gap that still exists between humans and LSA. Integrating LSA into the comprehension model developed here might help us to close this gap and at the same time obtain a better and more realistic model.

The vector representation of LSA is similar to the feature vectors popular in many psychological theories – except that we do not have to define, invent, or identify specific features. We need not interpret the values on the 300-dimensional LSA vector (in fact, we cannot), but we can objectively and automatically represent the meaning of various verbal units in this way and use these representations in computational models of comprehension and memory. The theory of memory based on vector representations has been relatively well explored (Estes, 1995) and hence can be used for modeling with LSA vectors. Latent semantic analysis needs no parser; it treats sentences, paragraphs, and whole texts holistically, representing each as a vector. As currently implemented, LSA has limitations that need to be explored. The very fact that it needs no parser also means that it does not take into account syntactic information, at least in its present form. It allows us to approximately represent global meaning but not the analytic, formal aspects of human thought. Therefore, for example, LSA cannot serve as a basis for computing truth values. There may be several ways to overcome this limitation, one of which I have begun to explore here, namely, to combine the LSA vector representation with the construction–integration model of comprehension.

Latent semantic analysis is a young technique, and the research described in this book involving LSA is only a beginning and still quite tentative.[2] Nevertheless, it opens exciting new possibilities that should be explored by discourse researchers.

How one represents the semantic structure of a text, the mental model that a reader forms when comprehending a text, as well as the reader's knowledge and experience that are needed for comprehension, are of fundamental importance for a psychological processing model of comprehension. The processing model itself is described in chapter 4 and then explored in the second part of the book. In this chapter, two representational formats were discussed. Both of them are language-based, that is, they are representations at the narrative–linguistic level, but they provide reasonably adequate approximations to other levels of representation as well, such as perception and action-based forms of mental representation. The first is the propositional representation that came into use in psychology and the study of language in the 1970s. It has been widely used since then and is by now quite familiar. The second is a vector representation that shares some features with propositional representations, but it is as yet not well known and remains to be explored further.

In the use of propositional representations of texts, we look back at a 20-year history of success. Much of what we have learned about text comprehension and memory in these decades we could not have discovered without a good system for representing the meaning of texts and the structure of texts. The propositional notation has served that purpose well. It is not an adequate notation for logic, semantics, or some branches of linguistics, but it was never intended for that use. It is a tool for research in the psychology of language, and much of the progress in that field has been based on the availability of that tool.

The use of propositional networks as knowledge representation is newer and not nearly as well established. It has several attractive features, however. Obviously, it is good to have the same

2   See sections 5.1.2 on words meaning, 5.3 on metaphor, 6.2.3 on macrostructures, 7.4 on retrieval structures, 8.2.2 on evaluation of summaries, 9.6 on learning from text, and 11.4 on decision processes. Readers may check (and extend on their own) these computations by using the LSA program available at http://samiam.colorado.edu /~lsi/Home.html

representational format for both the mental model a reader constructs from a text and the reader's knowledge. More important is the great flexibility of the propositional notation. Many different structures can be represented in a predicate–argument format: frames, schemas, scripts, even procedures. Thus, the propositional notation allows us to appropriate a wide variety of mental structures that have been found useful in cognitive science in one way or another, without forcing us to choose among alternatives that all have their advantages and disadvantages. Most important, however, propositional representations invite one to think about meaning in a different way. The meaning of a node in a propositional network needs to be constructed from the information the net provides. It is an active process of sampling related, neighboring nodes in the net and of integrating them into a coherent whole. This may be quite a superficial process or an extensive and deep one, but it always occurs in a specific context that crucially biases the final outcome. Thus, meaning is not fixed and ready-made but must be constructed anew in every new context.

The trouble with propositional nets as knowledge representations is that, although they work well in small, illustrative examples, it is impossible to create a large, realistic propositional knowledge net, for the whole net would have to be hand coded, just like a text representation. Latent Semantic Analysis may provide a practical alternative here. It can learn what it needs to know by reading very large amounts of texts. The information it needs is information about the higher-order correlations in the co-occurrence of words. As is the case with propositions, LSA treats meaning as a pattern of semantic relationships. Words, sentences, and whole texts can be represented as vectors in a high-dimensional semantic space and compared with one another. In the chapters that follow, some of the advantages of this alternative knowledge representation are explored when it is used in conjunction with the processing model originally developed for propositional representations. The preliminary results that are available at this point suggest a great potential for LSA for psychological knowledge representation.

4

Modeling comprehension processes
The construction–integration model

Language has been studied and analyzed for centuries. Philosophers, linguists, logicians, and others have accumulated a rich store of knowledge about language. What has emerged, however, is not a uniform, generally accepted theory but a rich picture full of salient details, brilliant insights, ambiguities, and contradictions. Most of this work has focused on analyzing language as an object, rather than on the process of language comprehension or production. The importance of the actual process of language comprehension has not gone unrecognized, for instance, by literary scholars who have understood very well the role that the process of reception plays in the appreciation of a literary work, yet the tools for explicit modeling of comprehension processes have not been available until quite recently. Progress in the building of artificial intelligence systems for natural language processing as well as in the techniques for the simulation of higher-order cognitive processes has provided the foundation upon which psychological process models of comprehension can now be built.

We comprehend a text, understand something, by building a mental model. To do so, we must form connections between things that were previously disparate: the ideas expressed in the text and relevant prior knowledge. Comprehension implies forming coherent wholes with Gestalt-like qualities out of elementary perceptual and conceptual features. It is a marvelous and wondrous achievement, for there are myriads of such features ready to yield many different configurations. How are the right ones selected from these all-too-rich offerings, and how do they cohere into an understanding that is attuned to our goals and motivations as well as the characteristics of the situation within which we find ourselves?

There is no question that this happens. But how? The traditional answer is that order is guaranteed because the process of understanding is under the control of a schema that guides it (Bartlett, 1932; Schank & Abelson, 1977; Selz, 1922). A schema in this view serves as a control structure that regulates comprehension processes in a top-down fashion. It works, on the one hand, like a perceptual filter, in that it admits material consistent with itself but blocks irrelevant materials, and, on the other hand, it serves as an inference machine, in that it fills in the gaps that are inevitably found in the actual stimulus material.

Schema theory has taken many forms in the years past, in both AI and psychology, and has become rather more sophisticated than the caricature just presented suggests. Nevertheless, it has its problems. First and foremost, there exist enough psychological data to question whether the top-down guidance of comprehension is as tight as schema theory suggests. I do not review these data here, but results are presented throughout this book that indicate the need for conceiving of comprehension as a more bottom-up, loosely structured process. Second, human comprehension is incredibly flexible and context-sensitive. It is hard to see how one could model that process with fixed control structures like schemas. It is, therefore, worth exploring an alternative.

A coherent model is certainly the outcome of comprehension, but it does not have to be the result of forcing comprehension into a procrustean schema. One can conceive of comprehension as a loosely structured, bottom-up process that is highly sensitive to context and that flexibly adjusts to shifts in the environment. Comprehension, in this view, may in fact be quite chaotic in its early stages. It becomes orderly and well behaved only when it reaches consciousness. Such a process can be modeled by a construction process that is only weakly controlled and proceeds largely in an associative, bottom-up manner that is followed by a constraint satisfaction process in the form of a spreading activation mechanism and that yields the coherence and order that we experience.

I have called this model the construction–integration (CI) model. In this model mental representations are formed by weak production rules that yield disorderly, redundant, and even contradictory output. However, this output undergoes a process of integration, which results in a well-structured mental representation. Thus, the end result is the same, both according to schema theory and the present proposal. But the way this structure is achieved is quite different.

According to schema theory, the *earthquake* schema would rule out the *chocolate* meaning of *mint* in *The earthquake destroyed all the buildings in town except the mint;* in the CI model propositions with both meanings of *mint* would be constructed, but the one that was irrelevant to the context would be rapidly suppressed. Again, according to schema theory, a reader might very well be reminded of *river* when reading *The car drove over the bridge,* but not of *cards,* which would be blocked by the schema, whereas such irrelevant associations should be commonplace (though fleeting) according to the CI model. Upon hearing *The hiker was surprised to see a bear blocking his path,* a schema-based inferencer might readily infer that *the hiker was scared* but hardly that *bears like honey.* Hence, on a naming task, schema theory would predict a priming effect for *scared* but not for *honey;* CI would predict priming effects for both, as long as the target word was presented right after *bear* in the sentence. In every case, the smart rules of a schema-based theory would prevent the wrong constructions from ever being formed. In contrast, the production rules in the CI model are weak and dumb and do not discriminate what is contextually appropriate from what is not; they are just as likely to instantiate the wrong as the right meaning of a word, or to form an irrelevant as a relevant inference. The construction of the "correct," contextually appropriate meaning results from the integration process that quickly deactivates contextually inappropriate constructions.

This chapter presents the basic elements of the construction-integration theory. After this initial sketch, the remaining chapters of this book will elaborate on the theory in the context of a wide range of issues concerning comprehension.

The process model to be described here was first described in Kintsch (1988; see also Kintsch & Welsch, 1991; Kintsch 1992a, 1992b). It continues and extends the earlier model of Kintsch and van Dijk (1978; see also van Dijk & Kintsch, 1983); van Dijk and Kintsch (1978) provided the basic process model but did not deal with knowledge use in comprehension; Kintsch (1988) added this feature, creating the construction–integration model.

4.1 Construction and integration

To say that construction rules are weak and bottom–up and require an integration process to function does not specify what these rules are. It merely characterizes an architecture within which various kinds of models can be developed. That is, to model a particular cognitive process, a set of (weak) construction rules must be formulated that are involved in this process. I discuss a few examples here that are important for understanding text. This discussion remains informal and relies on hand–simulation of the rules involved. Construction rules for a number of different cognitive processes are described and evaluated empirically in the remaining chapters of this book.

1. *Rules for the construction of propositions.* This is a large and important class of rules. An exhaustive and explicit statement of this set of rules would constitute the parsing component that is missing from the present model. In practice, we proceed as described in section 3.1.

2. *Rules for interconnecting the propositions in a network.* As discussed previously, three levels of connections among propositions can be distinguished: Propositions may be only indirectly related, they maybe directly related, or one proposition may be subordinated to another. Furthermore, propositions may be negatively linked, that is, interfere with each other. Whenever two alternative propositions are formed from the same sentence or phrase, this contradiction is indicated by a negative link. As an example, consider the syntactically ambiguous phrase *they are flying planes,* which yields the structure

FLY[THEY,PLANES]————————ISA[THEY,FLYING [PLANE]]

The negative link is assigned not because the two interpretations are logically incompatible, but because the two alternative propositions were formed from the same sentence. Thus, the system does not have to understand the contradiction in order to assign a negative link, but it does so on purely formal grounds. If the same string of words can be configured once into one proposition and once into another, the two constructions are mutually exclusive and inhibit each other.

A propositional network is thus formed. Link strengths may be chosen to be all equal, or they may be varied according to theoretical considerations. For instance, embedding relations may be given more weight than direct links, which in turn may be given more weight than indirect links. Link strengths may also be estimated empirically from free association data or by means of the cosine values in an LSA analysis. Different versions of the model may thus be obtained to be evaluated empirically for their adequacy.

3. *Rules for the activation of knowledge.* The basic mechanism for knowledge activation is assumed to be associative. Items in working memory activate some neighboring nodes in the knowledge net with probabilities proportional to the strengths with which they are linked to them. This mechanism may be modeled formally (see, for instance, Mannes & Kintsch, 1987, where the SAM theory of memory retrieval by Raajmakers & Shiffrin, 1981, is used for that purpose; likewise Doane, McNamara, Kintsch, Polson, & Clawson, 1992, or Kitajima & Polson, 1995, where memory retrieval processes are of central importance.) Sometimes, however, a more informal treatment is appropriate, as in many of the illustrative examples discussed later. Thus, Kintsch (1994a) obtained empirical estimates of what knowledge was likely to be retrieved but then made the simplifying assumption that all of it actually was retrieved. Even more informally, often only directly relevant knowledge is dealt with explicitly in uses of the model when the complete details of knowledge retrieval do not play a central role.

4. *Rules for constructing inferences.* Just as we are unable to state explicitly all the rules for deriving a propositional representation from a text, we cannot list all rules that people use for inferencing. Examples of such rules appear frequently throughout these chapters. For instance, a simple rule used in forming a situation model might involve the following transitive inference:

If A above B and B above C, then A above C.

As another example, a rule for constructing a macroproposition might take the following minitext:

(1) Jane drove to Alfalfa's, picked up some fresh fruit, a halibut steak, and some Italian cheese for dessert, and paid with her credit card.

into

(2) Jane went grocery shopping.

Rules like (1) and (2) are used intuitively in applications of the present model, just like the parsing rules. We are primarily concerned with the resulting structures, not with the parsing and inference rules themselves.

Once a network of propositions has been constructed through hand simulation of the kind of rules described here, and once these propositions have been linked into a network in a theoretically motivated and consistent way, a spreading activation process is used to stabilize the network. Activation is spread around the network until it stabilizes in a way that takes account of the pattern of mutual constraints that exists among the nodes of the network (the propositions of a text together with the inferences and knowledge elaborations a reader has produced). The final activation values of the nodes thus come to reflect the constraining properties of the network as a whole.

In a network of n nodes, at time t, each node has an activation value $a_i(t)$. The activation values of all nodes in the net at time t are given by the vector

$$A(t) = (a_1(t), a_2(t), \ldots a_n(t)) = \{a_i(t)\}$$

The initial activation vector is usually taken to be $A(1) = \{1\}$. The strength of the link between the nodes i and j in the network is w_{ij}. Thus, the total pattern of interconnections among the nodes is given by the connectivity matrix

$$W = \{w_{ij}\}$$

Activation spreads to a node from all of its neighboring nodes, so that the activation of a node at time $t + 1$ becomes

$$a_j(t + 1) = \frac{\sum_{i=1}^{n} a_i(t)w_{ij}}{\max a_j(t + 1)}$$

Dividing the activation value of a node after activation has spread to it by the maximum activation value in the net renormalizes the activation values and keeps them from growing without bounds. In earlier versions of the model, activation values were normalized by requiring the total activation in a net to sum to 1 by dividing each activation score by the sum of all scores. Other standard connectionist techniques could also be used for normalization – for example, a sigmoidal transformation, as in Goldman and Varma (1995).

The spreading activation process is continued for as many iterations as are necessary for the activation values to settle in a stable pattern. Once no activation value changes by more than some criterial amount, say .001 or .0001, the process is stopped. The conditions under which a spreading activation process stabilizes, that is, approaches an asymptotic activation vector $A(\infty)$, or simply A, are not known in general (though see Rodenhausen, 1992). Symmetric connectivity matrices with no negative values behave like ergodic Markov chains. That is, an asymptote exists and is independent of the starting vector.

The values of A indicate the strength of each node in the integrated network. Nodes that are positively connected to many other nodes in the net will be strengthened. Nodes that have few connections or are negatively connected will wither away or become suppressed. This is a process of constraint satisfaction: Nodes that satisfy the multiple constraints of the network become stronger, whereas nodes that do not become weaker. The resulting pattern of activation indicates for each node the role it plays in the network as a whole and can be considered a measure of the strength of that node in the mental representation.

A simple numerical example helps to form some intuitions about this integration mechanism. Consider the network of five nodes shown in Figure 4.1. The dashed line indicates a negative link. If we let all links have a strength of either 1 or –1, we obtain the following connectivity matrix, remembering that each node is linked to itself:

	A	B	C	D	E
A	1	1	1	1	0
B	1	1	0	1	0
C	1	0	1	0	1
D	1	1	0	1	–1
E	0	0	1	–1	1

We assume that each of the five nodes has an activation value of 1 initially:

$$A(1) = (1, 1, 1, 1, 1)$$

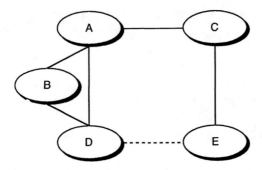

Figure 4.1

Multiplying this initial activation vector once by the connectivity matrix yields the following values:

(4, 3, 3, 2, 1)

The activation values after one iteration are obtained by dividing these scores by their maximum:

A(2) = (1.00, .75, .75, .50, .25)

If this new activation vector is repeatedly multiplied by the connectivity matrix, renormalizing it after each multiplication, the activation values stabilize after nine iterations. That is, the maximum change after nine iterations is less than .001. These final activation values for this network are as follows:

A(9) = A(∞) = (1.00, .85, .46, .85, .00)

Node E has become completely suppressed, in spite of its connection with node C, because of the strong inhibition from node D. Nodes A, B, and D support one another effectively, whereas C turns out to be only a marginal element in this net.

These calculations can be readily performed with a program written by Mross and Roberts (1992). This program for Macintosh is available on request.[1] It allows two kinds of input: Either proposition lists may be used that are automatically turned into a network and its corresponding coherence matrix by linking propositions with common arguments, or nets of any kind that are automatically translated into matrix form can be constructed graphically. The spread of activation can be calculated cycle by cycle or all at once until a stopping criterion is reached. Various display options are available, as well as a number of features that I introduce later. The program allows readers not only to check the results reported here, but it also provides an easy means of exploring on their own constraint satisfaction networks of the type described here.

4.2 Processing cycles in text comprehension

Text representations must be built up sequentially. It is not possible psychologically to construct and integrate a text representation for a whole book chapter or a whole lecture. The chapter and the lecture have to be processed word by word and sentence by sentence. As each text segment is processed, it is immediately integrated with the rest of the text that is currently being held in working memory. The immediate processing hypothesis, first put forward by Just and Carpenter (1987), generally holds, at least for lower-level processes in comprehension. Occasionally, however, readers use delay strategies when dealing with potentially ambiguous syntactic constructions (e.g., Ferstl, 1994b) or they continue reading when constructing a situation model when they do not understand something, in the hope that the succeeding text will clarify their problem. But in general information in a text is processed as soon as possible. In the model this means that as each text element is processed and a new proposition is added to the text representation, it is immediately integrated with the text representation. Thus, integration is not a sentence wrap-up phenomenon but is performed whenever a new element is added to the network under construction. Therefore, an ambiguous word in a discourse context will be disambiguated within about 350 ms after presentation – not just at the sentence end (Till, Mross, & Kintsch, 1988).

1 Send diskette to W. Kintsch, Institute of Cognitive Science, University of Colorado, Boulder, CO, 80309–0344.

The integration that takes place at the sentence end has a special status, however. Except for very short sentences, working memory at this point is usually loaded to capacity and must be cleared to make room for the next sentence. Whatever has been constructed is transferred to long-term memory. As a consequence, except for one or two central propositions that are retained in the focus of attention because of their presumed relevance to further processing, all that has been constructed up to this point in working memory is now lost from consciousness/primary memory. However, in a normal text, this information is still readily retrievable because the succeeding sentence most likely will contain retrieval cues that make it accessible in long-term working memory, as discussed in chapter 7. The active processing focuses on only the current sentence, plus whatever information had to be retrieved from long-term memory that is necessary for its processing. Thus, working memory is like a spotlight that moves across a text, sentence by sentence, constructing and integrating a mental representation in the process. The representation that results from this cyclical process is a coherent structure and not a sequence of disjoint structures, each corresponding to a sentence. The coherence is a result of the fact that propositions are kept in short-term memory from one sentence to the next to serve as bridging material and because earlier portions of the text as well as general knowledge items that were retrieved during processing provide a lattice of interconnections.

The number of propositions that are carried over from one cycle to the next is a free parameter of the model. The estimates that have been obtained so far suggest that it is a small number – generally 1. Just which proposition is carried over is determined by the activation values propositions receive at the end of a processing cycle. Typically, the strongest proposition of the previous cycle remains in the focus of attention as attention shifts to a new sentence. This strength criterion replaces the selection mechanisms that were introduced in earlier work, for example, the "leading edge strategy" of Kintsch and van Dijk (1978). A full discussion of memory use in comprehension is given in chapter 7.

As a result of this cyclical processing of a text, not all relations in a text that can be detected by linguistic analysis are actually realized in the mental representation. Only those relations that hold between propositions that were together in working memory at some time during the sentence-by-sentence process of comprehension play a role in the text representation.

As is common in connectionist models, the original coherence matrix **W** and the final activation vector **A** can be combined to give the outcome of the comprehension process, that is, the long-term memory strength of each element of the network and its interconnections. A new matrix **M** of memory strengths m_{ij} can be defined such that

$$m_{ij} = \sum_{c=1}^{k} w_{ij} * a_i * a_j$$

where w_{ij} is an element of **W** and a_i is the final activation value of the ith element; the summation is over the k processing cycles that the ith element has participated in, $k \geq 1$.

4.3 Textbase and situation model

The comprehension process yields as its end product a mental representation of a text, the episodic text memory. According to the theory presented here, it consists of a network of interrelated propositions of various strengths, given by the long-term memory strength matrix **M**.

This episodic text memory is a unitary structure, but for analytic purposes it is useful to distinguish two components – the textbase and the situation model. The textbase consists of those elements and relations that are directly derived from the text itself. It is what would be obtained if a patient linguist or psychologist were to translate the text into a propositional network and then integrate this network cycle by cycle, as described earlier, but without adding anything that is not explicitly specified in the text. In general, this procedure yields an impoverished and often even incoherent network. The reader must add nodes and establish links between nodes from his or her own knowledge and experience to make the structure coherent, to complete it, to interpret it in terms of the reader's prior knowledge, and last but not least to integrate it with prior knowledge. Various sources of knowledge must be used in the construction of situation models – knowledge about the language, about the world in general, and about the specific communicative situation. Furthermore, not only general knowledge enters this process but also the reader's personal experience. Such sources of knowledge may all be needed to complement the textual information and to transform what by itself is only an isolated memory structure into something that relates to and is integrated with the reader's personal store of knowledge and experience.

The extent to which a reader will actually perform the work of transforming a textbase into a situation model is subject to numerous influences. In a given comprehension episode, one influence or another may dominate, but it is generally the case that both play a role, complementing each other.

Figure 4.2 illustrates the relationship between textbase and situation model. The textbase can be more or less coherent and complete, and the situation model can be more or less adequate and precise. Mental text representations may fall anywhere in this quadrant. In the text-that-tells-it-all, in which every detail as well as the overall structure is made perfectly explicit (as far as that is possible!), the textbase is also a good situation model and no further knowledge elaborations on the part of the comprehender are required. Typically, however, the mental text representation is a mixture of text-derived and knowledge-derived information, not necessarily in equal parts. Extreme cases, in which either the

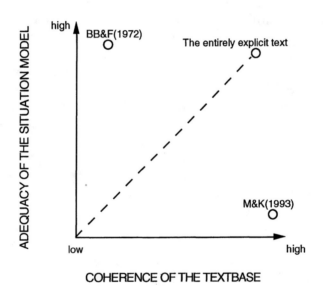

Figure 4.2   Textbase and situation model jointly determine the nature of the mental text representation. Extreme cases are Bransford, Barclay, and Franks (1972), where the situation model dominates at the expense of the textbase, and Moravcsik and Kintsch (1993), where the textbase dominates at the expense of the situation model.

textbase or the situation model dominates to the exclusion of the other, are instructive. Bransford, Barclay, and Franks (1972) and Bransford and Franks (1971) described some experiments in which they obtained no memory for the text itself – neither the actual words and phrases of the text (the surface structure of the text) nor its meaning (the propositional structure). However, subjects had understood the texts very well and were able to form stable situation models on the basis of which they could answer questions correctly and make inferences about the text. The experimenters produced these results by using artificial little texts that generated a great deal of intersentence interference so that subjects quickly forgot the text; however, subjects remembered very well the simple situations described by the text. At the other extreme, there were experiments such as that reported by Moravcsik and Kintsch (1993) in which subjects remembered a text reasonably well but failed to understand it at the level of the situation model. Their texts were well written and provided rich structural cues to the reader, so that skilled readers could construct a good, coherent textbase that was sufficient for the reproduction of the text. However, the texts concerned topics about which the subjects knew very little, so that they were unable to construct more than rudimentary situation models, which were insufficient for tasks that demanded more than the reproduction of the text.

The textbase consists of the network of propositions that represent the meaning of the text, as understood by a particular reader. Usually, an idealized "normal" reader is assumed, who reads everything carefully and constructs a proposition whenever the text invites one. This is not what real readers necessarily do, but it provides a baseline against which to score the performance of real readers. Thus, even if a text is written in such a way that an ideal reader could construct from it a highly coherent textbase, such will not necessarily be the case.

Another component of the textbase, in addition to the propositional structure, is the surface structure of the text. When the reader is reading a text or listening to a conversation, it is generally the case, that at least some of the exact words and phrases are remembered at least for a time. Under certain conditions, for example, in sentence recognition experiments or in memory for actual conversations, this surface memory may play a significant role. Thus, words, word groups (such as a noun phrase), or a prepositional phrase unit may be represented as nodes in the textbase, with links to their propositional counterparts as well as links between them, according to the linguistic relations involved. One does not have to stop there. For some texts, especially poetry, other relations among words or phrases such as rhymes, rhythm, or alliteration must be included as relations in the textbase if comprehension or memory for such texts is to be adequately simulated (Kintsch, 1994b).

All kinds of knowledge elements may be used in the construction of a situation model. The textbase is made coherent, for instance, by inferring a connective between only indirectly related propositions:

> (3)   Jane could not find the vegetable and the fruit she was looking for. She became upset.

Not finding something one is looking for is a common reason for becoming upset. Hence, a causal link is inferred between the two propositions, thus forming a simple situation model.

Elaborative inferences come in many kinds:

> (4)   Jack missed his class because he went to play golf. He told his teacher he was sick.

A situation model may be formed by the elaboration *Jack lied.*
In

> (5)   A turtle sat on a log. A fish swam under the log.

the situation model might be an image of a *lake,* a *log with a turtle,* and *a fish underneath.* Various elaborations are implied by such an image, for example, that *the turtle is above the fish, the fish is in the water,* and so on.

Situation models often involve more than filling gaps between propositions or local elaborations. They may provide a basis for the overall organization of the text even in cases where the text structure is not signaled explicitly in the text. Readers recognize certain text structures and can use this knowledge to impose an organization on the text. For instance, in a little story "Jane goes grocery shopping" readers can generate a macrostructure for the text even if none is signaled by reference to their grocery-shopping script, which identifies the episodes typically involved in grocery shopping (preparation, shopping, checkout, pay/ leave). The sentences of the text can be subordinated to these episode nodes, thus creating the macrostructure of the text via the schema-based situation model. If an episode (e.g., checkout) is not mentioned explicitly in the text, this schema can be a source for gap-filling elaborations.

A situation model is, therefore, a construction that integrates the textbase and relevant aspects of the comprehender's knowledge. No general rules can be stated, because knowledge elaborations may be of many different types, and the extent to which they occur may differ widely among readers and occasions. How much elaboration occurs depends on the text – whether it is self-sufficient or not – but also on the readers, their goals, motivation, and resources available.

In some cases it is necessary to distinguish between different kinds of situation models. Thus, in their work on how students understand and solve word algebra problems, Nathan, Kintsch, and Young (1992) found it useful to distinguish between the textbase, a situation model, and a problem model. In an overtake problem, for instance, the situation model represents the student's general understanding of what happens when two vehicles move along the same track at different speeds; the problem model represents the mathematization of this situational understanding in terms of algebraic entities and equations. Students have no difficulty with the former but may be unable to formulate the latter. Fischer, Henninger, and Redmiles (1991) have made a similar distinction with respect to computer systems. Users often do have a good understanding of the tasks they need to perform at a general level but do not know how to use their computer system for that purpose; they have an adequate situation model but do not know how to map it into a system model. The objects and relations in the situation model represent objects and relations in the world that we are familiar with; the objects and relations in the problem (or system) model represent objects and relations in a formal world, that of algebra or UNIX. Obviously, these two models have to be in correspondence, but they need to be differentiated, because they involve quite different processing demands.

We distinguish between textbases and situation models not because they are somehow different mental objects. On the contrary, there is a single, unitary mental representation of a text. To describe this representation and its genesis, it is useful to separate out textbases and situation models, as well as problem models and surface structures, as our analyses require.

To lend these discussion some concreteness, two simple examples are discussed to illustrate a few aspects of the construction of textbases and situation models.

4.3.1 Imagery as a situation model

The minitext (from Kintsch, 1994a) to be considered here is:

(6)   John traveled by car from the bridge to the house on the hill. A train passed under the bridge.

To form the textbase we assume that the two brief sentences are both processed in a single cycle. The first sentence yields a single proposition with a modifier; another proposition with a filled location slot is derived from the second sentence; the two propositions are only indirectly related (by the common argument BRIDGE), as shown in Figure 4.3. The textbase is thus strongly constrained by the text; most or all cooperative readers would be expected to form a propositional textbase like the one shown in the figure. Just what sort of situation model would be formed is much less constrained. We make the assumption here, which will be correct for at least some readers, that an image will be formed. For the first sentence, this image might be of a house on a hill, a bridge crossing a river, a road connecting the bridge and the river, and a car driving from the bridge up to the house. Note that this image does not include John, but there is a road and a river, as well as a particular spatial relationship between hill and river – for example, the hill might be to the left of the

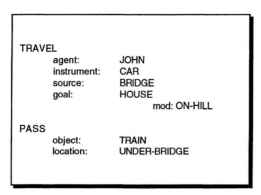

Figure 4.3

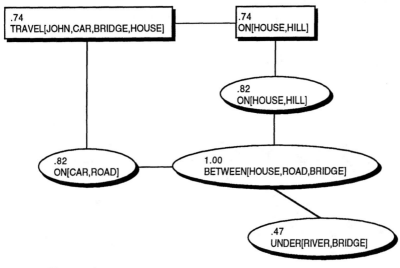

Figure 4.4

river, for which there is no license in the text. This image can be represented by the four spatial relations (shown in the ovals of Figure 4.4), which form a network together with the two textbase elements (shown in the rectangules). The TRAVEL proposition corresponds to the ON[CAR,ROAD] image element, which therefore links them together in the network, and the spatial and propositional ON[HOUSE,HILL] elements correspond to each other.

As each proposition or imagery element is formed, it is integrated into the network that is being formed in working memory. The status of the network after the elements shown in Figure 4.4 have been constructed and integrated is indicated by the activation values that are shown with each element. The main point is that the gratuitous elaboration of including a river in the image receives a low but positive activation value. This will change, as the next sentence becomes part of the network (see Figure 4.5).

We have the two propositional elements derived from the second sentence, which give rise to a new imagery element: a train under the bridge. This is linked to the previous image of the bridge, road, and house but is incompatible with the other element of the previous image of a river

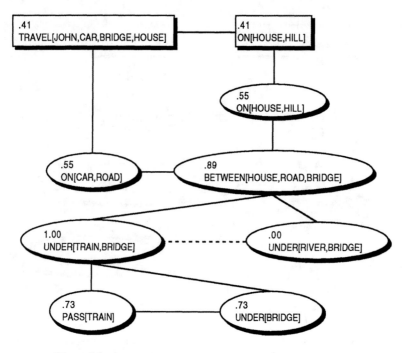

Figure 4.5

under the bridge. Thus, the negative link is based on an inference that a bridge over train tracks does not have a river underneath (neglecting the possibility that a bridge could span both train tracks and a river). The two UNDER nodes therefore interfere with each other and are linked by a value of –1 in the network (indicated by a broken line). The outcomes of the final integration cycle are shown at the top, with each node. The image of the train under the bridge dominates the net and completely suppresses the image of bridge and river.

This example was chosen to demonstrate two points. First, it shows how the model can deal with images – not very elegantly, but it can do so. Some imagery information can be presented in the way shown here but with some loss of information – the concreteness of the image together with some of its spatial implications. Second, it provides a good example of the operation of weak, dumb rules. In response to the first sentence, an image was constructed of a bridge and a river. The text said nothing about a river; it was imported as a part of the image of a bridge. In the second sentence, this image had to be corrected because a new image interfered with it. No damage was done by the gratuitous inclusion of a river in the budding situation model – it simply disappeared when better information became available. Knowledge (river-under-bridge) was activated associatively, that is, by a context-independent, dumb mechanism. But the mechanism need not be any smarter, because the network representation corrects errors easily and without requiring major repairs in the structure that has been generated.

4.3.2 A script-based situation model

Many texts contain linguistic markers of importance and structure that signal their macrostructure. The following example shows how a text that lacks such signals can nevertheless be assigned a macrostructure as part of the construction of a situation model if it fits a familiar schema. This text is slightly longer and must be processed in more than one processing cycle. We assume a cycle size of six elements. Once working memory contains six new elements, the model stops accepting further input as soon as it reaches a sentence (or, in some cases, phrase) boundary. In other words, working memory capacity is not inflexible, in that more than six new elements may be processed if it is necessary to avoid breaking up a complex proposition. The text is as follows:

(7) (S1) Jane went grocery shopping on Sunday afternoon. (S2) She had to park the car far away from the store because the parking lot was full. (S3) The aisles were as crowded as the parking lot. (S4) The lettuce was wilted and the fruit was picked over. (S5) She became upset. (S6) But she filled her cart with whatever she could find. (S7) The bill was larger than expected. (S8) She carried two heavy bags across the parking lot.

The first sentence (S1) retrieves the grocery-shopping script as in Figure 4.6. This script provides a macrostructure for the text, in that its slots become the superordinate macropropositions. The first sentence (S1) merely specifies the agent and time slot for this script. Because so far fewer than six network nodes have been created, the model continues to

GROCERY SHOPPING

    agent: PERSON

    event sequence: PREPARATION
                       SHOPPING
                       CHECKOUT
                       PAY-LEAVE

    place: GROCERY STORE
    time: $

Figure 4.6

read in the second sentence (S2). This sentence is assigned to the preparation slot of the grocery-shopping script, because preparation is associated in the knowledge base with making a shopping list, driving to the
store, parking, and entering store. Thus, the structure that is generated
when the first two sentences are processed now contains seven nodes
(Figure 4.7). All nodes and links are assigned a value of 1. The main
proposition is GROCERY-SHOPPING, with three filled slots; the
PREPARATION slot is connected to PARK, which has two modifiers
and is linked (via an explicit BECAUSE relation) to FULL. Working
memory is loaded to capacity, and the end-of-cycle integration determines the final activation values for these nodes, which are as shown in
Figure 4.7 before each element of the net.

The third sentence (S3) is associated with the SHOPPING slot of the
main proposition, and it also reinstates the FULL proposition from the
previous processing cycle. Because S3 is a short sentence and only three
new elements have been constructed at this point, the model goes on and
reads in S4 as part of the same cycle. It is also connected to the SHOP-
PING episode. In addition, the PARK proposition is carried over in the
short-term memory buffer as the most highly activated proposition from
the first processing cycle. This yields the network shown in Figure 4.8.
The third processing cycle comprises S4 and S5. The key element here is
the UPSET proposition. Because other information has already been

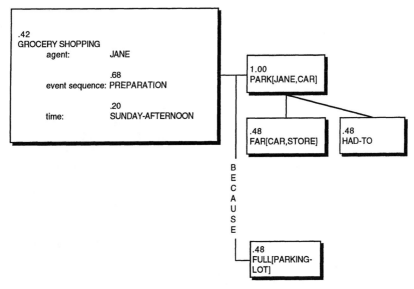

Figure 4.7

processed that constitutes normal conditions for getting annoyed, the reader may[2] generalize and form a macroproposition, ANNOYED, with the slots agent, condition, state, and consequence (the latter remains unspecified). The full parking lot, the crowded aisles, and the picked-over fruit all get connected to this new macroproposition as preconditions and hence are reinstated (Figure 4.9). The link between UPSET and FILL represents the sentence connective *but*. Again, activation values after the end-of-cycle integration are shown next to each propositional element.

The last processing cycle includes the final two sentences, S7 and S8. The ANNOY proposition is carried over as the most highly activated element on cycle 3 (Figure 4.10).

Thus, the processing of this text resulted in the creation of two macro-propositions, GROCERY-SHOPPING and ANNOYED, that serve to organize and interrelate the text. The first macroproposition was gener-

---

2   This is only one possible interpretation of this text – not all readers will follow this course.

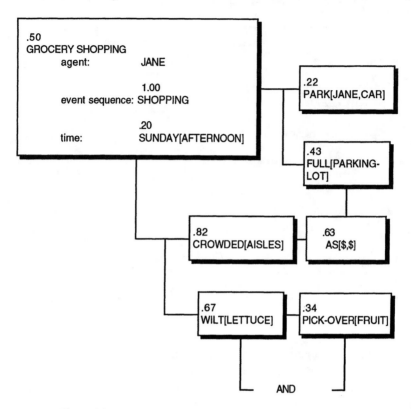

Figure 4.8

ated by the fact that a script that was retrieved on the basis of the first sentence proved to provide an appropriate organizational structure for the remainder of the text. Each sentence of the text was recognized as a possible filler for the slots of the script that was available. This computation involves matching each (complex) text proposition with propositions associated with the slots of the scripts in long-term memory. The second macroproposition involved a similar process. A proposition in the text – UPSET – retrieved information from long-term memory (let's call it an ANNOY schema) about normal conditions for becoming upset in a grocery store; text propositions were found that matched this information and hence were subordinated to the ANNOYED proposition. These two macropropositions provide an organization for the text. They are the core

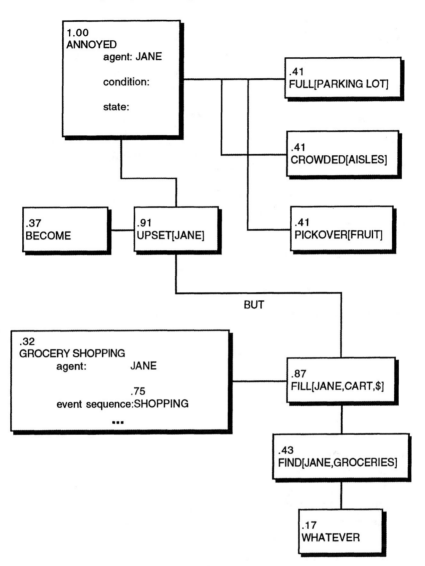

Figure 4.9

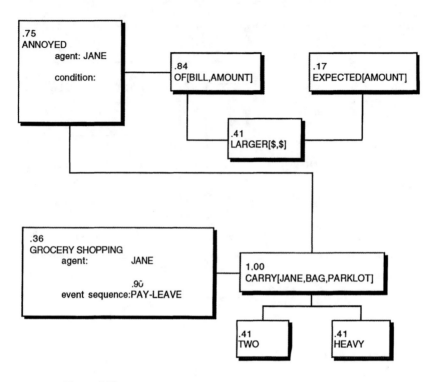

Figure 4.10

of the situation model; the rest of the text provides detail that fits into that model and supports the situation model. The situation model was of course constructed on the basis of that detail, but once the construction process is over, it becomes the dominant element in the episodic text structure.

Note that in all the preceeding examples one cannot make a strict distinction between situation model and textbase. Certain propositions are clearly text derived and hence belong to the textbase, but the way they are organized and indeed their very strength in the overall structure depend on the situation model that has been created of a woman getting annoyed while grocery shopping. A reader without knowledge about shopping in a supermarket who has not experienced the annoyances of such places could and would not create this kind of structure. His or her memory representation would therefore be quite different – more like a pure textbase.

To calculate the long-term memory strength of the nodes in the network (section 4.2), all activation values are squared, multiplied by the node strength in the network (which is always 1), and summed if a node participates in more than a single cycle. These strength values are most informative if calculated for complex propositions rather than for each propositional element separately, except that time or location slots are best kept separate (for purposes of scoring recall protocols). The resulting strength values are shown in Figure 4.11. For S1, the strength of the main proposition and the time element are shown separately. The other sentences correspond to complex propositions, except sentences S2 and S4, in which two propositions are linked by a *because* and *and,* respectively.

The strength values shown in Figure 4.11 can form the basis for various experimental predictions, as is illustrated in later chapters. For instance, they could be used to predict the rank order of recall frequencies for the complex propositions in this text. Or they could be used to form a predicted summary, which, if based on the three strongest propositions, would be something like

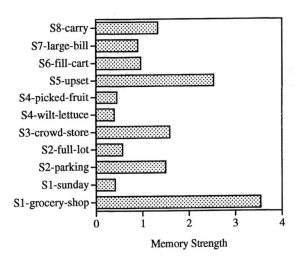

Figure 4.11 Long-term memory strengths for the propositions of the grocery-shopping text.

(8)   This woman went grocery shopping. She got upset because it
was crowded.

Indeed, a variety of theoretical summaries could be formed in this way,
with a relative likelihood associated with each one.

4.4 Earlier versions of the model

Although much has changed since Kintsch and van Dijk (1978) began
work on a process model of comprehension, the basic framework of that
model is still the same today: the propositional representation, the cyclical processing, the distinction between the micro- and macrostructure.
But the model has evolved and, indeed, changed in some important ways.

The year of the mental model was 1983. Johnson-Laird published his
influential book of that title, and van Dijk and I introduced the related
notion of situation model (van Dijk & Kintsch, 1983). This was a major
change in the theory, which shifted the emphasis away from the text itself
to the knowledge/text interaction. This emphasis has been retained and
strengthened here.

A more technical innovation made by van Dijk and Kintsch (1983) was
the use of complex propositions in contrast to atomic propositions, as in
the earlier work. However, in actual modeling work I continued to use
atomic propositions for some time thereafter, and only in the present
work have I employed complex propositions more consistently.

In 1988 the CI architecture was developed (Kintsch, 1988). It involved
a shift from a schema-based control system to a bottom–up system in
which context effects were viewed as constraint satisfaction. This made it
possible for the first time to deal seriously with the use of knowledge and
memory in comprehension. In the present book I have tried to develop in
detail the program laid out in 1988. In particular, the theory of long-term
working memory of Ericsson and Kintsch (1995) is used to specify the
details of the use of knowledge and memory in comprehension, as detailed
in chapter 7. Thus, the new framework has significantly modified earlier
views of working memory management, the use of episodic text memory
and knowledge in comprehension, and inferencing.

In the present book I also introduce Latent Semantic Analysis (LSA)
as an alternative to propositional representations. It is consistent with the
processing theory presented here, as I have tried to show with the various

illustrative examples to be analyzed in Part II of the book. Propositions have the advantage that we can interpret them easily, but they depend on hand coding. Thus, they are not suitable for large-scale applications because automation is impossible. The vectors of LSA, like distributed representations in a neural net, are not as readily interpreted, but they can be constructed automatically and objectively and do not impose limits on the size of the texts to be analyzed. It may be advantageous for the theorist to think in terms of propositions because of their concreteness, but the LSA format offers advantages of scale, objectivity, and automaticity that open up new horizons for the theory of comprehension.

A process model of text comprehension attempts to describe the step-by-step processes by which written or spoken language is transformed into a mental representation in the reader's or listener's mind. The construction-integration (CI) model assumes that this process involves two phases: a construction phase, in which an approximate but incoherent mental model is constructed locally from the textual input and the comprehender's goals and knowledge, and an integration phase that is essentially a constraint satisfaction process that rejects inappropriate local constructions in favor of those that fit together into a coherent whole. The construction rules in this model can be relatively simple and robust because they have to take into account only the local context. The global context becomes important only in the integration phase, when the tentative, incoherent network that has been formed by the context-free construction rules settles into a stable state.

The CI model differs thus from a strictly top-down, schema-controlled process that would require more sophisticated, fine-tuned, context-sensitive construction rules. Such rules tend to be brittle and unreliable in the face of the complexity and variability in the real world. Human comprehension processes do not appear to work this way but employ simpler and more robust local rules in conjunction with a holistic integration process.

Mental models of texts have two sources: the text itself, and what readers contribute to it from their knowledge and experience, after their own needs. Accordingly, it is often useful to distinguish between a textbase, which more or less reflects the text as it is, and a situation model, which includes the reader's elaborations. Different readers on different occasions will weight these two aspects of the text representation differently. The contrast between textbase and situation model is one of the main themes in this book, recurring in one form or another in just about every chapter to come.

The present chapter merely introduces a framework for building models for specific comprehension tasks. In Part II of the book, such models are constructed and empirically evaluated for a wide variety of tasks, ranging from simple word identification in discourse to learning from text, action planning on the basis of verbal instructions, and judgments based on verbal cover stories.

Part II

Models of comprehension

5

Word identification in discourse

5.1 The construction of word meanings

Newell (1990) observed that although the simplest experimental tasks may have the least ecological validity, they tend to provide the best opportunities for empirically testing assumptions about the basic architecture of a theory. Experiments on word identification in discourse have played this role for the construction–integration (CI) model. The primary claim of that model is that construction processes are relatively independent of context and that the contextual fine-tuning is achieved in a subsequent integration phase. Studies of word identification allow us to test these predictions.

How is the meaning of a word in a discourse constructed? Are there differences when words are used literally and when they are used metaphorically? How are anaphora identified, and how does the structure of a discourse emerge from this process? Rich linguistic and psycholinguistic results are available to significantly constrain answers to these questions. I sketch the principal features of these data and describe simple simulations with the CI model to show that the model provides a suitable framework for the discussion of how word meanings are constructed in discourse.

The process of identifying a word – in reading or listening – involves a complicated sequence of analyses – perceptual as well as conceptual – and takes considerable time to complete. As we shall see later in this section, the construction of a word meaning in a discourse context takes approximately 350 ms. Although an eye fixation during reading lasts only around

200 to 250 ms, word meanings in a discourse context need more time than that to stabilize. This means that meaning construction at the word level extends beyond the fixation time. In general, readers attempt to interpret whatever structure they encounter – lexical, syntactic, semantic, or discourse – immediately rather than engaging in a wait-and-see strategy (for a detailed review, see Just & Carpenter, 1987.) However, this means only that they begin the interpretive process as soon as possible. It is not necessarily the case that each word is fully encoded while it is being fixated. During the fixation, the perceptual construction processes are initiated and largely completed. According to the CI model, these do not produce a final product – a particular word meaning – but must be integrated into the discourse context. This process of contextual constraint satisfaction starts immediately, as soon as anything has been constructed to be integrated, but may not be completed until sufficient local context is available to allow the integration process to stabilize.

5.1.1 From the retina to working memory

The sequence of intermediate perceptual representations generated during reading has been studied extensively (see, for instance, Potter, 1983). First, light receptors register visual information on the retina; then, in a series of transformations, the neural information is analyzed en route to the associative cortex. Higher levels of representation are derived from the lower-level representations as the information at each lower level is maintained briefly in associated memory buffers. What is stored in these memory buffers are temporary representations, which are accessible to other cognitive processes only in highly restricted ways. Some low-order buffers can be accessed only by certain specialized processes. Their contents are never consciously experienced, and their existence can be demonstrated only by special experimental methods. The contents of other buffers, on the other hand, may be transferred to the level where conscious experience is possible; but at that point they become contents of working memory, characterized by the same properties as other contents of working memory. Thus, some results of intermediate perceptual and conceptual processing are only temporarily buffered and by their very nature are transitory and unconscious. Others are normally so but may become cognitive end products in their own right and are thus consciously experienced.

Some of these intermediate buffers receive input not only from the sensory, perceptual, and conceptual processes but also from working memory directly. That is, they serve as slave systems for the central executive, as Baddeley (1986) has shown. These are the articulatory loop and the visual-spatial scratch pad, which are capable of recycling special sorts of information under the control of the central executive.

Thus, putting some of the notions of Potter (1983) and Baddeley (1986) together, we arrive at the following sequence of intermediate buffers in reading a text. The neurophysiological bases of the first three buffers listed below, including the differentiation between space and pattern information, are relatively well understood. The remaining memory buffers with higher levels of representation involve learned recodings of visual stimuli.

1. *Retinotopic icon.* This buffer is the perceptible continuation of a single presented word resulting from photoreceptors and other neural mechanisms.

2. *Spatiotopic visual memory.* Retinal information from successive eye fixations is integrated at this level of processing. The printed text is represented as a stable structure located in space.

3. *Reatopic visual memory.* Spatial characteristics of the retinal information are less relevant at this level of transformation than are the configuration of visual features and patterns of the perceptually available text segment. Even when this text segment is removed and replaced with an irrelevant stimulus (visual mask), information about the original text segment is retained in this memory buffer for several seconds.

4. *Conceptual buffer.* At this level of representation, words and objects are perceived and understood. Experimental results show that words can be momentarily understood but are then lost because of interference from other cognitive processes. Conceptual representations become conscious and receive permanence only when transferred to working memory.

5. *The articulatory loop/acoustic buffer.* Even skilled, adult readers transform visual information in reading into an acoustic form (we ignore here the debate whether this level of representation is best understood as acoustic or articulatory-motoric). Articulatory representations not only are intermediate results in the sequence of cognitive processes but also may become contents of working memory, and material from working memory can be recycled in the articulatory loop. Thus, this buffer may function as a slave system for working memory (Baddeley, 1986).

6. *The visual-spatial scratch pad.* This is Baddeley's (1986) other slave system, which has much the same function in the visual-spatial domain as the articulatory loop in the acoustic domain.

7. *Working memory.* This is Baddeley's (1986) central executive. It comprises the entire cognitive work space (here I deviate from Potter, 1983) where information about the current text segment is stored in rapidly accessible form. Information in working memory is the cognitive end product of all the foregoing processes but is itself complex and structured and involves different levels of representation.

Figure 5.1 (modified from Potter, 1983) illustrates this temporal sequence of buffers. Positron emission tomography (PET) and event-related potential (ERP) studies indicate activity in the right posterior cortex during visual feature analysis (Posner & McCandliss, 1993), begin-

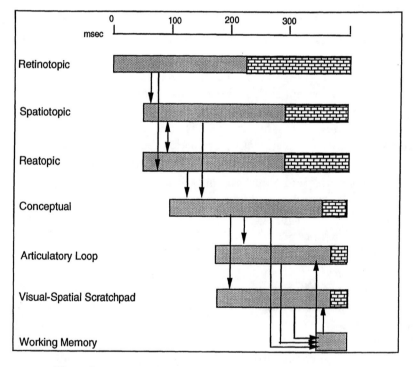

Figure 5.1   Intermediate processing stages with their associated memory buffers in word identification.

ning at about 100 ms. By 200 ms there is activity in the left-lateralized visual word form area if the strings analyzed are word candidates, but not otherwise. The time necessary to encode acoustical information can be estimated as about 175 ms: A reader needs at least 400 ms to pronounce a word, 225 of which appear to be needed for articulation (if a subject knows which word is to be pronounced, the time to articulate it is 225 ms). Conceptual processing begins about 100 ms after the fixation of a word. At 250 ms, PET and ERP results show diffuse activation in frontal brain regions of both hemispheres. Priming studies (e.g., Swinney, 1979) indicate that it takes about 350 ms for the meaning of a word to be fixated in context. PET studies indicate that if subjects are given enough time, the activity associated with semantic processing shifts from the frontal regions to posterior regions (Posner & McCandliss, 1993).

The sequence of buffers shown in Figure 5.1 is critical to the integration and comprehension of segments of text, such as phrases and sentences. Deficits in any one of these storage buffers may have complex results beyond the buffer in question. Thus, phonological storage deficits affect not only the acoustic/articulatory buffer itself but also general learning and comprehension capacities. Baddeley, Papagno, and Valla (1988) observed a patient with such a deficit and found a normal ability to associate meaningful, familiar word pairs, but an almost total inability to associate words with unfamiliar sounds (words in another language). Apparently, the patient could process familiar sound patterns adequately without having to maintain them in the acoustic buffer. But the patient did not have enough time to analyze unfamiliar sound patterns without maintaining them at least briefly in the acoustic buffer. Baddeley and Wilson (1988) observed a similar patient who had no trouble identifying single words and comprehending brief sentences, even syntactically complex ones. This patient, however, could not understand longer sentences because, although comprehension abilities were intact, the patient could not maintain speech sounds long enough in the acoustic store to complete a successful analysis. Analysis was unsuccessful, for instance, when an early word in a sentence could not be disambiguated until late in the sentence.

Figure 5.1 represents a best guess at this time. I am not strongly committed to this particular sequence of buffers and their time course, or to the way the arrows between these buffers have been drawn. Further research will change some of this detail; the important point concerns the existence of such a sequence of intermediate buffers and their relation to working memory. It is, of course, a highly significant research question to come up with a more accurate version of Figure 5.1, but it is not my question. What I want to focus on here is the question of how and where context effects enter into this picture. The CI model makes some clear predictions in this respect that can be tested empirically. The test case involves the identification of lexically ambiguous homographs.

5.1.2 Homographs

Many studies in recent years have explored how lexically ambiguous words are understood in a discourse context. Various forms of schema theory predict that the discourse context works like a filter that selects the contextually appropriate meaning of a homograph, so that the inappropriate word sense is never activated. This theory has the great advantage that it corresponds to our everyday experience. As readers and listeners we encounter numerous words that have more than one potential sense, but we usually do not become conscious of these contextually inappropriate meanings. The alternative theory, suggested by the CI model as well as by modular conceptions of cognition (Fodor, 1983), maintains that all meanings of a homograph are accessed initially but that the contextually appropriate meaning wins out before any of the alternate meanings reach consciousness. That is, the construction process itself is dumb and does not take the word context into account; it serves as a source of constraints, however, quickly eliminating inappropriate alternatives. This is the exhaustive access model, which seems best to correspond to the experimental facts.

The original demonstration of exhaustive access of homograph meanings was reported in 1979 by Swinney, who used a cross-modal lexical decision task in his study. Subjects listened to a disambiguating text, such as a man surreptitiously entering an office and planting a bug. Just as the word *bug* was heard, a letter string appeared on a screen in front of the subject, who had to decide by pressing an appropriate response key whether the string was an English word or not – that is, the subject made a "lexical decision." Four types of letter strings were presented: nonwords as a control, unrelated words, close associates of the contextually appropriate meaning of the homograph (e.g., *spy*), or close associates of the contextually inappropriate meaning of the homograph (e.g., *spider*).

The results were most interesting: The lexical decision times to words that were associates of either sense of the homograph were both primed, that is, they were about 40 ms shorter than the lexical decision times for unrelated control words. In further work, it was found that if the lexical decision task is not presented immediately after the target word but delayed for 350 ms, the contextually inappropriate associate is no longer primed. Swinney concluded that all meanings of a homograph were accessed initially but that the context quickly selects the appropriate one, so that the inappropriate one never even enters consciousness.

Following Swinney's original demonstration, a large number of studies of lexical access have appeared using either the lexical decision task or simply a naming task. Swinney's findings were replicated repeatedly, but the opposite result was obtained in a number of experiments, too. Despite this confusion, the issue seems to be settled today: Initial lexical access does appear to be exhaustive and context independent, at least for homographs with two balanced meanings. In a recent review of that literature, Rayner, Pacht, and Duffy (1994) conclude that the most likely reason for the repeated findings of context effects is that both the lexical decision task and the naming task are subject to postlexical influences. Thus, what appears to be a context effect on lexical access is really an effect of the context on the integration of the word into the discourse context subsequent to lexical access. They argue convincingly that measures of eye movement provide a better and less biased index of lexical access, and they report some data that let us observe both the context-independent access to multiple meanings of homographs and the process of contextual integration that begins the moment the multiple meanings have been generated.

Rayner et al. (1994) measure the fixation time on homographs embedded in a disambiguating prior discourse. They find that readers fixate longer on a homograph that has two meanings, one of which is much more frequent than the other, when the subordinate meaning is instantiated, than on balanced homographs or on unambiguous control words matched for length and frequency. They call this the subordinate bias effect. Presumably, the more frequent meaning is accessed first, and the longer initial fixation time is required to access the subordinate meaning required by the context.

Now what happens if a biased homograph is repeated, both times in its subordinate sense? If context can constrain access, it makes no sense for the reader to initially re-access the primary meaning of the homograph that has just been rejected. In actual fact nothing happens. Initial fixation times for the repeated homographs are just like the initial fixation times when the word was first read (290 ms for repeated homographs and 295 for first reading – both significantly longer than the fixation times for neutral control words, 275 ms). Thus, there is no selective access to the contextually appropriate word meaning when a homograph is repeated; instead, the reader must go through the same exhaustive access process as when the word was read for the first time. However, following this context-independent access, which is reflected in the initial fixation time, the integration process for homographs in the subordinate meaning is much faster when the words are repeated than when they are read for the first time: Total fixation time is 336 ms for repeated homographs, but 408 ms when the homograph is read for the first time. Thus, the discourse context effects are there and have a clear and immediate influence on total fixation time, though not on initial access. The process of constructing the alternate senses of a homograph is context-free – following the dumb construction rules of the CI model – but the contextual constraints become effective right away to ensure the integration of the word meaning into the ongoing discourse.

5.1.3 Local and global priming in discourse: What words mean

Our own studies of word identification in discourse are in good agreement with this picture that has emerged from the literature. Kintsch and Mross (1985) developed an all-visual lexical priming task in which subjects read a text and were interrupted at predetermined points for a lexical decision. Their results clearly favored an exhaustive access over a selective access model. Immediately after reading a balanced homograph in a disambiguating context, associates to both word senses are activated, but after 570 ms only the context-appropriate sense remains activated. Kintsch and Mross used texts based on simple, familiar scripts. Thus, they were able to investigate whether words that were part of the script but not associatively related to the target word were also primed immediately after the presentation of the target word. For instance, in a text describing someone boarding a plane, right after the priming word *plane* either an associated word – *fly* – or an unassociated word – *gate* – that was part of the boarding a plane script was presented. No priming was obtained for unassociated thematic words. Priming was clearly a matter of local associations. The theme neither helped to prime unassociated words related to it, nor did it suppress associated words unrelated to it.

Till, Mross, and Kintsch (1988) extended these results by including not only local associates but also thematic associates as test words in their study. An example of one of their experimental sentences was the following:

(1) The townspeople were amazed to find that all the buildings had collapsed except the **mint**.

After reading this sentence, subjects were given a lexical decision task with either one of four test words (nonword strings were, of course, also used in the experiment):

- *money* – an associate of the contextually appropriate sense of the homograph *mint*
- *candy* – an associate of the contextually inappropriate sense of the homograph *mint*
- *earthquake* – a thematic inference
- *breath* – an unrelated control word

These test words were presented either 200 ms after the last word in the sentence, 300, 400, 500, 1,000, or 1,500 ms later. Figure 5.2 shows the amount of priming that was obtained for these test words as a function of the stimulus onset asynchrony (SOA) as the difference between the lexical decision time for contextually inappropriate associates minus the lexical decision time for contextually appropriate associates. For short SOAs, the Till et al. (1988) data replicate the results of Swinney (1979) and Kintsch and Mross (1985). Both the contextually appropriate associates and the inappropriate associates are equally activated initially. We can explain this in the following way. The process of word–meaning construction is completed by 350 ms: The contextually appropriate word sense has been established, and its associate *money* remains activated. Because the alternate meaning is now deactivated, no priming effect is obtained for *candy* at this point.

However, globally relevant inference words corresponding to the theme of the sentence do become activated after a certain time even in the absence of any local associations, unlike the scriptally relevant test words

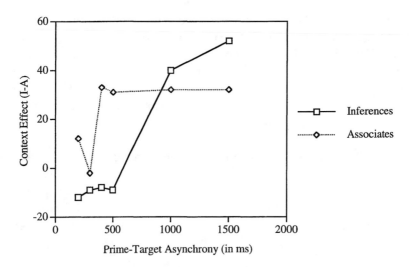

Figure 5.2   Time course of priming effects for associate and inference targets. Points represent the mean priming effect: response latencies for contextually inappropriate targets minus response latencies for contextually appropriate targets. After Till et al. (1988).

in Kintsch and Mross (1985), which had no global relevance.[1] Inference
activation was measured by the difference in the lexical decision times for
control words minus those for inference words. The thematic inference
was first activated at the 1,000 ms SOA. The construction of a thematic
inference apparently takes this much time. Presumably, the construction
of a thematic inference is part of the processing that goes on during the
well-known sentence wrap-up time, the extra reading time that is usually
observed at the end of a sentence (Figure 5.2).

Long, Oppy, and Seely (1994) reported an experiment that extends and
replicates Till et al. (1988) by including a 750 ms SOA. They observed
significant associative priming already at 300 ms. Evidence for topic
inferences was obtained earlier than in the Till et al. study: At the 500 ms
SOA, appropriate topic words were responded to significantly faster than
inappropriate topic words. This effect was even more pronounced at the
750 ms SOA. Thus, perhaps the best estimate we have at this time for the
fixation of word meanings is 300 to 350 ms, whereas 500 to 750 ms appear

---

1   E.g., "gate" is part of the boarding a plane script but may not be topically relevant in
    a story about someone almost missing a plane.

to be required for topic inferences. Meaning construction is not an instantaneous process. It takes time, and because it occurs in continuous interaction with the discourse context, it is a dynamic process.

The theory of meaning implied by these analyses is highly constructive and contextual. The clearest way to see this is to frame the discussion in terms of latent semantic analysis (LSA), which was introduced in section 3.3. In Kintsch and Mross (1985), we theorized that word identification involves the stages of sense activation and sense selection. Given a homonym like *mole*, the different senses $mole_1$ and $mole_2$ are looked up in a mental lexicon and then the contextually appropriate sense is selected. Latent Semantic Analysis implies a very different scenario that is more in agreement with the analyses presented in this chapter. A word meaning in LSA is a vector in a multidimensional semantic space. The vector for *mole* would be somewhere in between those for $mole_1$ and $mole_2$, right in the middle of no-man's-land; there are no separable senses that could be selected. Instead, when *mole* is used in a sentence, its meaning vector combines with the vectors of the other words in that sentence to form a new vector, the centroid of the word senses if all words are weighted equally. *Mole* in this context now has meaning, but its meaning is no longer separable from the context.

Whether a word is a homonym makes no difference for this argument. A word that has only a single sense in the traditional view is represented in LSA in the same way: as a vector in the semantic space. When it is used in a sentence context, it contributes its share to the sentence vector, merging with it and losing its identity.

In a master's thesis at the University of Colorado, Steinhart (1996) made some interesting observations. For certain types of sentences he found no priming effects, even though the target words were strongly associated with the final word in all the sentences according to associative norms, which he also collected. This failure is puzzling in the traditional view that word identification amounts to looking up the right sense of a word but is readily explained by a contextual account in which the meaning construction is inseparable from the context. Consider first an example from Till et al. (1988) for which reliable priming effects are obtained:

(2)   The gardener pulled the hose around to the holes in the yard. Perhaps the water would solve his problem with the **mole**.

Targets: *ground* and *face*

Landauer and Dumais (1997) have already shown that in an LSA simulation of the Till et al. (1988) materials the cosines between the target words and the experimental sentences mirror the obtained experimental results. We go a step further here by incorporating their semantic relatedness estimates into a construction–integration simulation, which allows us to model the changing time course of priming. Table 5.1 shows the cosines obtained from LSA, that is, the strength of the semantic relation, between the prime *mole* and the two target words, *ground* and *face*. Both targets are reasonably closely related to the prime; empirically, both are strong associates of the prime. In separate CI simulations, these two target words were then linked to the words in (2) according to their cosine values. The results of the spreading activation process are also shown in Table 5.1. *Ground* is strongly activated, because it has high or moderate cosines with several words in (2), whereas *face* ends up with a low activation value, because its cosines with all of the words in (2) except *mole* are low.

The implications of this analysis are in agreement with the Till et al. data: There is immediate priming for both *ground* and *face* because of their relatedness to *mole*. But once *mole* has been integrated into the sentence context, only *ground* will be primed; *face* is no longer semantically related to the *mole-in-the-yard*.

Now consider an example of the kind Steinhart used:

(3)   For his birthday last year, I wanted to give my brother something ugly. But no pet store in town would sell me a *mole*.

Targets: *ground* and *face*

Table 5.1. *Cosines and results of spreading activation process*

	cosine
mole – ground	.35
mole–face	.24
	activation
(2) + ground	.49
(2) + face	.06
(3) + ground	.08
(3) + face	.06

The two target words can be linked up with (3) in the same manner, employing the cosine values between the targets and the words in (3) as link strengths. However, now *ground,* the target related to the contextually appropriate sense of *mole,* fares no better than the target related to the inappropriate sense: All the cosines are low in both cases, as are the activation values resulting from a CI simulation, also shown in Table 5.1.

It does not seem that word identification is a look-up process in a mental lexicon. Otherwise, the *ground-mole* sense should have been selected in (3) as well as in (2), and *ground* should have been primed in both cases, because we know that it is a strong associate. On the other hand, suppose that in word identification there are no "senses" of words to be picked out of a lexicon. If words and sentences are represented as vectors in a semantic space, *mole* is a weird mixture of the *ground-mole* and the *face-mole,* by itself priming *ground* as well as *face.* Once *mole* is integrated into the sentence context of (3), it is no longer the *ground-mole* but a new construction, the *ugly-pet-mole.* The *ground-mole* burrows holes into the ground and annoys gardeners; none of this is important for the *ugly-pet-mole* – it is ugly and supposed to annoy my brother! Reading (3) does not select a particular sense of *mole* but constructs a new meaning of *mole* meticulously attuned to its context.

Results in the memory literature lend support to Steinhart's priming data. For instance, Barclay et al. (1974) had subjects study sentences like *The man lifted the piano* or *The man tuned the piano.* Later, two kinds of recall cues were provided: either *Pianos are heavy* or *Pianos make nice sounds.* The subjects had to recall the study sentences. Depending on which form of the study sentence they had read, one or the other of these cues was appropriate. Recall was significantly better (80%) with the appropriate cue than with the inappropriate cue (61%). Similar results were obtained in an experiment by Anderson and Ortony (1975), who found that the sentence *Television sets need expert repairmen* was recalled best with the cue *appliance,* and the sentence *Television sets look nice in the family room* was recalled best with the cue *furniture.* Clearly, both *appliance* and *furniture* are potential components of the meaning of *television set,* but only the contextually relevant feature was actually used in comprehension.

These memory data with unambiguous words support Steinhart's finding that priming effects for homonyms are influenced by their contextual use. However, negative results like Steinhart's are at best suggestive and need to be replicated with appropriate controls. If they do hold up, this would constitute strong evidence for the position advocated here. Word meanings are not something to be pulled from a mental lexicon but are ephemeral constructions that are generated during comprehension. In the next section, I explore in a little more detail the nature of this construction process as it is conceived by the CI model.

5.1.4 A simulation of priming effects in discourse[2]

Meaning construction is a bottom-up process that starts rather indiscriminately (the multiple activation of word senses). Meaning construction takes time (word meanings are fixed by 350 ms, but sentence themes require about twice as much time). Nevertheless, the process of meaning construction is highly interactive, with local and global factors jointly determining its course from the very beginning. Some interesting experimental results by Schwanenflugel and White (1991) and a simulation of these results by Kintsch (1994a) show how local and global processes occur at the same time and illustrate the complex dynamics of a growing network.

The brief text presented in Table 5.2 is taken (with slight simplifications) from a study by Schwanenflugel and White (1991). Consider how the CI model would simulate comprehension of this text and predict how it would be recalled. Let us assume that we want to simulate comprehension processes at the level of sentences or phrases, that is, in six processing cycles, as shown in Table 5.2. The first step is to construct a propositional representation, resulting in the list of atomic propositions also shown in the table.

Propositions P1 to P13 are connected in a network by argument overlap, and we could proceed cycle by cycle to calculate the outcome of the integration process in this network. However, the construction phase of comprehension is not yet finished, for we have not yet considered the construction of a situation model, the construction of a macrostructure, or associative knowledge activation processes.

In the present example, the strategic construction of a macrostructure involves the following steps. A hypothesis is made that the first sentence contains the macropropositions, and later statements are recognized as instances of the generalization given by the first sentence. This

2   This section is adapted from Kintsch (1994a).

Table 5.2. *Example of a text and proposition list*

1. The bar was designed for male professionals
2. and turned away all secretaries and nurses who tried to get in.
3. It had an exclusive look to it.
4. The bar was in a nice place located in the business district in town.
5. It was perfect to take clients to the bar.
6. The bar would not serve drinks to women.

Cycle Number	Proposition Number	Proposition
1	P1	DESIGN[BAR,P2]
1	P2	MALE[PROFESSIONALS]
2	P3	TURN-AWAY[BAR,SECRETARIES,NURSES]
2	P4	TRY[SECRETERIES,NURSES,P5]
2	P5	ENTER[SECRETARIES,NURSES]
3	P6	LUXURIOUS[BAR]
4	P7	LOCATION[BAR]
4	P8	IN[P7,NICEPLACE]
4	P9	IN[P7,BUSINESSDISTRICT]
4	P10	IN[P7,TOWN]
5	P11	PERFECT[BAR,P12]
5	P12	TAKE[CLIENTS,BAR]
6	P13	NOT-SERVE[BAR,DRINKS,WOMEN]

Source: From Schwanenflugel & White (1991).

strategy is plausible in the present case because in the experiment from which this text was taken, many texts of the same structure were read by the subjects.

In the simple, brief text used here, the situation model and the macrostructure of the text are largely the same. A great deal of domain knowledge is necessary for the construction of the macrostructure, so that in this process a situation model would also be obtained. One has to know what it means for a bar to be designed for male professionals in order to recognize that *turning away secretaries* and *taking clients to the bar* are instances of the general concept. Thus, we obtain a situation model in the form of a *bar-for-male-professionals* script with five slots – the same structure that results from the application of the macrostrategies.

Thus, we need to mark P1 and P2 as macropropositions and P3, P6,

P7, P12 and P13 as macrorelevant. This is done by increasing the strengths of the links between P1 and the macrorelevant propositions by a factor of 2, as well as the strength of the links from P1 and P2 to themselves. The choice of doubling link strengths is arbitrary and is merely intended to show that certain links in the net should be assigned more strength than others. Obviously, one cannot obtain precise quantitative predictions with such guesswork, but qualitative predictions can nevertheless be derived. The advantage of this procedure is that it avoids the objection that whatever success the model has is due only to skillful fine-tuning of the parameters in a very complex model.

Finally, associative knowledge elaboration during comprehension must be simulated. We have assumed that this occurs independently of context. Hence, free association data obtained in a situation outside the present discourse context for the concepts and propositions (expressed as simple declarative sentences) of the text provide an estimate for which items of knowledge are most likely to be activated when reading this text. In an informal experiment, the 12 associations shown in Table 5.3 were obtained. The 12 associates (k1–k12) were then added to the 13 propositional nodes constructed in Table 5.3 and connected to their source nodes

Table 5.3. *Content words from the experimental text shown in Table 5.2 and frequent free association responses*

Stimulus Item	Associated Response
bar	drink (k1)
design(person,building)	architect (k2)
male(person)	female (k3)
professional	lawyer (k4), doctor (k5)
turn-away (person,from-building)	door (k6)
secretary	typewriter (k7)
nurse	doctor (k5)
enter(person,building)	door (k6)
exclusive(object)	fashion (k8)
place	country (k9)
business district	shops (k10)
take(clients,to-bar)	lunch (k11)
not-serve(bar,drinks,to-person)	minors (k12)

with a value of .5, to indicate that an item retrieved from long-term memory during comprehension receives less weight than one that is explicit in the text.

We are now ready to start the integration process. The complete network that has been constructed is shown in Figure 5.3. A cycle size of five elements was assumed, but knowledge elaborations belonging to a text proposition were always included in the same cycle as the text proposition, even if more than five elements had to be processed in working memory because of that. A buffer size of 1 was assumed, that is, the most highly activated proposition on each cycle was carried over to the next processing cycle. Six cycles were required to process this text under these conditions. The long-term memory strengths of the 13 propositional nodes in the network that resulted from these six processing cycles are shown in Figure 5.4.[3]

The knowledge elaborations have been omitted from Figure 5.4 because none of them received enough strength to be experimentally significant. However, this does not always have to be the case. Imagine a reader who is reminded of *discrimination* every time she reads the six sentences of Table 5.2. For such a reader, the knowledge elaboration *discrimination* would achieve considerable strength. Specifically, the *discrimination* node will have a strength of .62 in the network, the eighth highest value. Thus, under appropriate circumstances it is quite possible that knowledge elaborations end up with greater memory strength than actually presented items.

In the experiment of Schwanenflugel and White (1991), subjects read texts like the one shown in Table 5.2 with an RSVP procedure, that is, one word at a time, appearing centered on a computer screen. It was a dual task experiment, because in addition to reading the text (and answering questions about it later), at certain points during reading subjects made rapid lexical decisions. The point of particular interest here concerns the last word of sentence 6, namely, *women*.

We make the assumption that priming effects will occur in the lexical decision task to the extent that the target words are activated by the con-

---

3   The normalization procedure used for these calculations required the total sum of activation to remain constant in each cycle and differs therefore from the one employed in the Mross and Roberts (1992) program.

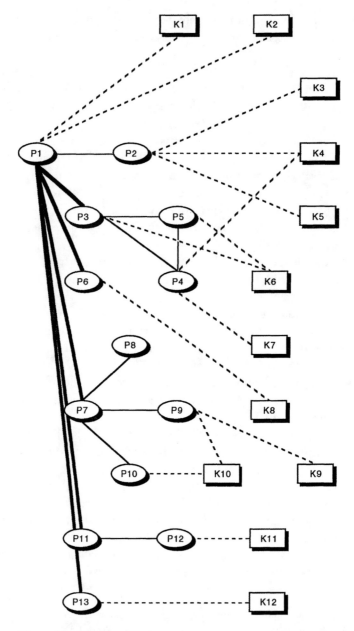

Figure 5.3   The network of propositions and knowledge elaborations for the
text (1) to (6). Plain links have an initial value of 1; heavy links have an initial
value of 2; broken links have an initial value of .5.

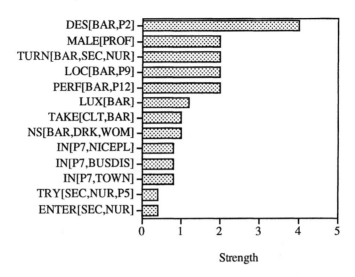

Figure 5.4   Final memory strengths for the propositions shown in Figure 5.3.

text of reading. Suppose that subjects are reading sentences 1 to 6 but that at the point where the last word should have been presented, a lexical decision trial occurs with the word *women*. We need to calculate how strongly this word will be activated by the memory structure for the text that already has been constructed at this point. This structure is identical with that shown in Figure 5.3, except that the last proposition, P13, is incomplete and has the form NOT-SERVE[BAR, DRINKS, $] – the recipient of the action has not yet been presented. How will this structure activate the target word *women*? *Women* is connected with the episodic text structure in two ways. First, it fits semantically into the slot of the incomplete NOT-SERVE proposition and hence receives activation from that source. However, we already have a potential slot filler for that proposition in the form of the knowledge elaboration *minors*, which became a part of the net as an associate of NOT-SERVE(BAR,DRINKS,TO-PERSON). Because *women* and *minors* are mutually exclusive alternatives for the same slot, they interfere with each other; thus, we add a link with a negative weight of –1 between them. Hence, there are two sources of activation for *women*, a positive and a negative. If we let activation spread to it from the incomplete network through the two links just mentioned, the positive is considerably stronger because it derives from the dominant discourse topic, whereas the negative source has only a weak associate to draw upon.

Now suppose that instead of *women* the word *students* had been presented as a target in the lexical decision task. Obviously, *students* also fits the slot of the NOT-SERVE proposition – *The bar did not serve drinks to students* is a perfectly acceptable English sentence – and, therefore, *students* also competes with the preexisting associate *minors*. Hence, it is connected to the net in exactly the same way as *women*. However, something else now changes in the net. When the NOT-SERVE proposition was completed with *women*, it formed a macrorelevant statement, as in the original text. However, the completion *student*, while semantically acceptable, no longer fits into the current discourse structure. In the context of the present discourse, *not serving drinks to students* is not an instance of *bar-designed-for-male-professionals,* and hence the link between the discourse topic P1 and the proposition completed with STUDENTS no longer receives extra weight. As a consequence, the target word *students* becomes less strongly activated than *women.* Thus, the model predicts discourse priming, in that items that fit into the discourse structure become more highly activated and hence have shorter reaction times. This was precisely what Schwanenflugel and White (1991) observed, from whose study the present text was borrowed. A priming effect occurred for discourse-relevant completions like *women* when compared with discourse-neutral control words like *students.*

Schwanenflugel and White (1991) also used *minors* as a target word in their experiment, in addition to *women* and *students,* and observed that *minors* was also primed when presented at the end of sentence 6. The priming effect for *minors* was more or less the same as for *women.* Thus, although *minors* never occurs as a knowledge intrusion in subjects' recall of the text (see Kintsch, 1994a), and the model predicts that it should not (the calculated LTM strength of the *minors* node is .001), it nevertheless yields a significant priming effect simply because it is a locally strong association. The model predicts this priming effect, too. The target *minors* is connected to the episodic text structure in two ways. First, it is a possible slot filler for the NOT-SERVE proposition, just as the other two targets were, yet, unlike the other two, it does not compete with the preexisting knowledge association *minors,* although it is activated from that source too. However, as was the case for *students*, the NOT-SERVE proposition completed with the object *minors* is no longer macrorelevant and hence receives no special activation from the discourse topic. As a consequence, *minors* ends up with an activation value not as high as that for *women* but higher than the activation of *students*.

The CI model therefore correctly predicts at the same time both local priming effects that are independent of context and priming through the discourse context. Purely associative models would predict the former, schema theories the latter, but what is needed to account for what actually happens is something like the marriage of bottom–up processes and contextual integration processes as postulated by the CI theory. Actually, the theory makes even more powerful predictions, for which, however, no empirical tests are available as yet. As shown in Figure 5.5, it predicts that the target *minors* is strongly activated from the very beginning (via the preexisting *minors* that is already a node in the network), but that its activation then decreases because it does not fit well into the discourse context. *Women* and *students*, in contrast, start out with zero activation but then become activated from the discourse structure to different degrees.

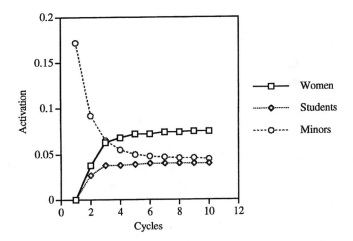

Figure 5.5   The settling process for the activation values of three target words in a lexical decision task on the CI model. The targets were presented in place of the last word of sentence 6.

Presumably, the Schwanenflugel and White data points fall somewhere near cycle 3 or 4 in the simulation results shown in Figure 5.5. A more stringent test of the theoretical predictions would require further experiments tracing out the complete speed–accuracy trade-off curves.

5.2 Anaphora

The Latin word *textus* is derived from a verb meaning "to weave." The warp of the fabric that is a text are the anaphora: repeated and reinstated discourse referents that are a major source of coherence in a text. The manner in which these repetitions and reinstatements occur is governed by an intricate set of rules that ensure that a speaker and a listener, or a writer and his readers, agree on the intended referent and where to look for it.

5.2.1 The psycholinguistics of anaphora resolution

Once a word has been introduced in a text, it is often repeated in some form, reference is made back to the already introduced concept by means of an anaphor: by repeating or paraphrasing the word, by a pronoun, or even implicitly (zero anaphora). What are the main experimental findings about anaphora, and can they be accounted for within the framework developed in the previous section?

Anaphora vary on a dimension of lexical content or specificity (e.g., Gernsbacher, 1989). Pronouns or demonstratives have little or no lexical content of their own and rely entirely on their context to provide their content. On the other hand, definite noun phrases and proper names have a specific lexical content of their own. Their meaning may be influenced and modified by the context in which they are used, just as the meaning of other words that are used for the first time must be constructed in the discourse context, but unlike pronouns they contribute lexical content of their own.

As we have seen in the previous section, readers fixate longer on a homograph that is biased toward its subordinate meaning by the text that precedes it, compared to an unambiguous control word. This is true even when the word has been encountered in its subordinate meaning earlier in the same passage of a text (Rayner et al., 1994). These results suggest that repeated words are identified in much the same bottom–up way as words that appear for the first time in a discourse context.

There is, of course, a difference in the way new words and repeated words are processed. Part of the process of meaning construction for the repeated word involves retrieving the context in which the word appeared earlier and incorporating it into the present context. This retrieval of prior information about a repeated word occurs quite rapidly, roughly in the same time that it takes to activate and fixate information about the word from semantic memory. A study by Dell, McKoon, and Ratcliff (1983) illustrates this process.

Dell et al. (1983) investigated the case in which a discourse referent is first introduced with one word (e.g., *burglar*) and then referred to with another, definite noun phrase (e.g., *the criminal*). One of their texts was the following:

(4)   A burglar surveyed the garage set back from the street.
      Several milk bottles were piled at the curb.
      The banker and her husband were on vacation.
      The$_1$ criminal slipped$_2$ away from the streetlamp$_3$.

At the positions labeled 1, 2, and 3 in the last sentence, subjects were given a single word recognition test with one of three test words: the prior referent of the noun phrase (*burglar*), a word appearing in the same proposition as the prior referent (*garage*), and a control word from a different sentence (*bottles*). The results are shown in Figure 5.6 as the difference in the recognition times between the test words and the control word. Before the anaphoric word (position 1), response times for all words were about equal. About 250 ms after the anaphor (position 2), both the prior referent and the word referring to a concept from the same proposition as the prior referent were recognized significantly faster than the control word, suggesting that both were activated in the reader's working memory. At position 3, the prior referent was still activated, but other concepts from the prior context of the anaphor were no longer activated.

This pattern of results is roughly what one would expect from the CI model. Figure 5.7a shows the network that a reader has constructed according to the model at position 2: It contains the two surface elements *the criminal* and *slipped*, the corresponding proposition, a bridging infer-

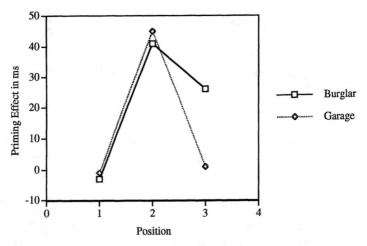

Figure 5.6   Priming effects (recognition time for test word minus recognition time for control word) for prior referent (*burglar*) and other concepts from the same proposition (*garage*) at three positions in text (4).

ence linking criminal to burglar, and the reinstated proposition containing BURGLAR from the first sentence, which includes GARAGE. The argument of the SLIP proposition has been written as CRIMINAL/ BURGLAR to indicate that as a result of a bridging inference and the retrieval of BURGLAR, CRIMINAL has been identified with BUR-GLAR. Integrating the network shown in Figure 5.7a yields an activation value of 1.00 for CRIMINAL/BURGLAR and .54 for GARAGE. Hence, both concepts are strongly activated at this point, compatible with the results in Figure 5.6 for position 2.

Once the whole sentence has been read (position 3), the full network shown in Figure 5.7b is obtained. In this network, the central concept CRIMINAL/BURGLAR still has an activation value of 1.00, but the proposition containing the related concept GARAGE has now become marginal and its activation value is reduced to .18. It is reasonable to assume that such a weak activation could not be detected by the experimental method of Dell et al. (1983).

Explicit anaphora are thus rapidly identified with their prior referent, reactivating in the process at least temporarily other related concepts from the prior context. It is probably safe to generalize Dell et al.'s results to other types of explicit anaphora such as proper names, which are iden-

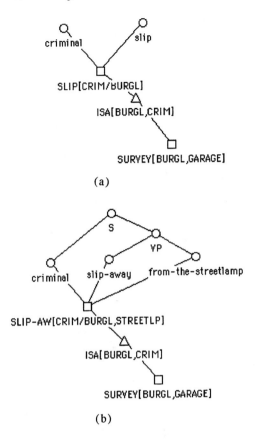

Figure 5.7 (a) The CI network at position 2. (b) The CI network at position 3. Circles are surface structure nodes, squares indicate text propositions, and the triangle indicates a bridging inference.

tified just as rapidly (Gernsbacher, 1989). Thus, explicit anaphora are treated much like other nonanaphoric words in a text, except that in the construction of their meaning the context of their prior appearance is integrated. This seems reasonable and plausible. After all, when readers encounter a definite noun phrase or proper name, these may be used as anaphora or they may not. Pronouns, on the other hand, are different; readers know they are dealing with anaphora (or perhaps kataphora – a pronoun whose referent has not yet been introduced).

What factors influence pronoun resolution and when does it occur?

The literature is rich but confusing. The results of many studies that vary by only a single factor are difficult to interpret because other confounding factors were not controlled. An overall picture emerges nevertheless.

1. Speakers use pronouns to refer to entities in the focus-of-attention/short-term-memory/consciousness (Chafe, 1974; Ehrlich, 1980; Fletcher, 1984).

2. When there are several antecedents, all of them tend to become activated. If there are enough contextual cues to disambiguate a pronoun, the irrelevant referents will become deactivated, but referents are not automatically identified when no individual one is sufficiently salient (Greene, McKoon, & Ratcliff, 1992).

3. Syntax does not dominate pronoun resolution. That is, even when a text is unambiguous (e.g., using *she* in the context of *John* and *Sally*), other salient referents are still considered (Garnham, Oakhill, & Johnson-Laird, 1982; Greene et al., 1992).

4. Referents in the discourse focus are more likely to be selected as the antecedent of a pronoun than referents that are less discourse relevant. This discourse bias is manifested in several ways. Recency of mention powerfully biases antecedent selection (Carpenter & Just, 1977; Clark & Sengul, 1979; Ehrlich & Rayner, 1983). Prior topicalization makes an antecedent more salient (Anderson, Garrod, & Sanford, 1983; Sanford, Moar, & Garrod, 1988). Antecedents that are part of the same scene or the common ground between speaker and listener are favored (Anderson et al., 1983; Gordon & Scearce, 1995; Greene, Gerrig, McKoon & Ratcliff, 1994; Lesgold, Roth, & Curtis, 1979).

5. Pragmatic information is used in pronoun resolution together with other types of information from the very beginning (Garrod, Freudenthal, & Boyle, 1994; Tyler & Marslen-Wilson, 1982), as soon as it becomes available (McDonald & MacWhinney, 1995).

Pronoun resolution is therefore best viewed as a multiple constraint satisfaction problem. Pronouns are used to create the textual web by making the reader engage in processes that serve to strengthen the links between its various parts. In the next section I show how these processes are modeled by the CI theory. The theory is particularly suited for combining many different effects to arrive at a global decision about meaning.

Hence, pronoun resolution becomes an especially interesting field of application for the theory.

5.2.2 Anaphora resolution in the CI model

An experiment that examines the interaction of several different factors in anaphora resolution is that of Garrod et al. (1994). It is an eye movement experiment whose dependent variables are the total reading time for the target sentence containing the anaphor and first-pass fixation durations for various regions of the sentence, in particular the anaphor and verb regions. The factors they vary are (1) whether or not the referent is in the discourse focus; (2) the form of the anaphor (either an ambiguous or unambiguous pronoun or an explicit anaphor – that is, a name or a definite description); and (3) the pragmatics of the verb of the target sentence that makes one or the other of two possible antecedents more suitable. The results of Garrod et al. (1994) are in general agreement with the conclusions reached in the foregoing sections – everything matters, and everything matters from the very beginning. For instance, pragmatic effects do not come in late, after an anaphor has been tentatively identified on the basis of its syntactic properties; instead syntactic and pragmatic factors both contribute to the resolution process from the very beginning, though some effects take longer to develop than others. Further details of their results are discussed in connection with the following simulations.

One of Garrod et al.'s examples (1994) is as follows:

(5)   Flying to America. Jane wasn't enjoying the flight at all. The dry air in the plane made her really thirsty. Just as she was about to call her, she noticed the stewardess coming down the aisle with the drinks trolley.

Continuation 1: Right away she ordered a large glass of Coke.
Continuation 2: Right away she poured a large glass of Coke.

What concerns us here is how readers interpret the "she" in the two continuation sentences – as *Jane* or as *stewardess*.

To simulate these conditions in the CI model, the comprehension of the text prior to the test sentence must be simulated. The resulting network is shown in Figure 5.8. It consists of the propositional textbase (squares; to simplify things, modifiers are merely indicated as "mod") corresponding to (5), the situation model based upon the FLYING schema (triangles), and the two alternative representations of continuation sentence 1 containing the pronoun "she": *Right away she ordered a large glass of Coke* (circles), which are connected by a negative link of −1 (all other links are +1). The nodes constructed during reading of (5), which are in long-term memory at the time the continuation sentence is presented, are filled in, and the test nodes are open. The parts of the FLYING schema that are used here are the prop, the PLANE, and two roles, the PASSENGER-JANE and STEWARDESS. SERVE is a characteristic activity for STEWARDESS, activated during reading of (5), and ORDER is a characteristic activity for PASSENGER, activated by the continuation sentence.

What is of interest is how the two continuation sentences are processed

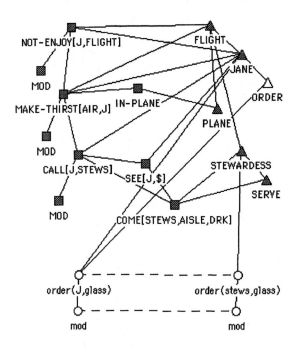

Figure 5.8   The network corresponding to text (5). The continuation sentence shown is *Right away she ordered a large glass of Coke.*

in the context of this LTM trace. Each continuation sentence was twice represented as a main proposition with a modifier: once for JANE and once for the STEWARDESS, connected with an inhibitory link. In the *order* case, the test proposition was connected to three situation model elements: the actors *Jane* and *stewardess* as possible antecedents of the pronoun *she* and, for the JANE version only, to *order* because ordering a drink is what passengers are supposed to do. In the case of the *pour* sentence, it was linked to the two possible antecedents and to *serve* in the situation model for the STEWARDESS version only. Because we are interested in the whole course of the integration process and not just the final outcome, the starting values of the test sentence elements were set to zero and those for prior test elements were set to their LTM values. Most of the prior text was deactivated, and only the three elements directly linked to the new input, plus the situation model header FLIGHT, were allowed to participate in the processing of the test sentences. Figure 5.9 shows the course of pronoun resolution in the two continuation cases. For the *order* sentence, the interpretation *she_{Jane}* orders a Coke gains quickly in activation, whereas *she_{stewardess}* orders a Coke never gathers much activation at all. Discourse focus and pragmatic acceptability combine in favor of the pas-

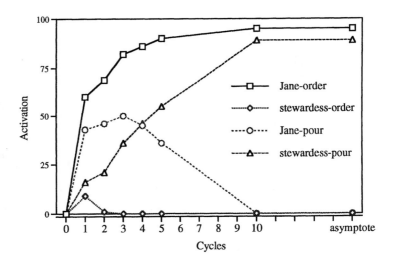

Figure 5.9   Activation values for the two referents *Jane* and *stewardess* in *she-orders* and *she-pours* sentences.

senger ordering the drink. The situation is quite different, however, for continuation 2. Initially, it is *Jane*, the referent in the discourse focus, that is more strongly activated, and only after four processing cycles does the fact that stewardesses are more likely to pour drinks than are passengers make itself felt. In the end, however, the model arrives at the correct, intended interpretation in both cases. Asymptotically, she_{Jane} *orders a Coke* and $she_{stewardess}$ *pours a Coke* are equally strong. Total reading times for these sentences in Garrod et al.'s (1994) experiment were not significantly different.

The pattern of results is quite different if the text (5) is altered so that it contains a *steward* rather than a *stewardess*. Now the pronoun *she* in the continuation sentences uniquely identifies JANE, but discourse focus and verb pragmatics still have their effects, as is shown in Figure 5.10. These simulations were performed in the same way as before, except that no link was made between $she_{steward}$ *pours a Coke* and STEWARD because of the incongruent pronoun. The model does arrive at the intended referent *Jane* for both continuation sentences, but she_{Jane} *pours a Coke* never catches up with she_{Jane} *orders a Coke*. There is a significant reading time difference in this case in the data of Garrod et al. (1994).

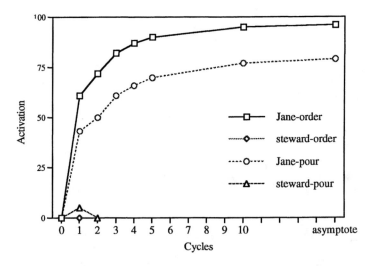

Figure 5.10   Activation values for the two referents *Jane* and *steward* in *she-orders* and *she-pours* sentences.

Figure 5.11 shows the results of another variation: Here the text contains *steward,* but the continuation sentences also contain *he.* A straightforward, totally unambiguous case, but the discourse focus effects in the model are powerful. Again, the model arrives at the intended interpretation of *he,* namely, the STEWARD, but it takes some time, and $he_{steward}$ *orders a Coke* never receives much strength. The Garrod et al. (1994) data show significant differences in reading times. The differences between Figures 5.10 and 5.11 reflect discourse focus effects: JANE has an LTM strength of 1.54 and STEWARD of 0.40, and the strong concept (i.e., the one in the discourse focus, in the terminology of Garrod et al.) is better able to violate pragmatic constraints than is the weak concept.

Figures 5.9 to 5.11 can hardly be considered decisive tests of the Garrod et al. (1994) data. It is not obvious just what feature of the simulations would predict reading times. I have suggested that when the activations of two continuation sentences reach the same asymptotic value, no reading time differences should be expected. Another possibility is that reading times for the continuation sentences might depend on the difference between how strongly and how long the intended and unintended alternatives were activated in the integration process. Thus, if one adds up all activation values in these figures for each pair of alternatives and takes the

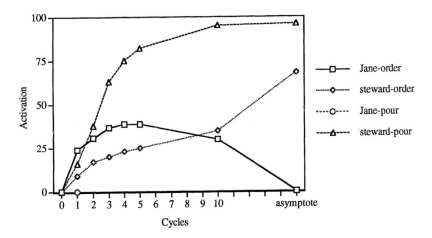

Figure 5.11   Activation values for the two referents *Jane* and *steward* in *he-orders* and *he-pours* sentences.

difference (e.g., the sum of activation values for *she*$_{Jane}$ *orders a Coke* minus the sum of activation values for *she*$_{stewardess}$ *pours a Coke*), one should get a predictor of reading times. Indeed, these differences are correlated $r = .84$ with the mean reading times reported by Garrod et al. (1994). There are, however, only six means, so one cannot make any strong claims about the goodness of fit of the model.

It is also of interest to examine with the CI model how explicit anaphors are identified in the context of Garrod et al.'s (1994) experiments. Consider, for instance, the case in which the continuations for text (5) do not involve a pronoun but either a name (*Jane*) or a definite description (*stewardess*). In this case, simulations can be performed just as before, except that now there is only a single alternative to be considered for each continuation sentence, either JANE or the STEWARDESS, whatever the sentence was. Figures 5.12 and 5.13 show what happens: Explicit anaphora are identified very rapidly, but there are still effects due to the pragmatics of the verb (*Jane orders* is activated more rapidly than *Jane pours,* and the reverse is true for *stewardess*). The effects are very small, however, and Garrod et al.'s (1994) results show no differences. The discourse focus effect, on the other hand, is a little bigger, as a comparison of Figures 5.12 and 5.13 reveals. Again, Garrod et al. observed no differences.

Thus, the model provides a framework within which we can simulate anaphora resolution in considerable detail, in fact, in more detail than the resolution power of our experimental procedures. These simulations summarize and organize what we know about pronoun resolution from the psycholinguistic literature as exemplified by the results of the Garrod et al. experiments. Furthermore, the simulations could be done without any really new theoretical machinery. It is true that some things were done differently here than in other simulations reported in this book. In particular, because we were interested in the time course of activation, the test sentence was started with an initial activation value of zero, and prior elements were given their LTM strengths as starting values. But these are technicalities, well within the general theoretical framework. They are not used elsewhere only because they are not needed and would simply add irrelevant complexities.

It would have been a significant ad hoc theoretical adjustment to introduce a new concept such as discourse focus into the theory. However, the

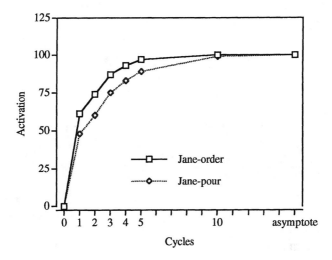

Figure 5.12   Activation values for the referent *Jane* in *Jane-orders* and *Jane-pours* sentences.

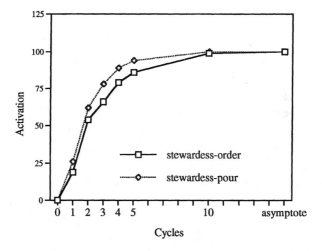

Figure 5.13   Activation values for the referent *stewardess* in *the-stewardess-orders* and *the stewardess-pours* sentences.

model could do very well without it because this concept was implicit in the CI theory all the time. Currently activated discourse entities that have acquired a high LTM strength in the process of comprehension are said to be in discourse focus. Thus, one can talk about discourse focus in the framework of the CI theory, as done here, where the use of that term was natural and convenient. However, discourse focus is not really a concept needed by the CI theory. For many theories of text comprehension, discourse focus is a central, explanatory concept (e.g., Greene et al., 1994; Grosz & Sidner, 1986; Sanford & Garrod, 1981). The CI model is more parsimonious in this respect, for discourse focus is simply a concept that falls right out of its basic architecture.

There is another context in which simulations such as the ones performed here may become relevant. Within functional linguistics, there are several studies that attempt to describe the factors that control the use of anaphora in discourse. This is essentially correlational work: A particular discourse characteristic is observed to be correlated with the use of, say, zero anaphora, pronouns, or full noun phrases. The most basic of these factors is linear distance (Givón, 1983). If few words intervene before a concept is repeated, many languages employ zero anaphora. If more words intervene between concept repetitions, pronouns are used, unstressed pronouns or stressed ones in English if the distance is larger. If the number of intervening words is high, noun phrases are normally used. These default cases can be overridden for specific linguistic purposes. For instance, pronoun use when zero anaphora would suffice may signal a topic shift (e.g., Fletcher, 1984; see also section 6.2.1). Thus, linear distance is by no means the only determinant of pronoun use. Fox (1987) shows that a theoretically motivated measure based on the distance in a theoretical structure provided a better fit than linear distance measures. A host of additional syntactic and semantic factors have been identified. These include, for example, the role of the antecedent (e.g., whether the antecedent concept was the subject or actor, whether it was the protagonist of a story, whether it was animate or not, and so on). It has been shown that not only linear distance in words matters, but also whether or not a paragraph boundary intervenes. By putting all these factors together in a multiple correlation, good accounts of pronoun use can be obtained.

It may be conjectured that the activation value in working memory of a repeated concept, as calculated in the foregoing simulations, reflects all these factors and, together with some considerations about the use of working memory in discourse comprehension (see chapter 7), could be used as the basis for determining the choice of anaphora in discourse. To test this conjecture, sufficiently extensive simulations would have to be performed. If the prediction envisaged here were successful, we would have a highly parsimonious theory of anaphora selection. No special mental computations would be required when a speaker or writer uses anaphora. The same processes that generate the discourse in the first place also determine which anaphor will be selected.

5.3 Metaphor

Metaphor, setting our mind to flying betwixt one Genus and another, allows us to discern in a single Word more than one Object.

Umberto Eco, The Island of the Day Before

   The process of meaning construction described so far has focused on literal meaning. Because figurative thought and figurative language are ubiquitous, however, one cannot discuss meaning construction without taking into account nonliteral meaning. It is no longer the case that metaphors are considered a peculiarity of poetic language that might as well be disregarded; rather, we have come to realize that figurative language exists everywhere we look (e.g., Gibbs, 1994), as does figurative thought (e.g., Lakoff, 1987).

   How do people understand figurative language, metaphors in particular? Metaphors consist of some kind of comparison by means of which features are transferred to the metaphor topic that are not normally associated with it. Thus, in *Sermons are sleeping pills* a low-salience feature of *sermon* is pushed into the foreground, whereas in *Atoms are little solar systems* certain properties of solar systems are assigned to *atoms*. How does the comprehender know to make such a feature transfer, rather than include sermon in the class of sleeping pill and atom in the class of solar systems? The classical answer has been that the comprehender recognizes that the literal interpretation of the sentence is impossible – sermons have properties that do not allow them to be included in the class of small white pills. Once the incoherence of the metaphorical sentence has been recognized, the comprehender attempts to find a metaphorical comparison. Early theories of metaphor in linguistics, philosophy, and psychology (including Kintsch, 1974) were all of this kind. Psychological research results quickly showed that these theories were wrong. If comprehenders first interpret a metaphorical statement literally, recognize its incoherence, and then get to work on a nonliteral interpretation, the metaphor comprehension must involve more processing, require more resources, and take more time than literal comprehension. A number of studies have shown convincingly that this is not the case (for a review see Cacciari & Glucksberg, 1994). Metaphors are as easy to comprehend as literal sentences. Sometimes a literal interpretation is easier to arrive at, but just as often the metaphorical reading is more readily attained.

It is probably fair to say that the view is commonly accepted today that there exist no essential processing differences between metaphors and literal sentences. As long as the semantic interpretation of a sentence is conceived as a process of looking up the appropriate word meanings in a mental lexicon and then computing the total meaning from the concatenation of the word meanings, metaphors have to be regarded as something abnormal. If, however, there is not that much to be looked up, and most of the meaning construction occurs in context and with the particular material at hand, there is no reason literal constructions should always be the default and metaphorical interpretations be the last resort.

The proof of this claim requires actually showing that the process of meaning construction proceeds along much the same line for metaphors as for literal sentences. Three simple simulations show that this can be the case for the CI model. The examples chosen are simple indeed and therefore possibly misleading (not the general theory; just that these examples are so trivial), but they are easy to understand and serve to illustrate the general principle involved.

First, consider the metaphor *The theory is a laser beam*, which predicates something about *laser beams* to *theory*. But what is being predicated? One way to find out is to construct a simulation with some degree of objectivity by using LSA as a guide (see section 3.3). Latent semantic analysis can indicate what some of the strong neighboring nodes are of

Table 5.4. *Four neighbors of* theory *(top four items) and four neighbors of* laser beam *(bottom four items) and their cosines in the LSA space*

	Cosine with Theory	Cosine with Laser Beam
relativity	.64	.14
bang	.64	.04
propose	.60	.02
explain	.60	.08
light	.09	.68
coherent	.06	.65
illuminates	.01	.44
polarizer	−.03	.60

both *theory* and *laser beam,* and it tells us how strong these links are. With this information we can construct a CI model network, integrate it, and obtain some predictions as to the meaning of the metaphorical statement. Specifically, the four nearest neighbors of *theory* in the encyclopedia-based LSA space (excluding proper names, morphologically related words, and function words) are the first four nodes shown in the first column of Table 5.4 together with their link strengths (the cosine between the respective vectors in the LSA space). The table also shows four neighbors of *laser beam* – the last four items in column 1 – and the cosines between all these vectors.

A network consisting of the text nodes THEORY, LASER-BEAM, and ISA[THEORY,LASERBEAM] and the eight knowledge elaborations in Table 5.4, with all their pairwise cosine values as link strengths, yields the activation values shown in Figure 5.14 when integrated. Although I have no data to evaluate these predictions, they seem intuitively acceptable. The dominant features of *theory* in isolation are deemphasized, and several features derived from *laser beam* become relatively strong: *coherent, light,* and *illuminates.* However, note that this feature transfer is quite crude. Features like *polarizer,* which seem intuitively irrelevant, also are introduced at a fairly high level of strength.

As another example, consider the famous opening line of Carl Sandburg's poem: *The fog comes on little cat feet.* Again, I selected four neigh-

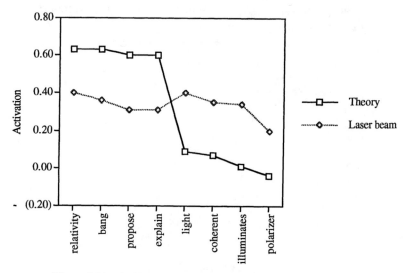

Figure 5.14   Activation strength of nodes related to *theory* in isolation and to the metaphorical statement *The theory is a laser beam.*

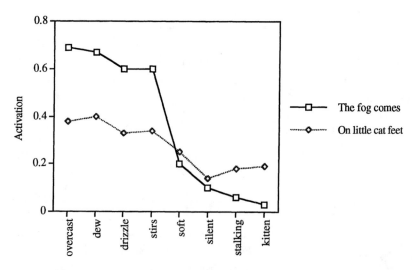

Figure 5.15   Activation strength of nodes related to *The fog comes* in isolation and to the metaphorical statement *The fog comes on little cat feet.*

bors of *The fog comes* from the LSA space as well as four neighbors of *on little cat feet*. The text propositions

(6) P1 COME[FOG]
     P2 LITTLE[CAT[FEET]]
     P3 ON[P1,P2]

are integrated together with the eight semantic neighbors that have been retrieved by LSA, with the cosine values from the LSA serving as link strengths. Figure 5.15 shows the results. Dominant features of *The fog comes*, such as *drizzle*, become less central to the meaning of the whole sentence, and some new features are introduced, such as *stalk* and *kitten*. Note that *The fog comes* already was somewhat *soft*, and although this node is even more strongly related to *little cat feet*, its absolute activation did not increase much, but its relative weight in the pattern that constitutes the meaning of text (6) certainly has increased.

Note that if I had used the sentence *The theory is abstract*, the process of meaning construction would have been essentially the same, though quite nonmetaphorical. Some of the things we associate with *theory* would be deemphasized, whereas some features of *abstract* would transfer, creating a new concept.

My next example makes this equivalence between metaphorical and literal processes explicit. Consider *The old rock had become brittle with age*, uttered about a former professor and the wall of a medieval monastery, respectively (adapted from Gibbs, 1994):

(7a) John was in for a surprise when he visited his former professor after many years. The old rock had become brittle with age.
(7b) John was in for a surprise when he touched the wall of the monastery tower. The old rock had become brittle with age.

The inference ISA[FORMER[PROFESSOR], OLD[ROCK]] is required in (7a) and PART-OF[MONASTERY[WALL], OLD[ROCK]] is required to understand (7b). Both are presumably made on formal grounds: The definite determiner *the* signals a prior referent, and the *wall* and the *professor* are the nearest candidates. Sentence (7a) is metaphoric and (7b) is literal. Yet the process of meaning construction is the same for both. To construct an illustrative example, I have assumed that each noun phrase retrieves from long-term memory four of its most strongly associated neighbors. To reduce the arbitrariness of the example, I used LSA

Table 5.5. *Four strongly associated neighbors of key
noun phrases in examples (7a) and (7b)*

former professor:	university
	emeritus
	faculty
	*Nicolaas Bloembergen
wall of monastery tower:	vaulted
	buttresses
	masonry
	*Westminster Abbey
old rock:	old
	monolith
	volcanic
	*Dome of the Rock

to determine what these neighbors are and how strongly they are associated to the noun phrases in the (7a) and (7b) sentences. Thus, I assumed that the items shown in Table 5.5 will be retrieved; in each case I selected three word concepts, that is, words that have a high cosine between their vector and the eliciting noun phrase in the LSA space, and one document (the starred item) – the LSA analog of a memory episode.

Latent semantic analysis knows the world only through reading documents, whereas people have real experiences, episodes they remember and use to understand and interpret language. Nicolaas Bloembergen, I suppose, must be a famous old professor to whom an encyclopedia article was dedicated, and when LSA read the phrase *old professor* it was reminded of that article, much as a human might be reminded of some old professor or of a particular encounter with a member of that curious species.

If we construct a network linking the two noun phrases in (7a) and (7b) in the same way as in Figure 5.14 and integrate these networks, the activation patterns shown in Figures 5.16 and 5.17 are obtained. Whether metaphoric or not, the results are much the same: Features of *old rock* are transferred to *wall* as well as to *professor,* and some of the original features of these terms are muted, though by no means effaced. The *wall* reminds us now more of the *Dome of the Rock* than *Westminster Abbey* and becomes *old* and more like a *monolith;* it is less likely to be composed of *masonry.* The *professor,* too, ages and assumes some features of the *Dome of the Rock*

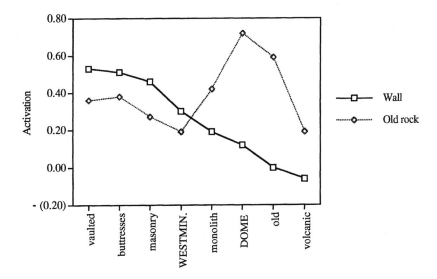

Figure 5.16 The activation of eight nodes linked to *wall of monastery tower* alone and linked to *the wall of the monastery tower is an old rock.* The first four items have been retrieved from the neighborhood of *wall of monastery tower,* and the last four items have been retrieved from the neighborhood of *old rock.*

and a *monolith;* his university associations become less prominent. Previously characterized only quite blandly by his role, this simple metaphor creates a better specified individual characterization for the *professor.* Presumably this is the reason people use figurative language. It allows them to say things compactly and effectively that would be cumbersome and perhaps impossible to say otherwise. But the process involved is no different from the nonmetaphoric example.

If there is no processing difference between metaphoric and nonmetaphoric language use, how can people tell what is a metaphor and what is not?[4] Judgments of metaphoricity might be a matter of semantic distance: If two quite unrelated noun phrases are put together in a sentence, we call it nonliteral. However, the semantic relatedness between the noun phrases in (7a) and (7b), as measured by the cosine between

4 Actually, there may be less agreement than linguists think concerning what a metaphor is. I often have trouble convincing my class that "the stock market crashed" is a metaphor.

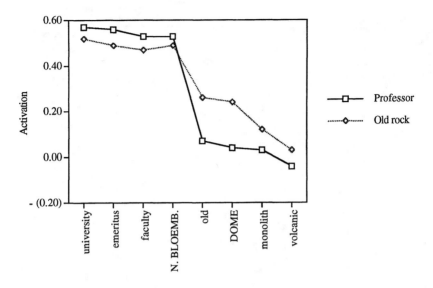

Figure 5.17   The activation of eight nodes linked to *old professor* alone and linked to *the old professor is an old rock*. The first four items have been retrieved from the neighborhood of *old professor*, and the last four items have been retrieved from the neighborhood of *old rock*.

their vector in the LSA space is .07 and .04, respectively. *Old rock* is just as unrelated to *wall of the monastery tower* as to *former professor*. Perhaps judging whether a sentence or phrase is or is not a metaphor involves more analysis and is not directly based on semantic distance. Perhaps the aesthetic pleasure one derives from reading figurative or poetic language is also based on such a postcomprehension analysis. For instance, a reader might detect a category violation in the case of the simple IS-A metaphors we have discussed here: We say (7a) is a metaphor because we know that rocks and professors belong to different conceptual categories, and we take pleasure in understanding the sentence nevertheless.

The illustrations of metaphor comprehension described here show that it is feasible to use the CI model together with semantic relatedness data obtained from LSA to simulate metaphor comprehension. However, many aspects of metaphor comprehension and usage have not been addressed here (such as asymmetries in metaphorical comparisons). To demonstrate the general validity of the points made here will require a great deal of further work with representative examples of sentences and corresponding human judgment data.

The construction of meaning does not stop with the construction of word meanings, but it must start there. Constructing the meaning of a word is a highly contextualized process, so much so that it becomes misleading to talk about constructing word meanings. The process might be better described as one of constructing the meaning of phrases, sentences, or even larger text units of which the word is a part. The meaning of the word, then, is intertwined with the meaning of these larger units and indeed difficult to separate from them. "A rose is a rose is a rose" is false – it is a somewhat different rose in every new context. Because the contexts in which the rose will appear are not arbitrary but are interrelated, not all these roses will be totally different but will share overlapping sets of features. But these shared features are not a common core meaning, the essence of the rose, but are much more widely variable, depending upon the use that is made of the word.

The CI model describes this process of meaning construction as starting with a bottom–up activation of a vague and nonspecific potential meaning and the gradual formation of a specific meaning in the process of integrating the word into larger sentence and text units. In the case of a content word encountered for the first time in a discourse context, information linked to the word in long-term memory, semantic as well as personal-episodic, is instantiated in working memory and participates in the integration process. The result of the integration process is a coherent structure into which the word meaning has become embedded. Anaphora of all kinds – specific repeated words as well as pronouns – are treated in much the same way, except that prior information in the text plays a stronger role. Various potential interpretations are interpreted in parallel, with the one that fits best into the discourse context winning out in the integration process.

The distinction between literal and nonliteral language is not well defined in such a framework. The process of meaning construction is one of constraint satisfaction and contextual elaboration that is basically the same whether a word is used literally or not. It is possible to simulate how literal as well as nonliteral word meanings are constructed in a discourse context at least for some simple cases. The empirical data on word identification, anaphora resolution, and metaphor interpretation are in good agreement with these simulations, providing a reasonably firm, though still incomplete, basis for the further exploration of meaning construction in discourse, beyond the word level.

6

Textbases and situation models

A parser in the CI model should take text as its input and generate as its output a network of propositions that then could be used as a foundation for the further modeling of comprehension processes. We do not have such a parser and must do with hand coding as an unsatisfactory (but workable) substitute. Nevertheless, there are at least the beginnings of some research on parsing processes within the CI framework, which I discuss in the first section of this chapter. The main focus of the CI model has always been on how textbases and situation models are put together, once the elementary propositions that are their building blocks have been constructed. Thus, I review recent research on the formation of macrostructures and the role they play in comprehension. This leads to the general topic of inferences, which is discussed in some detail here, in part because there has been a great deal of controversy in this field in recent years and in part because of their acknowledged central role in comprehension. Inferences (though that term, I argue, is misleading) are involved in both the formation of the textbase and the construction of the situation model. In particular, I discuss the construction of spatial situation models because of the special challenges this topic provides for a propositional theory.

Although most research on text comprehension has been done with narrative or descriptive texts, the principles of comprehension are very general. How they might be applied to literary texts is explored in section 6.5. A good argument can be made that the comprehension of literary texts is not different at the level of the basic architecture from the comprehension of the kinds of texts we typically study in our laboratories, although it demands special strategies and knowledge. However, all text genres require domain-specific strategies and knowledge.

6.1 Parsing

When the CI model was first presented in Kintsch (1988), I suggested that it might provide a plausible account of parsing processes. Relatively general and robust parsing rules might be used, and much of the burden of arriving at an unambiguous parse could be shifted to the contextual integration process. The only researcher who has followed up these ideas is Ferstl (1994a, 1994b). I therefore describe her work in some detail here.

The basic idea is simple. Instead of sophisticated, context-sensitive parsing operators, simple operators are employed that use little information but are easy to apply. Similar to the process of establishing word meanings, the parsing operators generate a network full of contradictions, for whenever there are choices, they yield both alternatives. However, these alternatives inhibit each other, and during the integration process the right alternative should win out because it fits better into the given context. I illustrated this model of parsing with the garden-path sentence

(1)   The linguists knew the solution of the problem would not be easy.

The parser would create a network containing two mutually inhibitory nodes, as shown in Figure 6.1. Following standard parsing heuristics ("minimal attachment"), it creates the proposition KNOW [LINGUISTS,SOLUTION], but it cannot complete the parse. The WOULD-NOT-BE-EASY must be attached to SOLUTION, but that contradicts the proposition just created. The alternative is to treat SOLUTION not as the object of KNOW but as the beginning of a new phrase. This way, the NOT-EASY can be readily incorporated. The resulting structure, of course, contains contradictions that must be resolved by the integration process. The final activation values displayed in Figure 6.1 show that the integration process does not do a clean job, assuming that all links have strength either 1 or −1. Although the correct alternative is more activated than the incorrect one, the troublesome NOT-EASY??? still retains some activation. But perhaps this account is not so far off and actually describes the mental representation of a garden-path sentence.

The model can generate a more unambiguous interpretation of example (1) if we allow changes in the link strength. Suppose a comprehender is not satisfied with the result of the integration process in Figure 6.1 and

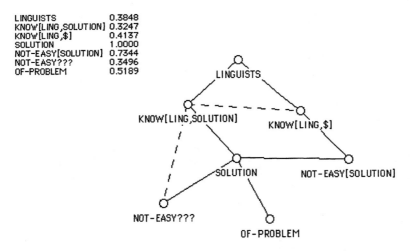

```
LINGUISTS               0.3848
KNOW[LING,SOLUTION] 0.3247
KNOW[LING,$]            0.4137
SOLUTION                1.0000
NOT-EASY[SOLUTION]  0.7344
NOT-EASY???             0.3496
OF-PROBLEM              0.5189
```

Figure 6.1 The network constructed to process the linguist-sentence (1).
All links are either 1 (solid lines) or –1 (broken lines). Final activation values
after the integration phase are displayed on the left.

decides that ungrammatical nodes like NOT-EASY??? are unacceptable
and that the constructions responsible for their creation should be more
strongly inhibited than was the case in Figure 6.1. In Figure 6.2, the same
net is shown, except that the link between NOT-EASY??? and KNOW
[LINGUISTS,SOLUTION] has been given a value of –2. In this case,
the offending proposition is now completely deactivated, but the NOT-
EASY node itself retains considerable activation as a sort of memory of
past trouble.[1]

How could the model make such a decision to increase an inhibitory
link? One way would be to calculate a statistic that indicates how well the
results of integration satisfy the initial constraints in the network. Such a
statistic is the *harmony* statistic of Smolensky (1986; see also Britton &
Eisenhart, 1993). Harmony is a function of the products of the initial and
final link and node strengths in the net. These products are large when
the initial and final strength value agree, that is, when the final solution
respects the initial constraints. In the case of Figure 6.1, the harmony is
quite low, with a value of .18. It is conceivable that a harmony monitor
would reject such a solution and make changes in the network designed

1 It remains to be seen whether this is an empirically correct prediction; according to
   Gernsbacher (1993), rejected nodes are suppressed, that is, their activation is negative or below baseline!

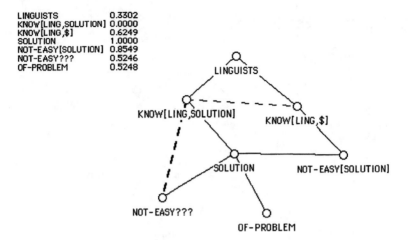

```
LINGUISTS               0.3302
KNOW[LING,SOLUTION]     0.0000
KNOW[LING,$]            0.6249
SOLUTION                1.0000
NOT-EASY[SOLUTION]      0.8549
NOT-EASY???             0.5246
OF-PROBLEM              0.5248
```

Figure 6.2   The same network as in Figure 6.1, except that the broken link in boldface has a strength of –2. Final activation values after the integration phase are displayed on the left.

to provide a better solution with a higher harmony value. Indeed, the harmony for the network shown in Figure 6.2 increases to a value of .30.

Ferstl (1994a) discusses a parsing problem that parallels (1). She is concerned with another well-known garden-path sentence:

(2)   The horse raced past the barn fell.

Again, a network is constructed representing RACE[HORSE] and PAST-BARN, but the FALL??? node cannot be syntactically connected to this network, as shown in Figure 6.3. The alternative RACE[SOME-ONE,HORSE] and FALL[HORSE], on the other hand, provides no problem. The integration process suppresses the incorrect constructions entirely, as shown in Figure 6.3. The difficulty in this case appears to be in constructing the correct alternative in the first place, for informal observations suggest that many undergraduate students have trouble with this construction.

What is interesting about these examples is that the interpretation proceeds using only syntactic cues. This is not generally the case, for semantic and pragmatic cues usually play a role as well. Consider the following sentence pair, from an experiment by Taraban and McClelland (1988):

(3)   The janitor cleaned the room with the broom.
(4)   The janitor cleaned the room with the window.

```
fall??                        0.0000
RACE[HORSE]                   0.0000
LOC[R[H],PAST-BARN]           0.0000
HORSE                         0.8236
BARN                          0.2567
FALL[HORSE]                   0.8236
RACE[SOMEONE,HORSE]           1.0000
LOC[R[S,H],PAST-BARN]         0.5677
```

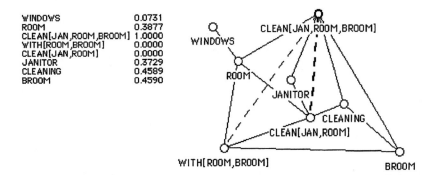

Figure 6.3   The network constructed to process the sentence *The horse raced past the barn fell*. Final activation values after the integration phase are shown on the left. Positive links are indicated by solid lines, negative links by broken lines. After Ferstl (1994a).

These sentences have the propositional representations CLEAN[JANITOR,ROOM,BROOM] and CLEAN[JANITOR, ROOM] and WITH [ROOM,WINDOW], respectively. Out of context, subjects prefer the "broom" sentence over the "window" sentence, but they correctly parse both sentences (Taraban & McClelland, 1988). Ferstl (1994a) shows that the CI model can find the correct interpretation of these sentences without explicit representation of the verb's thematic roles or selection restrictions. All it needs are a few associative knowledge elaborations. The network the model constructs for (3), according to Ferstl (1994a) is shown in Figure 6.4.

```
WINDOWS                       0.0731
ROOM                          0.3877
CLEAN[JAN,ROOM,BROOM]         1.0000
WITH[ROOM,BROOM]              0.0000
CLEAN[JAN,ROOM]               0.0000
JANITOR                       0.3729
CLEANING                      0.4589
BROOM                         0.4590
```

Figure 6.4   The network constructed to process the sentence *The janitor cleaned the room with the broom*. Final activation values after the integration phase are shown on the left. Positive links are indicated by solid lines, negative links by broken lines. After Ferstl (1994a).

To represent the verb attachment bias of subjects in Figure 6.4, the self activation of the preferred CLEAN[JANITOR,ROOM,BROOM] node was increased, as was the inhibitory link between the two alternatives. ROOM was associated with WINDOW, and CLEANING was associated with BROOM. and JANITOR (association strengths were assumed to be .5). As a result of these minimal knowledge elaborations, the model correctly computes the verb attachment for BROOM in (3) and (a network analogous to Figure 6.4) the noun attachment for WINDOW in (4).

A final example from Ferstl (1994a) illustrates how the CI model takes account of the discourse context in parsing a sentence. It has already been mentioned that the noun attachment required by (4) is less preferred than the verb attachment. This bias can be overcome by an appropriate discourse context. For instance, if the sentence

(5)   There was a room with plants and a room with windows.

precedes (4), the nonpreferred noun-attachment becomes easier. In contrast, if the sentence

(6)   There was a lounge with plants and a room with windows.

precedes (4), this effect is not obtained. Altmann and Steedman (1988) have called this the principle of referential support: Example (5) has the effect of introducing a *room with windows* into the discourse, to distinguish it from the *room with plants*, whereas the *window* modifier is redundant in (6).

Ferstl (1994a) simulated this effect by first integrating (5) and carrying over in the short-term memory buffer the two most highly activated propositions for the second processing cycle, which involved the integration of *The janitor cleaned the room with the window.* The propositions carried over were WITH[ROOM$_1$,PLANT] and WITH[ROOM$_2$,WINDOW]. Similarly, (6) adds WITH[LOUNGE, PLANT] to the network. In either case, whether (5) or (6) preceded it, the noun attachment was successfully made (i.e., the proposition with the instrument interpretation was correctly deactivated). However, the time course of integration was quite different, depending upon whether the discourse context was (5) or (6). Ferstl's results (1994a) are shown in Figure 6.5. In the context when only one room was mentioned, the preferred (but incorrect) instrument interpretation for *window* was slightly more activated for the first 14 iterations and did not become fully deactivated until after 27 iterations. In contrast, when two rooms were mentioned so that a discourse object

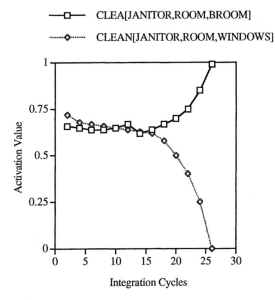

Figure 6.5 The time course of activation for the two propositions
CLEAN[JANITOR,ROOM,BROOM] and
CLEAN[JANITOR,ROOM,WINDOWS]. After Ferstl (1994a).

room-with-windows had already been established, the instrument proposition weakens much earlier and is fully deactivated after 20 iterations.
Similarly, the correct *room-with-window* proposition increases in strength
more rapidly when it receives referential support than when it does not.

Ferstl (1994a,1994b) also discusses other experiments in the literature
in which results were obtained that were seemingly contradictory to those
of Altmann and Steedman (1988), such as an experiment by Ferreira and
Clifton (1986). She points out that the negative results of Ferreira and
Clifton could be expected according to the CI model, because the materials used in their experiment were written in such a way that the referential information was no longer in the discourse focus when the target
sentence was read. Hence, the WITH[ROOM$_2$,WINDOW] proposition,
although it had been constructed earlier, was not carried over in the
buffer and did not participate in the processing of the target sentence,
and therefore could not have had an effect.

Ferstl's simulations and her discussion of the literature are interesting
and provoking. Looking at the parsing literature through the eyes of the
CI model can be instructive. However, a really systematic treatment of

parsing within the CI framework is yet to come.[2] Such a task may need to wait until we have acquired a more extensive database on the parsing strategies people actually use than is available now. Richer empirical studies of parsing strategies, data as in Ferstl (1994b), would substantially help our progress theoretically.

6.2 Macrostructure formation

According to the model of text processing of Kintsch and van Dijk (1978) and van Dijk and Kintsch (1983), the formation of a macrostructure is an integral part of normal text comprehension. It does not occur merely in response to special task demands, such as instructions to summarize the text, but is an automatic component of the process of comprehension that cannot be separated from it.

That readers are able to recognize topic sentences that are expressed in a text has been shown many times with a variety of procedures, including reading times, think aloud protocols, and importance ratings (e.g., by Kieras, 1980). Similarly, it has been shown that readers can produce adequate summaries of simple texts on demand (e.g., Kintsch & Kozminsky, 1977). However, there also exist good experimental data to support the stronger claim of the theory that macrostructure formation occurs as an integral part of comprehension.

If subjects read a text as part of a word recognition experiment, there is no reason to think that they would intentionally engage in macroprocessing if such processing were an optional, strategic part of comprehension. Thus, if one can show that readers under these conditions form macrostructures anyway, this would provide evidence for the automatic nature of macroprocesses. Guindon and Kintsch (1984) produced such evidence in a study that relied on the recognition priming method of Ratcliff and McKoon (1978).

Ratcliff and McKoon had shown that recognition priming can provide a very sensitive and at the same time nonintrusive measure for the analysis of the memory structures generated during reading. Their method was exceedingly simple. They gave subjects sentences to read, followed by a word-recognition test. They looked at the speed with which words from

2   The present approach has some similarities to the probabilistic parsers that have recently been developed within computational linguistics (Charniak, 1993; Jurafsky, 1996), but the compatibility of these approaches needs to be investigated further.

the sentences were recognized as a function of the word that preceded the test word on the recognition test: whether or not the preceding word was from the same sentence as the target word, and whether or not it was from the same proposition. In the first case, they observed a priming effect of 110 ms over different-sentences controls. When the preceding word and the target word not only came from the same sentence but also from the same proposition, an additional small, but statistically significant priming effect of 20 ms was obtained.

Guindon and Kintsch (1984) used this procedure to study macroprocessing in comprehension. In experiment 1, their subjects read paragraphs with an initial topic sentence. For instance, a text describing the training of decathloners might start with the topic sentence *A decathloner develops* a **well-rounded athletic** body and contain as one of the sentences in the body of the paragraph the statement *A decathloner also builds* up **strong** hands. In what we called macropairs, both the preceding word and the target word came from a topic sentence (e.g., *develop, body*); in micropairs, both words came from a detail sentence (e.g., *build, hand*); in control pairs, words that appeared in the text but in different sentences succeeded each other. Hence, the correct response to all target words was "yes." The priming effect was computed as the difference between the recognition time for control target words minus the recognition time for macro- and microtarget words. Figure 6.6 (left panel) shows that the priming effect was substantially larger for macro words than for micro words.[3]

Similar results were obtained in experiment 2 of Guindon and Kintsch (1984), except that in this experiment the paragraphs were shown without the topic sentences, so that macropropositions had to be inferred rather than constructed on the basis of an actual topic sentence. Control word pairs were used (words that had not appeared in the paragraphs), as well as word pairs thematically related to the paragraph but that did not function as macrowords. Thus, we compare the recognition times for *body* as a macroword and *feet* as a thematically related nonmacroword with a thematically unrelated control word. Because the subject had not seen any of these words before, the correct response in all cases was "no" in this experiment. The results are shown in the right panel of Figure 6.6: A

---

3   In a recognition experiment reported by Albrecht and O'Brien (1991), similar results were obtained: macrorelevant, central concepts were more rapidly recognized than peripheral concepts.

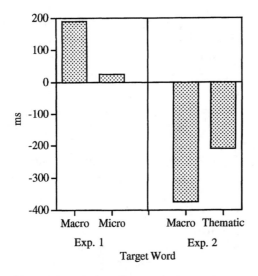

Figure 6.6   Priming effects in word recognition for macro words and non-macro words. After Guindon and Kintsch (1984).

stronger (negative) priming effect was obtained for macrowords than for thematically related nonmacrowords.

Figure 6.6 provides evidence that readers react to macro words differently than to nonmacrowords, even though this was only a word recognition task. Readers did not even have to understand what they read. However, just as they could not help understanding the texts they read, they could not help generating a macrostructure for these texts. Macrostructure formation indeed appears to be an automatic and integral part of reading comprehension.

A study by Lorch, Lorch, and Mathews (1985) adds further support to this conclusion by means of a different experimental methodology. Lorch and his colleagues constructed texts that were hierarchically organized into major and minor subcategories. They compared reading times for topic sentences after a major and a minor topic shift and found that after a major shift topic sentences required 300 ms more reading time than after a minor shift. However, there were no shift effects on sentence reading times when the sentences were presented in a disorganized fashion, thus preventing readers from generating an orderly macrostructure. It is interesting that these effects occurred when subjects were reading without special instructions. When the subjects were informed that they would have to outline the text, these effects became even larger. Thus, macroprocessing occurs during normal reading but can be enhanced strategically when there are appropriate task demands.

The generation of macropropositions can be considered as some kind of inference – an inference that does not add information to the text but that reduces information (Kintsch, 1993). In selecting a macroproposition, micropropositions are deleted, and in forming a generalization or construction, several micropropositions are replaced by an appropriate macroproposition. Information is reduced in all these cases, as a summary replaces lower-level detail. In the studies reviewed here, this reduction process was largely automatic because they dealt with familiar domains for which the appropriate generalizations and constructions are readily available to the comprehenders. For instance, if we are told that

(7) John bought a ticket, went to the airport in Denver, got on a plane, ordered some drinks and dozed off, and finally got off the plane in Chicago,

the construction of the macroproposition *John flew to Chicago* is fully automatic because the information we were given is connected in a stable retrieval structure (see chapter 7 for more detail) to *flying* in long-term memory. Hence, *John flew to Chicago* does not have to be inferred by some special inference procedure but becomes available automatically in long-term working memory. It is in these situations, when such retrieval structures are available in long-term memory, that macropropositions become automatically available during comprehension. As a consequence, they do not have to be formed at all; the process of textbase construction simply makes them potentially available. However, in unfamiliar domains, where the comprehender lacks retrieval structures, macrostructure formation for texts cannot be automatic and is not an inherent component of comprehension. In fact, it may not take place at all, or if a macrostructure is formed, it requires controlled processing – explicit reasoning procedures as well as memory search for potentially relevant information. This distinction between automatic and controlled processes in inferencing is discussed more fully in section 6.3.

6.2.1 Signaling the macrostructure

Mross (1989), as part of a dissertation at the University of Colorado, used an experimental design that allowed him to study another feature of macroprocessing: the signals by means of which macropropositions are linguistically marked in a text. He had subjects read texts that consisted of three subtopics. Each of the three subtopics was introduced by an explicit topic statement, as in the following example:

(8)   One form of business organization is that of sole proprietorship. There are no legal requirements for this form of organization. (Marked text)

In the implicit version of the texts these topic statements were omitted.

(9)   There are no legal requirements for the sole proprietorship form of organization. (Unmarked text)

In his first experiment, Mross used an item recognition task to study the speed and accuracy with which words from topic statements and words from detail sentences were recognized. These recognition probes were presented at two points during the reading of each paragraph. Macro-probes (*sole proprietorship*) were recognized more accurately (93% vs. 76%) than microprobes (*legal requirements*) and were responded to faster than microprobes (487 ms vs. 524 ms, respectively), in agreement with Guindon and Kintsch's (1984) results.

In another experiment (experiment 3), Mross (1989) recorded reading times for both topic sentences and detail sentences in the marked as well as the unmarked texts. These results are shown in Figure 6.7. Topic sentences were read more slowly than detail sentences, replicating the results

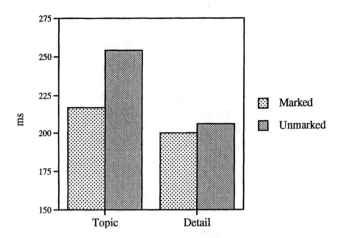

Figure 6.7   Reading time per syllable in ms for topic and detail sentences in the marked and unmarked condition. After Mross (1989).

of Lorch et al. (1985). In addition, we observe an interesting interaction in Figure 6.7: topic sentences are read much more slowly when they are not marked linguistically. Readers apparently need extra time to figure out the topical status of these sentences when they are not given a linguistic cue.

Mross also asked his subjects to summarize the texts they read, and he scored these summaries for completeness. It turned out that the subjects who read the marked texts wrote significantly better summaries than the subjects who read the unmarked texts (5.6 subtopic statements included in the summary for marked texts vs. 4.6 subtopic statements for unmarked texts). Linguistic marking not only allowed readers to process the texts faster but also helped them to write better summaries.

Topic marking thus appears to be a powerful means for facilitating macroprocessing. Mross used summary sentences for this purpose, but headings and previews work equally well for this purpose (e.g., Lorch, Lorch, & Inman, 1993). Indeed, the language makes available a variety of more subtle means to signal whether we are continuing with a topic or shifting to a new one, and speakers and writers use these means liberally. One technique used to signal a topic shift is to overspecify anaphora. We have seen (section 5.2.1) that as long as a concept is available in working memory, writers tend to refer to it by zero anaphora or pronoun. Full noun phrases are typically used only when the concept must be reinstated into working memory. Violating this convention signals a topic shift. If one refers to a concept with a full noun phrase when a less specific reference would have sufficed, a topic shift is signaled thereby. Linguists have shown this to be the case in the texts they have analyzed (e.g., Fox, 1984; Linde, 1979), and several experimental demonstrations of this effect also exist. Fletcher (1984) gave subjects sentence pairs to read, such as the following:

(10) 1a. Peter intended to go bowling last night.
    1b. Peter intended to go bowling with Sam last night.
    1c. Sam intended to go bowling with Peter last night.
    2. Peter broke his leg.

and asked them to rewrite the second sentence to make it sound more natural. His striking results are shown in Figure 6.8. For the highly coherent (1a)–(2) pair, subjects almost always chose either zero anaphora or a pronoun. For the (1c)–(2) pair, which involves a clear topic shift, a

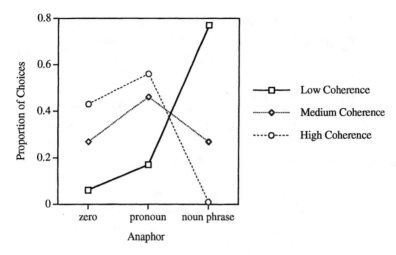

Figure 6.8   The choice of zero anaphora, pronouns, or noun phrases as a function of the coherence between sentence pairs. After Fletcher (1984).

full noun phrase was the overwhelming choice, and intermediate results were observed for the pair with medium coherence.

Fletcher's result were corroborated by Vonk, Hustinx, and Simons (1992), who had subjects provide verbal descriptions of picture stories that did or did not involve a topic shift. Because there was only a single actor in these picture stories, no linguistic ambiguity was involved. Nevertheless, topic shifts in the pictures were signaled linguistically by a full noun phrase in 88% of all continuations, which contrasts with 83% pronoun choices when no topic shift was involved.

The experiments reviewed here clearly show that macroprocesses are real. They are as much part of discourse comprehension as microprocesses are. These experiments also allow us to glimpse how readers form macrostructures. In particular, we note that natural language has available rich means, including syntactic ones, to help the reader to generate macrostructures. What the experiments discussed here do not make clear is the enormous importance of macroprocesses for text understanding: how easy a text is, how well readers understand it, how well they can remember it, what they learn from it – all this is strongly dependent on a successful macrostructure. Local comprehension problems may be a nuisance, but problems at the macro level tend to be a disaster.

6.2.2 Dominance of the macrostructure: Contradictions in the text

A well-organized macrostructure is crucial for understanding and remembering a text. Texts that are locally coherent but that contain global inconsistencies are read more slowly and remembered less well (Albrecht, O'Brien, Mason, & Myers, 1995; Albrecht & O'Brien, 1993). But too much of a good thing can make readers misunderstand and misremember a text. An excessive emphasis on the macrostructure can lead to serious distortions of the meaning of a text. Otero and Kintsch (1992) have shown how certain pathological interpretations of texts containing an outright contradiction can arise as a consequence of such an overemphasis on the macrostructure of the text.

It is well known that readers often do not notice even direct contradictions in a text. Just how frequent such mistakes are depends on the readers and the task demands generated by the experimental situation, but the basic phenomenon has been observed in a number of studies under a variety of conditions. In the data of Otero and Kintsch (1992), for example, 40.3% of the contradictions in a text were not noticed by the reader, either during reading or afterward. This is a striking result, because the texts used in this experiment were brief and simple (though scientific descriptions, rather than stories), and the contradictions were blatant, as in the following example:

(11) Superconductivity. Superconductivity is the disappearance of resistance to the flow of electric current. **Until now it has been obtained only by cooling certain materials to low temperatures near absolute zero.** That made its technical application very difficult. Many laboratories now are trying to produce superconducting alloys. Many materials with this property, with immediate technical applicability, have recently been discovered. **Until now, superconductivity has been achieved by considerably increasing the temperature of certain materials.**[4]

The two contradictory sentences (in boldface type) are separated by only two sentences; all sentences in the paragraph are on the topic of superconductivity; the contradiction is explicit (*cooling* vs. *increasing the temperature*). The readers were asked to report any comprehension problems

---

4   The actual texts used in the experiment were written in Spanish.

while reading and later recalled the paragraph. They were not warned of contradictions in the texts (four of the six experimental texts contained a contradiction). Most of the failures (82%) to notice a contradiction in a text were of three types:

1. Subjects reproduced the definition of superconductivity but did not mention in their recall protocols either of the contradictory sentences.
2. Subjects mentioned that superconductivity is achieved by cooling but said nothing about the contradictory sentence.
3. Subjects mentioned both cooling and heating but explained away the contradiction by some unwarranted, fanciful inference, such as "Up to now superconductivity was achieved by cooling, but now it can be achieved by heating certain materials."

Thus, we have a high incidence of errors, and errors that are highly systematic rather than random – a phenomenon that cries for an explanation.

To simulate comprehension of the superconductivity paragraph, the text (11) was represented as a list of propositions. Because subjects read a series of texts that all had the same structure (definitional sentence plus three elaborative sentences), it is highly likely that they would have considered SUPERCONDUCTIVITY and IS[SUPERCONDUCT-IVITY,DISAPPEARANCE] as macropropositions. As an additional macroproposition, we assumed that subjects would use either OF [DIS-APPAEARANCE,RESISTANCE] or OBTAIN [SUPERCODUCTIV-ITY[COOL [TEMPERATURE]], corresponding to the type 1 and type 2 readers. The network contains the two contradictory propositions OBTAIN [SUPERCODUCTIVITY[COOL [TEMPERATURE]] and OBTAIN[SUPERCONDUCTIVITY,INCREASE[TEMPERATURE, OF MATERIAL]], which are linked by an inhibitory link of strength -1. All other links have strength $+1$.

Integrating the propositinal network thus generated in cycles yields the long-term memory strength values for the two contradictory propositions shown in Figure 6.9 ("normal"). The strength values are unequal, but both propositions have substantial strength, and one would expect that the contradiction would be noted.

Type 1 and type 2 errors can be created in the model by increasing the weights of the macropropositions in the network. If we increase the strength of the links between macropropositions from 1 to a value of 10, the model makes type 1 and type 2 errors, depending on which macrostructure we assume. If OF[DISPPEARANCE, RESISTANCE] is

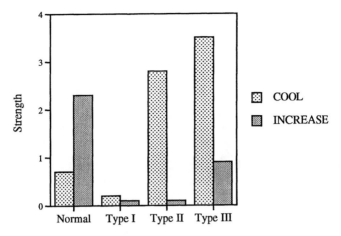

Figure 6.9   Strength values for the two contradictory propositions for normal readers and three types of nondetectors.

included in the macrostructure, the definitional component becomes so strong that both contradictory propositions receive only negligible activation. Hence, they most likely would be overlooked, as type 1 readers overlooked them in the experiment. On the other hand, if OBTAIN [SUPERCODUCTIVITY[COOL [TEMPERATURE]] becomes part of the macrostructure, the first proposition becomes so strong that it inhibits the contradictory proposition later in the text, which is what happened with type 2 readers.

Some readers did not report a contradiction because they explained it away by an unwarranted inference, usually by assuming that one way of generating superconductivity was used in the past but that now there is a second way. We simulate these type 3 readers as normal readers who detect the contradiction but add another proposition, FROM-NOW-ON [OBTAIN[SUPERCONDUCTIVITY[HOT[TEMPRETAURE]]]. As Figure 6.9 shows, both contradictory propositions receive high strengths in this case, but there is no contradiction to report any more because UNTIL-NOW has been arbitrarily replaced by FROM-NOW-ON.

Note that these type 3 readers employ a strategy for resolving the contradiction that is applicable in many cases, because contradictions are often resolved by noting a difference in time or place. The present text, however, does not warrant the use of this strategy.

Otero and Kintsch (1992) do not claim that every failure to note a contradiction in a text is the result of an overemphasis on macroprocesses. However, under the conditions of their experiment, this is a reasonable hypothesis, and, as has been shown, it explains their data in some detail. No new model had to be constructed for this purpose. All we did was to assign an extra weight to an important and integral component of normal comprehension processes. Comprehension of anything but the shortest texts strongly depends on the successful construction of an adequate macrostructure for the text. The macropropositions must be emphasized in normal comprehension and are recalled better than the microprop-ositions of a text. However, if that emphasis is exaggerated, the model becomes pathological and starts missing information in the text in ways that parallel what real subjects do in certain experimental situations.

6.2.3 Macrostructures as vectors in the LSA space

How are macrostructures generated? According to the theory of van Dijk (1980), macrostructures are derived from a text through the applica-tion of *macrorules:* Less important portions of the text may be *deleted,* instances may be *generalized,* and summaries of events may be *constructed.* A difficulty with this theory is that the macrorules are easy to describe and readily illustrated by examples but cannot be automated. Given a paragraph, it is not possible to say what its macrostructure, or gist, is. We can suggest plausible macropropositions for it and show how these are derivable via van Dijk's macrorules, but these rules do not specify a unique solution.

Latent semantic analysis may provide a useful alternative, in that it permits us to represent macrostructures as vectors in the semantic space, in the same way as words or sentences are represented. A macrostructure in the LSA representation is thus the vector corresponding to a para-graph, and a higher-order macrostructure is simply the vector of several paragraphs or the whole text. Thus, macrostructures in LSA are easily computable and are unique. They are not, however, intuitively plausible sentences or phrases, such as those generated by the macrorules, but an uninterpreted vector in a high-dimensional semantic space that we can know only by its neighbors. For some purposes this may be quite suffi-cient, however, and in fact advantageous, because we now have the capa-bility to calculate the semantic distance of this macrovector with other vectors of potential interest, as the following example illustrates.

Consider the following ministory, a text T, consisting of a setting (the first paragraph, ¶1) and an event (the second paragraph, ¶2):

(12) T ¶1 S1 John was driving his new car on a lonely country road.

S2 The air was warm and full of the smell of spring flowers.

¶2 S3 He hit a hole in the road and a spring broke.

S4 John lost control and the car hit a tree.

Latent semantic analysis lets us represent as vectors the content words in S1 to S4 as well as the four sentences themselves. Thus, we can compute the semantic relatedness between each word in a sentence and the sentence as a whole – the cosine between the respective vectors. Figure 6.10 shows the results.[5] What is interesting here is that some words have a big effect on the sentence meaning (high cosine between word and sentence vector, e.g., *car* in S1), whereas others have very little effect (word meaning and sentence meaning are only weakly related, e.g., *lonely* in S1). Do ratings by readers of the contribution that each word makes to a sentence reflect these LSA relations? Furthermore, one can also compute a cosine between a word in a sentence and the other words in the sentence, indicating how interrelated the words of a sentence are. If these values are high, are sentences faster or easier to comprehend than when these values are low?

Different sentences make different contributions to a paragraph, and the two paragraphs make different contributions to the text as a whole. Do readers judge the importance of sentences to a paragraph, or paragraphs to a text as a whole, in the same way as does LSA? The necessary experiments to answer these questions are quite straightforward. If the answers are positive, there appear to be numerous theoretical as well as practical implications.

The paragraph representations ¶1 and ¶2 in Figure 6.10 are uninterpreted vectors without an English-language counterpart. Using macro-

5   The fact that these results are based on a semantic space derived from reading an encyclopedia must be borne in mind. An adult human semantic space is based on much more experience with words, and with words from different kinds of texts – encyclopedias focus on that part of human knowledge that is not common sense, whereas common sense knowledge is what is most involved in understanding simple texts like the ones analyzed here.

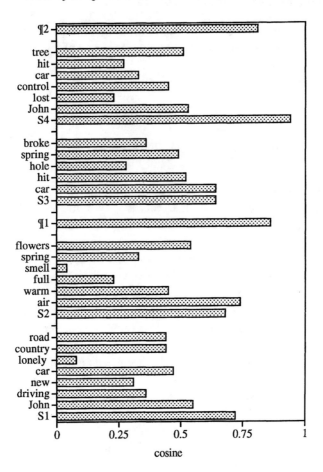

Figure 6.10   Cosines between words and sentences, sentences and paragraphs, and paragraphs and the whole text.

rules, one might generate the following summary sentences for ¶1, ¶2, and the whole text, T, respectively:

(12)   S (¶1)   An automobile ride in the spring.
       S (¶2)   An automobile accident.
       S (T)   An automobile ride in the spring ends in an accident.

Obviously, however, there are other plausible alternatives. However, we can easily test whether these suggested summary sentences or phrases adequately express their respective macronodes. For instance, the two summary sentences, S(¶1) and S(¶2), for the two paragraphs suggested have cosines with the ¶1 and ¶2 vectors of .39 and .42, respectively, and the cosine between the summary sentence S(T) and the whole text vector T is also .42. These are fairly high values (compare them to the cosines between words and sentences in Figure 6.10), indicating that we have constructed good summaries. This technique may prove useful for evaluating summaries objectively and automatically.[6]

The cosine values between words and sentences, sentences and paragraphs, and paragraphs and the whole text shown in Figure 6.10 can be used to implement a CI-model simulation of the text together with its macrostructure. We add to the atomic propositions of the text the complex propositions S1 to S4 corresponding to the four sentences, and a macrostructure consisting of ¶1 and ¶2 for the two paragraphs, and T for the text as a whole, and link them with the cosine values obtained from the LSA. The resulting network is shown in Figure 6.11. Sentence 2 fills the time–circumstance slot of DRIVE; DRIVE provides the setting for the events described by S3 and S4; the propositions of S3 and S4 are all causally linked. The microstructure consists of the atomic text propositions and the four complex propositions corresponding to sentences S1 to S4. The macrostructure consists of the two paragraph vectors ¶1 and ¶2 (P1 and P2), and the whole-text vector T. Links between atomic propositions have a value of 1; all other links have values equal to the strength of their relationship as assessed by LSA and shown in Figure 6.10. The numbers after each label are the long-term memory strength values computed from the CI simulation.

Comprehension of this network was simulated in four cycles, each cycle comprising one sentence, including its superordinate macronodes. For each cycle, the most strongly activated node from the previous cycle was held over in the short-term memory buffer. The results, shown in terms of long-term memory strengths in Figure 6.11, are interesting. The strongest nodes are the DRIVE proposition from the first sentence and sentence vectors S2, S3, and S4. On the other hand, the paragraph representations ¶1 and ¶2 and the whole-text vector T end up with relatively low strengths.

Does including the macrostructure in this way make a difference for the model? It certainly does, for if we simulate comprehension of this text without the complex propositions and macronodes in Figure 6.11, the strengths values obtained for the atomic text propositions correlate only

6   Some empirical results are reported in section 8.2.2.

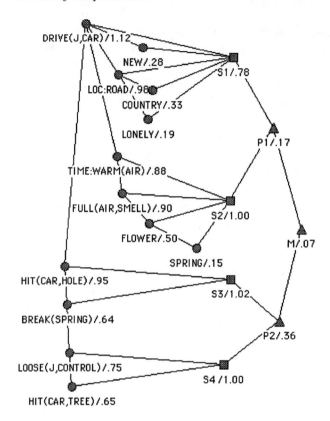

Figure 6.11   A simulation of the comprehension of text (12).

$r = .50$ with the values obtained by including the macrostructure. Which version is better can be determined only by a systematic comparison of such model predictions with recall and summary data for a sufficiently large number of texts. Furthermore, although it seems reasonable that the link weights of the macronodes should be proportional to their cosines in the LSA analysis, setting them equal to those values as was done here is probably an oversimplification. Just how the micro- and macrostructures should be weighted relative to each other remains an issue to be explored.

6.3 Inferences

Text comprehension depends as much on the reader and the pragmatic situation as on the text itself. What readers bring to the text, their goals and prior experience, has been studied under the label of inferencing in text comprehension. In particular, the process of knowledge use that every reader must engage in to properly understand a text has been characterized as making inferences in text comprehension. This is a regrettable terminology that has caused a great deal of confusion, for much of what we call inferencing has very little to do with real inferences.

6.3.1 Classification of inferences

A distinction should be made between problem-solving processes when there are premises from which some conclusions are drawn (not necessarily by the rules of logic) that may be justly called inferences, and knowledge retrieval processes in which a gap in the text is bridged by some piece of preexisting knowledge that has been retrieved (Kintsch, 1993). Both inferences proper and knowledge retrieval may be either automatic (and usually unconscious) or controlled (and usually conscious and strategic). This classification results in Table 6.1.

The classification in Table 6.1 is based on a proposal by Guthke (1991) and is described in detail in Kintsch (1993). Retrieval adds preexisting information to a text from long-term memory. Generation, in contrast, produces new information by deriving it from information in the text by some inference procedure. Thus, although the term *inference* is suitable for information generation processes, it is a misnomer for retrieval processes.

A prototypical example for cell A, the automatic retrieval process that

Table 6.1. *A classification system for inferences in text comprehension. After Kintsch (1993)*

	Retrieval	Generation
	A	C
Automatic Processes	Bridging inferences, associative elaborations	Transitive inferences in a familiar domain
	B	D
Controlled Processes	Search for bridging knowledge	Logical inferences

enriches the information in a text, would be the activation of *with a hammer* by *John nailed down a board*, or *cars have doors* by *A car stopped. The door opened.*[7] In both cases sufficient retrieval cues for the information retrieved exist in short-term memory and are linked with pertinent information in long-term memory. Under such conditions a long-term working memory forms, which means that the linked information in long-term memory becomes readily available in working memory (see Ericsson & Kintsch, 1995, and the discussion in chapter 7 for details on the operation of long-term working memory). In the terminology of Ericsson and Kintsch (1995), a retrieval structure exists that links the cues in short-term working memory to particular contents of long-term memory, thereby expanding the capacity of working memory. Such knowledge use is automatic, rapid, and places no demands on cognitive resources. An alternative model for this kind of knowledge retrieval is the resonance theory of Myers (Myers, O'Brien, Albrecht, & Mason, 1994), a well-developed mathematical model employing a resonance analogy for memory retrieval. According to this model, cues in short-term memory produce a resonance in long-term memory, so that the resonating items become available for further processing in working memory. Thus, either via retrieval structures or resonance, relevant, strongly related items in long-term memory become potential parts of working memory, creating a long-term working memory that is much richer than short-term working memory, which is severely restricted in capacity. Indeed, it is only this long-term working memory that makes discourse comprehension (or, indeed, any other expert performance) possible. Smooth, efficient functioning would be impossible if we had no way of expanding the capacity of working memory beyond the rigid limits of short-term memory. These issues are discussed in greater detail in chapter 7; the point here is that making long-term memory contents available via retrieval structures or resonance should hardly be called "inference."

In cell B of Table 6.1 are cases in which automatic retrieval is not possible. That is, the cues present in short-term memory do not retrieve relevant information that bridge whatever gap exists in the text. An extended search of memory is required to yield the needed information. A memory search is a strategic, controlled, resource-demanding process in which

---

7   I am not claiming that this sort of inference does or does not occur "naturally" during comprehension. I am simply classifying inferences.

the cues available in short-term memory are used to retrieve other likely cues from long-term memory that in turn are capable of retrieving what is needed. Consider the following:

(13) Danny wanted a new bike. He worked as a waiter.

Purely automatic, associative elaboration might not retrieve the causal chain from *want-bike* to *buy-bike* to *money* to *work*. However, a directed search for causal connections between the two sentences would easily generate these by no means obscure links. In all probability, genre-specific strategies exist to guide such search processes. In a story, one would look for causal links. In a legal argument, one routinely looks for contradictions. In an algebra word problem, algebra formulas guide the search. The difficulty of such procedures and the resource demands they make vary widely.

Retrieval processes merely access information available in long-term memory, either automatically or by a resource-demanding search. Generation processes actually compute new information on the basis of the text and relevant background information in long-term memory. They, too, may be either automatic or controlled.

On the one extreme, there are the fully automatic generation procedures (cell C of Table 6.1). For instance, given the sentence

(14) Three turtles rested on a floating log, and a fish swam beneath them.

the statement *The turtles are above the fish* is immediately available to a reader. Indeed, readers often are unable to distinguish whether they were explicitly told this information or not (e.g., Bransford, Barclay, & Franks, 1972). Note, however, that this is not merely a question of knowledge retrieval as in *doors are parts of cars*. The statement *the turtles are above the fish* is not something that already exists in long-term memory and is now retrieved, but it is generated during the comprehension process. The reason it is so highly available in the reader's working memory is presumably that the fish-log-and-turtle scene is encoded as an image, and this mental image constitutes a highly effective retrieval structure that provides ready access to all its parts – not just the verbal expression used in its construction.

Here is an instructive case in which the decision to represent mental representations by propositions can easily get us into trouble. In a propositional system, it would appear that some inference rule, for instance, transitivity, would be needed to derive that *the turtles are above the fish*. Instead, this information is given directly by the image that serves as the situation-model representation of the sentence in question. Indeed, at this level of representation there is no difference between explicit and implicit statements. A difference exists only at the level of the textbase and surface representation, which, however, may not always be effective (as in the experiments of Bransford et al., 1972, in which subjects could not distinguish between explicit and implicit statements, given study and test sentences as in the example discussed here). These facts do not argue against propositional representations. Instead, they argue that propositional representations for imagery must be constructed with great care, so that the salient aspects of the image are indeed represented in the propositional network.

However, what happens in cell C of Table 6.1 should hardly be called an inference either. It is simply a case in which, because of the analog nature of the mental representation involved, more information is generated in forming a situation model than was explicit in the text. The term *inference* really should be reserved for cell D of Table 6.1. This is the domain of deductive reasoning and extends far beyond text comprehension, though deductive reasoning undoubtedly plays an important role in text comprehension, too. Explicit reasoning comes into play when comprehension proper breaks down. When the network does not integrate and the gaps in the text cannot be bridged any other way, then reasoning is called for as the ultimate repair procedure.

Inferences (real inferences, as in cell D) require specific inference procedures. It is a matter of considerable controversy in psychology what these inference operations are – whether inference proceeds by rule (Rips, 1994) or mental model (Johnson-Laird, Byrne, & Schaecken, 1992). The issue is beyond the scope of this book, but the stand taken in chapter 2 on multiple levels of mental representation implies a definite position in this controversy. Inferences in domains where the basic representation is an action or perceptual representation – that is, analog rather than linguistic or abstract – must involve operations on mental models. Inferences in truly symbolic, abstract domains must be by rule. Inferences in the linguistic domain, where the representation is at the narrative level, may be based on mental models (to the extent that language is embodied, as discussed in chapter 2) but also could involve purely verbal inference rules.[8]

6.3.2 Inference generation during discourse comprehension

The literature on inferences in discourse comprehension is for the most part not concerned with cell D of Table 6.1. Indeed, it concentrates heavily on cell A, the processes that are the least like inference, according to the argument presented here.[9] A major focus of the recent research has been on the question of to what extent inferences are made during normal comprehension. On the one hand, it is clear that if the readers of a story are asked to make inferences and are given sufficient time and incentive, there is almost no limit to what they will produce (Graesser, 1981). On the other hand, there is good evidence that much of the time, and in particular in many psychology experiments, readers are lazy and get away with a minimum of work (e.g., Foertsch & Gernsbacher, 1994). McKoon and Ratcliff (1992; 1995) have elaborated on the latter position as the *minimalist hypothesis,* which holds that the only inferences readers normally make are bridging inferences required for the maintenance of local coherence and knowledge elaboration in which there are strong preexisting multiple associations. Many text researchers (e.g., Graesser & Kreuz, 1993; Graesser, Singer, & Trabasso, 1994; Singer, Graesser, & Trabasso, 1994), however, feel that this minimalist position underestimates the amount of inferencing that occurs during normal reading and would at least add inferences that are necessary for global coherence to the list (superordinate goal inferences, thematic inferences, and character emotional reactions). Although this controversy has contributed a great deal to our understanding of the role of inferences in text comprehension, it has also shown that the question concerning which inferences are necessary for, and are normally made during, text comprehension has no simple answer. Text characteristics (much of the research is based on stories, mostly ministories), task demands, and individual differences among readers create a complex, though orderly picture.

---

8 Good experimental evidence exists on both sides of the rule versus model controversy; whether it can be aligned along levels of representation, as suggested here, is another question.

9 Nevertheless, I shall drop the quotation marks from "inference" after this sentence in deference to the commonly accepted terminology.

Trabasso and Suh (1993) have combined discourse analysis, talk-aloud procedures, and experimental measures, such as recognition priming, reading times, coherence ratings and story recall, to show that their readers did make causal inferences in reading a story and that these inferences could be predicted by their analysis.

In an illuminating series of studies O'Brien and his co-workers have shown that causal inferences in story understanding should best be regarded as a passive operation that makes available background and causal antecedents via a resonance-like mechanism (or what I would call a retrieval structure). Such a process contributes to the coherence of the text representation (Garrod, O'Brien, Morris, & Rayner, 1990) but is not predictive. Readers refrain from prediction unless there is absolutely no chance of being discomfirmed (O'Brien, Shank, Myers, & Rayner, 1988). Global automatic goal inferences occur only under limited conditions (Albrecht, O'Brien, Mason, & Myers, 1995), probably because such inferences are as risky as predictions – they are frequently discomfirmed as the later text reveals a different goal. When global goal inferences occur, resonance describes what happens better than the notion of inference does. Through resonance, related parts of a text are connected because of preexisting retrieval structures. In contrast, the construction of a full mental model with rich causal connections appears rather as a nonautomatic, controlled process (Albrecht & O'Brien, 1995; O'Brien, 1995).

How much time and resources the reader has strongly determine the amount of inferencing that occurs. Magliano, Baggett, Johnson, and Graesser (1993), using a lexical decision task, found that causal antecedent inferences were not made when texts were presented with an RSVP procedure at a 250 ms rate but were made when the presentation rate was 400 ms. Long, Golding, and Graesser (1992) found that superordinate goal inferences linking various episodes of a story (but not subordinated goal inferences) were made by readers when they were given lots of time. But with a rapid presentation rate, only good comprehenders made such inferences, and there was no evidence for goal inferences by poor comprehenders (Long & Golding, 1993).

Readers are much more likely to make antecedent causal inferences than consequent causal inferences (e.g., Magliano et al., 1993). For instance, readers of *The clouds gathered quickly, and it became ominously dark. The downpour lasted only 10 minutes* infer the causal antecedent *the clouds caused the rain*. But given *The clouds gathered quickly, and it became ominously dark*, they do not infer the consequent *the clouds caused rain*. This finding that antecedents, though not consequent causal inferences, are made in text comprehension is readily accounted for by the CI model. Suppose a text describes a situation that is a common cause of some event, and then asserts that this event occurred, without mentioning an explicit causal connection between the antecedent and the event. Preexisting retrieval structures causally link the antecedent and the event in the reader's memory; the causal link is activated and is likely to become a permanent part of the reader's episodic text memory because it connects two highly activated nodes in the memory structure.

The situation is different for the consequent inferences. The same retrieval structures that made available the causal antecedent will make available the causal consequent, too. But at that point in the reading process, the consequent is a dangling node in the episodic text structure because it is connected to nothing else in the network but the antecedent. Therefore, the consequent will not receive much activation in the integration process and will be excluded from episodic memory. Thus, *The clouds gathered quickly, and it became ominously dark* might make available *the clouds caused rain,* but if nothing else in the text connects to *rain*, this node will become quickly deactivated in the network. When in a later processing cycle other information becomes available that could have linked up with *rain*, that node is most likely lost from working memory. Hence, although the retrieval structures in the reader's long-term memory make available both antecedent and consequent information, only the former is likely to survive the integration process and become a stable component of the reader's text memory.

According to Table 6.1, it should make a great deal of difference whether bridging inferences occur in a familiar domain or in an unfamiliar domain. In the former case, preexisting retrieval structures make available the information that fills the gap. The process of retrieving information from long-term memory via a retrieval structure takes about 400 ms, as is shown in chapter 7. Hence, reading times for sentence pairs for which a bridging inference is required should be increased by at most 400 ms in comparison with sentence pairs for which this information has been explicitly stated. In fact, 400 ms is an upper limit, because the retrieval from long-term working memory most likely occurs at least partly in parallel with other ongoing reading processes. Noordman and

Vonk (1992) provide some data that allow us to test this prediction. In one of their texts about a woman looking for an apartment to rent, the following sentence pair occurred:

(15) The room was large, but one was not allowed to make music in the room.

In the explicit condition, this was preceded by

(16) The girl wanted to play music in her room.

Sentence (16) was missing in the implicit condition. Noordman and Vonk's (1992) results are shown in Table 6.2. Statistically reliable differences are marked by an asterisk (*), nonsignificant differences are indicated by *ns*. Reading times for the *but* phrase in (15) were slightly but significantly longer in the implicit condition than in the explicit condition, as predicted by the retrieval structure hypothesis, but no differences in verification times were found between conditions.

The results contrast with another experiment with a similar design in which the texts were in an unfamiliar domain. The sentence pair requiring a bridging inference in this study is exemplified by

(17) Connors used Kevlar sails because he expected little wind.

The text is about a sailboat race, and the required inference, which is provided in the explicit condition, is

(18) Kevlar sails are advantageous when the weather is calm.

Presumably, the subjects in this experiment did not know this fact about Kevlar sails before reading this text. The results are also shown in Table 6.2. Reading times for the *because* phrase in (17) are equal in the explicit and implicit conditions; that is, subjects wasted no time on figuring out the obscure relationship between the Kevlar sails and the wind while reading this sentence. On the other hand, when forced to make the inference in a sentence verification task, they were considerably faster to verify (18) in the explicit than in the implicit condition. Noordman and Vonk (1992) also report a version of this experiment in which the same texts on economics were used in the familiar and unfamiliar condition, but the readers were either novice students in economics or expert economists. The results are analogous to those in Table 6.2.

The *but* and *because* in (15) and (17) play a crucial role in this experiment. Keenan and I have reported an analogous experiment with familiar

Table 6.2. *Phrase reading times for the second phrase in (15)* *(familiar text) and (17) (unfamiliar text) and inference verifi-* *cation times in ms for explicit and implicit conditions. After* *Noordman and Vonk (1992)*

	Reading Times	Verification Times
Familiar		
Explicit	1,473	2,169
	*	ns
Implicit	1,536	2,198
Unfamiliar		
Explicit	3,910	3,179
	ns	*
Implicit	3,934	3,512

materials, such as those in examples (15) and (16) but without linguistic signals like *but* and *because* (Kintsch & Keenan, 1973). Our results were completely different: Reading times for explicit and implicit sentences were not significantly different, but verification times were 400 ms longer in the implicit condition (these results are discussed in section 7.3.2). However, I do not believe that these results contradict Noordman and Vonk (1992). By using a sentence connective such as *but* or *because*, Noordman and Vonk invite their subjects to find a connection between the two phrases. When that is easy, because the bridging inference involves no more than a retrieval from long-term working memory, subjects comply, resulting in longer reading times for the to-be-linked phrase but verification times that are the same as for explicit sentences. When that is diffi- cult, because the domain is unfamiliar and suitable retrieval structures are lacking, readers do not construct the link they are invited to form. Hence, they have to do it in the verification phase of the experiment. In the exper- iment by Keenan and me, the domain was familiar enough and readers could have retrieved the missing link readily enough, but being lazy read- ers and lacking a linguistic cue specifically requesting a bridging infer- ence, they did not make the effort. This added 400 ms to the verification time, because the linking proposition had to be retrieved at that point from long-term working memory. Thus, the question "Are inferences made during reading?" needs to be approached with great care: Background knowledge, task demands, and linguistic cues in the text all interact in determining what will happen in a particular case.

6.3.3 Time course for constructing knowledge-based inferences

Of considerable interest is the time course of constructing knowledge-based inferences in text comprehension. We know that it takes about 300 to 350 ms for word meanings to become fixed in a discourse context (section 5.1). Inferences require more time. In Till et al. (1988; see also section 5.1.3) no evidence for topic inferences was obtained at an SOA of 500 ms, but topic inferences were clearly made at an SOA of 1,000 ms (there were no data points in between). In contrast, Magliano et al. (1993) found that antecedent causal inferences required an SOA of only 400 ms. Long et al. (1994), in a study modeled after Till et al. (1988), have used SOAs of 200, 300, 400, 500, 750, and 1,000 ms. Associative effects are fully apparent in their data already at 300 ms. Topic effects develop gradually: they are already apparent at 500 ms but increase in strength up to 750 ms. Because different materials and conditions were used in all these studies, the differences in the results are not surprising.[10] It seems that sentence-level inferences require from 400 to 750 ms, depending on experimental conditions. Thus, sentence meanings take roughly twice as long as word meanings to fixate.

6.3.4 The construction of situation models

Much recent research has been concerned with the construction of situation models (e.g., Glenberg, Kruley, & Langston, 1994; Glenberg & Langston, 1992; Graesser & Zwaan, 1995; Zwaan, Langston, & Graesser, 1995; Mani & Johnson-Laird, 1982; Trabasso & Suh, 1993; van den Broek, Risden, Fletcher, & Thurlow, 1996). It should be clear from everything that has been said so far that there is not a single type of situation model and not a single process for the construction of such models. Situation models are a form of inference by definition, and Table 6.1 is as relevant for situation models as it is for any other inference in discourse

---

10 Because poor readers do not always make inferences even when more skillful readers do, some of these estimates (in particular, the Till study) may be unduly inflated by averaging results over skilled and less skilled readers.

comprehension. That is, situation models may vary widely in their character. In the simplest case, their construction is automatic. Relevant information is furnished by existing retrieval structures, as in the examples given for cell A in Table 6.1. Or it may be available simply as a consequence of a particular form of representation, such as imagery in (14). Such situation-model inferences do not add new propositions to the memory representation of the text but simply make available information in long-term memory via retrieval structures, or information that is implicit in the mental representation, such as an image (see Fincher-Kiefer, 1993, and Perfetti, 1993, for similar suggestions). On the other hand, situation models can be much more complex and result from extended, resource-demanding, controlled processes. All kinds of representations and constructions may be involved. The process may be shared by a social group or even by a whole culture and extend over prolonged periods. Text interpretation is not confined to the laboratory. At least some experimental methods for studying more complex cases are being developed today. Trabasso and Suh's three-pronged method that combines theoretical analysis, verbal protocols, and experimental procedures is a promising development in this respect, as is the simple but very effective "landscape" method of van den Broek et al. (1996). However, for the most part current research on situation models prudently sticks to rather simple cases, as I do in the next section, where the formation of spatial situation models is discussed, a topic that presents a particular challenge to a propositional theory such as the CI model.

6.4 Spatial situation models

For certain kinds of texts, full understanding requires the construction of a spatial situation model. If readers form only a textbase, they can achieve only a superficial understanding of such texts, sufficient for reproductive recall and recognition but not for reconstructive recall and inferences. The latter require a workable model of the spatial situation implied by the text. This distinction between text-based behaviors and behaviors based on situation models was demonstrated in experiment 1 of Perrig and Kintsch (1985), who wrote two texts describing the spatial layout of a small town. Each text had 24 sentences, six of which contained nonlocative information. The same town was described in both texts, but in one case a route description was used to present the information and in the other the same information was provided in the form of a survey description. Thus, where one text might say

(19) After two blocks, turn right on 6th Street to reach the school house.

the other might read

(20) Sixth Street crosses Main Street two blocks north. The school house is on 6th Street just west of its intersection with Main Street.

Each subject read either the route or the survey text. Reading rate was controlled by the experimenter. Half of the subjects read the text once, and half were given three presentations of the text. After reading, subjects were given a free recall test and a sentence verification test, with true old sentences, paraphrases, and inferences, and false distractor sentences.

Reproductive memory, tested either by free recall or verification of sentences actually in the text (verbatim or not), was quite good. Across both texts, subjects recalled 22% of the propositions after one reading and 40% after three readings. Similarly, the d' for the verification of old test sentences was 1.63 after one presentation and 2.36 after three presentations, attesting to the fact that these subjects had been able to form an adequate textbase. However, the subjects had not been able to form a situation model that would have allowed them to verify the inference questions correctly. The d' value for inference sentences was a mere .20 after one presentation and rose to only .85 after three presentations. Thus, we have here a good textbase enabling normal reproductive memory but a weak situation model that yielded poor performance on inference sentences.

In their experiment 2, Perrig and Kintsch (1985) used briefer texts (14 sentences), describing a simpler geographic layout, so that readers would be better able to form a usable situation model. Furthermore, subjects were allowed to study the text at their leisure. Again, both a route and a survey version of the text were used. These changes in the experiment had the desired effects. Overall, reproductive memory remained at a high level, as in experiment 1: The average recall was 40% of the text propositions, and the d' for old test sentences was 3.01. However, unlike in experiment 1, the verification of spatial inference sentences was also good, with an average d' of 1.79. Thus, with a simpler task and more time, these subjects were able to form an adequate situation model that enabled them to verify inference sentences fairly accurately.

Although in both experiments the route text led to better performance than the survey text, readers formed routelike situation models when they read the route text and maplike situation models when they read the survey text. Thus, when subjects who read one version of the text were asked to verify inference sentences in the same version, their performance was better ($d' = 2.11$) than when they were unexpectedly asked to verify sentences in the alternate version ($d' = 1.46$). We also observed an interesting interaction, in the sense that female subjects showed a preference for the route version of the text, whereas male subjects preferred the survey version. However, because this interaction was not replicated in other studies following up this line of research (Taylor & Tversky, 1992), there is no need to discuss it here.

Perrig and Kintsch (1985) demonstrate the importance of distinguishing between the textbase and situation model in studies of text comprehension. For this reason, the study is of central importance for the theory presented here, but it did not include an actual simulation of their data. Such a simulation was performed for an interesting set of data involving a spatial situation model by Haenggi, Kintsch, and Gernsbacher (1995).

Haenggi, Kintsch, and Gernsbacher (1995) replicated a well-known experiment by Morrow, Greenspan, and Bower (1987) in which the incidental formation of a spatial situation model during story comprehension was investigated. Perrig and Kintsch (1985) used texts that had only one goal: to describe the spatial layout of a town. Morrow et al., in contrast, wrote texts that told a story about a character moving around in a particular spatial setting that was only incidental to the action described. Hence, there was no strong task demand to form a spatial situation model. Nevertheless, using a clever experimental procedure, Morrow et al. showed that their subjects indeed were forming and updating a spatial model. A number of later studies show that this outcome is by no means necessarily the case. Whether or not subjects spontaneously form spatial models depends on a number of subtle factors, but that is not the issue here. It is sufficient for us that readers under the conditions of the Morrow et al. experiment do form such models.

Haenggi et al. (1995), in their replication of Morrow et al. (1987), had subjects first memorize a floor plan of a castle, as shown in Figure 6.12. The castle had four rooms, which could be reached via certain doorways. In each room were four distinct objects, such as the carafe and the rug in the dining room. After the subjects had thoroughly memorized this floor plan, they read a brief story in the course of which the main character

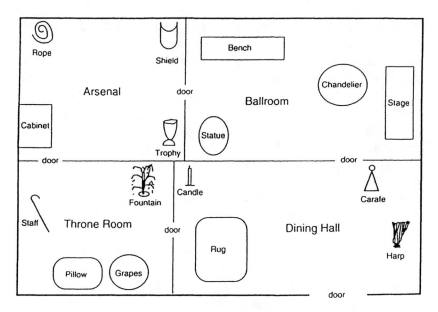

Figure 6.12   Floor plan of the castle that subjects had to memorize for the spatial inference task in experiment 1. From Haenggi et al. (1995).

moved through the rooms of the castle. At four points during the story two objects were presented on the computer screen, and the subjects had to decide whether the objects were in the same room or in different rooms. For instance, just after the main character walked into the ball-room, CARAFE-RUG was presented as the test pair, requiring a "same" response. In this case the objects were in a different room than the actor. On another test both objects were in the same room as the actor, and there were tests where the objects belonged to different rooms. The main result of the experiment, just as in Morrow et al., was that the decision time for "same" responses depended on whether the objects were in the same room as the actor in the story or in another room. In experiment 1, for instance, the mean response time for "same" responses was 2.108 s when the objects were in the same room as the actor, and 2.782 s when they were in a different room. Readers seem to focus on the location of the actor, so that objects close to that location become more available than objects farther away. Obviously this is a dynamic process, for the readers must update their situation model throughout the story.

In simulating these results, we face a challenging problem because the spatial layout must be translated into a propositional representation in such a way that the relevant spatial relations are preserved. Figure 6.12 shows that this can be done in a perfectly simple and straightforward way. The castle has four rooms, some of which are connected by doors, and each room contains four distinct objects. Comprehension is then simulated sentence by sentence in the usual way, and any time an object or location is mentioned in the story, a link is formed between the knowledge representation and the text representation. Figure 6.13 shows the network that is being generated when the sentence.

(21) Penelope walked from the arsenal to the ballroom

is processed. Forming a spatial situation model means that location inferences are made, in this case IS[PENELOPE,IN-BALLROOM]. Because

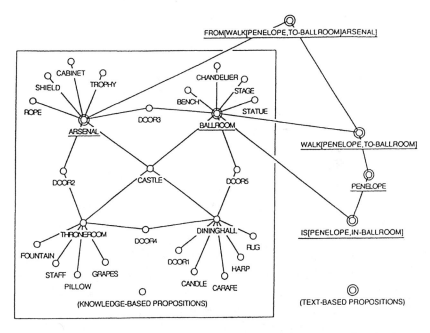

Figure 6.13 The associative network of propositions generated to simulate the integration of text- and knowledge-based information in experiment 1. Text-based propositions are underlined, and the frame designates the area of knowledge-based propositions in the network. From Haenggi et al. (1995).

we wanted to weigh knowledge less strongly than information explicitly mentioned in the text, all link weights among knowledge propositions were given a value of 0.5, and the links among text propositions were given a value of 1. Starting values of 0 and 1 were assumed for knowledge and text propositions, respectively. The statistic of interest was the average final activation values for all test pairs that were presented at various points in the story. These values were higher when both objects were in the same room as the actor than when they were in a different room (.25 versus .12, respectively, for experiment 1).

Haenggi et al. (1995) performed two variations on this basic experimental design (using a linear sequence of rooms, for instance, rather than a circular layout as in Figure 6.12). Under those conditions, the reaction times to objects differed depending on which room they were in. For the most part, the pattern of activation produced by the simulation faithfully reflected these differences. Thus, the simulation not only accounted for the main results of these experiments but also duplicated some of the detailed patterns of the data produced by idiosyncratic features of the experimental materials, the particular layouts, and the stories used.

The Haenggi et al. (1995) simulations show that it is possible to simulate the construction of spatial situation models with a propositional network. It may not always be as easy as it was here to preserve the crucial spatial information in a propositional network as the spatial information becomes richer and more complex, but we have shown that the model can handle spatial imagery, at least in simple cases.

6.5 Literary texts[11]

Der Gedanke geht nach allen Richtungen sofort immer weiter, die Einfälle wachsen an allen Seiten auseinander heraus, das Resultat ist ein ungegliederter, amorpher Komplex. Im exakten Denken nun wird er durch das Ziel der Arbeit, die Beschränkung auf das Beweisbare, die Trennung in Wahrscheinliches und Gewisses usw., kurz durch die aus dem Gegenstand kommenden methodischen Forderungen verschnürt, begrenzt, artikuliert. Diese Auslese fehlt hier. An ihre Stelle tritt die durch die Bilder, den Stil, die Stimmung des Ganzen.

11   This section is based on Kintsch (1994b).

The thought immediately proceeds in all directions; remindings branch out from each other on all sides; the result is an unstructured, amorphous complex. In rigorous thought, this complex is reined in, delimited, articulated through the goal of the task, through being restricted to what is provable, through separation into what is probable, what is certain, and so on, in short, through the systematic demands that emanate from the object itself. This selection process is missing here [in artistic thinking]. It is replaced by selection through the images, style and mood of the whole.

Robert Musil,
Diaries (August 13, 1910)

Studies of discourse processing, such as the ones presented here, have traditionally employed brief artificial texts that truly deserve to be called trivial. The reasons we restrict ourselves to such texts should be obvious: Their complexity is all we can handle, both in the theoretical analysis and in most of our experiments. Long natural texts are not only difficult to simulate with the means at our disposal, but they also provide the subject with too many opportunities for misunderstandings, slips of attention, and a sheer unwillingness to cooperate, which makes illusory the predictions derived from the model of an ideal reader that assumes that everything in the text is processed equally completely and equally perfectly.

Thus, there are compelling reasons for the choice of such texts. The practice does not introduce distortions that are too serious (except when text genres are confused – a miniature description of Margie watering her flowers is not a story), but it does raise questions about the generality of the theory. Apart from the practical difficulties involved in working with very long naturalistic texts, are there in principle limitations that restrict the theory to simple stories, essays, and descriptions? In particular, how would the theory handle literary language?

My hypothesis is that the comprehension processes, the basic strategies, the role of knowledge and experience, as well as the memory products generated, are the same for literary texts as for the simple narratives and descriptive texts we have used in our research. That is not to say that there is no difference, but the difference is in the "what," not the "how." Literary language presents a novel and powerful set of constraints not present in everyday texts, but these new and different constraints are processed in the same way as other more familiar constraints.

Although there are only a few experimental studies of the comprehension of literary texts and how they are remembered, it seems certain that the surface structure of such texts plays a much bigger role in determining comprehension and memory than for nonliterary texts. Long texts are typically reconstructed rather than reproduced faithfully from memory. In the kinds of texts we have studied earlier, this reconstruction was based on the situation model. Properties of the surface structure or even the textbase play a negligible role in the reconstruction process. They are secondary in comprehension, an arbitrary vehicle for the construction of a situation model that then becomes the basis of remembering Not so for literary texts. Surface structure and textbase are carefully coordinated with the situation model. What words are used, how sentences are formed, the precise pattern of semantic relationships in the textbase are not arbitrary but rather are calculated by the author to produce particular effects. They function as a set of nonsemantic and nonpragmatic formal constraints that can play a crucial role in the reader's integration process. Not only syntactic constraints are important here but also poetic forms such as verse, rhyme, alliteration, and so on, which establish formal relations among elements in the surface structure that affect comprehension and memory. Similarly, the textbase is more than the chaff to be disregarded as the situation model is extracted from it. It is calculated to produce remindings that are essential to the effect of the text. In some literary texts, the situation model itself may be trivial and unimportant. In others, there may be several coordinated or competing situation models that the reader is invited to construct. In the quotation that I used as a preface for this section, Musil sketches a picture of comprehension that is not too far removed from the construction–integration model. For scientific texts, the bottom-up proliferation of ideas generated by a text is controlled and ordered by the constraints imposed by scientific analysis – logical argument, scientific theory, and methodology. For literary texts, textual relations, images, and style, as well as emotional reactions, the mood of the whole, serve as the effective constraints instead.

6.5.1 Versification as a source of constraints

As a demonstration of the feasibility of this approach the reader by now surely expects something like a simulation of one of Shakespeare's sonnets. Alas, all I have to offer is a nursery rhyme! It is not only that I do not dare to be more ambitious; there is also no psychological research to fall back on in the case of the sonnets. However, there are some rather useful studies of nursery rhymes.

It often happens in such cases that rhyme and rhythm completely overshadow meaning. As a child, Eileen Kintsch knew the following nonsense rhyme:

(22) Mersidotes and dosidotes
      and little lambs eat ivy.
      Diddely-divey-do,
      Wouldn't you?

Only later, after she had acquired more vocabulary and learned to read, she found out that it wasn't a nonsense rhyme at all:

(23) Mares eat oats and does eat oats,
      and little lambs eat ivy.
      Kids'll eat ivy too,
      Wouldn't you?

The rhyme in this case had overpowered the semantics. It is not an isolated instance. In comprehending and remembering rhymes, the poetic language is at least as essential a factor as the meaning. How can the CI model deal with such observations?

Kelly and Rubin (1988) have collected a large number of observations about the following nursery rhyme, which therefore is an ideal object for our analysis:

(24) Eenie, meenie, minie, mo.
      Catch a tiger by the toe.
      When he hollers let him go.
      Eenie, meenie, minie, mo.

Figure 6.14 shows an analysis of the first two lines of this nursery rhyme. The surface structure has been subdivided into two parts, the phonology and the versification. The first text element – (1) in Figure 6.14 – is identified phonologically as /ee/. It is linked to the second element /nie/, as is /ie/, with /mee/, and so on. At the level of versification /ee/ is not directly linked to /nie/ but with the verse markers VOWEL[1], BEGINNING-OF-LINE[1], RHYME[1,3], and RHYTHM[1,3,5,7, STRESSED]. The same element, therefore, enters into a different set of

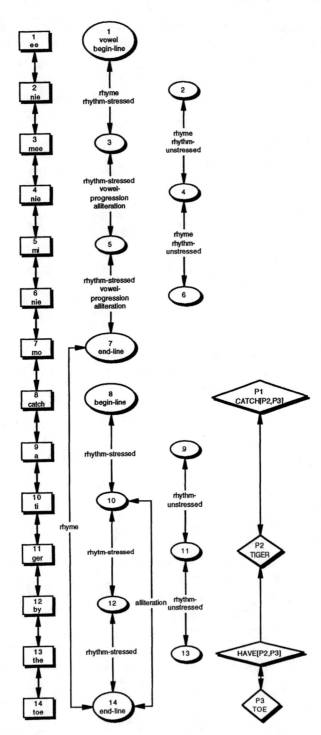

Figure 6.14 The network generated by the phonological, versification, and semantic relations for the first two lines of *Eenie, Meenie, Minie, Mo.*

relationships, depending on whether we analyze its phonological or verse properties. This is true for all other elements, too. For instance, text element (2) is related at the phonological level to element (1) as predecessor and (3) as successor, but at the versification level (2) is related to RHYME[2,4,6] and RHYTHM[2,4,6, UNSTRESSED]. The nonsense syllables (1) to (7), which are not interpretable semantically, do not enter into semantic relations with other elements. The text elements (8) to (14), however, are linked via the relations among the propositions derived from them.

We have, therefore, in Figure 6.14 three sets of overlapping relations: at the phonological level a simple string of successive text elements, at the versification level a rich and complex network, and at the semantic level, which again is rather impoverished. It is obvious that in such a network the versification relations will dominate the integration process and not the semantics. (There are no situation models to speak of with rhymes like these.)

The CI model, equipped with the proper construction rules for the versification level, should construct precisely such a network as in Figure 6.14. In the integration phase, activation flows through this network until it settles into a stable pattern (for simplicity, I have assumed all links and all starting values to be 1). Figure 6.15 shows the results of this integration process. The activation of the text elements from Figure 6.14 is shown in the bottom part of Figure 6.15. The stressed syllables of the first line, as well as *toe*, have the highest activation values, and *a* and *the* have the lowest activation values. The activation of the verse markers is shown in the middle part of Figure 6.15. On the average, the activation is highest in this part of the network. The semantic elements – the propositions – end up with very little activation, as seen in top part of the illustration.

The model thus predicts that the versification relations in this rhyme should be dominant in memory. This is precisely what Kelly and Rubin (1988) observed. Historically, this popular rhyme has changed in many ways, but rhythm and rhyme have remained constant. One finds *eena, dena, dina, do* but never *eenie, meenie, diney, mo*.

6.5.2 Multilevel situation models

For most genres that have been studied so far (descriptive texts, stories, manuals), a single situation model is assigned to a text. The author's

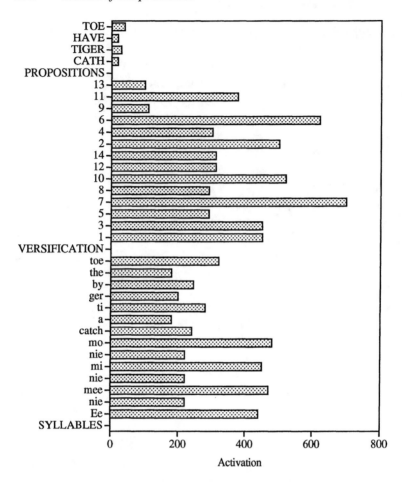

Figure 6.15   The activation values for the network shown in Figure 6.14.

intent is to communicate this model to the reader via the text. How effective a textbook or a manual is depends on how well the author succeeds with this communication. If competent readers construct the wrong model, the author has failed. Not so for literature. It is almost always the case that the author intends the reader to construct situation models at more than one level: At one level there may be an action sequence, at another a commentary about the social condition, at yet another a moral message, and so on. It is also not necessary or even possible for the author to define the intended situation model precisely and uniquely, for what readers make of a text depends on their personal experiences and the way they read the text.

As yet, only very little research in psychology and cognitive science has been concerned with the comprehension processes involving multilevel situation models. Story grammars, for instance, have focused primarily on the action sequence in a story, with the moral of the story as a sort of afterthought (Mandler & Johnson, 1977). On the other hand, there have been attempts in the context of artificial intelligence to describe the constellation of actions that can be considered as "betrayal," or "seduction" (Lehnert, 1981). Multiple situation models are more familiar in a different context – the study of word arithmetic problems and the use of computers, for instance, as discussed later this book. There we distinguish between the situational understanding of a word problem and the formal problem model, its mathematization (chapter 10), or between the task model that a computer user might have and the device model that is necessary to perform this task on the machine in question (chapter 11). There has also been some work on the role that personal experiences play in interpreting new situations, although not in a literary context (such as "reminding" in Schank, 1982, or the work on case-based reasoning by Kolodner, 1993).

There are no simulations of how multilevel situation models are formed for literary texts. The general theory for such a task exists, and there are no compelling reasons why it could not be undertaken. Such a project would have to be conceived as an interdisciplinary enterprise, for although the principles of comprehension are presumably the same for literary texts as for other genres, only literary experts could tell us what the content of the multilevel situation models ought to be. The cognitive scientist can construct the situation model, but the content of the model and the strategies used in its construction are domain specific. This is no different from other cases – for example, when we must ask a computer expert what the device model should be, or when we consult a biologist about the biology content of an instructional text.

6.5.3 Comprehension strategies for literary language

Do the strategies used for comprehending literary text differ from those used in other genres? This issue has received little attention among cognitive psychologists, but there are some interesting studies on how balladeers in primitive societies without a written record reproduce their songs from memory or, rather, reconstruct them (Lord, 1960; Wallace & Rubin, 1988). Strategies similar to those these singers use to reconstruct their songs are employed by educated persons in comprehending literary texts. We thus can gain an impression of the rather complex strategies that must be acquired before literary texts can be appreciated.

Lord (1960) describes a well-known Serbo-Croatian singer of ballads who was able to repeat a 2,294-line ballad he had never heard before after listening to it once. His reproduction was 6,313 lines long and contained many embellishments, character descriptions, and an emotional depth that were lacking in the somewhat naive original. The strategies that make such a feat possible are reasonably well understood (Lord, 1960; Rubin, 1988).

The songs of the balladeers – in Homer's day as well as in our own (Wallace & Rubin, 1988) – largely consist of metric formulas (90% in the *Odyssey*) that can be used whenever needed, irrespective of the semantics. Thus, we find "brilliant Odysseus," "resourceful Odysseus," or "long-suffering, brilliant Odysseus," depending on whether the verse requires two syllables, three, or more. In composing the song, this metric vocabulary is organized around particular topics. A large variety of scripts is used for this purpose. For instance, the topic "council meeting" is used over and over again in just as stereotyped a manner as the restaurant script in AI. This includes various subscripts, such as the arrival of the hero, with horse and weapons always being described in the same order.[12] Equipped with this vocabulary and his scripts, the balladeer is able to concentrate entirely on the action and characters of the story – not unlike musical improvisation, especially in jazz.

The balladeer employs a variety of strategies that enable him to regenerate songs of a certain kind. (There is no claim to originality here; the balladeer insists that he merely reproduces faithfully what he has heard.) These generative strategies are employed effortlessly, automatically, and unconsciously. Thus, they must be well rehearsed before they can be used. Furthermore, the singer's memory must contain a rich store of similar songs as well as related usable information and episodes from everyday life. According to the findings of Ericsson and Chase (1982), we can safely assume that this material is organized in memory in certain ways. Thus, what we have here is a form of expert memory, which, as is well

---

12   These examples are quoted after Wallace and Rubin (1988).

known, enables one to achieve a great deal but which can be acquired only with much effort and over an extended period (e.g., Ericsson, 1985).

Comprehending literary texts makes similar demands. The reader must be able to employ the required encoding strategies automatically and must have readily available the knowledge basis needed for the use of these strategies. Everyone can read and remember a trite newspaper story. We are all experts in this regard, the required linguistic encoding strategies and the necessary domain specific knowledge having been practiced over a whole lifetime (Ericsson & Kintsch, 1995, chap. 7). Literary texts are different. Unfamiliar linguistic strategies are needed for comprehension, beginning with verse and rhyme, all the way to schemes for the organizational principles of the novel. Information about the author and the time and social context in which the text was generated may be relevant. Remindings and reminiscences of related texts may be fundamental for the interpretation of the text. I am suggesting, therefore, that the comprehension of literary texts should be regarded in the same way as any other expert performance. Peak performance, accordingly, would probably require a decade of intensive study. Of course, a literary text can be enjoyed at some level even without that expertise, but deep understanding is reserved for the expert.

Returning to the question posed at the beginning of this section – Is the comprehension of literary texts different from that of nonliterary texts? – the answer must be "yes" and "no." Yes, because literary texts demand specific encoding strategies and specific knowledge that do not play a role in comprehending nonliterary texts. Specifically, the encoding strategies for literary language are different from those employed for everyday language, and specific domain knowledge is required to understand literary texts. No, because the psychological processes involved are the same in both cases: The "what" is different, but the "how" is the same. A simulation of a literary text more complex than *Eenie, meenie, minie, mo* is quite conceivable, but it would be unwise to attempt it until the comprehension theory can be expanded beyond the realm of the purely cognitive. Without a computational account of the emotional reactions (chapter 11) and aesthetic experiences that play a central role in understanding literary text, such a simulation would be unsatisfactory.

The macrostructure of a text – intuitively, its gist – plays a major role in memory and comprehension, especially for longer texts.

Texts differ in the extent to which this structure is made explicit. Several experimental studies are discussed here. The first is concerned with the question whether the formation of a macrostructure is an optional process in text comprehension, or whether it is an integral, automatic part of understanding. We provide evidence that macrostructures are formed automatically even in the absence of task demands. In a second study, we investigate the linguistic markers that authors employ to signal the macrostructure of a text. We also show that the macrostructure of a text may dominate the comprehension process to such an extent that material contradictory to what the reader takes to be the text's macrostructure is simply ignored.

Inferences are involved in the construction of situation models. I argue that different types of "inferences" in text comprehension must be distinguished. On the one hand, a distinction exists between information that is retrieved from long-term memory and information that is newly constructed by some sort of inference rule. On the other hand, a distinction must be made whether the process is automatic or controlled. Thus, we have automatic retrieval (as in most of the classical bridging inferences), automatic generation (as in a transitive spatial inference), controlled retrieval (e.g., when a memory search is required for a bridging inference), and controlled generation (real inferences based on some specific rule, including the rules of logic).

Two special cases of situation models are explored in greater detail, both through simulations and experimentation. One is spatial inference: keeping track of the location and movements of an actor in a story. It is shown that the CI model does this as a normal by-product of comprehension, without having to postulate special strategies or processes. The second case we have investigated is the comprehension of literary texts, with a simulation of a simple example in which various literary constraints (such as rhyme) play a significant role.

7

The role of working memory
in comprehension

The differences between how much people remember in one situation and how little in another can be dramatic. I listen to a child tell a friend what happened at a party she attended a few days ago. Now, I wasn't there and cannot vouch for the accuracy of everything she said, but the impression she gives is that she remembers a lot about who said and did and wore what. And she had fun when she was there, she wasn't memorizing anything. Laboratory experiments on memory provide a stark contrast to this scene. Years ago, when psychologists did paired-associate experiments with nonsense syllables as stimuli, being an experimenter was very boring; you sat there and watched helplessly as your subject tried over and over again to reach criterion on that list. When finally the list was reproduced correctly twice in a row, the experimenter was just as grateful as the student that the torture was over. No wonder theorists of verbal learning were obsessed with the idea of interference!

Memory for text is usually quite good, and often very good. There is an issue here, because if the same memory system is used for remembering text as for learning the nonsense syllables and word lists we study in the laboratory, the discrepancy between the good text memory and the poor list memory needs to be explained.

The span of immediate memory is plus or minus seven items. From a list of 30 random words, college students recall about 12 to 14 after one reading, adults somewhat fewer. It takes about one hour to memorize 100 random words. How can people live with such a terrible memory?

They can't and they don't. The memory demands of many cognitive tasks exceed the memory capacities we observe in the typical laboratory experiment by a large margin, but memory outside certain kinds of laboratory situations is really quite good. Analyses of complex cognitive tasks, such as playing chess or making medical diagnoses, or, indeed, text comprehension, reveal significant memory demands. For instance, in van Dijk and Kintsch (1983, p. 347) we presented a figure that summarized the contents of working memory assumed to be involved in text comprehension. These ranged from sensory features, linguistic expressions, propositional structures, and situation models to control structures, goals, lexical knowledge, frames, and schemata, as well as episodic memory traces of prior text and context. Because all these demonstrably play a role in text comprehension, they must somehow be available in working memory during comprehension. This amount of material is nowhere to be fitted into a classical short-term working memory of seven chunks. Analyses of other problem-solving tasks have come to the same conclusion (e.g., Newell, 1990).

Furthermore, it is clearly not the case that memory for text is as poor as studies of list learning suggest. After one reading of a story, free recall is quite good, and cued recall is excellent. Similarly, cued recall of lectures, conversations, newspapers, and so on is generally good and is adequate to support us in our daily life. Recall of a news story in the laboratory was comparable to incidental recall when the news item was read in the course of everyday activities (Singer, 1982).

Thus, the contrast between the extremely limited memory found in the laboratory and memory in everyday situations, as well as certain expert activities such as playing chess, solving physics problems, or making medical diagnoses is striking, indeed. What does it mean? Some researchers have concluded from these observations that the laboratory study of memory is ecologically invalid and has produced misleading and useless results. Jenkins suggested that possibility as early as 1974 in his influential article "Remember that old theory of memory? Well forget it!" and he has had many followers since. I propose a very different solution to this dilemma. There is nothing wrong with the findings from studies of list learning and the theories of memory based on them; all they need is an extension to everyday and expert activities. This extension is provided by the theory of long-term working memory of Ericsson and Kintsch (1995). It accepts memory theory as it is and shows how it can be extended to account for the good or excellent memory found in certain activities by means of concepts developed within the framework of the classical theory.

7.1 Working memory and skilled memory

Long-term memory (LTM) is everything a person knows and remembers: episodic memory, semantic memory, as well as declarative and procedural knowledge.[1] Just because a person remembers something or knows something does not guarantee that this memory or knowledge participates in a given cognitive process at a given time, even though it would be relevant for that process. The analogy with a computer may help to understand the issue: A great deal of information is stored in various forms accessible to the computer, but this information does not affect processing unless it is retrieved and installed in the computer's central processor. The human central processor is called working memory (WM). To affect a cognitive process, items in long-term memory must be retrieved and inserted into working memory. Working memory is thus the active part of long-term memory, as shown in Figure 7.1a. There are other names for the active part of long-term memory – short-term memory (STM), the focus of attention, and consciousness. At least for present purposes these names refer to roughly the same phenomena. Psychologists were therefore quick to identify working memory with short-term working memory. Baddeley, our foremost authority on working memory, defines working memory as "the temporary storage of information that is being processed in any range of cognitive tasks" (Baddeley, 1986, p. 43).

This short-term working memory (ST-WM) is insufficient to account for the role of memory in cognitive processes. This problem is discussed in considerable detail in Ericsson and Kintsch (1995), and I only summarize briefly the arguments presented there. The capacity of STM is severely limited. Miller (1956) suggested that STM contains as many as 7 ± 2 chunks, but the best current estimate of STM capacity is about 4 chunks (Broadbent, 1975). This capacity is sufficient to account for the phenomena of list learning in the laboratory, which explains why researchers were satisfied for so long with the equation of WM and STM.

---

1 The distinctions between these different types of memory, such as episodic and semantic memory, are irrelevant for present purposes, although they may be important in other contexts.

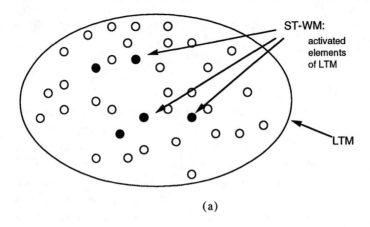

(a)

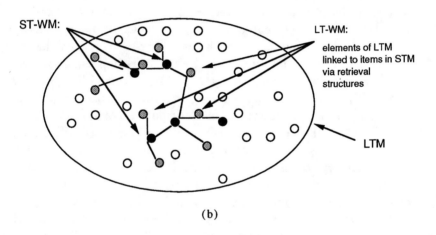

(b)

Figure 7.1   (a) The classical theory of working memory: ST-WM is the activated portion of LTM, containing no more than 4 to 7 chunks. (b) The long-
term working memory theory of Ericsson and Kintsch: LT-WM is the part
of LTM (gray circles) linked to the chunks in STM (circles) by retrieval
structures.

It is only when we study expert memory, inside and outside the laboratory,
that this severe capacity constraint becomes intolerable. I have already
mentioned the many things a discourse comprehender must maintain in
working memory in order to succeed at comprehension. Expert performance in chess, mental calculation, scientific problem solving, and medical diagnosis makes similar demands on working memory. Furthermore,

in all these tasks one can show that working memory involves a long-term component, not some sort of expanded temporary storage in a super-STM. This is implied by the repeated findings of insensitivity to interruption, good incidental long-term recall, and resistance to interference. Apparently, these experts have learned to use parts of their long-term memory as working memory – the long-term working memory, or LT-WM.

Figure 7.1b illustrates how LT-WM functions. The items available in the capacity-limited STM serve as retrieval cues for those parts of LTM that are connected to them by retrieval structures (as explained in section 7.3). A single retrieval operation, using one of the cues in STM, makes available that subset of LTM memory that is linked to the cue by such a retrieval structure. A retrieval from LTM by a cue in STM requires about 300 to 400 ms (see Ericsson & Kintsch, 1995). Hence, the amount of information in working memory consists of two sets of items: those already in ST–WM, which are accessible very rapidly though not instantaneously (Sternberg, 1969), and those reachable by a retrieval structure in about 400 ms. Whereas the capacity of ST-WM is strictly limited, that of LT-WM is constrained only by the extent and nature of the retrieval structures that can be accessed via the contents of STM.

Retrieval structures were first studied in detail by Chase and Ericsson (1982), who investigated a subject who was able to increase his digit span to more than 90 digits after extended training. Later, many other subjects were taught to extend their digit span to 30 or more items. Such feats were achieved by developing and automating efficient encoding strategies to store digits in LTM. This requires a large body of relevant knowledge, for the encoder must be able to perceive familiar patterns in the digit sequences that are to be memorized and to associate these patterns with retrieval cues. Schemata retrieved from LTM must be used to further organize these retrieval cues into stable retrieval structures that will support the quick and reliable recall of the digit sequence to be learned. For instance, S. F., Chase and Ericsson's original subject, was a runner who used his extensive knowledge about running times as an encoding scheme. Typically, he formed four-digit chunks by associating the digits with some remembered numerical fact about running — for example, 3,596 might be coded as 3 m 59.6 s, or just under a four-minute mile. He then used spatial relations to encode these chunks into higher-order groups, forming a hierarchical retrieval scheme, as shown in the upper part of Figure 7.2. Having formed such a structure, S. F. was able to recall

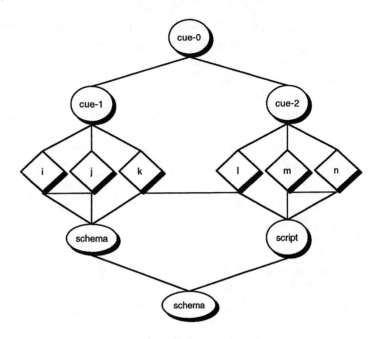

Figure 7.2   A retrieval structure for digits *i* to *n* stored in long-term working memory. On top is the hierarchical organization of retrieval cues associated with groups of digits. On the bottom are the knowledge-based associations relating units of encoded information with patterns and schemas. After Ericsson and Kintsch (1995).

the corresponding digits at any location in this structure that the experimenter requested.

Subject S. F. further strengthened this retrieval scheme through elaborative encoding. He not only associated digits with a retrieval cue but used higher-order relations among the encodings he had generated to organize his retrieval structure. He might, for instance, have noted that several successive chunks were all related to running times for a mile, thereby forming a supergroup. The resulting retrieval structure thus was organized both hierarchically and elaboratively, as shown in Figure 7.2.

There are several important things to keep in mind about retrieval structures such as that shown in Figure 7.2. Only a very rich knowledge base enables one to form such structures, because many different patterns and associations must be readily available for encoding. Suitable knowledge bases exist only in areas where a person has reached a high level of expertise in a special expert domain, or in everyday life situations where everyone is an expert. Knowledge alone, however, is not sufficient; one also needs well-developed and well-practiced encoding strategies. In the case of text comprehension, these encoding strategies are the normal operations engaged in during comprehension, but in other instances, for example, a waiter memorizing dinner orders, they must be specifically learned and practiced. A great deal of practice is required for encoding to be successful, given the real-time constraints of most tasks: Only rapid, reliable, automatic operations will be effective. Thus, LT-WM is severely constrained and does not come easily. It is restricted to situations in which people have true expertise – knowledge as well as encoding skills.

Long-term working memory provides the basis for reconciling the poor performance in traditional laboratory tasks and the very good memory in some everyday situations and expert domains. If people have the knowledge and the encoding skills in a domain, they are able to use their LT-WM to extend working memory by building retrieval structures that allow them to access LTM. For text comprehension, the skills that build retrieval structures are the same skills that are involved in comprehension in the first place, and hence, unlike domain-specific encoding strategies, do not have to be acquired specifically. Thus, in domains in which a reader has a good knowledge background, LT-WM can be used. To the extent that knowledge is lacking, LT-WM is unavailable. As a consequence, both comprehension and memory should be affected. Stories, for instance, are about human goals and human actions, something all of us are very familiar with. Scientific or other technical texts, on the other hand, require domain knowledge not shared by everyone. Therefore, stories are better remembered than technical texts (see Kintsch, Kozminsky, Streby, Mc-Koon & Keenan, 1975, for a comparison of narratives and history texts).

7.2 Long-term working memory in text comprehension

In the traditional memory laboratory, conditions were intentionally arranged so that the role of knowledge was minimized. Subjects therefore had to rely on their ST-WM exclusively. Thus, memorizing became a difficult, strenuous task, and its outcome was unreliable. Subjects in these experiments had no chance to concentrate their efforts on important information. They could not be selective, because the experimenter had set up the experiment so that every item was equally important. Text comprehension is different. It is rapid and, if the text is well written and the domain familiar, effortless. Immediate cued recall is virtually perfect. And the reader knows which aspects of the text to concentrate on and which can be neglected, so that important information is much more likely to be encoded than insignificant details (the "levels" effect in recall, as reported by Kintsch, 1974; Meyer, 1975; and many others).

Retrieval from long-term memory varies, depending on whether or not LT-WM is involved. In the traditional experiment, retrieval is slow and unreliable. The principle of encoding specificity severely restricts the effectiveness of retrieval cues because only cues encoded with the material to be learned at the time of learning will be effective. Proactive inhibition limits the retrieval of stimuli that are similar. In domains where LT-WM can be used, retrieval is rapid, reliable, and flexible. It is flexible not because the encoding specificity principle has lost its validity, but because the material that is encoded in a retrieval structure is richly linked to various regions of LTM, from which it can be successfully retrieved. Proactive inhibition is either absent or greatly reduced because of this use of elaborate retrieval structures.

Ericsson and Kintsch (1995) discuss these differences between ST-WM and LT-WM in detail, and they also describe a number of different theoretical predictions that flow from this distinction and that can be tested empirically. I focus here on one of these predictions.

A particularly striking instance of the theory of LT-WM making different predictions from the classical theory concerns the effect of interrupting reading comprehension. Glanzer and his colleagues (Fischer & Glanzer, 1986; Glanzer, Dorfman, & Kaplan, 1981; Glanzer, Fischer, & Dorfman, 1984) have reported a series of experiments in which reading was interrupted after each sentence of a text by various activities and for various lengths of time. As a prototypical example, consider the study described in Table 7.1. After each sentence of a text, the subject read another unrelated sentence. After the eight-sentence text had been read, with or without interruptions, the subject was given a number of comprehension questions. The results were quite striking: The interruptions had no effect whatever on comprehension. Subjects answered correctly as many questions about the interrupted text as they did when they read the text without any interruptions. The only effect was an increase of about 400 ms in the reading time per sentence after an interruption.

These results are difficult to interpret within the classical theory of

Table 7.1. *Example of a text used in the interruption experiment by Glanzer et al. (1981). Sentences 1, 3, 5, . . . comprise a connected discourse; the interspersed sentences 2 ,4, 6, . . . are unrelated*

S1	James Watts' first steam engine was completed after many years of thought and labor.
S2	Honeybees gather nectar from flowers of a particular kind during spring.
S3	Even then much work was needed to make it practical.
S4	Democratic principles are not always observed in the developing countries of Asia.
S5	He supplied enough money to make the machine a success.
S6	Water management in the arid states of the Southwest is affected by legal issues.
S7	Mine owners came from all over to see the engine work.
	Etc.

working memory, for reading an unrelated sentence surely must wipe out any traces of the prior text from the reader's STM. Resource-consuming reinstatement searches should be required, and comprehension should be badly degraded. The theory of LT–WM, however, readily accounts for the observed results. The next sentence of a text following an interruption provides the cues in STM that can retrieve the LTM trace of the previous text from LT–WM. The mental structure that the reader has created in the process of comprehending the text itself functions as a retrieval structure. Hence, with every new sentence, the reader gains access to the previous memory trace of the text in LTM, at the cost of a single retrieval from LT–WM, which takes about 400 ms.

Many versions of the Glanzer experiment exist, with longer and shorter interruption intervals and different interrupting activities such as doing simple arithmetic problems. A full discussion of their results can be found in Ericsson and Kintsch (1995). All these results are in agreement with the interpretation in terms of LT–WM offered here. Interrupting a text does not interfere with comprehension because LT–WM allows the reader reliable access to the LTM trace of the prior text with a single retrieval operation. Similar observations have been reported concerning the interruption of other highly skilled cognitive operations, such as playing a chess game.

Text comprehension is structure building. To comprehend a text means forming a mental structure that represents the meaning and message of the text. Different theories of text comprehension (e.g., Gernsbacher, 1990; Just & Carpenter, 1987; van Dijk & Kintsch, 1983) differ on the precise characteristics of that structure, but they agree on the central issue of structure building. Any one of these theories could therefore in principle serve as a theory of LT–WM. Whatever mental structure is incidentally generated in the process of comprehension also serves as a retrieval structure, thereby generating LT–WM. In the next section I explore in somewhat more detail how the text representations generated by the CI model function as retrieval structures.

7.3 Retrieval structures in the CI model

Memory plays two distinct roles in text comprehension. First, texts must be comprehended sequentially, one sentence after another; therefore, when focusing on one sentence, memory is needed to provide access to the prior text. Second, text representations are not based solely on the text but require significant contributions from the comprehender's long-term memory. Hence, relevant structures and facts must be continuously retrieved from long-term memory during comprehension.

7.3.1 Episodic text memory during comprehension

Comprehension implies the creation of a coherent mental representation of a text. The reader can focus on only a small portion of the text at any time – typically, a sentence – and to establish coherence must frequently reinstate in the focus of attention items from the episodic text memory under construction. Normally, texts are written in such a way that a sentence contains cues (e.g., overlapping word concepts or explicit connectives) that link it with previous sentences in the text. These cues provide access to the episodic text structure in LT–WM. Figure 7.3 illustrates how retrieval structures function in text comprehension. The elements of the structure, the propositions derived from the text, are connected in a hierarchical macrostructure. The text propositions become linked in with various LTM structures – schemas, frames, scripts, associations, or episodic memory units, as shown in the lower part of Figure 7.3. The end result, the episodic text memory, is a tightly interconnected structure, in part through already established links in LTM as the text becomes integrated into the reader's knowledge and experience, and in part through novel links – the links among propositions generated in the construction of the micro- and macrostructure. Note the similarity between Figures 7.2 and 7.3. The episodic text representation that is formed in the CI

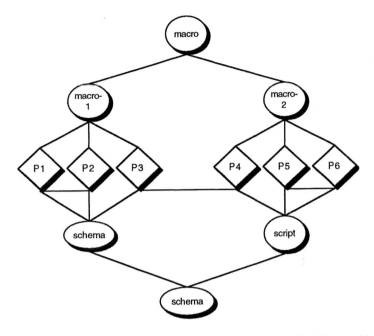

Figure 7.3   A retrieval structure for a text (the propositions P1–P6) stored in long-term working memory. On top is the hierarchical macrostructure of the text. On the bottom are the knowledge-based associations relating units of encoded information with scripts, frames, and schemas.

model, the textbase/situation model, has all the formal properties of a retrieval structure as described in skilled-memory theory. Our claim is that it also functions as one.

When a new proposition is formed as a sentence is being read, it becomes part of the textbase/situation model structure. It is linked to other propositions in that structure to which it is related in various ways. In the microstructure, propositions may be linked because they share a common argument, because of temporal, spatial, or causal relations, or because of a common schema; further links are generated by the macrostructure, because groups of micropropositions are subordinated under a common macroproposition. Thus, a newly constructed proposition is associated with other propositions in working memory, some of which are already linked to propositions in LTM. It thereby becomes capable of retrieving propositions that have been generated previously in the process of comprehension but are now part of the network stored in LTM. An LT-WM has been created.

Givón (1995) has pointed out that the syntax of a sentence serves as processing instructions to the comprehender for the formation of a discourse representation. For instance, different forms of anaphora indicate to the comprehender in which part of memory a referent is likely to be found. In English, one can refer to a prior referent via zero anaphora, a pronoun, or a full noun phrase. Zero anaphora or an unstressed pronoun is used when the writer (or speaker) expects the referent still to be available in ST-WM. When the referent is more distant but still retrievable via LT-WM, a stressed pronoun is used. When the referent was last mentioned in some other, not directly related part of the text, requiring a more complex LTM retrieval, it is reintroduced by a full noun phrase. Consider the following example:

> (1)   John hit a deer driving [0] late at night on a forest road. It was dark and at first he [$P_{unstressed}$] did not realize how much damage had been done. However, the mechanic at the garage said that the bill would be very large. The insurance agent took a long time to inspect the damage, and he [$P_{stressed}$] got quite impatient. In the meantime in the forest, three vultures circled the dead deer [NP].

In the first sentence, zero anaphora is used for *John* as the agent of *driving*. In the second sentence, *John* is referred to with an unstressed pronoun. In both cases *John* is presumably still available in the reader's focus of attention. The stressed pronoun in the fourth sentence signals a referent in LT-WM, namely *John*. When the deer is mentioned in the last sentence, it is reintroduced with a full, definite noun phrase, *the dead deer*. Needless to say, there is a great deal more to say about the use of anaphora in English (e.g., Chafe, 1974; Greene et al., 1994; see also section 5.2). Besides their other roles, anaphora also serve as directives for the use of memory. They are by no means the only processing signals. Givón (1995) has discussed other signals of this kind. His evidence is based on the linguistic analysis of texts that shows that anaphora are indeed employed in the way he claims. For example, the distance between a referent and its anaphora is generally short for zero anaphora, moderate for stressed pronouns, and long for full noun phrases. Such data are very important and strongly support his analyses. It is to be hoped that psycholinguists will also find ways to test these claims with their methods.

7.3.2 The activation of knowledge during comprehension

In the foregoing example, the retrieval structure was constructed by the comprehender on the spot. Next we turn to retrieval structures that pre-exist in long-term memory and that are used during comprehension in building new structures.

Figure 7.4 shows a simple sentence and some putative knowledge that would have been available for activation during comprehension. Actually, all the LTM items to which the various elements of the sentence are linked should be on this list. However, I have selected only a few examples, including some weird, highly idiosyncratic, and context-inappropriate ones, just to illustrate the context-independent nature of the process. For *bank* a context-appropriate and a context-inappropriate associate are shown; *robbery* is related to a compound cue that comprises all the elements of the sentence. If all the elements shown were actually retrieved and took part in the integration process, the ones related only to a single item would become deactivated, and *robbery* would become the strongest node in the network because of its centrality.

None of these associations are actually retrieved in the normal process of comprehension. They and the many others not shown in Figure 7.4 are all available and could be retrieved because they all lie within the reader's LT-WM. But they are not retrieved and do not enter the reader's

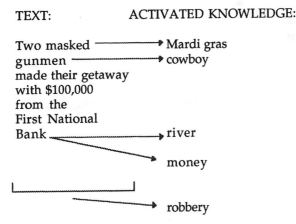

Figure 7.4   Long-term working memory: some links between the words of a sentence and items in LTM.

STM/consciousness/focus of attention unless there is some reason for it. If a reason exists, they can be accessed within the time that a LT-WM retrieval requires, that is, 400 ms. One reason for retrieval is, for instance, that the reader is participating in a priming experiment and is shown either *river* or *money* after the word *bank* in a sentence of a lexical decision task. The word *bank* is embedded in a LT-WM retrieval structure that has been generated through a lifetime experience with the use of that word. It includes both *river* and *money*. Thus, both are accessible right after the presentation of the word, before integration has taken place. Hence, when either *river* or *money* appears as a test word, it has a small advantage over unrelated control words that are not part of the reader's LT-WM. To recognize a test word as an English word, the corresponding lexical node must be sufficiently activated. This activation process is strengthened and speeded up when the lexical node in question is already linked to a structure in the reader's STM, which is the case for *river* and *money* right after *bank* appears in the example given.

If the lexical decision test is delayed for at least 350 ms after *bank,* the word has become integrated into the discourse context and its context-appropriate meaning has become fixed, whereas its context-inappropriate meaning has become deactivated. Hence, associates such as *river* that belong to the context-inappropriate sense of *bank* are no longer accessible via the reader's LT-WM and are therefore no longer primed.

It takes even longer (at least 750 ms; the time estimates given here are based on Till et al., 1988) for the test word *robbery* to be primed. For that to happen, the meaning of all the words in the sentence must be fixed, that is, a complete sentence representation must have been formed. Only such a compound cue, rather than a single word of the sentence, is likely to retrieve *robbery,* which does not occur in the sentence. Thus, it takes about 750 ms to infer the sentence topic in this case. Note, however, just what "infer" means here: not that *robbery* has become an element of STM/consciousness but that the sentence representation that has been constructed is linked by LT-WM to that concept. If it is introduced into STM (by being used as a test word in a lexical decision task, as in our example, or because of other task demands, such as the question "What is the topic of the sentence?"), it is readily available from LT-WM.

The theory of LT-WM requires us to reinterpret many other observations that have been labeled traditionally as inferences. As another example, consider the bridging inferences studied by Kintsch and Keenan (1973). Subjects received such texts to read as the following:

(2) *Implicit*
A burning cigarette was carelessly discarded. The fire destroyed many acres of virgin forest.

(3) *Explicit*
A burning cigarette was carelessly discarded. It caused a fire that destroyed many acres of virgin forest.

Immediately afterward subjects were shown the following test sentence for verification:

(4) The burning cigarette caused the fire.

On the immediate test, verification times for explicit test sentences were 400 ms faster on the average than for implicit test sentences. In the case of the explicit sentences, all three propositions CAUSE [CIGARETTE,FIRE], DISCARD[BURNING[CIGARETTE]] and [DESTROY[FIRE,FOREST]] were active in STM, and hence the test sentence could be verified quickly. In the case of the implicit sentence, only DISCARD[BURNING[CIGARETTE]] and [DESTROY[FIRE,FOREST]] were in STM, but because both are linked associatively to CAUSE[CIGARETTE,FIRE], this proposition could be retrieved from LT-WM within about 400 ms, which added that much to the verification time for the implicit test sentence.

It is misleading, however, to talk about a bridging inference in this case, because that would imply that by some inference operation the proposition CAUSE[CIGARETTE,FIRE] was inserted into the reader's working memory independently of the test statement. What happened, instead, was that as a normal consequence of comprehension, the bridging proposition became part of the reader's LT-WM, and when the test statement required it, it was readily accessible.

Given the right knowledge about what happens when burning cigarettes are thrown away in dry forests, comprehension assured that this linking knowledge was available when needed. Without the right knowledge, this bridging cannot happen. Consider the following sentence pair:

(5)   An abnormally low amount of hydrocele was found. The spermatic cord was quite dry.

For most readers, *hydrocele* and *spermatic cord* retrieve nothing. A real
bridging inference is required to establish the coherence of such a text. A
reader might reason that the spermatic cord is some sort of place where
hydrocele, which seems to be a kind of fluid, is located. This is deliberate,
conscious inferencing, reflected in the reader's verbal protocol, unlike the
automatic knowledge access that occurs in a familiar domain.

The is not the place for a comprehensive discussion of either the priming data or of topical inferences. (For another discussion of these issues,
see chapters 5 and 6, respectively). My goal here is merely to show how
the theory of LT-WM is relevant to the interpretation of these phenomena.

We have already discussed the interruption studies of Glanzer and his
colleagues (e.g., Glanzer et al., 1981). Their studies constitute strong
empirical evidence for the operation of LT-WM. In comprehending easy
texts in familiar domains, readers construct coherent, orderly text representations, tied into their LTM, which serve as efficient retrieval structures, almost obviating the effects of the interruption. If the textbase
formed were incoherent, however, no effective retrieval structure would
be available, and interruptions should have a deleterious effect. McNamara and Kintsch (1996) tried to arrange for such conditions. Instead of
the simple story Glanzer used, we chose difficult scientific, technical
texts in domains with which our subjects were unfamiliar. Furthermore,
instead of interrupting after each sentence of a text, we interrupted in the
middle of each sentence. A subject read the last half of the prior sentence
plus the first half of the present sentence and was then interrupted by an
unrelated sentence. Thus, at the time of interruption whatever representation a subject had formed was necessarily incomplete, so it would be
less likely to function as a retrieval structure.

The results of this modified interruption procedure are shown in Figure 7.5, together with the results of a replication of Glanzer's work with
familiar texts and interruptions after complete sentences. In neither case
was there an effect on comprehension as measured by the subjects' free
recall. Subjects recalled as much with midsentence interruptions as with
end-of-sentence interruptions as with no interruptions at all. However,

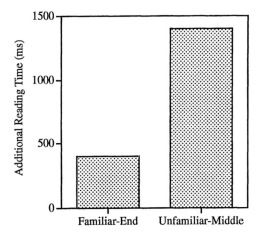

Figure 7.5   The difference in reading times per sentence between normal reading and interrupted reading for familiar texts with end-of-sentence interruptions and for unfamiliar texts with midsentence interruptions. After McNamara and Kintsch (1996).

there was an effect on reading times. The interpolation effect shown in Figure 7.5 is the additional reading time per sentence that subjects needed when the text was interrupted by unrelated sentences. For familiar text with end-of-sentence interruptions, we replicated Glanzer almost precisely – reading times were 400 ms longer on the average, indicating LT-WM retrieval. For midsentence interruptions with difficult texts, however, reading times per sentence increased by about 1,400 ms. As expected, our procedure made it impossible for the subjects to use their LT-WM, but they were able to retrieve the previous sentence context from LTM in spite of that, using whatever cues, temporal as well as content, they had available. The time required for reinstating the previous sentence context under these conditions agrees well with other estimates of retrieval times from LTM (Ericsson & Kintsch, 1995).

A final illustration of the role of LT-WM in discourse comprehension concerns the consequences of forming different kinds of text representations. On the one hand, readers might form a representation that is based primarily on the meaning and rhetorical structure of a text, with minimal links to LTM. On the other hand, a text representation may reflect the actual text and its organization only sketchily, whereas LTM structures are used to organize and elaborate the textual material. Text representations are always a mixture of textbase and situation model, but one or the other component may predominate. In other words, either the top or bottom half of the structure shown in Figure 7.3 is emphasized. Furthermore, depending on their knowledge base, different readers may form quite different situation models.

This argument can be elaborated by considering in more detail the role of LT-WM in the process of comprehension.

Textbase dominance. Textbase dominance typically occurs when a reader lacks the background knowledge necessary for a full understanding of the text. Each word of the text (or, in any case, most words) is understood, that is, it is linked to its lexical node and the associative neighborhood of that node, thus generating a LT-WM. But this LT-WM consists of many different unconnected islands in the LTM structure, because the reader does not have the knowledge necessary to form associative links between the separate words of the text. Thus, LT-WM cannot play a major role. Any item retrieved from such a fragmented LT-WM will become deactivated because it is connected to the text structure merely by a single link. Hence, recall will be reproductive and remain close to the text structure.

Textbase dominance may also occur when a reader has relevant background knowledge but does not use it during comprehension. Passive readers are not rare, and to ensure learning from text, such readers have to be jolted out of their passivity and induced to assume a more active comprehension strategy. These issues are further discussed in chapter 9.

It is not clear, however, what it means in terms of LT-WM theory to say "a reader does not use his knowledge during comprehension." If the knowledge is there, it ought to be automatically linked to the text, forming an LT-WM. Surely, the elicitation of *river* and *money* by *bank* is not under strategic control, but perhaps the use of the whole sentence as a compound cue (to retrieve *robbery* in Figure 7.5) is under strategic control. Thus, good readers, who infer sentence topics (Long et al., 1994), may use compound retrieval strategies, whereas poor readers do not. Alternatively, it might be a question of the strength of the associations: LTM items are included in LT-WM only if they are connected to an element of STM with a sufficiently high strength. The difference between good and poor readers in that case would be that the former have not only more but also stronger links in their LTM structure. Poor readers may need some sort of help to bring their text-LTM associations above threshold strength so that an effective LT-WM is formed.

Situation model dominance. At the other extreme, a person with rich background knowledge forms a very different LT-WM. The text is not only linked to (mostly useless) single-word associates but also to rich and extensively interconnected larger knowledge structures that connect different text elements. Thus, activation of a schema or script might connect a large number of text propositions in different parts of a text. When such a structure is retrieved from LT-WM, it tends to assume a dominating position in the integration process because of its centrality in the network. High-knowledge persons, therefore, will tend to reconstruct a text when trying to recall it in terms of these general knowledge structures and will reproduce correspondingly fewer text propositions and less of the text structure.

These different outcomes can be observed in studies in which persons at different levels of expertise recall medical case records and diagnoses (Groen & Patel, 1988; Schmidt & Boshuizen, 1993). Interns behave like readers who mostly depend on the textbase and have only a weak situation model. Thus, they reproduce parts of the text without clearly differentiating essential and inessential information and make few knowledge intrusions. The recall of doctors with several years of practice, in contrast, clearly reflects their situation model. It is very rich, and much material is included that was not in the case record but was inferred in the process of arriving at a diagnosis. In particular, this includes general medical and physiological knowledge that is relevant to their understanding of these cases. Interns do not include such material in their recall protocols either because they do not have the requisite knowledge or because, although they learned these things in medical school, their knowledge is too weak and insufficiently situated to be used in diagnosis.

Interestingly, the real experts, doctors with many years of practice, produced much briefer and quite different recall protocols than the doctors with less experience. They too relied on their LT-WM and reconstructed rather than reproduced the protocols, but because their situation model was very different from that of less experienced doctors, their LT-WM and what they recalled were different, too. Expert doctors gave brief recalls concerned with the essential symptoms and diagnosis of a case.

This information was not embedded in general medical knowledge, suggesting that these experts no longer used that knowledge in understanding a case. Instead, their rich experience gave them an alternative basis for organizing and understanding this material. Their extensive direct experience provided them with the requisite LTM structures, and they no longer needed their school knowledge as a crutch. One can be quite confident that their medical knowledge was still intact; however, the links between observations and medical knowledge had become rather weak, and their representations were dominated by their much stronger links between observation and experience.

7.3.3 The short-term memory buffer

In the text-processing theory of Kintsch and van Dijk (1978), the STM buffer played a crucial role. It was the only way a coherent text representation could be constructed. According to that theory, a few elements, or at least one, from one processing cycle must be maintained in the STM buffer to be reprocessed together with the elements of the next cycle, in the hope that some link (argument overlap) will be found so that a coherent text representation can be formed. The buffer was the bridge in the model between processing cycles that permitted the formation of a coherent mental representation of the text, which had to be processed sentence by sentence. The capacity of the buffer became an important issue, though most estimates suggested that it remained relatively constant at one or at most two propositions.

This picture must now be modified in some important respects. First, the Glanzer data discussed earlier (Glanzer et al., 1981) clearly demonstrate that comprehension is possible without the use of an STM buffer. The interruption procedure surely wipes out the contents of STM – yet comprehension is unaffected, except for a slight increase in reading times. Second, the theory of LT-WM provides an alternative mechanism for the construction of a coherent text representation. Links between text elements from different processing cycles are formed via LT-WM.

Thus, both empirically and theoretically, comprehension can do without an STM buffer. However, there is good evidence (Fletcher, 1981; Fletcher & Bloom, 1988) that an STM buffer is used in normal uninterrupted comprehension. One may question why an STM buffer is used when comprehension obviously can proceed without it, but just because a mechanism is redundant does not mean that it is useless. The STM buffer, for instance, allows for the formation of a more coherent textbase. Propositions maintained in the buffer can be linked with the propositions derived from the next sentence on the basis of purely textual relations, whereas LT-WM links must be based on prior knowledge. High-knowledge readers are probably not as dependent on the buffer, but interference with the STM buffer might have stronger effects for low-knowledge readers.

7.4 An LSA model of retrieval structures

The notion of retrieval structure has appeared in several places in the literature on comprehension and problem solving in recent years. Richman, Staszewski, and Simon (1995) propose a formal model of retrieval structures in recall in the context of the EPAM theory of memory. Clark and Marshall (1981) describe how what they call "reference diaries" function as retrieval structures in a conversation, somewhat like macrostructures do in reading a text (Figure 7.4). Myers, O'Brien, Albrecht, & Mason have reported a series of experiments in which they explore how the content that is in the focus of attention during reading accesses related prior information in the text or in the reader's knowledge base (e.g., Albrecht & Myers, 1995; O'Brien, 1995; O'Brien & Albrecht, 1991). Myers uses a well-chosen metaphor for this process, namely, that long-term memory resonates with the contents of short-term memory; the items that resonate most strongly become accessible in working memory (Myers et al., 1994). Myers's *resonance theory* is a specific, mathematical model of retrieval structures in comprehension. It builds on memory theory, in particular the SAM formulation of Gillund and Shiffrin (1984), to describe how resonance works in comprehension and is in principle quite compatible with the CI model. Indeed, Varma and Goldman (1996) have implemented a version of the CI model that includes a resonance-based reinstatement mechanism.

Retrieval structure, therefore, is not just a useful but vague concept; rather, it is something that can be modeled formally. The possibility of formally specifying retrieval structures brings up another problem, however. How can we objectively and with some degree of accuracy hope to model the reader's long-term memory? As suggested in section 3.3, latent semantic analysis may provide at least a partial solution to this problem.

Latent semantic analysis (LSA) can be used to model retrieval structures. Retrieval structures are fixed, well-established links in long-term memory. Such links should be related to semantic distance as measured by LSA. Therefore, one may hypothesize that in text comprehension the probability that a particular piece of knowledge is activated in long-term memory is proportional to the cosine between the vector of the eliciting item and the knowledge item.

With this assumption, we can readily model knowledge elicitation, or reminding, in discourse comprehension. Consider example (12) discussed in section 6.2.3, which is reprinted here.

(6)   S1   John was driving his new car on a lonely country road.
       S2   The air was warm and full of the smell of spring flowers.
       S3   He hit a hole in the road and a spring broke.
       S4   John lost control and the car hit a tree.

What are likely words that LSA might be reminded of when reading S1, *John was driving his new car on a lonely country road?* Table 7.2 shows two of the 10 most closely related terms in the encyclopedia LSA space for each of the content words in that sentence.

For *John,* LSA thinks of two historical Johns; for *new* it knows no better than New York and New Jersey. But suppose we add these remindings to the network created for that sentence in (6), using the cosines from the LSA analysis for link strengths. Integrating, we obtain the results shown in Figure 7.6, where the areas of the squares used for each node are approximately proportional to the final activation value of that node. Note that *lonely* has completely disappeared from the network, as have most of the intuitively irrelevant remindings from the list in Table 7.2. Only *rail* and *York* remain as obviously irrelevant associations but with activation values barely above zero.

If we similarly select two associates from the top 10 neighbors of each

Table 7.2. *Most closely related terms in the LSA space for each content word in example (6)*

John	Butterfield, Milton
drive	driver, gears
car	driver, automobile
new	York, Jersey
lonely	tomboy, girl
country	nation, landlocked
road	rail, highway

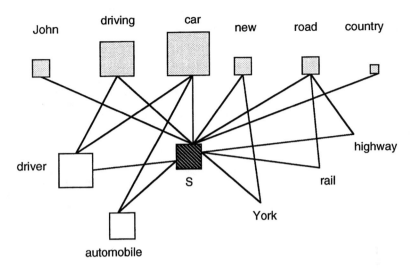

Figure 7.6   The activation values for the words from the sentence *John was driving his new car on a lonely country road* (gray squares) as well as for several remindings (white squares) and the sentence node S (black square). The area of each square indicates the activation value of the node.

content word in the other three sentences of example (6), the following knowledge intrusions can be obtained.

S2   The air was warm and full of the smell of spring flowers:
       smell drops out, *humidity, dew, showy,* and *leaves* are added.
S3   The car hit a hole and a spring broke:
       driver, automobile, smash, and *album* are added.
S4   John lost control and the car hit a tree:
       automobile, trunk, and *bark* are added.

Obviously we have a method to predict knowledge intrusions in reading comprehension, which may eventually lead to some empirical tests. Equally obviously, the method is not perfect yet, probably because of the nature of the LSA space used. As discussed in section 3.3, the LSA space on which all calculations are based is derived from the analysis of about 4 million words from an encyclopedia. Thus, what LSA knows is heavily weighted toward technical information such as one finds in an encyclopedia, but its knowledge of everyday things is woefully inadequate. For instance, all top 10 neighbors of *hit* from example (1) have to do with popular music, and it knows nothing about cars hitting a hole in the road or a tree along the road. Therefore, LSA misunderstands things because of its inadequate knowledge base. For instance, the nearest neighbor in the LSA space for the sentence S1, John driving his car around, is the document "New Frontier." This is not as puzzling as it appears: Put together *John, country, new, road* – quickly you get into Camelot country. One might say LSA is doing a good job here. If it knew more about the everyday worlds – knowledge that LSA might get from reading newspapers, novels, movie scripts – it might also be reminded of more prosaic drives in the country. The example also illustrates another limitation of the present version of LSA: its disregard of syntax. Sentence S1 is not about John (FK) leading his country along a new road but about driving on a country road.

In spite of these caveats about LSA, its use for modeling the operation of retrieval structures in comprehension opens exciting new possibilities. Only further research will show how much of this promise can be realized. It should be possible, however, to employ LSA to derive specific, a priori predictions for experiments such as those of Myers and his colleagues – with a better, more informed LSA space.

7.5 Capacity differences in working memory?

In section 9.1 there is a discussion of the factors that make for a good or a poor reader. Decoding skills, language skills, and domain knowledge are emphasized. Another factor that has often been suggested as a determinant of reading comprehension is the capacity of working memory. The theory of long-term working memory described earlier implies that individual differences in comprehension may be the result of skill and knowledge differences. Capacity differences in working memory may or may not play an additional role (see also Ericsson & Kintsch, 1995).

At first glance, the data seem to contradict any relation between reading comprehension and STM capacity. Reading comprehension improves enormously between childhood and adulthood, but measures of STM capacity such as the digit span show only a slight improvement (e.g., Chi, 1976; Huttenlocher & Burke, 1976; and others). Good and poor readers cannot be distinguished on the basis of their memory span (e.g., Farnham-Diggory & Gregg, 1975; Rizzo, 1939). However, such data are not really conclusive, because the memory span merely measures a subject's ability to store unfamiliar digit sequences and does not provide a direct indication of the STM capacity available during reading. Daneman and

Carpenter (1980), therefore, developed an alternative measure of STM capacity, called the *reading span*, which directly indicates how much capacity a reader has available during reading. They gave subjects a list of unrelated sentences to read and later questioned the readers about the content of these sentence to make sure the readers actually comprehended them. After reading the sentences, subjects were asked to recall as many of the last words of the sentences as they could. The reading span was defined in terms of the number of words subjects could recall in this task. Thus, it provides a measure of memory during reading. Unlike the traditional memory span, the reading span correlates highly with reading comprehension on a variety of tasks. In the studies reported by Daneman and Carpenter (1980) and others, correlations between reading span and text comprehension have ranged from .5 to .9.

Thus, a clear and strong relation between STM capacity and reading comprehension appeared to have been established. Cantor, Engle, and Hamilton (1991) and Just and Carpenter (1992) further developed the notion that STM memory capacity, as measured by the reading span, is the basis for individual differences in reading comprehension.

However, questions arose early on whether the reading span really was a measure of STM at all. Masson and Miller (1983) reported evidence that the whole sentences were stored in LTM (rather than the final word being maintained in STM). Similarly, Baddeley (1986) showed that measures of reading span could be obtained in situations in which the subjects were not told beforehand which word to recall and hence had to retain the whole string in memory. Baddeley's measures of reading span correlated with text comprehension just as well as the original one, but they must have been based on LTM storage, for such a large amount of information could hardly be retained in STM. Thus, the reading span is certainly a good predictor of reading comprehension but apparently not a measure of STM capacity.

The theory of long-term working memory proposed by Ericsson and Kintsch (1995) provides an alternative interpretation for these findings. What the reading span measures is the efficiency with which readers can comprehend sentences and hence store them in long-term memory. More skilled readers construct better representations and hence have available more effective retrieval structures; if they recall anything at all from a sentence, they are more likely to reintegrate the whole sentence and retrieve the last word than are low-skill readers. To use a metaphor, it is not that good readers have a larger box to put things in for temporary storage, but that they are more skilled in putting things into long-term storage and retrieving them again.

This reinterpretation of the findings of Daneman and Carpenter (1980) fits many of the results that have been reported in support of the capacity theory. Differences in language skills, not STM capacity, explain these findings. Cantor and Engle (1993), for instance, had subjects with high and low reading spans memorize either a list of unrelated sentences or a list of thematically related sentences. The number of statements in these sentences that related to a particular concept was varied. A fan effect is typically observed in such situations when subjects are asked to verify these statements: The more statements there are about a particular concept, the slower the verification time. Indeed, this was what Cantor and Engle observed in both low- and high-span readers when the sentences were unrelated. When the sentences were related, however, low-span readers still showed the typical fan effect, whereas this effect was reversed for high-span readers: The more statements about a particular concept, the faster were the latters' verification times. The fan effect occurs because the more unrelated statements subjects have to remember, the larger the search set becomes on a verification test. For thematically related sentences, however, high-span readers could use their superior organizational skills to construct a single, coherent representation. The more information there was about a given concept, the more strongly integrated this representation became and the better it was able to serve as a retrieval structure. Hence, the negative fan effect. The low-span readers, on the other hand, did not fully succeed in constructing a coherent representation of the thematically related sentences because of their inferior organizational skills. The mental representation they created was therefore only partially coherent, which resulted in a typical fan effect.

We can similarly explain the results of Just and Carpenter (1992) in terms of LT-WM processes. In one of their experiments, Just and Carpenter showed that only high-span subjects took advantage of pragmatic cues when comprehending reduced relative clauses. Consider the following two sentences with unreduced relative clauses:

(7) The evidence that was examined by the lawyer shocked the jury.
(8) The defendant who was examined by the lawyer shocked the jury.

From these sentences, a baseline measure can be obtained for the reading time for the phrase *by the lawyer*. Reduced relative clauses can be constructed by omitting the *that was* or *who was* from the original sentences:

(9) The evidence examined by the lawyer shocked the jury.
(10) The defendant examined by the lawyer shocked the jury.

Omitting this important syntactic cue makes the sentence harder to understand, which should increase the reading time for the *by the lawyer* phrase. However, there is a difference between these sentences: The reduction in the *defendant* sentence created an ambiguity that is not present in the *evidence* sentence. A natural way to continue *The defendant examined . . .* would be with an object of *examine*, such as *the documents*. The continuation with *by the lawyer* is unexpected and should create a garden-path effect – the reader needs to take extra time to correct wrong expectations. This is not the case for the *evidence* sentence, because we know that an inanimate noun could not be the subject of *examine*. High-span readers in fact react like this; they read sentences of the *evidence* type about 50 ms faster than ambiguous sentences with animate subject nouns (*defendant*). Low-span readers read both sentences equally fast, that is, they do not take advantage of the pragmatic cue provided by the inanimacy of the sentence subject. Just and Carpenter (1992) claim that this is so because they do not have the STM capacity to take pragmatic information into account. Ericsson and Kintsch (1995) claim that this effect is a consequence of the fact that low-span readers are low-skill readers. They know how to use obvious syntactic cues like *that*, but they cannot take advantage of more subtle cues such as the animacy of the noun and hence do not form expectations about the continuation of the sentence based on it. High-span readers, in contrast, know and use such information in the comprehension process.

In another, very informative experiment, Just and Carpenter (1992) show that knowing a lot is not always helpful but may even work against a good reader. They used sentences like:

(11) The experienced soldiers warned about the danger before the midnight raid.

This sentence has a simple structure, and low-span readers read through it without difficulties. High-span readers, on the other hand, pay more attention to the subtle cues the language provides and notice a potential syntactic ambiguity; this might be another reduced relative clause, in which case it might continue something like

(12) The experienced soldiers (who were) warned about the danger were ready.

Readers who form an expectation like this will stumble over the last word of the actual sentence and experience a garden-path effect. Indeed, that is what happened to high-span readers, who took about 130 ms longer to read *raid* than did mid- and low-span readers.

   Just and Carpenter (1992) attribute this result to STM capacity. Low-span and high-span readers alike form both expectations (that the sentence will continue as a normal sentence, as it actually does, or that there is a reduced relative clause). However, low-span readers have insufficient memory capacity to retain both alternatives in STM and hence drop the less likely parse before they come to the end of the sentence. High-capacity readers retain both parses to the end, which results in unnecessary processing difficulties. An alternative possibility is that the less skilled low-span readers never consider the possibility of a reduced relative clause and hence have no difficulty. High-span readers habitually use more of the information available to them in the parsing process, which in this case gets them into trouble. Pearlmutter and MacDonald (1995) have actually investigated whether both low- and high-span readers are sensitive to the cues in question and found results in accord with our claims. They found that only high-span readers were sensitive to probabilistic constraints in the sentences used in their experiment. Low-span readers ignored these constraints. It was not that low-span readers did not know about these constraints. They had the knowledge when appropriately questioned, but that knowledge was not sufficiently automated to be used for the encoding of sentences in an actual comprehension task. This illustrates a very important feature of retrieval structures. Simply knowing something – that is, being able to retrieve it under optimal circumstances – is not sufficient for a retrieval structure; the knowledge must also be strong, stable, well practiced, and automated, so that it can be employed for encoding without additional resource demands. Retrieval structures are a characteristic of expert memory. Unskilled, low-span readers may have the knowledge, but it is not in readily usable form.

   Thus, much of what has been taken as studies of working memory capacity turn out to be studies of comprehension skills. This may also be the case in an experiment on lexical ambiguity resolution by Miyake, Just, and Carpenter (1994), who wrote sentences in such a way that a lexically ambiguous term does not become resolved until several words later, as in (13):

(13) Since Ken liked the boxer, he took a bus to the nearest pet store to buy the animal.

There were large differences between high- and low-span readers with such sentences. Low-span readers became confused when they had to activate the nonpreferred sense of the ambiguous noun at the end of the sentence, whereas high-span readers had no such difficulties. However, when the disambiguating phrase followed right after the homograph, low-span readers performed just like high-span readers. Clearly, low-span readers knew both word senses.

The capacity interpretation of this finding is that both low- and high-span readers activated both word senses, but only the high-span readers had enough working memory capacity to maintain both meanings until the end of the sentence, when it was needed for understanding. Low-span readers were forced to drop the less likely meaning because of the limitations of their working memory capacity, and hence they had difficulties understanding the end of the sentence. The trouble with this interpretation is that we know (e.g., section 5.1.2) that word meanings in context are fixed in about 350 msec; hence, by the end of (7) all readers must have deactivated the nonpreferred word sense. However, high-span readers had built a good retrieval structure that enabled them to reactivate without difficulties the lost word sense when it was needed, whereas low-span readers had to engage in more cumbersome recovery processes because the tentative sentence structure they had built did not serve them as an efficient retrieval structure.

This interpretation is strengthened by another finding Miyake et al. (1994) reported. Differences between high- and low-span readers were observed only with sentences like (13), where the homograph has a preferred and a nonpreferred meaning. With equibiased homographs, there were no differences between high- and low-span readers. This observation is difficult for a capacity theory but is readily explained if knowledge and skill differences are involved. Low-span readers know all about word senses, but only in the case of the more frequent, equibiased homographs is that knowledge sufficiently automated and usable. Again, knowledge of word meanings is not sufficient to support the formation of a retrieval structure – the knowledge must be well integrated and well connected to the knowledge base.

There is also considerable evidence that high- and low-span readers employ different strategies. In a study of discourse ambiguity, resolution of Whitney, Ritchie, and Clark (1991) used texts like the well-known washing-machine story of Bransford and Johnson (1972) without titles and obtained think-aloud protocols from subjects reading these texts. High-span readers maintained several possible scenarios while they were reading, which they tested against each new sentence. Low-span readers, in contrast, either made numerous wild guesses, or they gave up trying to make sense out of these stories. Thus, the discourse processing of high-span readers was characterized by orderly, systematic, and effective strategies, whereas low-span readers simply did not know what to do. Low- and high-span readers do different things when it comes to discourse processing, with the result that high-span readers are able to make more efficient use their ST-WM and LT-WM capacity.

Singer and Ritchot (1996) argue quite plausibly that individual differences abound everywhere we look in cognition, and they report a study that they interpret as evidence that both knowledge/skill and capacity differences play a role in comprehension. However, their results can be reinterpreted as showing the effects of two types of retrieval structure: general knowledge and skills involved in reading, as measured by the reading span test and specific fact and world knowledge, which was needed in their experimental task to make certain required inferences. Perhaps it is true that eventually there will be a place for both capacity and skill explanations of individual differences in comprehension. Further research that more clearly differentiates these two aspects will be needed. It is quite clear, however, even at this point, that the availability of reliable retrieval structures is a major factor in reading comprehension, as Ericsson and Kintsch (1995) have argued.

This chapter started out with a well-known dilemma for memory theory; it suggested a solution for it and then went on to explore the rich and manifold implication this solution has for the understanding of the role of memory in discourse comprehension. The dilemma for memory theory lies in the contradiction between the laboratory findings of severe capacity limitations of short-term memory and the immense demand most higher cognitive processes make on short-term memory capacity and the apparent ease with which real people meet these demands. Memory theorists usually prefer to forget this dilemma, and ecologically minded psychologists use it as an argument against laboratory psychology. Ericsson and Kintsch (1995) have shown that the solution to this dilemma lies well within the laboratory and that, indeed, the knowledge that we have gained through laboratory research provides a ready explanation for it. Retrieval structures help people to overcome the capacity limits of short-term memory and thus make possible all higher cognitive functions. All information that is linked by a retrieval structure to a cue in short-term memory can be retrieved in a single retrieval operation. Thus, as long as we can rely on retrieval structures, all potentially relevant and necessary information in long-term memory is just one retrieval step away during problem solving and comprehension. However, retrieval structures are not a naturally given part of memory but must be acquired through long and hard practice. Retrieval structures are not just knowledge links, but links that are strong and allow fully automatic performance. Such structures are typically acquired in becoming an expert in a cognitive domain – chess, medical diagnosis, and so on. They are relevant to text comprehension because most educated adults are experts in text comprehension, at least in familiar domains.

It has been argued in earlier chapters of this book that the term *inference* is too loosely applied in text comprehension. When one reads in a familiar domain in which stable retrieval structures have been acquired through lifelong practice, any item in working memory that is linked to long-term memory is able to tap into a system of rich retrieval structures that makes available a large body of relevant information on demand. The comprehender does not have to "infer" this body of information, or even less, install it in short-term memory/consciousness. It is just there if it is needed for one reason or another. It is there only if the comprehender stays within his or her area of expertise, however. Take the scholar away from his specialty and the scientist from her subject, let the chess player play bridge instead, and give a college student a philosophical essay to read instead of the sports page of the newspaper or a trite little story, and their memory for what they read and did and their ability to activate relevant knowledge will not be characterized by the theory of retrieval structures but by the classical theory of short-term working memory.

8

Memory for text

I am intrigued as I continually rediscover that what looks effortless in nature can be so laborious to compute.

Brian Hayes in an article on the collision of billiard balls
in American Scientist (July 1996)

8.1 Recognition memory

8.1.1 List-learning data and theory

The typical recognition memory experiment consists of a study trial followed by a test trial. On the study trial, subjects are shown a list of items
– words, for instance. On the test trial, subjects are shown a test list consisting of the previously shown ("old") items and a set of new, "distractor" items. Their task is to say "yes" or "no" whether each test item has
been presented before. The principal features of the results of item recognition experiments are as follows.

1. Recognition memory is very good and long-lasting in contrast to
other memory tests. In a classical experiment, Shepard (1967) employed
a pool of 300 frequent and 300 infrequent words, of which 540 were
shown on a study trial. Recognition memory was then tested with a
forced-choice test: 60 of the study words were randomly selected, and
each word was paired with one of the 60 words not shown. Recognition
was 88% correct, which means that subjects were able to remember about
475 of the 540 words they had seen. Similar results were obtained with a
pool of 612 sentences; performance was at 89% correct. Even more
impressive were Shepard's results on picture memory. After seeing 612

pictures a single time, subjects were tested for forced-choice recognition immediately and after two hours, three days, one week, or four months. The percentage of correct recognitions were 97%, 100%, 92%, 87%, and 58%, respectively. Thus, there was very little memory loss even after seven days. After four months, however, performance was no longer significantly different from the 50% chance level.

2. As described by signal detection theory for sensory detection, recognition performance must also be decomposed into two separate components: (a) the discriminability of old items and distractor items in memory, and (b) the decision criterion adopted by the subject. Discriminability depends on the way study items are encoded, the length of the retention interval, and, most important, the similarity between study and test items (e.g., Underwood & Freund, 1968). By varying the similarity between study and test items, recognition can be made arbitrarily easy or difficult. The decision criterion depends on instructions, the retention interval, and the benefits or costs associated with the decisions.

3. In many ways, recognition memory is like recall memory. For instance, context effects are as important in recognition (Thomson, 1972) as in recall; the short-term memory function for recognition (Shepard & Tegthsoonian, 1961) looks much like the short-term memory functions for other memory tests. The main difference between recognition and recall is that recognition is much less sensitive to organizational factors. The structure and organization of a memory trace are central for retrieval in recall tasks but play a much lesser role in recognition (e.g., Kintsch, 1977a).

4. The primary recognition procedure can be described as a familiarity judgment. On a recognition test, the subject assesses how "familiar" a test item is and responds "yes" if the familiarity exceeds some criterion value. Models of recognition memory describe how this familiarity assessment is achieved.

Early models of recognition memory, such as Anderson and Bower (1972) and Kintsch (1966), were flawed because their central assumption about the recognition process was wrong. In these models, a familiarity value was computed by comparing a test item to its corresponding memory image and computing a match score. Empirical evidence failed to support this assumption, and it is rejected by all current models of recognition memory. Instead, it is assumed that a test item is compared to the whole set of study items in memory. Several recognition models have been proposed that share this common assumption. These models differ radically in the form of the memory representation they use. In Murdock's TODAM, for instance, all items in a list are represented by a single vector (Murdock, 1993); in contrast, in Hintzman's MINERVA, not only each item but each presentation of each item results in a separate memory trace (Hintzman, 1988). In Gillund and Shiffrin's (1984) model, the representation of memory is a network, or matrix. In spite of these differences about what memory really is, all these models make rather similar predictions that account quite well for the existing data.

Perhaps behavioral data alone cannot settle the basic issues about the nature of memory representations. But they certainly have provided good models that describe and predict recognition data, and they have allowed us to identify the essential features of recognition processes: that strength and bias must be distinguished according to signal detection theory, and that a test item must be matched against the whole memory set.

I propose here to model sentence recognition data by using the CI model to describe the memory representations generated from sentences in a discourse and a recognition model to describe the recognition process. Because none of the three recognition models is obviously superior to the others, we are free to choose our favorite on the basis of other considerations. The Gillund and Shiffrin (1984) model is most suitable for our purposes because it employs a matrix representation that is closely related to the one used in the CI model. Hence, structures generated in the CI model can be directly used as input to the Gillund and Shiffrin model, whereas they would have to be transformed in nontrivial ways to make them suitable for the other two models.

Gillund and Shiffrin (1984) analyze item recognition experiments. A list of items is studied, resulting in an interconnected network of memory images. On a recognition test, old items (I_j) as well as distractor items (D) serve as cues. In addition, the general list context (CX) is a cue that plays an important role. The strength values $S(I_i, I_j)$ of the links between the various cues and memory images are given by a cues-by-memory images matrix:

MEMORY IMAGES

Cues		I_1	I_2	I_j	. . .	I_n
	CX	$S(CX,I_1)$	. . .	$S(CX,I_j)$		$S(CX,I_n)$
	I_1					
	I_2					
	. . .					
	I_i	$S(I_i,I_1)$		$S(I_i,I_j)$		$SI_i,I_n)$
	. . .					
	I_n					
	D	$S(D, I_1)$		$S(D, I_j)$		$S(D, I_n)$

If a cue is used to probe memory, its effectiveness depends not only on how strongly it is linked to a memory image but also how strongly that image is linked to the current list context. In fact, for cue i and memory image j, the probe strength is given by the multiplicative rule:

$$S(CX,I_j) * S(I_i,I_j) \tag{1}$$

Even though items *i* and *j* may be strongly associated in memory, if item *j* is unrelated to the list context, it will not be linked to the probe. Associations unrelated to the context play no role, as demanded by Tulving's encoding specificity principle (Tulving & Thomson, 1973).

The familiarity of a test item *i* is the sum of the strength values of the links between all probe sets of which it is a part and the images in memory:

$$\sum_{\text{all } j} S_j(CX,I_j) * S(I_i,I_j). \tag{2}$$

In many situations, we are interested in the familiarity value of a compound cue consisting of more than two items in which case the products in equations 1 and 2 will contain more than two terms (see equation 3).

A yes–no recognition decision is made by employing a signal–detection decision rule with the familiarity values calculated in this manner: If the familiarity of a test item is greater than some critical value, respond "yes"; if it is less, respond "no."

This brief excursion into the results and theories of recognition memory experiments prepares the ground for a discussion of sentence recognition.

8.1.2 Sentence recognition

How well does the CI model account for the data from sentence recognition experiments? An earlier attempt was made by Kintsch, Welsch, Schmalhofer, and Zimny (1990) to answer this question. Some simulations consistent with the present version of the model are presented below (see also Singer & Kintsch, in preparation).

Sentence recognition data. Sentence recognition data have much in common with list item recognition data. Recognition performance with sentences is generally very good, decreases relatively little with delay, and the probability of a false alarm is a function of the similarity of old and distractor items. Beyond that, sentence recognition data are much more complex and richer than item recognition data. Whereas a word list is either unstructured or minimally structured (e.g., by categories), texts are highly structured, which has important implications for the results of sentence recognition experiments.

In particular, the probability of recognizing a sentence from a text can be predicted from the position of the sentence in the text hierarchy, with structurally important propositions, especially macropropositions, being recognized better than unimportant, detail propositions (e.g., Walker & Yekovich, 1984).

The probability of a false alarm to a distractor sentence depends on the nature of the relationship between the text and the distractor sentence. False alarm probabilities are ordered from highest to lowest for paraphrases, inferences, topically related distractor sentences, and unrelated distractor sentences (Kintsch et al., 1990). Delay has only minor effects on the hit rate for old items but raises the false alarm rate for paraphrases, inferences, and related distractors. Figure 8.1 shows the data of Zimny (from Kintsch et al., 1990) on which these conclusions are based.

Kintsch et al. (1990) have further analyzed this pattern of delay effects in terms of the levels of representation of a text in episodic memory by computing separate decay rates for the situation model, the propositional textbase representation, and surface memory. Surface memory was estimated by the difference between verbatim sentences and paraphrases; textbase memory was estimated by the difference between paraphrases (in the text but not verbatim) and inferences (true, but not in the text); and situation model memory was estimated by the difference between inferences and distractors (true vs. false; neither appeared in the text).

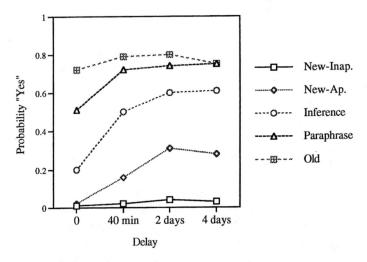

Figure 8.1 Recognition probabilities for old sentences, paraphrases, inferences, contextually appropriate new sentences, and contextually inappropriate
new sentences as a function of delay. After Kintsch et al. (1990).

Their results are shown in Figure 8.2. Under the conditions of their
experiment, no memory loss was observed for the situation model in a
four-day period; the propositional textbase lost about half of its strength
over that period, and surface memory was lost completely.

Differences in instructions are another factor that contributes significantly to the complexity of sentence recognition data. Results are similar
whether subjects recognize a sentence as having been part of a text or
whether the sentence is true with respect to that text (Schmalhofer,
1986). However, differences are obtained when subjects are asked to recognize a sentence or to judge its plausibility (Reder, 1982, 1987). Her
recognition data are about the same as those shown in Figure 8.1, but the
plausibility data show a different pattern of results. There are almost the
same number of "yes" responses to old sentences and inferences (roughly
an 8% difference), on both the immediate and delayed test, and there is
essentially no forgetting.

Sentence recognition data, therefore, are fairly complex. The challenge
to the CI model is to account for this pattern of results. Which of the
empirical phenomena are simply a consequence of the basic architecture
of the CI model? What additional assumptions are needed to account for
these data, and how justifiable are these assumptions?

The CI model is not a model of recognition memory and hence it must

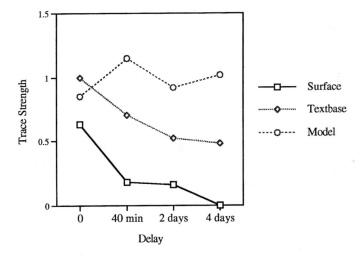

Figure 8.2   Estimates of trace strengths for surface, textbase, and situation model traces as a function of delay. After Kintsch et al. (1990).

be combined with one. As stated earlier, the easiest choice for that purpose is the recognition memory model of Gillund and Shiffrin (1984). This model represents memory in the same form as the CI model does, as a network of interconnected nodes. The CI computation generates a network that can be used as an input to the Gillund and Shiffrin memory model. Other memory models, such as TODAM (Murdock, 1993) and MINERVA (Hintzman, 1988), use different representations that would require a transformation from the network representation of the CI model to the format appropriate for TODAM or MINERVA.

To model delay effects, we need to know what happens to the memory trace as a function of delay. Figure 8.2 provides the necessary constraints. Thus, the simulations of sentence recognition are constructed from three components: the simulation of comprehension by the CI model, the simulation of recognition by the Gillund and Shiffrin model, and the empirically determined decay functions for different levels of sentence memory.

The effects of importance in sentence recognition. Lists of words in a recognition experiment are usually constructed in such a way that all items are as much alike as possible. That is, relevant variables such as word frequency, length, imagery value, and the like are controlled. Any remaining differences between items are random to the extent that other factors have been successfully controlled.

Sentence recognition experiments are fundamentally different in this respect, because the sentences in a natural text are never equal. Indeed, it has been shown that important, central sentences in a text are recognized better than unimportant, less central sentences (Walker & Yekovich, 1984). The CI model allows one to calculate the strength of each sentence in a textbase. Hence, if we use these calculations as the input to the Gillund and Shiffrin recognition model, the model should predict correctly that sentences high in the textbase hierarchy should be recognized better than sentences low in the hierarchy.

A simple test of this prediction can be obtained by constructing an arbitrary textbase and then computing how well a sentence corresponding to a proposition high in the hierarchy is recognized versus a sentence corresponding to a lower-order proposition. Figure 8.3 shows the network I have used for that purpose. It contains seven nodes forming a textbase, the propositions P1 to P7, the corresponding surface structure nodes S1 to S7, and a situation model consisting of a general context node, CX, and two macropropositions, M1 and M2. This is an abstract example, in that no particular text is associated with it. Its structure is arbitrary but designed to allow us to investigate recognition for important and unimportant sentences, that is, sentences high or low in the textbase hierarchy. Thus, the propositional nodes are arranged so that they occupy three levels of a hierarchy: P3 and P6 are at the top of the hierarchy (directly subordinated to the macropropositions), P2, P4, P5, and P7 are at the intermediate level (subordinated either to P3 or P6), and P1 is at the lowest level (subordinated to P2). This allows us to test recognition for sentences based on P1 and P3, that is, for a low-importance and for a high-importance sentence.

As a first step, comprehension of the structure shown in Figure 8.3 was simulated. (At this point, the stars in the upper left corner of Figure 8.3 play no role.) The simulation was done in two cycles: The first contained CX, M1, and all nodes under M1; the second cycle included CX and M2 and all the nodes dominated by M2, plus P3, which was retained in the STM buffer as the most strongly activated proposition from the first cycle. Thus, a long-term memory matrix L_{text}, which became the basis for the recognition tests, was calculated. The program of Mross and Roberts (1992) was used for these calculations.

The recognition probe is represented in Figure 8.3 by the stars labeled

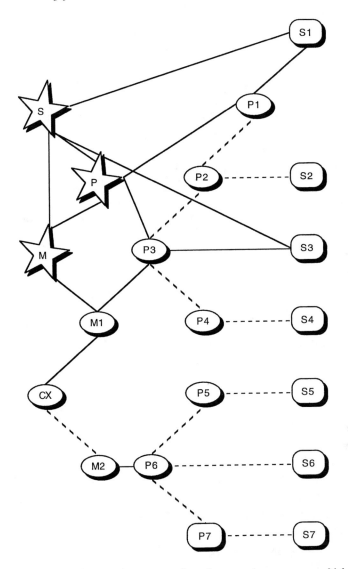

Figure 8.3   A network representation of a text and a test sentence high in the
textbase hierarchy. Nodes that do not participate in the test are linked by
dashed lines.

M, P, and S for its three components at the situation model (MOD), propositional (PRO), and surface levels (SUR). When the high-importance sentence (P3–S3) was tested for recognition, the PRO element was connected to its counterpart, P3, and the SUR element was connected to its counterpart, S3, as shown in Figure 8.3. The MOD element was connected to M1, because the test sentence fits into that part of the situation model. All other elements in Figure 8.3 were deactivated, that is, they did not take part in the processing of the test sentence. The activated structure was then integrated and the results added to the existing LTM matrix, L_{text}. The resulting matrix L_{high} was then used as the input to the recognition module.

For the test of the low-importance P1–S1 sentence, SUR was connected to S1, PRO to P1, and MOD as before to M1, because that sentence, too, is part of the same portion of the situation model. All other elements (including P3, etc.) were deactivated. Once again, the remaining network was integrated and the results added to the original LTM values. Thus, another LTM matrix L_{low} was obtained that could be used as input to the recognition module.

The matrices L_{high} and L_{low} are both sparse – that is, most of the entries are zero, because only the direct links between nodes have strength values in the LTM matrices generated by the CI model. The Gillund and Shiffrin model (1984), however, requires information not only about the direct links between items but also about indirect links. Hence, full matrices have to be calculated from L_{high} and L_{low}. To illustrate this problem, note that in Figure 8.3 there is no direct link between S1 and S2. However, there is a third-order connection between these two nodes by P1 and P2. The strength of this connection can be calculated by multiplying the strengths of the path segments: $r(S1,S2) = r(S1,P1)$ * $r(P1,P2)$ * $r(P2,S2)$. In this manner, full matrices R_{high} and R_{low} can be obtained that give the strength values of all interconnections between all nodes in the network for the high- and low-importance test sentences.[1] These matrices correspond to the retrieval structures of Gillund and Shiffrin (1984).

Because the Gillund and Shiffrin model does not care whether an element in memory is a proposition or a surface feature, the Ms, Ps, and Ss in Figure 8.3 will be relabeled as memory images, $I_1, I_2, \ldots, I_{16}$. The retrieval cues CX, MOD, PRO, and SUR will be relabeled as $Q_1, \ldots Q_4$.

---

1   I thank Ernie Mross for writing the "Matrix" program that performs these operations.

Then the familiarity of the probe $(Q_1, \ldots Q_4)$ is given by equation 1 of Gillund and Shiffrin as

$$F(Q_1, \ldots, Q_4) = \sum_{k=1}^{16} \prod_{j=1}^{4} S(Q_j, I_k) \qquad (3)$$

For the high-importance sentence, the familiarity value calculated in this way is .536; for the low-importance sentence, the familiarity value is .038. These values are sensible, given our expectations. Transforming them into observable statistics such as the probability of a "yes" response, requires some further calculations, however.

Gillund and Shiffrin (1984) suggest a signal-detection model for calculating the probability of "yes" or "no" decisions based on familiarity values. Assume that the familiarity values we have calculated are the mean values of normally distributed random variables. A plausible source of this variability may be subject differences. Thus, we need to obtain from the familiarity values we have calculated d' and β values. For this purpose, we arbitrarily fix the d' value of the high-importance sentence to be $d'_{high} = 2.00$ and $\beta_{high} = -.84$, so that $P(yes)_{high}$ becomes .80, which is a reasonable value according to Figure 8.1. Assuming that the standard deviations of the familiarity values for the high- and low-importance sentences are the same, we can calculate $d'_{low} = .14$. Therefore, $\beta_{low} = 1.02$, and $P(yes)_{low} = .17.$[2]

Thus, in our example, a high-importance sentence is recognized much more often than a low-importance sentence. Of course, these values depend on how the example has been constructed; a different and considerably higher value would be obtained had we chosen P2 as the low-importance proposition. Yet different values would be obtained with different networks. The point here is merely that when we compare recognition of a high-importance sentence and a low-importance sentence, the former is correctly predicted to be higher than the latter. This prediction is obtained without ad hoc assumptions, merely by using the CI model together with an off-the-shelf recognition model and standard signal detection analyses.

---

2   $m_{high} = .536$ and $d'_{high} = 2$ implies $s_{high} = .536/2 = .268$. For $d' = 2$, a b value of $-.84$ corresponds to a b value of 1.16 for $d' = 0$. For the distribution of the low-importance sentence with a mean of .038, $d' = .038/.268 = .142$. The criterion value of 1.16 corresponds to $1.16 - .142 = 1.02$ on the low-importance distribution. Hence $P(yes)_{low} = .172$.

The effects of level of representation in sentence recognition. Now let us turn to a somewhat more complex task, namely, modeling the pattern of results seen in Figure 8.1 for recognition of old sentences, paraphrases, inferences, and distractors. Two phenomena in Figure 8.1 deserve attention. First, old sentences, paraphrases, inferences, and unrelated distractor sentences yield systematically different recognition probabilities. Second, recognition probabilities remain essentially constant over a four-day period for old sentences but increase systematically for paraphrases, inferences, and distractors.

To keep this illustrative example as simple as possible, a smaller net was used than the one in Figure 8.3. This is sufficient, because there is no need here to distinguish between high- and low-importance propositions. Figure 8.4 shows the net chosen for this simulation. The network is similar to the previous one, but the number of propositions and surface nodes has been reduced to four. The test item is always related to P1, but there are three different cases. (1) If the old sentence is tested, all three test nodes are linked to corresponding nodes in the LTM structure. (2) If a paraphrase of that sentence is tested, the link between SUR and S1 is deleted because the surface structure is no longer the same. (One could make more subtle distinctions, of course, such as decreasing the strength of the link between SUR and S1 proportionally to the amount of change in the paraphrase). (3) If an inference is tested, neither the SUR node nor the PRO node is directly linked to the LTM structure because both the surface form and the propositional content are new. Only the link between the model component of the test sentence (MOD) and the situation model component of the text (M1) remains because the inference pertains to the situation model that was constructed for this particular recognition test.

Comprehension of the network in Figure 8.4 was simulated in two cycles, the first comprising the upper branch, dominated by M1; the second the lower branch, dominated by M2. The situation model element M1 was retained from the first to the second cycle in the STM buffer because it was the most strongly activated node in the first processing cycle. The CX node also participated in both processing cycles because it is connected to both parts of the network. The resulting LTM strengths are shown in the first column of Table 8.1.

Recognition of an old sentence (P1–S1) was simulated by adding three test nodes to the network, MOD, PRO, and SUR, corresponding to the situation model, proposition, and surface components of the test sentence, as shown by the stars in Figure 8.4. These three nodes were linked to their

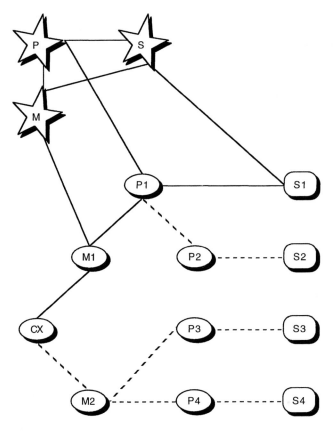

Figure 8.4   A network representation of a text and an old test sentence. Nodes that do not participate in the test are linked by dashed lines.

corresponding nodes in the LTM structure, as has been described. All other nodes in the LTM structure were deactivated, and the test nodes were integrated together with the active portion of the text. The resulting LTM values were added to the LTM values calculated from the comprehension simulation, as shown in column 2 of Table 8.1. Column 3 of Table 8.1 shows the results of testing a paraphrase of P1–S1. For these calculations, the node S1 was deactivated. Otherwise the calculations were the same as for the old test sentence. Finally, testing an inference was simulated, for which purpose the P1 node was also deactivated. These results are shown in the last column of Table 8.1. Note the changes in the memory strength values for the test nodes MOD, PRO, and SUR in Table 8.1 (last three rows) for old, paraphrase, and inference test items: All three

Table 8.1. *The LTM strength values for the network shown in Figure 8.4 and the strength values calculated for the recognition of an old sentence, a paraphrase sentence, and an inference sentence*

	LTM	OLD TEST	PARA TEST	INF TEST
CX	.712	.787	.810	.779
CX,M1	.740	.949	.987	.886
CX,M2	.669	.667	.667	.667
M1	1.112	1.691	1.739	1.436
M1,P1	.708	1.000	1.000	.708
M1,P2	.708	.708	.708	.708
M1,MOD		.740	.792	.568
P1	.501	1.253	.984	.501
P1,S1	.260	.824	.260	.260
P1,PRO		.867	.676	
S1	.135	.558	.135	.135
S1,SUR		.613		
P2	.501	.501	.501	.501
P2,S2	.260	.260	.260	.260
S2	.135	.135	.135	.135
M2	1.000	1.000	1.000	1.000
M2,P3	.667	.667	.667	.667
M2,P4	.667	.667	.667	.667
P3	.445	.445	.445	.445
P3,S3	.223	.223	.223	.223
P4	.445	.445	.445	.445
P4,S4	.223	.223	.223	.223
S3	.112	.112	.112	.112
S4	.112	.112	.112	.112
MOD		.945	1.000	1.000
PRO		1.000	.946	.677
SUR		.888	.602	.677

nodes are strong for old items, whereas for paraphrases only the MOD and PRO nodes are high, and for inferences only the MOD node is high.

The CI model having done its work, we turn to the recognition module. We first need to transform the sparse matrices obtained from the CI model into full matrices, showing indirect as well as direct connections between all nodes in the network. Table 8.2 shows the sparse matrix obtained from testing the old sentence; this is equivalent to column 2 of Table 8.1, except presented in a different form.

Table 8.2. *The sparse matrix showing the direct links between nodes for an old test sentence*

	Memory Images												
Cues	M1	P1	S1	P2	S2	M2	P3	P4	S3	S4	MO	PRO	SUR
CX	0.95	0	0	0	0	0.67	0	0	0	0	0	0	0
M1	1.69	1	0	0.71	0	0	0	0	0	0	0.74	0	0
P1	1	1.25	0.82	0	0	0	0	0	0	0	0	0.87	0
S1	0	0.82	0.56	0	0	0	0	0	0	0	0	0	0.61
P2	0.71	0	0	0.5	0.26	0	0	0	0	0	0	0	0
S2	0	0	0	0.26	0.14	0	0	0	0	0	0	0	0
M2	0	0	0	0	0	1	0.67	0.67	0	0	0	0	0
P3	0	0	0	0	0	0.67	0.45	0	0.22	0	0	0	0
P4	0	0	0	0	0	0.67	0	0.45	0	0.22	0	0	0
S3	0	0	0	0	0	0	0.22	0	0.11	0	0	0	0
S4	0	0	0	0	0	0	0	0.22	0	0.11	0	0	0
MOD	0.74	0	0	0	0	0	0	0	0	0	0.95	0.97	0.92
PRO	0	0.87	0	0	0	0	0	0	0	0	0.97	1	0.94
SUR	0	0	0.61	0	0	0	0	0	0	0	0.92	0.94	0.89

Table 8.3 shows the corresponding full matrix, in which the strengths of all indirect paths have been computed by multiplying together the strengths values of all path segments connecting to nodes. Because the network in Figure 8.4 is fully connected, all entries in this matrix are nonzero. These entries are the strengths values with which nodes i and j are connected in memory, $S(I_i,I_j)$.

In the Gillund and Shiffrin model (1984), the Ms, Ps, and Ss of Figure 8.4 are the memory images, which we now label as I_k. The recognition probe consists of the context element CX and the test sentence, which are represented by the three elements MOD, PRO, and SUR in Figure 8.4. The familiarity of the probe (CX, MOD, PRO, SUR) according to equation 1 of Gillund and Shiffrin is given by

$$F(CX,MOD,PRO,SUR) = \sum_{k=1}^{9} S(CX,I_k) * S(MOD,I_k) * S(PRO,I_k) * S(SUR,I_k). \quad (4)$$

The familiarity values calculated in this way for OLD sentences from Table 8.3 is 1.378. These calculations were repeated for paraphrases and inferences, starting with the values for these test sentences shown in Table 8.1. The familiarity value of the paraphrase test sentence turns out to be

Table 8.3. *The full matrix showing both direct and indirect links between nodes for an old test sentence*

	Memory Images												
Cues	M1	P1	S1	P2	S2	M2	P3	P4	S3	S4	MOD	PRO	SUR
CX	0.95	0.95	0.78	0.67	0.17	0.67	0.44	0.44	0.1	0.1	0.7	0.82	0.64
M1	1.69	1	0.82	0.71	0.18	0.63	0.42	0.42	0.09	0.09	0.74	0.87	0.68
P1	1	1.25	0.82	0.71	0.18	0.63	0.42	0.42	0.09	0.09	0.84	0.87	0.82
S1	0.82	0.82	0.56	0.58	0.15	0.52	0.35	0.35	0.08	0.08	0.56	0.71	0.61
P2	0.71	0.71	0.58	0.5	0.26	0.45	0.3	0.3	0.07	0.07	0.52	0.61	0.48
S2	0.18	0.18	0.15	0.26	0.14	0.12	0.08	0.08	0.02	0.02	0.14	0.16	0.12
M2	0.63	0.63	0.52	0.45	0.12	1	0.67	0.67	0.15	0.15	0.47	0.55	0.43
P3	0.42	0.42	0.35	0.3	0.08	0.67	0.45	0.44	0.22	0.1	0.31	0.37	0.29
P4	0.42	0.42	0.35	0.3	0.08	0.67	0.44	0.45	0.1	0.22	0.31	0.37	0.29
S3	0.09	0.09	0.08	0.07	0.02	0.15	0.22	0.1	0.11	0.02	0.07	0.08	0.06
S4	0.09	0.09	0.08	0.07	0.02	0.15	0.1	0.22	0.02	0.11	0.07	0.08	0.06
MOD	0.74	0.84	0.56	0.52	0.14	0.47	0.31	0.31	0.07	0.07	0.95	0.97	0.92
PRO	0.87	0.87	0.71	0.61	0.16	0.55	0.37	0.37	0.08	0.08	0.97	1	0.94
SUR	0.68	0.82	0.61	0.48	0.12	0.43	0.29	0.29	0.06	0.06	0.92	0.94	0.89

.834, and of the inference test sentence .221. These values are shown in Table 8.4.

Familiarity values for test sentences after a delay can also be calculated by making suitable assumptions about the decay of probe strengths as a function of delay. These assumptions were motivated by Figure 8.2. Specifically, it was assumed that there was no loss of strength as a function of delay for situation model nodes in memory but that propositional nodes lost half their strength and surface elements all their strength. Thus, the terms in equation 2 were multiplied by .5 if the imagery element was a proposition and by 0 if it was a surface element. The resulting familiarity values for old sentences, paraphrases, and inference test sentences are also shown in Table 8.4.

Finally, a signal-detection model was used to calculate recognition probabilities from the familiarity values of the test sentences. As in the previous example, d'_{old} was arbitrarily set to 2, and β_{old} was chosen so that $P(yes)_{old} = .80$, as suggested by Figure 8.1. The d' values for paraphrases and inferences were obtained by scaling their familiarity values in the

Table 8.4. *Familiarity values, d'- and β-values and P(yes) for old sentences, paraphrases, inferences, and unrelated distractor sentences for immediate and delayed recognition*

	Immediate			
	Familiarity	d'	β	P(yes)
Old	1.38	2.00	−.84	.80
Paraphrase	.83	1.20		.52
Inference	.22	.32		.20
Distractor	0	0		.12

	Delay			
	Familiarity	d'	β	P(yes)
Old	.84	1.21	−.84	.80
Paraphrase	.64	.93		.71
Inference	.16	.23		.44
Distractor	0	0		.36

same way as for old sentences (i.e., dividing by .69). The β and P(yes) values could then be calculated for paraphrases, inferences, and distractors, as shown in the table. The calculations for the delayed recognition test were identical, again choosing a criterion value that yields a recognition probability of .80 for old test sentences. Figure 8.5 summarizes the predicted recognition probabilities for both the immediate and delayed test. These predictions capture the essential features of the empirical data of Figure 8.1. That the "yes" probability for old sentences remains at .80 for both immediate and delayed tests was built into Figure 8.5 by the way the parameters of the signal detection model were estimated. What the model predicts correctly is the ordering of the test items and the increase with delay in false alarms for items that were not actually part of the original text (paraphrases, inferences, and distractors).

The two examples of how well-known phenomena of sentence recognition can be derived from the CI model and current memory theory make an important point. We don't need a special theory of sentence memory: If we understand sentence comprehension (the CI theory) and recognition memory (the list-learning literature), we have all the parts we need for a sentence recognition model. Conceptually it is very simple.

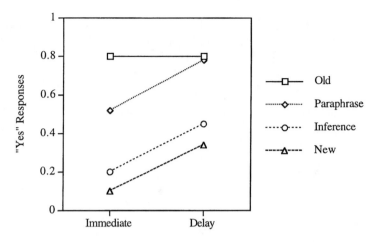

Figure 8.5   The predicted probabilities of recognizing old sentences, paraphrases, inferences, and unrelated distractor items on an immediate and delayed recognition test.

The actual calculations are complex, and the pattern of data that must be accounted for is complex, too. But underlying all this complexity is a simple model of comprehension and a simple memory model.

The examples discussed have been intentionally simplified in order to be able to work through the actual calculations step by step. This is important if one wants to show that a complex new phenomenon can be accounted for by simple old theories. It is, of course, also necessary to work with real, nonarbitrary texts, fitting actual data, and to extend the domain of phenomena modeled – for example, by including the plausibility results mentioned in the introduction to this section. Singer and Kintsch (in preparation) attempt to do so, thus demonstrating that the kind of account proposed here of sentence recognition in terms of familiar theories about comprehension and memory is indeed feasible, and not just a theoretical possibility.

8.2 Recall and summarization

To provide an account of how readers recall a text they have read has been one of the oldest and most important applications of the CI theory and its predecessors (Kintsch, 1974, 1976, 1977b; Kintsch & van Dijk, 1978; Miller & Kintsch, 1980; van Dijk & Kintsch, 1983). In general, one can say that the theory has done a reasonably good job of predicting recall, especially for short texts and stories. The way these predictions were derived was to simulate comprehension of a text and then assume that recall probabilities for propositions are a monotonic function of the activation values, or better, the long-term memory strength values calculated in the simulation. Correlations between predicted recall and observed recall frequencies typically range between .4 and .8. This is as good as or better than intuitive judgments of what will or will not be recalled from a text.

Exceptions have been encountered, however. In my experience, there are two cases in which the theory regularly yields poor predictions. First, recall for long texts cannot be predicted without an explicit account of macrostructure formation. Brief, paragraph-long texts are recalled reproductively, but longer texts are summarized. Their macrostructure may be reproduced, but the microstructure is either deleted or reconstructed, as Bartlett (1932) showed long ago. The solution to this problem is to include the macrostructure explicitly in the simulation. When this is done, as in Kintsch and van Dijk (1978), the predictions of the model can be substantially improved.

Another reason for prediction failures of the model occurs when readers do not properly understand the text that they are recalling. The model assumes an ideal reader, that is, it assumes that the reader has processed the whole text and has formed a mental representation of the text as the author intended – essentially complete and essentially correct. If the reader misunderstands the text and makes various kinds of errors in recall, the model simply does not apply. Such misunderstandings occur quite frequently, especially with scientific texts. For instance, recall data recently collected in my laboratory on a text discussing several hypotheses concerning the extinction of the Irish elk – a huge animal with giant antlers – were beyond the scope of the comprehension theory because most subjects egregiously misunderstood the discussion of the competing hypotheses. They formed idiosyncratic mental text representations, depending on the nature of their misconceptions, which is unpredictable. Thus, some conspicuous failures of the model to predict recall data that have been reported in the literature may very well be attributable to the subjects' inadequate comprehension of the text they had read.

The model does, overall, a fairly good and reliable job of predicting story recall. Some issues, however, need to be considered and might help us to improve the model predictions further. These concern parameter estimations, the propositional unit of analysis, and the possibility of combining an explicit model of free recall with the comprehension theory, as was done for recognition.

The CI model has a large number of parameters, at least potentially. Might not the success of the model be due the fact that the model judiciously exploits this parameter space? One often hears the complaint that with that many degrees of freedom, any structure could predict any data set. It is an ill-founded complaint, however. It is the structure of the model that yields the good predictions, not the free parameters. Although the model has many potential parameters (conceivably, every link strength might be estimated separately), actual simulations use this freedom with restraint. Some research has begun to explore the parameter space of the model with respect to free recall predictions (Miller & Kintsch, 1980; Tapiero & Denhière, 1995). Their conclusions are rather reassuring, in that the model does not appear to be overly sensitive to the selection of particular parameter values within some reasonable range. Direct links may be assigned a value of 1 and all other links a value of 0; short-term memory buffer values between 1 and 4 have been used, with 1 or 2 yielding the best results; the appropriate cycle size (i.e., the number of atomic propositions included in a processing cycle) appears to be around 7. Tapiero and Denhière (1995) obtained better results when links were defined by "minimal predication" than by strict argument overlap: If A is an argument and P and Q are predicates, P[A] is linked to Q[P[A]] by argument overlap, but not by Tapiero and Denhière's criterion of predication. Thus, not only does the CI model use only relatively few parameters in practice, but these remain mostly the same from one application to the next. Parameter estimates don't have much to do with the good fit of the model, at least at the qualitative level. More careful parameter estimation would be required if quantitative fits were desired.

Most published research involving the CI model and its predecessors use atomic propositions as the unit of analysis. The simulations presented in the following section employ complex propositions, instead. There are several reasons to prefer complex propositions. First, the data are often difficult to score in terms of atomic propositions. Higher scoring reliability can usually be obtained for complex propositions. Second, atomic propositions may or may not be expressed in a recall protocol for a variety of reasons, even if they are remembered. For instance, a modifier may be omitted in a recall protocol, not because it was not encoded as part of the text representation, but because it was considered redundant in the production phase. Such editing processes introduce further and spurious variability into data scored in terms of atomic propositions. Thus, complex propositions appear to be better units for analyzing recall data and for comparing predictions with data.

In the previous section I showed how memory strength estimates derived from the CI model of comprehension can predict sentence recognition data when plugged into a standard model of recognition memory. In contrast, no recall theory was used in deriving recall predictions in the studies of story recall; it was simply assumed that recall was proportional to the activation values calculated in the comprehension simulation. Although this simplifying assumption yielded reasonable predictions, it is certainly as questionable as in the case of sentence recognition. Why should activation values predict frequency of recall? In theories of list recall, we do not assume that memory strengths *directly* predict recall; instead, it has been necessary to introduce complex processing assumptions in order to describe the experimental phenomena typically observed in list recall experiments. Thus, the SAM theory of Gillund and Shiffrin (1984) assumes recall to be a complex process of cue-based retrieval and recovery. Whatever cues are present in short-term memory (for example, a context cue plus an already recalled list item) serve as retrieval cues. The retrieval process then may or may not produce implicitly another as yet not recalled item from the list, depending on the strength of the relation between the retrieval cue and the items of the list. This implicitly retrieved item may then be recovered with a probability depending on its memory strength. This process is formulated mathematically, and predictions derived in this way indeed mimic all the major features of list recall data that have been observed in the laboratory. Why should text recall be different? Should not the same model of recall that has proven its worth elsewhere also be used to derive predictions for text recall? The current practice in predicting story recall from comprehension simulations assumes without any justification that recall is directly determined by memory strength. Can we enhance our predictions based on the CI model by using a proven memory theory to model the recall process, as we did for the recognition process in the previous section?

8.2.1 Simulations of story recall

To address this question, I simulate the comprehension of two stories and then derive recall predictions from these simulations in the traditional oversimplified way (that is, by assuming that the long-term memory strength values in the CI simulations are proportional to recall frequency), as well as in ways suggested by memory theory. Specifically, I adapt the Gillund and Shiffrin (1984) theory of list recall to story recall. The stories are two Aesop fables previously used by R. M. Golden (personal communication). The first text is shown in Table 8.5.

The propositionalized text is shown in Table 8.6. There are thirteen complex propositions, each corresponding to a sentence. Links among complex propositions are shown in Figure 8.6. Repeated arguments are indicated by first letters in bold face type. Note that verbs of psychological state and verbs of saying and thinking are treated as modifiers. Thus, for The *frogs decided to find a new home* the core proposition is FIND [FROGS,HOME], which has the modifiers DECIDE[FROGS, FIND [. . .]] and NEW[HOME], as shown in Table 8.6 in a abbreviated form. Similarly, *The second frog replied: Suppose the well's bottom is not a good home* has the core proposition NOT-GOOD[BOTTOM,HOME] with the modifiers REPLY[SECOND-FROG,NOT-GOOD[. . .]], SUPPOSE [NOT-GOOD[. . .]], and OF[BOTTOM,WELL].

For the simulations, a buffer size of 1 atomic proposition was used. Cycle size was varied systematically between 4 and 8 atomic propositions. Thus, for a cycle size of 4 the first processing cycle would contain only

Table 8.5. *The* Frog *story: Two Frogs and the Well*

Two frogs dwelt in the same pool of water.
The pool dried up in the summer heat.
The frogs decided to find a new home.
The two frogs left the pool of water.
The two frogs began their search for another pool of water.
As the two frogs traveled along, they reached a well.
The well was very deep.
The first frog said the well would provide them with shelter and food.
The first frog wanted to enter the well.
The second frog wanted to think about the well as a new home.
The second frog replied: "Suppose the well's bottom is not a good home."
The second frog said, "How will we get out of the deep well in that case?"

Table 8.6. *Propositional analysis of the Frog story*

P1   Two frogs and the well.

$$\text{AND[FROGS,WELL]}$$
$$\underline{\quad\quad\quad}\text{ TWO}$$

P2   Two frogs dwelt in the same pool of water.

$$\text{DWELL[F, POOL]}$$
$$\vdash \text{SAME}$$
$$\llcorner \text{OF-WATER}$$

P3   The pool dried up in the summer heat.

$$\text{DRY [P]}$$
$$\vdash \text{SUMMER}$$
$$\llcorner \text{IN-HEAT}$$

P4   The frogs decided to find a new home.

$$\text{FIND [F, HOME]]}$$
$$|\quad\quad \llcorner \text{NEW}$$
$$\text{DECIDE}$$

P5   The two frogs left the pool of water.

$$\text{LEAVE [F, P]}$$

P6   The two frogs began their search for another pool of water.

$$\text{SEARCH[F, POOL]]}$$
$$|\quad\quad \llcorner \text{OF-WATER}$$
$$\llcorner \text{BEGIN}$$

P7   As the two frogs traveled along, they reached a well.

$$\text{REACH [F, W]}$$
$$\underline{\quad\quad\quad}\text{ AS-TRAVEL}$$

P8   The well was very deep.

$$\text{DEEP [W]}$$
$$\llcorner \text{VERY}$$

P9   The first frog said the well would provide them with shelter and food.

$$\text{PROVIDE[W,SHELTER,FOOD]}$$
$$\llcorner \text{SAID[FIRST-FROG]}$$

P10 The first frog wanted to enter the well.

$$\text{ENTER[F, W]}$$
$$\llcorner \text{WANT[FF]}$$

P11 The second frog wanted to think about the well as a new home.

$$\text{THINK [F, W, H]}$$
$$\llcorner \text{WANT[SEC-FROG]}$$

P12 The second frog replied:

"Suppose the well's bottom is not a good home."

$$\text{NOT-GOOD[BOTTOM,H]}$$
$$\llcorner \text{SUPPOSE} \quad \llcorner \text{OF-W}$$

P13 The second frog said,

"How will we get out of the deep well in that case?"

$$\text{HOW-GET-OUT[F, W]}$$
$$|\quad\quad\quad \llcorner \text{IF-N-G}$$
$$\llcorner \text{SAID[SF]}$$

the first two complex propositions (which actually contain 5 atomic propositions, because the second complex proposition consists of 3 atomic propositions that cannot be split apart). For a cycle size of 7, the first three complex propositions would be included in the first cycle, by the same argument.

Repeated arguments were introduced as separate nodes in the network, Thus, a node FROGS was formed that was connected to all propositions with that argument, (FROGS or F in Table 8.6). In this way, repeated arguments were treated as separate discourse entities.

All links were assigned a value of 1. Links were constructed between a proposition and its modifiers and between a discourse entity node and the propositions containing that discourse entity. These links are shown in Figure 8.6.

Trabasso and van den Broek (1985) and others have shown that causal links in a story are more important than other types of links. Hence, a sec–

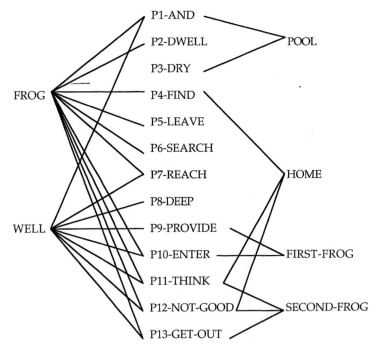

Figure 8.6   The argument–repetition network constructed for the proposition list in Table 8.6. Only predicates and repeated arguments are shown; modifiers and the links among them have been omitted for clarity.

ond coherence network was constructed in addition to Figure 8.6 that included causal links in addition to the links established by mere argument overlap. Whenever a causal relation was found between two complex propositions (e.g., between P3 and P4 or between P5 and P6), another link was added to the argument overlap network. Comprehension was simulated for this causal net with an input size of 7 atomic propositions only.

Tables 8.7 and 8.8 show the text and proposition list for a second story, the *Miser* story. There are seventeen complex propositions, each corresponding to a sentence. Links among complex propositions are not shown. Repeated arguments are indicated by first letters in boldface type.

Thirty-two college students were asked to read and recall both the *Frog* and the *Miser* stories. Figure 8.7 shows the correlations between the activation values of atomic propositions and the observed recall frequencies as a function of cycle size. It is reassuring that these correlations are not strongly affected by cycle size. The highest correlations for the two stories were obtained for cycle sizes of 6 and 7. Adding causal links did not help; indeed, it significantly decreased the correlation with the data in the case of the *Miser* story. Note the relative robustness of these results with respect to input size. Input size is the most important parameter in this model (more than, say, link strength or buffer size), but it is reassuring to

Table 8.7. *The* Miser *story. The Miser, the Neighbor, and the Gold*

A miser bought a lump of gold using all his money.
The miser buried the gold in the ground.
The miser looked at the buried gold each day.
One of the miser's servants discovered the buried gold.
The servant wanted the miser's gold.
The servant stole the gold.
The miser, on his next visit, found the hole empty.
The miser was very upset.
The miser pulled his hair.
The neighbor wanted to make the miser feel better.
The neighbor wanted the miser to realize a stone was as useless as the gold.
The neighbor told the miser not to be upset.
The neighbor said, "Go and take a stone and bury it in the hole."
The neighbor said, "And imagine that the gold is still lying there."
The neighbor said, "The stone will be as useful to you as the gold."
The neighbor said, "When you had the gold, you never used it."

Table 8.8. *Propositional analysis of the* Miser *story*

P1   The miser, the neighbor, and the gold.
          AND [MISER,NEIGHBOR,GOLD]

P2   A miser bought a lump of gold using all his money.
          BUY [M, G,USE[MONEY]]
                    └ ALL

P3   The miser buried the gold in the ground.
          BURY [M, G,GROUND]

P4   The miser looked at the buried gold each day.
          LOOK [M, G]
            └ EACH-DAY

P5   One of the miser's servants discovered the buried gold.
          DISCOVER [SERVANT, G]
                └ OF-M

P6   The servant wanted the miser's gold.
          WANT [S, G]

P7   The servant stole the gold.
          STEAL [S, G]

P8   The miser, on his next visit, found the hole empty.
          FIND [M,HOLE]
                └ EMPTY
            └───────── NEXT-VISIT

P9   The miser was very upset.
          UPSET [M]

P10 The miser pulled his hair.
          PULL [M,HAIR]

P11 The neighbor wanted to make the miser feel better
          MAKE[N, FEEL-BETTER [M]]
            └ WANT[N]

P12 The neighbor wanted the miser to realize a stone was as useless as the gold.
          REALIZE [M, AS [USELESS [STONE],USELESS [G]]]
            └ WANT[N]

P13 The neighbor told the miser not to be upset.
          NOT-UPSET [M]
            └ SAY[N]

P14 The neighbor said, "Go and take a stone and bury it in the hole."
          BURY [M, ST, IN-H]
            └ SAY[N]

P15 The neighbor said, "And imagine that the gold is still lying there."
          IMAGINE [M, G, IN-H]
            └ SAY [N]

P16 The neighbor said: "The stone will be as useful to you as the gold."
          AS [USEFUL[ST,TO-M],USEFUL[G,TO-M]]
            └ SAY [N]

P17 The neighbor said "When you had the gold, you never used it."
          NOT-USE [M, G]
               └ WHEN [HAVE [M, G]
           └ SAY [N]

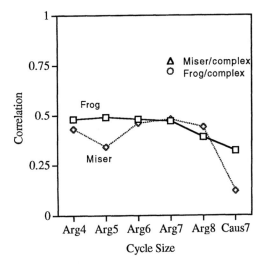

Figure 8.7   The correlations between observed recall frequencies and model predictions for two stories. The connected lines show the correlations with models based on argument repetition only (Arg) or argument repetition plus causal links (Caus) for input cycle sizes between 4 and 8 atomic propositions. The correlations between predictions and recall with complex propositions as units, with links based on argument repetition and an input size of 7, are also shown.

see that not even that matters very much. It is the structure of the model that yields the predictions, not the specific parameter values chosen. However, an input size of 7 appears to be best for these two stories.

Figure 8.7 also shows the correlations for complex propositions, for cycle size 7 only. These were obtained by adding together the activation values of all atomic propositions as well as the corresponding recall frequencies. The activation values for complex propositions predict recall much better than do the activation values for atomic propositions and indeed, account for over half of the variance in the recall data.

Although correlating activation values for complex propositions with recall data gives good predictions, it remains to be investigated how much better can we do if we use an established memory model for free recall, such as the Gillund and Shiffrin (1984) theory. In the present case there is probably not much to be gained because, for these very simple stories, activation values predict recall quite well – the reliability of the data is probably not much better than the predictions! Nevertheless, it is worth investigating how better-motivated theoretical recall predictions could be derived from the Gillund and Shiffrin model.

Unlike in the case of sentence recognition, however, we cannot simply take over Gillund and Shiffrin's recall model wholesale and apply it to story recall. Much of that model is designed to deal with features of list recall that are absent or different in story recall. When subjects recall a list of words, they exhaust their current retrieval cue and then return to the context cue to construct a new retrieval cue, using that as long as it is productive. Thus, a recall episode typically involves many new starts, resulting in bursts of recall separated by pauses during which the retrieval cue is being reconstructed. Story recall is quite different: It is ordered, backtracking is rare, and the bursts characteristic of list recall are absent because each recalled story proposition serves as a retrieval cue for a later one. Thus, lists are recalled like semantic categories, whereas stories are recalled like scripts (Walker & Kintsch, 1985; see also the discussion in section 3.2.2). The control strategies for list recall and story recall are therefore quite different, and the portions of the Gillund and Shiffrin model that deal with these aspects do not apply to story recall.

It is informative, however, to calculate the predictions of the Gillund and Shiffrin model for story recall in spite of these reservations. To do so, we must first compute the full matrix of links between propositions. The CI model generates only direct links (as in Table 8.2), but what we need are the strengths between all interitem links, direct links as well as indirect links (as in Table 8.3). For instance, although proposition 3 DRY [POND], and proposition 4, FIND[FROGS,HOME], in the *Frog* story are not directly connected (Figure 8.6), there is an indirect connection via POOL, DWELL, and FROG. The strength of that indirect connection can be computed as the product of the strength values of the links that form the path between proposition 3 and proposition 4.[3]

Recall that predictions from the Gillund and Shiffrin model were obtained through a Monte Carlo simulation, using the full link matrices and the same parameter values that Gillund and Shiffrin employed in their study of list recall.

These computations are performed on the matrix of atomic propositions (37 for *Frog* and 42 for *Miser*). Link strengths for complex proposi-

---

3   However, path strengths are never allowed to be greater than 1.

tions (13 for *Frog,* 17 for *Miser*) can be calculated by summing the strength values of all atomic propositions that belong to the same complex proposition. Note that the self strengths thus calculated are not just the sum of the self-activation values but include also the links between the atomic propositions that make up the complex proposition.

Table 8.9 shows the correlations between predictions and recall data for complex propositions when the activation values obtained from the CI simulation of comprehension were used directly as predictors and when these values were used in conjunction with the Gillund and Shiffrin model, as it has been described. Both sets of predictions are about equally good in predicting the overall frequency with which complex text propositions were recalled. Neither predicts the order of recall: The Gillund and Shiffrin model makes order predictions, but, as has been discussed, the list-learning control structure is not suited for story recall. Thus, there are numerous jumps from one part of the story to another, forward and backward, in the Monte Carlo simulations, that have no counterpart in the data.

Wolfe and Kintsch (in preparation) have explored modifications of the control structure of the Gillund and Shiffrin (1984) model that would allow the model to predict the order in which stories are recalled. The Gillund and Shiffrin model of recall is a two-stage model. In the first stage, memory nodes (text propositions in our case) are implicitly retrieved with probabilities proportional to their relative memory strength; in the second stage, an attempt is made to recover these implicitly retrieved memory items, the success of which depends on the absolute memory strength of the item. In our simulations, this recovery process played no role, because absolute memory strength was so high that recovery was almost assured. The recovery process may be likened to a recognition judgment of implicitly retrieved items: Does the item that was retrieved come from the right

Table 8.9. *Correlations between observed and predicted recall*

	Frog	Miser
Activation–recall	.77	.72
G&S–recall	.63	.73
G&S(order)–recall	.66	.68

list? With stories, such a decision seems straightforward, so the recovery process plays no important role. But suppose we assign the recovery process a more useful control function in story recall: Propositions out of order, or propositions far away in the story may have a reduced recovery probability. It would be unreasonable to assume that readers sequentially number the propositions of a story during comprehension and then use this information in the recovery process. However, we know that readers categorize story propositions in terms of story schema categories such as setting, problem, and resolution. In Wolfe and Kintsch (in preparation), we manipulated recovery probabilities in such a way that (1) transitions to a distant category (e.g., from setting to resolution) were prohibited, (2) transitions to the next category (e.g., from setting to problem) had a much lower recovery probability than within-category retrievals, and (3) even within a category, forward transitions had a higher recovery probability than backward transitions (such decisions can be made on the basis of local cues – e.g., if a subject has already recalled that the servant stole the gold, he or she is unlikely to say next that the servant discovered the gold). This control structure was devised simply to reflect the empirical data on recall order without making psychologically implausible assumptions. It did what it was supposed to. With this modification, the Gillund and Shiffrin model predicts recall order quite well (less than one within-category reversal per protocol and none between categories in both data and simulations), and the overall recall frequencies are still predicted as well as before (the last line in Table 8.9).

Figures 8.8 and 8.9 show the detailed correspondence between observed and predicted values (total activation) for atomic propositions for the *Frog* and *Miser* texts, respectively. The predictions for *Frog* roughly correspond to the trends in the data. For *Miser,* there is one exception, when a proposition that was recalled very well by the subjects did not get a particularly high activation value in the simulation (*The miser found the hole empty.*).

Overall, therefore, the recall predictions of the model are quite good. Furthermore, it mattered little whether a formal theory of recall – Gillund and Shiffrin (1984) – was used to derive the predictions, or whether the activation values of propositions, as calculated by the CI model directly, were used to predict recall. This may not always be the case, however, because the stories used here were extremely simple. With longer, structurally complex texts, the power of the memory module may be required for adequate recall predictions.

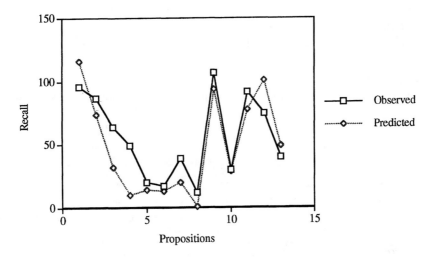

Figure 8.8   Observed and predicted recall frequencies for the *Frog* story.

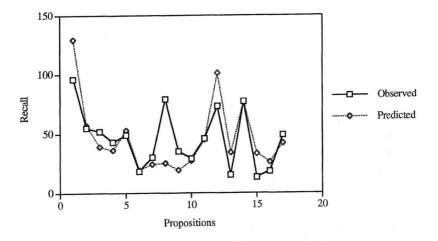

Figure 8.9   Observed and predicted recall frequencies for the *Miser* story.

8.2.2 Evaluation of summaries

The most straightforward way to derive predictions from the model for summarization would be to assume that subjects employ the same memory representation as for recall but that their output criterion is higher. Thus, the implicit retrieval process would remain the same as has been described for recall, except that when a story proposition is retrieved, recovery is attempted only if its self-strength is above a threshold value. This threshold value may vary, depending on whether the subject is trying to construct a high-level summary or a more detailed one. The two stories used here are not suitable for the empirical investigation of summarization because of their extreme simplicity, but an early version of such a model has been used successfully for a longer story by Kintsch (1976).

Summaries generated in this way are strictly reproductive, however. That is, they are based on only one of van Dijk's macrorules, the selection of important propositions (van Dijk, 1980). The other two macrorules – generalization and construction – are just as important, however, and summaries are usually generated by applying all three rules. As was discussed in section 6.2, the theory therefore can explain summaries after the fact, but it is not easy to predict what a summary will look like, because we cannot anticipate when the generalization and construction operations will be used.

What we can do is to analyze the summaries people have produced to determine whether they can in fact be accounted for by the operations of selection, generalization, and construction. However, until these operations are precisely formulated in a simulation model, such judgments are difficult to validate. A better way to evaluate summaries, as was suggested in section 6.2.3, is to employ LSA to measure how close a particular summary is to the text it was derived from.

This was done in a study by Nathan Chatfield at the University of Colorado. This study had two parts. In one condition, the participants, 33 undergraduate students, read 15 unrelated paragraphs selected from a wide variety of texts, essays as well as stories, and underlined what they judged to be the most important sentence in each paragraph. They then wrote summaries for three of the paragraphs. Their instructions were simply to write a one-sentence summary for each paragraph. In the second part of the experiment, the participants read 10 three-paragraph texts and rank-ordered the three paragraphs of each text in the order of their importance "to the overall meaning of the passage." Again, a variety of texts was used, varying in length between a page and half of a page. Finally, the subjects summarized three of these texts in no more than two sentences. All summaries, for the passages as well as for the single paragraphs, were graded by two judges on a scale from A to F. The judges were instructed to use all five grades approximately equally often.

Consider the rating results for the single paragraphs first. The empirical data consist of the frequencies with which each sentence of a paragraph was chosen as the most important one. To see whether this pattern of choices agrees with LSA, all paragraphs and their sentences were expressed as vectors in the LSA space obtained from the encyclopedia scaling (see section 3.3). The cosines were computed between a paragraph and each sentence in the paragraph. These cosines indicate the strength of the semantic relationship between a sentence and the paragraph. More important sentences should be closer to the overall meaning of the paragraph than less important sentences. Hence, these cosines should predict the frequency with which readers choose each sentence as most important in a paragraph. The overall correlation between the frequency judgments and the cosines was $r = .51$, $p < .01$. The split-half reliability of the frequency data is $r = .75$. Thus, the LSA predictions are not quite as good as the agreement among subjects but are reasonably close to human performance.

The importance ranking data for the three-paragraph passages were analyzed in the same way: The mean empirical rank for each paragraph was compared with the cosine between the paragraph and the whole passage. The overall correlation was $r = .58$, $p < .01$. To obtain an idea of how high a correlation might be expected, a split-half reliability coefficient was computed for the empirical rankings. This correlation was $r = .80$. As was the case for sentence judgments in paragraphs, LSA's ability to predict the importance ranking of paragraphs in a text is not quite as good as human judgments. This may indicate a weakness of LSA (almost certainly the fact that LSA was trained on an encyclopedia limits its performance in the present case, where commonsense knowledge is more relevant than the kind of formal knowledge that is usually found in an encyclopedia), or it may indicate that semantic relatedness is not the only factor in importance judgments. Further research is needed to clarify this question.

The summaries for the single paragraphs as well as the whole texts were evaluated by computing the cosine for each summary with the text it was supposed to summarize. The better a summary, the closer its vector in the LSA space should be to the text it summarizes. Not surprisingly, there were substantial differences between paragraphs. The first paragraph was summarized quite well (the average cosine between all summaries and the paragraph was .57), the second paragraph was summarized quite poorly (average cosine .28), and third paragraph was intermediate (average cosine .42). The overall correlation between the cosines and the average grade assigned to a summary was r = .57, p < .01. The correlation between the two human graders was only r = .48, however. Thus, LSA did even a little better than the two human graders in this case.

Similar results were obtained for the passage summaries. The differences between texts were less pronounced (the average cosines for the three texts were .36, .43, and .38, respectively). The overall correlation between the average grade and cosines was r = .48, p < .01, about the same as the correlation between the two human graders, r = .45.

Although these results need to be extended with more texts, systematic variation between text types, summaries of different length, and human graders who achieve a higher level of agreement, they suggest that LSA is quite successful as an automatic method for evaluating the quality of summaries, thus opening up a new research area as a well as a potentially fruitful field of application.

The details of the simulations described in this chapter should not obfuscate its message. A model of text comprehension does not by itself provide an account of all behaviors that have something to do with text understanding. The model takes care of only the input side – the transformation of the text into a mental representation. We need a separate, additional model to account for any behavior based on this mental representation, whether this is a lexical decision response, a comprehensibility judgment, a recognition response, the free recall of a whole text, solving a mathematical problem, or an action, as discussed in later chapters. In some cases these behavioral output models are trivial and the theorist gets away with assumptions like "behavior is proportional to activation strength," or the like. Even then one must not forget that this is merely a shortcut, a simplifying assumption that happens to be adequate in some cases. In general, an explicit account of the behavioral module is required.

In the two applications discussed here, this explicit account of the behavioral module is simple conceptually but complex to implement. At the rational level of theorizing, it is enough to say that the comprehension module feeds into a standard recognition or free-recall module. At the implementational level, however, fairly extensive calculations are required. Perhaps one should not be surprised at the complexity of these computations.

The phenomena we are dealing with here are indeed complex, and to get from simple principles to complex phenomena by extensive but mechanical straightforward computations may not be too serious a price to pay.

Using a standard theory for recognition memory and recall, which was developed for quite different purposes and on the basis of totally different empirical data, in combination with the CI theory of text comprehension is also a way of working toward a unified theory of cognition. The unified theory does not have to come from a single overarching theoretical scheme, but may also be constructed from the bottom up by building on prior established theories.

9

Learning from text

9.1 What makes for a good reader?

The answer to that simple question is surprisingly complicated. Reading is a complex activity, with several factors that can compensate for one another to a considerable extent. Thus, many highly intelligent persons and fluent readers may be poor decoders, and a person who knows a great deal about a particular domain but has low reading skills can outperform a highly skilled reader under the right set of circumstances.

This chapter discusses three factors that determine whether a person is a good reader and what kind of a reader the person is: decoding skills, language skills, and domain knowledge. All three are important for reading but in different ways.

9.1.1 Decoding skills

For a large sector of the reading research and instruction community, it often seems as if decoding and reading were one and the same. Decoding is certainly a very important component of the reading process, but there is obviously more to reading than that.

Good readers are good decoders (Perfetti, 1985). They recognize words almost twice as fast as poor readers do. Graesser, Hoffman, and Clark (1980), for instance, have estimated the reading time per word for poor adult readers to range from 198 to 227 ms, depending on the text, compared to 114 to 135 ms for good readers. Bisanz, Das, Varnhagen, and

Henderson (1992) obtained estimates ranging from 355 ms per word for poor fifth-grade readers to 170 ms for good seventh-grade readers. Rapid decoding is important because better word recognition frees up resources for higher-level processing (Perfetti's verbal efficiency hypothesis). Thus, better decoders build more accurate and complete representations of text content. Their decoding capabilities feed the growth of vocabulary, they know more word meanings, and they tend to have richer representations of individual word meanings.

However, slow decoders can use higher-order processes to compensate for their lack of decoding skills. Stanovich (1980) has shown that poor readers can use the sentence context to speed up their word recognition. Good readers, on the other hand, can recognize words rapidly and accurately either within a sentence context or without context; although context may speed their processing, they do not depend on it. Many studies investigating this phenomenon are summarized and discussed in Perfetti (1985, pp. 143ff): vocalization latency to words in context and in isolation, word identification latencies, predicting next word, and degrading of visual stimuli. A number of other studies are in agreement with these findings. Good readers, for example, fixate every word in a sentence, whereas poor readers show more irregular fixation patterns (Just & Carpenter, 1980). Therefore, good readers detect misspellings better than poor readers (McConkie & Zola, 1981). Note that poor readers, according to Perfetti, also are less able to exploit orthographic patterns in decoding when processing demands are high, even though they apparently do not lack knowledge of such structures.

Good decoding skills make good readers less dependent on discourse context in order to recognize a word, but certainly they are able to use contextual information when they need to, and furthermore they do so more effectively than poor readers. Frederiksen (1981) provided compelling evidence of this ability in comparing good and poor readers on a word recognition task. The target word was shown either without context or as the last word of a sentence. When the sentence made the target word highly predictable, both good and poor readers saved 125 ms in comparison to the context-free presentation. However, when the sentence context was only mildly constraining, poor readers could not take advantage of such a context, whereas good readers still showed a saving. Thus, good readers are not only better decoders but also better top-down processors.

9.1.2 Language skills

Most of the variance in reading times is taken up by the number of words, which is unfortunate because this factor overshadows everything else. It is not surprising that this is so because word recognition is executed more frequently in reading a sentence than anything else, and hence decoding must play a dominant role. However, other skills are involved in text comprehension in addition to word decoding, and they have been studied experimentally. These skills are those involved in constructing the kind of mental representations discussed in this book: figuring out the propositional elements of a text and organizing them into a coherent structure, including a macrostructure.

Lexical factors are obviously relevant. Just and Carpenter (1980) have shown that word frequency is related to reading speed in adults. Indeed, the very process of meaning construction for a word may be different in good and poor readers. Long, Oppy, and Seely (1994) observed that for both good and poor readers 300 ms after the presentation of a homonym lexical decision responses to context-appropriate associates of the homonym were faster than lexical decision responses to context-inappropriate associates. Thus, both good and poor readers were sensitive to the context of a word at this point. However, using a somewhat different procedure Gernsbacher and Faust (1991) and Gernsbacher, Varner, and Faust (1990) suggested that there were nevertheless important differences between good and poor readers in the way word meanings are constructed. Gernsbacher and her co-workers gave subjects sentences to read such as *He dug with the spade* versus *He dug with the shovel,* followed by a test word, such as *ace*. Subjects were asked to judge whether the test word matched the meaning of the sentence. Significant interference was observed for the test word right after reading the sentence by both good and bad readers. That is, both good and bad readers took longer to reject *ace* after reading the *spade* sentence than after reading the *shovel* sentence. After a 850-ms delay, poor readers still were slower to reject the test word *ace*, whereas there was no interference for good readers. Gernsbacher et al. (1990) argue that once the contextual meaning of a homonym is established, it suppresses the inappropriate meaning in good readers but not in poor readers. In terms of the CI model, this might mean that the integration process reduces the activation of contextually inappropriate associates of a homonym essentially to zero for good readers, whereas context only weakens (the Long et al. results) but does not fully suppress (the Gerns-bacher et al. results) such associations for less skilled readers. Further research is clearly needed to clarify these issues.

Efforts to determine the role of syntactic complexity in reading have not yielded uniform results. Graesser et al. (1980; also Haberlandt & Graesser, 1989) have used as a measure of syntactic complexity an aug-mented transition network analysis but without notable success. Simpler measures, such as the number of main and subordinate clauses per sen-tence, tend to be redundant with propositional analyses.

The number of propositions per sentence is indeed related to reading speed and recall. In an early study, Kintsch and Keenan (1973) observed an increase in reading times of 1 sec per proposition recalled. However, the effects of other potentially important variables were not partialled out in this study. When this is done, estimates of the additional reading time per proposition range from 191 to 238 ms for poor readers and 75 to 122 ms for good readers in the Graesser et al. (1980) experiment. Estimates obtained by Bisanz et al. (1992) for younger readers are consistent with these values: 166 ms per proposition for fifth-grade poor readers, down to 94 ms for seventh-grade good readers.

Of the skills that are important for the organization of the textbase, especially its macrostructure, the ones that have been studied most thor-oughly are the role of new propositional arguments in the coherence structure and the reader's use of causal relations in narratives. Kintsch et al. (1975) found longer reading times and poorer recall for paragraphs containing many new arguments than for paragraphs containing few new arguments. For short history and science paragraphs, subjects required on the average 1.6 s of reading time per proposition recalled when the paragraphs contained few new arguments, versus 2.5 s reading per proposition recalled when the paragraphs contained many new argu-ments. The overall level of recall was 75% for the paragraphs with few new arguments and 58% for those with many new arguments. In other words, subjects read at a fairly constant rate but recalled more from the paragraphs with few new arguments than from the paragraphs with many new arguments. Haberlandt et al. (1986) and others obtained similar results for reading times, and Bisanz et al. (1992) for recall.

A number of studies have pointed out the important role that causal links play in a text. For instance, Trabasso and van den Broek (1985) have shown that for both adults and children recall of a text unit is a function of the number of causal links connecting it with other text units. If stories are analyzed into units that fall on the primary causal chain of states, events, and actions that make up the story and dead-end units that are not located on this causal chain, units on the causal chain are recalled better than units off the chain (e.g., Omanson, 1982; Trabasso & van den Broek, 1985).

Bisanz et al. (1992) have shown that poor readers (fifth- and seventh-grade pupils) employ their causal knowledge in a compensatory manner. The more causal relations there were in a text, the faster poor readers could read it. In contrast, the number of causal relations had no effect on reading times for good readers. Thus, we have here another instance when readers are using a top-down process (causal inferences) to compensate for a weakness in other components of the reading process (they are slow at decoding, require more time to form propositions).

Bisanz et al. (1992) also make the interesting observation that different skills are related to reading times and recall. Specifically, reading time is primarily a function of the number of words and the number of propositions in a sentence, whereas recall is a function of the causal links in a text and the number of new arguments, both of which are important for the overall organization of the textbase.

Topic inferences by skilled and less skilled readers have also been investigated in the study by Long et al. (1994) already cited. Their experiment used a design like that of Till et al. (1988): At SOA intervals between 200 and 1,000 ms after reading a sentence, lexical decision responses were made to appropriate and inappropriate topic words. Response times to appropriate topic words were significantly faster than to inappropriate topic words at the 500 ms SOA for good readers, and an even larger difference was observed at the 750 ms SOA, but no differences in the lexical decision times for appropriate and inappropriate topic words were observed for poor readers, even after 1 s. It was not the case that poor readers could not infer the topic of these sentences, however, because when asked to provide topics for these sentences they performed just as well as skilled readers. Thus, they had the knowledge, but what was missing was the automatic retrieval structure necessary to make available this knowledge during normal reading. Referring back to Table 6.1, for good readers, the topic inference belonged to the inference category in cell A of that table (automatic retrieval of bridging information), whereas it fell into cell B (controlled search for bridging information) for poor readers. Or, expressed as a tautology, we might say that skilled readers were experts in this task and less skilled readers were not.

9.1.3 Domain knowledge

In addition to decoding and language skills, domain knowledge is the third factor that determines whether someone is a good reader. Readers with high domain knowledge tend to understand texts better and remember them better than readers with low domain knowledge. Domain knowledge may even compensate for other factors, such as low IQ, low verbal ability, or low reading ability. Recht and Leslie (1988) and Walker (1987) performed factorial experiments in which reading ability and domain knowledge – knowledge about baseball – were either high or low. Their subjects read a description of a baseball game and then answered memory and comprehension questions. Similarly, Schneider, Körkel, and Weinert (1989) designed a study comparing high and low IQ against high or low knowledge of soccer. In every case, readers with high domain knowledge outperformed readers with low domain knowledge, irrespective of their general ability. Thus, low IQ or low verbal ability could be fully compensated for by domain knowledge.

Three factors were varied in an experiment by Moravcsik and Kintsch (1993): (1) domain knowledge (high or low), (2) the way the text was written (good writing, well organized, vs. poor writing, disorganized), and (3) reading ability (high or low scores on the comprehension subtest of the Nelson-Denny Reading Test). Domain knowledge was manipulated in a different way in this study. Subjects read texts, such as the washing-machine paragraph from Bransford and Johnson (1972), that could easily be understood when given a title. The title allowed subjects to use their knowledge and to disambiguate the otherwise obscure text. Without the title, the texts were difficult to understand, because subjects could not interpret the situation as a familiar one. Hence, subjects could use their knowledge in the title condition but not in the no-title condition. The texts were either well written or poorly written. In the well-written versions, syntactic cues as well as the overall organization of the text allowed the reader to identify the significant elements of a text and their relationship to each other, even without knowing what was really going on. The poorly written texts provided no such cues to facilitate the construction of a textbase.

All three factors – knowledge, writing quality, and reading ability – significantly influenced the amount of reproductive recall (Figure 9.1). These effects were additive. There was no indication of an interaction and hence of compensation (see also Voss & Silfies, 1996). However, there was an interesting difference in the kind of mental representation subjects constructed in the different experimental conditions. Even though high skill and good writing enabled low-knowledge readers to form adequate textbases that were capable of supporting reproductive recall, these readers could not form correct situation models to support their elaborative recall.[1] Their elaborations tended to be wrong and fanciful. Only high-knowledge readers were capable of good elaborations. Figure 9.2 shows that inadequate situation models did not keep the subjects from elaborating but that their elaborations and inferences were erroneous, whereas the elaborations of readers who could use their knowledge to construct an adequate situation model were appropriate.

It is interesting to note the effects of writing quality in this study. All passages were written in two versions, preserving their content but vary-

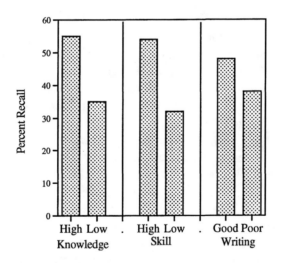

Figure 9.1   Reproductive recall: The mean number of propositions recalled as a function of knowledge, reading skill, and writing style. After Moravcsik and Kintsch (1993).

1   Elaborative recall is that portion of a recall protocol that is left over when verbatim or paraphrased reproductions of the text are deleted.

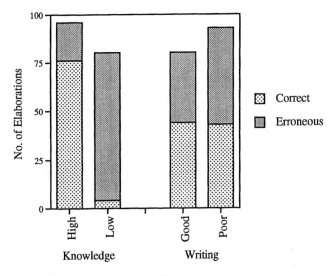

Figure 9.2   Reconstructive recall. Correct and erroneous elaborations and inferences as a function of knowledge and writing style. After Moravcsik and Kintsch (1993).

ing their style. In one version, the language was as helpful as we could make it in signaling discourse importance to the reader. The other version was as unhelpful as we could make it and still write an English text. Writing quality had a major effect on reproductive recall, facilitating reproduction about as much as domain knowledge did, but it did not help understanding. Whether or not a text was well written did not have a statistically significant effect on the proportion of erroneous elaborations. Thus, although good writing can help the reader to construct a better textbase that is sufficient for recall, it does not by itself guarantee the deeper understanding that is a prerequisite for learning.

   Just how low-ability students go about using their domain knowledge to achieve good comprehension results was investigated by Yekovich, Walker, Ogle, and Thompson (1990). One group of their subjects had high knowledge of football, and one had low knowledge. With texts that had nothing to do with football, the two groups performed equivalently. With a football text, the high-knowledge subjects outperformed the low-knowledge subjects, as in the other studies reported here. The questions on which the high-knowledge subjects showed the greatest advantage over low-knowledge subjects were inference questions and integrative summary statements. There was less of a difference on memory and detail questions. This is exactly what the theory of comprehension would lead one to expect. Even readers with little domain knowledge can understand information that is explicitly given in the text (though they might not remember it because their retrieval structures might not be rich enough). However, inferences and thematic integration that build retrieval structures require knowledge.

The study that most thoroughly investigates the relationship between reading skills and domain knowledge is one by Voss and Silfies (1996), who observed what students learned from history texts that were either causally explicit or not. They clearly identified two sets of relevant variables, one having to do with reading skills in general and one with knowledge of history. But Voss and Silfies are no longer concerned only with whether students are good readers; they also ask whether the students are good learners. The CI model provides the background for this shift in focus from text memory to learning, and that is where we turn next.

9.2 Learning and memory

There are important psychological differences between learning from a text and remembering the text. Text memory – that is, the ability to reproduce the text verbatim, in paraphrase, or by summarizing it – may be achieved on the basis of only superficial understanding. In the extreme case, one can learn to recite a text by rote without understanding it at all. Learning from text, on the other hand, requires deeper understanding. I define learning from text as the ability to use the information acquired from the text productively in novel environments. This requires that the text information be integrated with the reader's prior knowledge and become a part of it, so that it can support comprehension and problem solving in new situations. Mere text memory, on the other hand, may remain inert knowledge – reproducible given the right retrieval cues but not an active component of the reader's knowledge base.

This distinction is not always made in the literature. In the memory literature, for instance, one talks about a subject learning a list of paired associates or, synonymously, remembering it. On the other hand, there is an analogous distinction in the problem-solving literature, made especially by Wertheimer (1945), in differentiating superficial problem solving, which is only mechanical, from real problem solving, which involves deep understanding. The same difference exists in text comprehension. In most cases, deep understanding and mere memory for the words of a text are intermingled to various degrees, but there are experiments in the literature that represent fairly pure cases of one or the other extreme.

One is the well-known study of Bransford and Franks (1971), which can be characterized as all understanding and no memory. In this study, the texts consisted of four simple sentences, such as *The ants were in the kitchen. The ants ate the jelly,* and so on. These ideas could also be expressed in more complex sentences, such as *The ants in the kitchen ate the jelly.* Subjects were given several such texts, either in the form of four one-idea sentences, two two-idea sentences, one three-idea sentence, and one one-idea sentence, and other such combinations. Later, they were given a recognition test consisting of some sentences they had actually read and others they had not seen before. The results of the study were clear: Subjects remembered very well the stories they had read (e.g., they remembered the ants and the jelly and whatever else there was to that text) but did not know which particular sentences they had read. They remembered the meaning of each minitext, a scene, an image, perhaps – but not the way it had been presented verbally. The memory for the actual text they had read was wiped out by heavy interference (the subjects read many sentences, all very similar), but they had no trouble keeping in mind the few simple and distinct situation models they had formed for each of the several texts they had read.

Close to the other extreme – all memory and little understanding – is the study by Moravcsik and Kintsch (1993). Their readers had formed a good textbase but only a very sketchy or erroneous situation model. The subjects in the Bransford and Franks experiment had formed a good situation model but no textbase at all. Given the extreme simplicity and artificiality of the texts used by Bransford and Franks, it seems likely that their subjects merely combined what was in the text into an integrated scene to form a situation model.

9.2.1 *Textbase and situation model*

Because the distinction between textbase and situation model is important for the work discussed in this chapter, it is worth reviewing the main points here. First, it must be remembered that the textbase and the situation model are aspects of the same episodic memory trace of a text. We distinguish these aspects for the purposes of scientific analysis because this distinction is often useful in research as well as instruction.

1. Those elements or links in the mental representation that have a direct correspondence to elements in the text make up the textbase; to construct the textbase one needs syntactic, semantic, and (some, depending on how this is defined) pragmatic knowledge.

2. Texts usually describe real or imaginary situations in the world. The situation description that a comprehender constructs on the basis of a text as well as prior knowledge and experience is called the situation model.

3. In a totally complete, explicit text, a complete and adequate situation model is described. Thus, the textbase that tells it all is also a good situation model. Usually, however, texts are incomplete and rely on the comprehender to fill in gaps and make links to prior knowledge. This must be done on the basis of the comprehender's general knowledge – domain knowledge, knowledge of the world, and knowledge of the specific communicative situation. Therefore, in the general case, the situation model that a reader generates from a text is a mixture of text-derived (the textbase) and knowledge-derived elements. If the reader has no relevant background knowledge or does not employ it in understanding a text, the text representation will be dominated by the textbase. At the other extreme, if rich, relevant background knowledge is available and the text itself is poorly written and disorganized, the reader's knowledge elaborations may come to dominate the mental representation of the text, and a good situation model may be obtained at the expense of the textbase. Normally the two components, text-derived and knowledge-derived, are more balanced, resulting in a more or less complete textbase and a more or less adequate situation model.

4. The distinction between the micro- and macrostructure of a text is orthogonal to the textbase–situation model distinction. Microstructure refers to local text properties, macrostructure to the global organization of text. Either may be directly cued by the text or constructed on the basis of the comprehender's knowledge (e.g., by using a schema to organize a text whose macrostructure is not made explicit in the text, or by adding some detail to the text representation that would be expected on

the basis of the comprehender's knowledge but was not actually stated in the text).

5. A third distinction that must be kept in mind is how complete and good each one of these structures is. One may have a poor textbase (either at the micro- or macrolevel), perhaps because the text is poorly written or perhaps because the comprehender did not encode properly what was there. One may have a poor situation model, perhaps because the comprehender lacked the required knowledge, perhaps because he or she failed to apply it. A poor textbase may be combined with a poor situation model but may also be associated with a good situation model (as was shown in Figure 4.1 earlier).

6. As long as one tests for information that is directly given in the text, one is measuring textbases. For instance, in many laboratory experiments recall is almost purely reproductive, as are summaries. They may involve some semantic knowledge, as in generalizing a concept, but that still remains at the textbase level. Recall and summaries are not always reproductive, of course, and can be perfectly good indicators of well-developed situation models, when and if they go beyond the text.

As soon as one tests for things not directly in the text, one is testing for aspects of the situation model. Inference questions and sorting tasks are obvious examples. In some cases, recall or summaries may also function as situation model measures to the extent that they go beyond reproduction.

7. Bridging inferences often involve merely semantic information; one does not need a situation model construct for that case. They may, however, involve more than that in some texts. Often a comprehender needs a good model of the situation under discussion in order to make some of the bridging inferences required by the text.

9.2.2 Learning

Situation models not only integrate the text but integrate the text with the reader's knowledge. An example from Kintsch (1994c) makes this clear. In Figure 9.3 a brief text is shown, together with its propositional textbase and a situation model in the form of a graph. The textbase consists of three complex propositions linked by sentence connectives. The situation model consists of an image (shown here as a graph), plus back-

Text

When a baby has a septal defect, the blood cannot get rid of enough carbon dioxide through the lungs. Therefore, it looks purple.

Textbase and Situation Model:

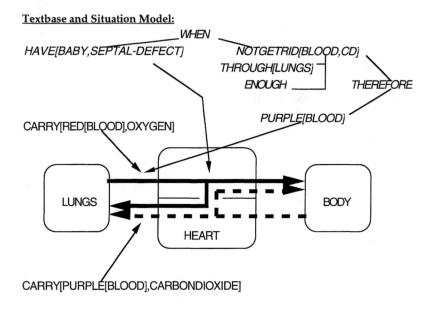

Figure 9.3   A text, its textbase, and situation model. The textbase is printed in italics and is linked to prior knowledge, forming a situation model. After Kintsch (1994c).

ground information about the role of some of the components of the image. It is mostly based on the reader's knowledge about the circulatory system, rather than on the text directly. Only the fact that there is a gap in the septal wall so that purple blood gets mixed with the red blood is derived from the text itself.

I do not claim that every reader will construct exactly this textbase and situation model. There may be some variation in the textbase (e.g., some readers probably will not encode the modifier ENOUGH). And there will certainly be even more variation in the situation model; not every reader will employ imagery. Some readers may form an even more sketchy model (or even none at all); others a much more elaborated one. Some readers will undoubtedly get some of the model wrong.

Text memory may be reproductive (e.g., the subject retrieves the textbase that has been formed and reproduces it), or it may be reconstructive (e.g., the subject retrieves the situation model that has been formed and reconstructs the text on this basis). Obviously, the two cases are not mutually exclusive. Learning from text, according to the definition given earlier, requires the formation of a situation model. Thus, the subject has learned something from the text in Figure 9.3 if the septal gap is added to the reader's knowledge about how the blood circulates in the heart.

9.3 The measurement of learning

To be useful in research, the theoretical distinction between learning from a text and memory for a text requires empirical methods to assess learning separately from memory. However, because learning and memory cannot be separated cleanly even in the theory (textbase and situation model are not two separate structures, but the text-derived and knowledge-derived components of a single structure, as in Figure 9.3), measurement procedures are not precisely separable into textbase and situation model measures, either. Instead, empirical measures reflect one or the other aspect of the structure to a stronger degree. Thus, one can ask questions that demand a specific detail from the text – or that require the integration of textual information and prior knowledge – in order to solve a new problem. Even recall reflects both aspects: the textbase to the extent that the recall is reproductive, and the situation model to the extent that it is reconstructive. Usually, recall is a mixture of the two, but in some cases it is primarily one or the other.

Text memory is measured in the conventional way, as described in the previous chapter: through free recall, cued recall, summarization, various types of recognition tests, and text-based questions. Different methods are needed, however, for the measurement of learning. Psychology shares the need for such measures with AI, insofar as AI is interested in the construction of knowledge-rich expert systems (e.g., Olson & Biolsi, 1991), and with education, where the assessment of learning is of obvious importance. Education and AI have relied for the most part on direct methods for knowledge assessment, that is, various forms of question asking. That is still by far the most widely used method in psychology too, although more indirect scaling methods have also been developed for purposes of psychological research.

Asking questions as a method for the assessment of knowledge is fraught with problems. Developers of expert systems rely on this method almost exclusively, but it is difficult to determine the correctness or completeness of the answers that are elicited. Educationally, the problem is that asking questions is artificial and sometimes yields invalid results. It is an unnatural act when a teacher asks a student for something the teacher knows better than the student. Furthermore, the answers that the students give may indicate much else besides real learning. Students may acquire specific strategies that allow them to generate acceptable answers without having deeper understanding. Or questions may be answered correctly or wrongly for various accidental reasons that have nothing to do with the students' understanding. These problems are widely appreciated but not easily avoided.

Asking questions to assess knowledge for scientific purposes is limited in its effectiveness because we do not have a detailed theory of question answering. As long as it is not known just what psychological processes and what knowledge are involved in answering a particular question, we simply do not have a reliable way of constructing the right questions for our purposes. Psychologists, like teachers, must and do rely on their intuition, which sometimes yields satisfactory results and sometimes does not. It is not surprising, therefore, that psychologists have looked for alternative and more objective ways of assessing knowledge. In particular, various scaling methods have been developed for the indirect assessment of knowledge.

Scaling methods require a set of key words or phrases that are characteristic of a certain knowledge domain. (One can ask experts for such words, or use more objective methods, such as frequency counts of technical terms in relevant scientific publications.) The knowledge of a subject is inferred from the way the subject organizes these key words. If the structure generated by the subject resembles the structure generated by domain experts, we infer that the subject's knowledge organization is similar to that of the experts. To the extent that the subject structures the set of key words in ways that differ from the experts, a lack of correct domain knowledge is revealed.

The basic technique for finding out how a subject organizes a set of key words is to ask the subject for relatedness judgments between all pairs of key words in the set. A similarity matrix between all keywords is thus obtained, showing the rated closeness between all word pairs. Such a matrix can then be used as the basis for multidimensional scaling (e.g., Bisanz, LaPorte, Vesonder, & Voss, 1978; Henley, 1969; Stanners, Price, & Painton, 1982). A low-dimensional space is generated in which the key words are embedded. One can then ask whether the space is the same for the students as for the experts, and whether the location of the key words in this space is similar for students and experts. This method has been used successfully a number of times. For instance, the semantic field of animal names has been scaled in this way, yielding a space with the two dimensions of size and ferocity, which account for 59% of the variance of the paired-comparison judgments (Henley, 1969).

However, these scaling methods are of limited usefulness. The pairwise comparison method is laborious for the subject and rapidly becomes impossible to use as the number of keywords increases. Furthermore, multidimensional scaling methods work with group data, but we often need to work with data from individual subjects. Most important, however, it has become apparent that very few knowledge domains (other than animal names) are regular and simple enough to be described by a space of a few namable dimensions.

A more practical method for indirect knowledge assessment has been developed by Ferstl and Kintsch (in press). It applies to the problem of measuring the amount of learning that occurs from reading a text. If the text has an effect on the reader's memory and knowledge, it should change the way the reader organizes a knowledge domain, and the change should be in the direction of the text organization. Thus, we assess a reader's knowledge about a particular domain, have the reader study a related text, and reassess the reader's knowledge organization to see whether it has changed in accordance with the text organization.

Ferstl and Kintsch chose a knowledge domain that is quite rich for most subjects and fairly stereotyped: the birthday party. We then wrote a story about a somewhat weird birthday party, designed to distort our readers' conventional birthday party schema. We assessed this particular schema both before and after reading the story. The question we were concerned with was whether the story had an effect on the way subjects organized the birthday party domain, whether this effect could be attributed to reading the story, and whether we could measure this effect with our procedures.

We selected a set of 30 key words characteristic of the birthday party domain from free associations subjects gave to the stimulus word *birthday party*. To these we added 30 words that were important in the story we had written about a birthday party but that were not otherwise associated with birthday party (such as *clown, credit card*). It is, of course, impossible to do pairwise comparisons with such a large set of keywords. Instead, we used two less demanding methods to obtain relatedness matrices from our subjects. One was a sorting task for which we gave each subject a stack of 60 index cards, each printed with one of the key words, and asked them to sort these cards into piles according to relatedness. We made sure that the subjects understood that there was no right or wrong way of sorting, that we were interested only in their intuitions about which of these words were related to each other. Thirty-two subjects performed this sorting task, and from their results a relatedness matrix was constructed, showing for each word pair how many times it had been sorted together into the same group.

The other method we used was cued association. The subjects were asked to read silently through the list of key words twice (to familiarize themselves with this word set), and then they were asked to generate up to three associations to each keyword. No restrictions were placed on the associations subjects generated, but because most of our keywords were associated with the birthday party theme and because subjects were primed by having just read these words, most of the associations they generated were actually from our set of key words. Thus, the number of times a key word was given as a response to another key word could be used as a measure of relatedness between the two words. Notice that the relatedness matrix generated in this way is asymmetric, whereas the matrix generated from the sorting data is necessarily symmetric.

Two analyses were performed on these relatedness matrices, a hierarchical clustering analysis after Johnson (1967) and a Pathfinder analysis after Schvaneveldt (1990). The former is particularly suited for symmetric relatedness matrices, the latter for asymmetric matrices. The results of the clustering analysis of the sorting data prior to reading are shown in Figure 9.4. The results of the Pathfinder analysis of the cued association data prior to reading are shown in Figure 9.5.

Figure 9.4 shows that the sorting procedure and cluster analysis yields readily interpretable results. The key words are neatly organized by cate-

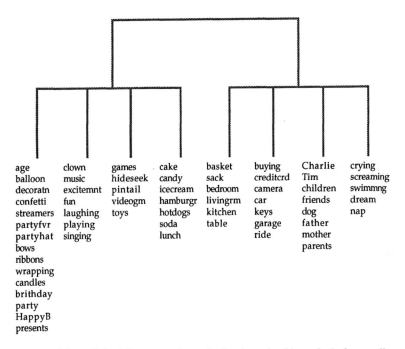

age   clown   games   cake   basket   buying   Charlie   crying
balloon   music   hideseek   candy   sack   creditcrd Tim   screaming
decoratn   excitemnt pintail   icecream   bedroom   camera   children   swimmng
confetti   fun   videogm   hamburgr   livingrm   car   friends   dream
streamers laughing   toys   hotdogs   kitchen   keys   dog   nap
partyfvr   playing   soda   table   garage   father
partyhat   singing   lunch   ride   mother
bows   parents
ribbons
wrapping
candles
brithday
party
HappyB
presents

Figure 9.4   The two top layers in the clustering hierarchy before reading based on sorting data. Only the two top layers are shown; long words and compounds are abbreviated. After Ferstl and Kintsch (in press).

gory membership. Indeed, the results are almost too neat, suggesting that subjects performed some sort of semantic analysis when sorting the key words. We have previously argued (Walker & Kintsch, 1985) that the sorting task produces results that are a bit too orderly and logical and do not necessarily reflect the memory structures that are operative in memory retrieval. In comparison, the structure derived from the cued association data (Figure 9.5) is much richer. It still shows much the same clusters as Figure 9.4, but there is a complex, rich pattern of interconnections evident that Figure 9.4 lacks. My guess is that the cued association data more accurately reflect knowledge organization than the less spontaneous sorting data do, but whether or not this is so would have to be established empirically.

If Figures 9.4 and 9.5 represent our subjects' birthday party schema,

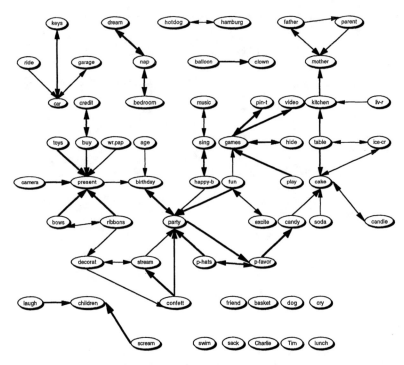

Figure 9.5   Part of the Pathfinder structure based on the cued association data. Only the links that were present both before and after reading are shown. Heavy lines indicate links that were stronger after reading, and thin lines indicate links that were stronger before reading. After Ferstl and Kintsch (in press).

how did this structure change after they read the birthday party story? One obvious way to answer this question is to have subjects re-sort the key words after reading the story, or ask them again for their cued associations, and construct from the resulting data postreading structures to be compared with Figures 9.4 and 9.5. Ferstl and Kintsch showed that it is indeed possible to see how these structures changed as a result of reading and argue that the changes that have taken place can be attributed to the new relations among the key words that were established by the story the subjects had read. However, this is a bit like interpreting inkblots, and there is certainly a danger of reading more into the data in accord with one's expectations than the facts warrant.

Fortunately, objective measures of change can be devised that have the advantage that they are not restricted to group data but can be computed for individual subjects, hence making standard statistical hypothesis testing procedures available. The strength with which two concepts are linked in a text can be determined from the propositional structure of the text. If the concepts belong to the same propositions, they are strongly linked; if they belong to different propositions, they are linked to the degree that these propositions are related in the textbase. Thus, the number of links that must be traversed from a proposition containing one concept to reach a proposition containing the other concept provides a convenient metric for the relatedness of concepts in the text structure. It is therefore possible to determine the extent to which the associations a subject gives coincide with the text structure. Figure 9.6 shows the proportion of associations subjects gave in the Ferstl and Kintsch experiment that coincide with text links before they read the text, immediately after reading the text, and one week after reading. Because a percentage value can be computed for each subject, these values can be analyzed statistically. In this case, we can conclude that the proportion of associations coinciding with text links is significantly higher after reading than before

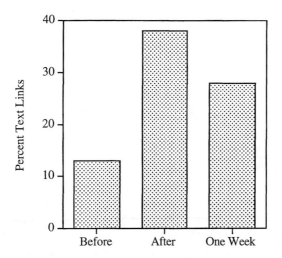

Figure 9.6   The percentage of associations before reading, immediately after reading, and one week after reading that coincide with text links. After Ferstl and Kintsch (in press).

reading the text, both immediately after reading and one week later. However, the proportion after one week is significantly lower than the proportion immediately after reading.

The story subjects read thus clearly influenced the pattern of associations they produced. Was their knowledge changed thereby, or was what we see in Figure 9.6 merely due to the influence of the episodic text representation they had formed? We don't know this, but if episodic memory and knowledge are all part of the same dynamic network, this is not a question we necessarily have to answer. Our subjects had learned something new that changed the way they thought about birthday parties, more strongly right after they read the story than a week later, but even then some change could still be documented.

The measurement of learning from text, as distinct from text memory, is probably best approached through a combination of direct and indirect procedures: questions that require inferencing and problem solving on the one hand and scaling methods based on sorting or association tasks, as in Ferstl and Kintsch (in press), on the other. Both approaches have their limitations, so it is important to obtain results with different methods that confirm each other. The experiments discussed in the next section demonstrate the practicality of this approach.

9.4 A simulation of learning with the CI model

In what way is learning from a text different, in terms of the construction-integration model, from text memory, which was investigated in chapter 8? I have discussed this question in Kintsch (1994c) and have provided a simulation to illustrate the crucial differences. It is assumed that the goal of learning is to form a situation model that integrates the textual information with prior knowledge, as in Figure 9.3, not merely the formation of a textbase. Thus, any simulation of learning from text must explicitly include a knowledge component.

In Kintsch (1994c) this was done by first assessing a subject's knowledge about a particular domain (heart disease) by means of a large set of questions. The questions that were answered correctly were used to construct a knowledge map for each subject. Figure 9.7a shows an example of such a knowledge map for a high-knowledge subject. All questions that were correctly answered are turned into statements and expressed as

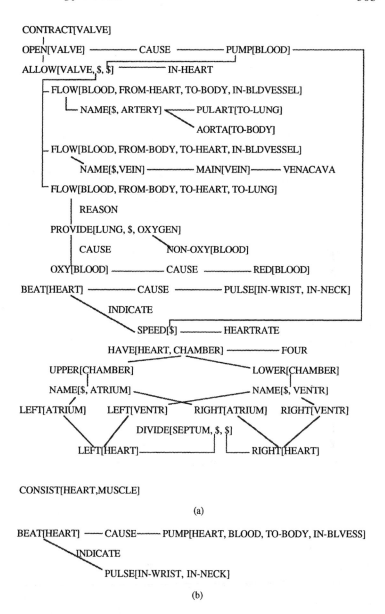

Figure 9.7 Knowledge maps for (a) a high–knowledge subject and (b) a low–knowledge subject. After Kintsch (1994c).

propositions. Links are drawn between core propositions and their modifiers, and whenever propositions are linked by a specific semantic relation (like CAUSE, or CONSEQUENCE), or when one proposition is embedded as an argument of another proposition. An inspection of Figure 9.7a shows that this subject knew quite a bit about the heart and that his understanding about the functioning of the heart was basically correct. Compare this with the skimpy knowledge map also shown in Figure 9.7b for a low-knowledge subject.

Two separate processing simulations of a text about heart disease (not shown here) were performed, one for the high- and one for the low-knowledge reader. The assumption was made that whenever a concept occurred in the text, it retrieved all the knowledge the reader had about this concept. Thus, the phrase *the heart supplies blood to the body* retrieved PUMP[HEART,BLOOD] for the low-knowledge subject, and FLOW [BLOOD, FROM-HEART,TO-BODY] for the high-knowledge subject. *Valve* retrieved ALLOW[VALVE,PUMP[BLOOD], FLOW [BLOOD, FROM-HEART,TO-BODY]] for the high-knowledge subject and nothing for the low-knowledge subject, and so on. In this manner 15 nodes from the knowledge map for the high-knowledge subject and one node from the knowledge map of the low-knowledge subject (the nodes printed in boldface in Figure 9.7) were added to the simulation at the appropriate points. It is not necessarily the case that every bit of knowledge a reader knows that is relevant to a certain text is actually retrieved when processing this text, but for present purposes this is a reasonable simplifying assumption.

For the simulation, working memory was set to five atomic propositions. Hence, the model reads the proposition(s) from the first sentence, goes on to the next sentence, and continues until it has read at least five elements. The model then retrieves from its knowledge base (the maps shown in Figure 9.7) any related information and adds these elements to the network. The network in working memory is then integrated. The most strongly activated proposition in each processing cycle is carried over to the next processing cycle in the short-term memory buffer.

The results of the simulation (not shown here) were not very different for high- and low-knowledge subjects so far as text propositions are concerned. The pattern of activation is similar, and the average activation strengths are about the same. However, there are two important differences. First, because 15 knowledge nodes were combined with the text structure for the high-knowledge subject but only one for the low-knowledge subject, the text representation generated by the high-knowledge subject is solidly anchored to the subjects' prior knowledge. This is not the case for the low-knowledge subject. Second, the prior knowledge that has become incorporated into the text representation for the high-knowledge subject bridges some coherence gaps in the textbase of the low-knowledge subject. Where the text is coherent, the textbase for the low-knowledge subject is also coherent, but where there is a gap in the text, requiring special knowledge for a bridging inference, the textbase lacks coherence. This is not the case for the high-knowledge reader, where gaps in the text can be bridged by prior knowledge.

What empirical predictions do these simulations imply? Behaviors that depend mostly on the textbase, such as questions about facts explicitly stated in the text, should not differ much for high- and low-knowledge subjects. High-knowledge subjects, however, should be better on questions requiring inferences or problem-solving tasks. The predictions for free recall are somewhat ambiguous. The reproductive component should be about equal for high- and low-knowledge readers, especially for a text that does not require many bridging inferences, but the former readers could successfully reconstruct portions of the text on the basis of their deeper understanding of the situation and hence end up with higher recall scores overall.

Predictions for the sorting task are illustrated in Figure 9.8. Consider how subjects with different knowledge would sort the four key words *oxygen*, *purple*, *septal defect*, and *brain defect* before reading the text on heart disease. A subject who knows nothing about septal defects would put the two defects together and sort the remaining two words into separate categories. A more knowledgeable reader, on the other hand, should sort the first three words together and use a separate category for *brain defect*. Figure 9.8 shows that the simulation makes just these predictions. The figure shows a segment of the mental representation constructed by the high-knowledge reader, together with the four key words. An inspection of the figure shows that there exist pathways with strong links between *oxygen*, *purple*, and *septal defect*, which therefore would tend to be sorted together, whereas *brain defect* is only weakly linked to *septal defect*. The predictions are quite different for the low-knowledge reader, however. The low-knowledge reader's text representation is the same as that of the high-knowledge reader, except that it lacks the knowledge component (all the

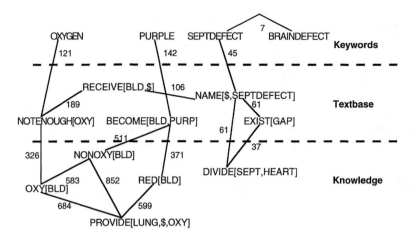

Figure 9.8   Network formed by four key words from the sorting task, related text propositions from reading, and related knowledge items. The numbers refer to the memory strengths of the links. After Kintsch (1994c).

nodes below the lower dashed line in Figure 9.8). It is easy to see that in this case there are no pathways linking *purple* with any of the other words. Hence, after reading the text a low-knowledge subject should keep *purple* separate in sorting these four key words but group *oxygen* and *septal defect,* which are linked together on the basis of the text alone. A low-knowledge subject who had not read the text would group the two defects only on the basis of their preexperimental association.

The most important predictions that can be derived from the simulation described concern learning from text, that is, the usability of the textual information in novel situations, which should be fairly high for the high-knowledge subject. According to the simulation, there are 12 entry points that allow access to the textual information from the reader's knowledge base – the items in boldface type in Figure 9.7 that form links between the text representation and background knowledge. Thus, even at a time after reading when the contextual and temporal cues no longer permit retrieval of the episodic text structure, it remains still accessible via the reader's general knowledge. Indeed, it has become a part of it and ceased to exist effectively as a separate episodic memory structure. Learning has occurred. With only one reading, the links may be too weak to permit reliable retrieval at a later date – typically one does not learn much from a single reading – but they could be strengthened through further study. The high-knowledge reader of our simulation is on the way to learning something he or she did not know before about the heart.

This is not the case for the low-knowledge reader, who in the simulation forms much the same text structure as does the high-knowledge reader, except that it is only very weakly linked to his knowledge base. This reader has stored in his memory the same information as the high-knowledge fellow student, but the only way to retrieve it is through the contextual and temporal retrieval cues associated with the episodic text memory. It is thus inert knowledge – the student knows something but cannot spontaneously make use of this knowledge in novel tasks because what is known is not tied in with the rest of his knowledge. The information may be retrievable given a retrieval cue such as "Think of the chapter on heart disease that you read here the other day," but once such episodic retrieval is no longer effective, the text information is lost.

9.5 Using coherent text to improve learning

According to the simulation described in the previous section, learning from text requires that the learner construct a coherent mental representation of the text, and that this representation be anchored in the learner's background knowledge. Thus, one reason students might fail to learn something from reading a text could be that they are unable to form a coherent textbase linked to their pre-knowledge.

It is easy to see why this might be the case for low-knowledge readers. Not all links either within a text or between the text and the readers' knowledge are always spelled out in a text but are often left for the reader to fill in, for example, as *bridging inferences*. This is fine and, as we shall see in the next section of this chapter, can be quite advantageous, but it often creates problems for low-knowledge readers. If readers simply do not have the necessary background knowledge to fill in the gaps in the text that an author has left, they will be unable to form a coherent representation of the text or to link it with whatever little they do know. Consider some trivial examples.

(1) The heart is connected to the arteries. The blood in the aorta is red.

For a reader who does not know what the relationship between *arteries* and *aorta* is, there will be a coherence problem. Or consider

(2)   To stop the North Vietnamese aggressors, the Pentagon decided to bomb Hanoi.

which may present all kinds of problems to a low-knowledge reader. Namely, what is the *Pentagon* and how does *Hanoi* get into this sentence? A little rewriting of these problem texts to make the relations between items in the text or between general knowledge and the text fully explicit can avoid these problems. Thus, we might define *aorta* for a low-knowledge reader by rewriting (1) as

(1a)   The heart is connected to the arteries. The blood in the aorta, the artery that carries blood from the heart to the body, is red.

And we can help with (2) by inserting explicit links between the unknown terms and what a reader might be expected to know.

(2a)   To stop the North Vietnamese aggressors, the U.S. Defense Department in the Pentagon decided to bomb Hanoi, the capital of North Vietnam.

So far we have considered only local coherence problems, but the global coherence of a text can often also be made more explicit. The macrostructure of a text is not always explicitly signaled in the text but is left for the reader to deduce. This is fine for knowledgeable readers but can be a major source of confusion when the requisite background knowledge is lacking. Thus, most of us need no help to understand the structure of a four-paragraph text, each describing the anatomical details of one of the chambers of the heart. However, for a reader who does not know that the heart has four chambers, a title like *The four chambers of the heart,* plus appropriate subtitles or clearly marked topic sentences for each paragraph, can be of great help.

Such relatively minor revisions of texts that ensure coherence at both the local and global levels facilitates text memory as well as learning for readers who lack background knowledge. Figure 9.9 summarizes the results of three studies in which the effectiveness of such revisions were explored.

Beyer (1990) used a computer manual as his learning material. He

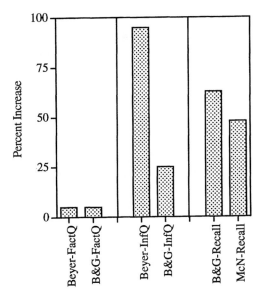

Figure 9.9 The effectiveness of text revisions in the experiments of Beyer (1990), Britton and Gulgoz (1991), and McNamara, Kintsch, Singer, and Kintsch (1996, Exp. 1). To make the data comparable, the improvement in performance after reading the revised text is expressed as a percentage of the performance with the original text.

revised the original manual by making its macrostructure explicit by means of titles and subheadings and by improving the comprehensibility of the instructions contained in the manual with illustrative examples. The revised text proved to be significantly better than the original version, but the improvement was restricted to problem-solving tasks. When questions were asked about facts that were explicitly stated in the text, the original text and the revised text yielded about equal performance. However, the students learned better with the revised text, as measured by their performance on inference questions (Figure 9.9).

A more systematic approach to filling in the local coherence gaps in a text was employed by Britton and Gulgoz (1991), who used a history text as their learning material that described the U.S. air war in Vietnam. The text was written at the time of the war and presumed considerable prior knowledge on the part of the reader – knowledge that at the time was probably readily available among the population to which the text was addressed. Many years after the war, the people who participated in Britton and Gulgoz's study had very little specific information about the war and hence found the text hard going. Although they were able to recall quite a bit from the text and answered more than half of the fact questions correctly, their performance was poor on the inference questions. In fact, they really did not understand the text at all. This conclusion follows from an analysis of the conceptual understanding of the situation as it was assessed by a key word comparison task.

Britton and Gulgoz (1991) selected 12 key words that were of crucial importance for the understanding of the text and had students give pairwise relatedness judgments for these key words. They also had the original author of the text plus several other experts on the Vietnam war provide relatedness judgments for the same set of key words. The author and experts agreed quite well among themselves (average intercorrelation $r = .80$). But the students who had obtained their information from reading the text did not agree with the author or the experts at all (average $r = .08$). Their understanding of the air war in Vietnam on the basis of reading this text was quite different from the one the author had intended (and which the experts achieved from reading the same text). Thus, even though the students recalled a good part of the text and answered questions about it reasonably well, they really did not understand what they were saying! Britton and Gulgoz also report a Pathfinder analysis of the key word judgment data that makes clear some of the fundamental misconceptions of these readers. For instance, whereas the text emphasized the failure of the operation *Rolling Thunder,* in the students' judgments *Rolling Thunder* was linked to *success,* instead. Britton likens this result to reading the Bible and concluding that the devil was the good guy.

This dismal performance could be significantly improved by some rather simple revisions of the original text to make it understandable to readers without adequate background knowledge. Britton and Gulgoz (1991) used the Miller and Kintsch (1980) simulation program to locate all coherence gaps in their original text. Whenever that program encounters a coherence gap (no argument overlap between propositions), it stops and asks the operator to supply a bridging inference. For instance, if in one sentence *North Vietnam* is mentioned, and the next sentence begins with *In response to the American threats, Hanoi decided,* Britton and Gulgoz might have made this sentence pair coherent by adding to the second sentence the *North Vietnamese government in Hanoi decided.* These revisions were highly effective. Recall increased significantly, as did the performance on inference questions. The improvement on fact questions was not significant, as in Beyer's experiment (Figure 9.9). Most important, however, readers now understood the text more or less correctly. Their relatedness judgments after reading the revised text correlate reasonably well with those of the experts (r = .52), and if one looks at the structure of their judgments as revealed by a Pathfinder analysis (not shown here), no glaring misunderstandings are apparent, as was the case for the readers of the original version of the text. Hence, making this text locally coherent by filling in the gaps that required bridging inferences yielded a text that readers could understand, even though their background knowledge was lacking.

A third experiment comparing the effectiveness of revising a text for greater coherence has been reported by McNamara, E. Kintsch, Songer, & W. Kintsch (exp. 1, 1996). In this study, the subjects were students in grades seven through nine. As learning material, we used a junior high biology text describing characteristics of mammals. The text was 1.5 pages long and was well written from the standpoint of local coherence, so that there were no local coherence gaps that had to be filled in the revision. However, the text had a listlike macrostructure that was not clearly signaled, and the paragraph structure did not always correspond to the subtopic structure of the text. Hence, revising the text amounted to adding material that explicitly identified the major subtopics as traits of mammals and reorganizing the paragraphs so that they corresponded to the subtopic structure. Subjects were given a prior knowledge questionnaire, after which they read either the revised or the original text at their own rate. They then were given a recall test, a postreading questionnaire, and a sorting test. For the latter, subjects were given 16 key phrases to sort, which could be sorted in multiple ways. Eleven of these key phrases were characteristics of mammals (e.g., *has hair or fur*) and five were non-mammalian traits (e.g., *is cold blooded*). We were interested in learning whether reading the text on mammalian traits increased the subjects' tendency to use "mammalian" as a sorting criterion.

The recall data replicate Britton and Gulgoz (1991), in that subjects recalled the revised text significantly better than the original text (Figure 9.8). Further analysis showed that this improvement was mainly a consequence of the better recall of macropropositions in the revised text, which would be expected, because the revision involved primarily the macrostructure of the text.

An indication that the way our subjects thought about this knowledge domain was indeed influenced by reading the text – and evidence that this influence was more pronounced for the revised text – could be obtained from an analysis of the sorting data. Each subject sorted mammalian traits together with some likelihood before reading the text on mammals. From these data, change scores could be computed. These change scores reveal an increase of 23% in mammal groupings after subjects read the revised text, compared with only a 10% increase for the original text. In addition, there was a corresponding decrease in the tendency to combine mammal characteristics with nonmammal characteristics (–1% for the original text, –7% for the revised text). Thus, subjects were more likely to employ "mammal" as a sorting criterion after reading, and especially after reading the revised text.

Several other studies confirm and extend these results. Beck, McKeown, Sinatra, and Loxterman (1991), working with fourth- and fifth-grade students who studied a text about the American Revolutionary War, significantly improved performance on open-ended questions and recall by adding explanatory coherence to the text, especially emphasizing causal relations. Similarly, McKeown, Beck, Sinatra, and Loxterman (1992) manipulated prior knowledge by means of a 35-minute instructional unit and text coherence (original and revised text) with fifth-grade students. Recall and open-ended questions both improved by coherent texts more than by knowledge alone, but the effects of the two factors were cumulative. The authors suggest that background knowledge alone was not sufficient to compensate for the poorly written text. Both prior knowledge and a coherent text were necessary to construct a good text representation.

Revising a text for coherence is thus clearly an effective technique to further understanding and learning. Students without adequate background knowledge cannot fill in gaps in the text on their own that readers with greater familiarity with the domain bridge effortlessly and in fact unconsciously. For such readers without background knowledge, providing explicit bridging material in the text, at both the local and global level, is a prerequisite for understanding and learning.

If this is so, why do authors ever leave gaps in their texts? Why do we not write fully coherent, explicit texts all the time? The answer is that to write such a text is an elusive goal; a writer must always rely on the reader's knowledge to some degree. There is no text comprehension that does not require the reader to apply knowledge: lexical knowledge, syntactic and semantic knowledge, domain knowledge, personal experience, and so on. The printed words on the page or the sound waves in the air are but one source of constraints that must be satisfied. The reader's knowledge provides the other. Ideally, a text should contain the new information a reader needs to know, plus just enough old information to allow the reader to link the new information with what is already known. Texts that contain too much that the reader already knows are boring to read and, indeed, confusing (e.g., legal and insurance documents that leave nothing to be taken for granted). Hence, too much coherence and explication may not necessarily be a good thing.

9.6 Improving learning by stimulating active processing

McNamara et al. (1996) conducted a second experiment that explores the contention that if readers possess adequate knowledge, a fully explicit text is not optimal for them. Such readers remember more and learn better from texts that require them to assume a more active role in comprehension. Specifically, we hypothesized that the results obtained by Beyer, Britton, and Gulgoz, and in our experiment 1, which were described in the previous section, pertain to low-knowledge readers. Readers with good domain knowledge might react in very different ways.

As the learning material for our experiment, we chose an encyclopedia article at the junior-high level on heart disease. We assumed that there would be a great deal of variability in background knowledge among junior-high students in this area, so that we could meaningfully distinguish between high- and low-knowledge students. We rewrote this text in several ways, only two of which concern us here. In one case we attempted to produce a text that was maximally coherent and explicit at both the local and global level. For this purpose, we replaced potentially ambiguous pronouns with full noun phrases, added elaborations that linked unfamiliar concepts to familiar ones, added sentence connectives whenever possible, and made sure that the same concept was always referred to in the same way (rather than by a synonym or paraphrase). In addition, we added titles and subtitles to indicate the macrostructure of the text, as well as explicit macropropositions to mark the role of each paragraph in the text. The resulting version was our high-coherence text. The low-coherence version was constructed by deleting all these signals but not otherwise changing the content of the text. Of course, the high-coherence text was quite a bit longer (1,053 words) than the low-coherence text (683 words).

The prior knowledge of our subjects was assessed by a knowledge assessment test consisting of a series of questions on the basic anatomy and functioning of the heart and a recognition test in which subjects were asked to match parts of the heart to a diagram showing a cross-section of the heart and its major blood vessels.

After taking this test, subjects read either the high- or the low-coherence text twice, and then responded to a series of posttests. First they were asked to recall the text in their own words. Then they were given 41 questions of four types: (1) text-based questions, (2) elaboration questions that required relating text information to the reader's background knowledge, (3) bridging inference questions that required connecting two or more separate text segments, and (4) problem-solving questions that required applying text information in a novel situation. Finally, subjects performed a sorting task consisting of 18 keywords, some from the text and others not, that could be grouped in various ways, but for which there existed only a single text-driven sorting principle.

The results of this study reveal a strong interaction between the level of prior knowledge of the students, the coherence of the text, and the method of testing. High-knowledge students always perform better than low-knowledge students do. But when tests are used that assess primarily text memory, the high-coherence text is better for all types of students. This is shown in Figure 9.10 for free recall and in Figure 9.11 for text-based questions. However, when tests are used that depend on the construction of a good situation model, the low-coherence text actually yields better results for high-knowledge subjects than the high-coherence text does. For low-knowledge subjects, the usual superiority of the high-coherence version over the low-coherence version is observed. Figure 9.12 shows this interaction for the problem-solving questions and Figure 9.13 for the sorting task. As mentioned before, the sorting task admitted to several rational groupings of the key words. Figure 9.13 shows the extent to which subjects changed from whatever grouping they employed before reading the text to a sorting principle that corresponded to the text. That score was close to zero for the low-knowledge subjects reading

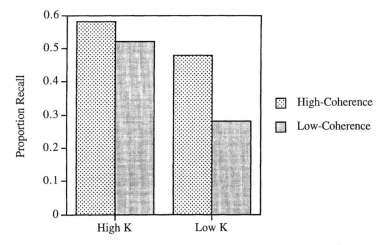

Figure 9.10   Proportion of text propositions recalled as a function of prior knowledge for high- and low-coherence texts. After McNamara et al. (1996).

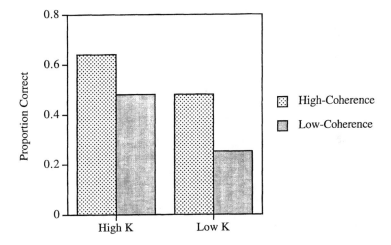

Figure 9.11   Proportion correct for text-based questions as a function of prior knowledge for high- and low-coherence texts. After McNamara et al. (1996).

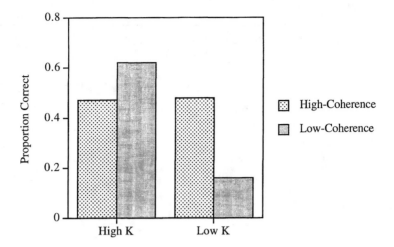

Figure 9.12   Proportion correct for problem-solving questions as a function of prior knowledge for high- and low-coherence texts. After McNamara et al. (1996).

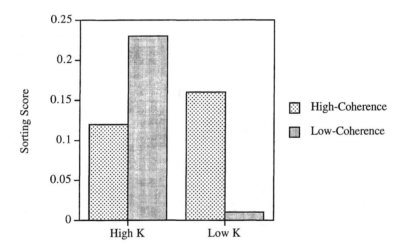

Figure 9.13   Sorting scores as a function of prior knowledge for high- and low-coherence texts. After McNamara et al. (1996).

the low-coherence text. That text was apparently just too difficult for these subjects, and they could get nothing out of it. However, the conceptual change induced by the low-coherence text in readers with a good knowledge background, as indexed by the sorting scores in Figure 9.13, was almost twice as great as for the high-coherence text. It appears that the high-coherence text that spelled out everything these readers already knew quite well induced an illusory feeling of knowing that prevented them from processing the text deeply. They were satisfied with a superficial understanding, which was good enough for recall and answering text-based questions, but they failed to construct an adequate situation model combining their prior knowledge with the information from the text. Hence, their relatively poor performance with the text that should have been the easiest and most effective text.

The interaction shown in Figure 9.13 has been replicated by McNamara and Kintsch (1996) with a different text and a different knowledge manipulation. In this experiment, we used the original and revised versions of the Vietnam text of Britton and Gulgoz (1991). The goal of the experiment was to replicate Britton and Gulgoz but at the same time to investigate whether their results depended on a low level of background knowledge, as we have argued. To achieve more variation in background knowledge among our subjects, we pretrained half of our subjects. These subjects received a brief, 20-minute history lesson designed to teach them the knowledge that was needed to understand the original version of the Britton and Gulgoz text – a few facts about the geography and history of Vietnam and about the role of the United States and its South Vietnamese allies in the war. Perhaps not surprisingly, this minilesson was not very effective. There was a considerable overlap in scores on the preknowledge test for subjects with and without pretraining. Hence, not all of our pretrained subjects had become high-knowledge subjects, and the division between high- and low-knowledge subjects had to be made strictly on the basis of the knowledge pretest, without regard to the subject's pretraining condition.

The results of this study were similar for both recall and questions (text-based questions and bridging inferences). Subjects who read the revised, coherent text performed better than subjects who read the original text, and high-knowledge subjects did better than low-knowledge subjects. There were no significant interactions. Thus, these results replicate both Britton and Gulgoz (1991) and Figures 9.10 and 9.11. The crucial results, however, are the sorting data (no problem-solving questions were given in this study), which are shown in Figure 9.14. Obviously, the same kind of interaction between prior knowledge and the coherence of the text was obtained as in McNamara et al. (1996) (Figure 9.13). For low-knowledge subjects, the original low-coherence text is quite ineffective, as is the revised, high-coherence text for high-knowledge subjects. However, if readers who know very little about Vietnam read the coherent, well-written text, their sorting is influenced by it. Similarly, if the better informed readers are given the more challenging text, the text clearly influences the way they sort the key words.

These results are paradoxical. Should we start writing incoherent texts and give disorganized lectures so that our better students will benefit from them? The answer to this question seems to be a qualified "yes." Making things too easy for a student may be a significant impediment to learning. However, just messing up a lecture is not a solution. Instead, we need to challenge the student to engage in active, deep processing of a text. This can be done, as we have shown here, by placing impediments in the path of comprehension, but impediments of the right kind and in the right amount. They must be impediments we have reason to think the student can overcome with enough effort, and the activity of overcoming

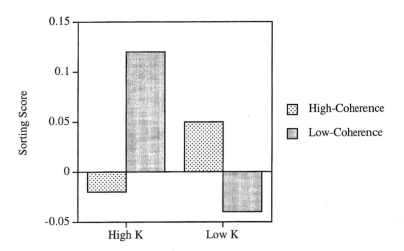

Figure 9.14   Sorting scores as a function of prior knowledge for high- and low-coherence texts. After McNamara & Kintsch (1996).

these impediments must be relevant to learning. We have shown that giving students a study text with coherence gaps, for which they do not have adequate background knowledge, is self-defeating. Such students need all the help they can get, and we need to organize and explicate the text for them as well as we can. But, as the literature on generation effects in memory also demonstrates (e.g., McNamara & Healy, 1995), students who are able to perform a task unaided should be encouraged to do so. They remember better and learn better to the extent that the activity they are engaging in is task relevant. This was certainly the case in the experiments we have discussed in which the incoherent texts forced the high-knowledge students to establish local coherence relations on the basis of their own knowledge, to figure out the macrostructure of the text on their own, and to elaborate the textual material with what they already knew. As shown by the simulation described in section 9.4, that is exactly what is required for learning from text.

The fact that not just any self-generated activity is helpful for text memory has been shown in a series of studies discussed in McDaniel, Blischak, and Einstein (1995). Story recall can be improved by omitting occasional letters from words so that the reader must fill in the missing information from the context. Filling in missing letters forces readers to focus on the details of the stories that readers often disregard in favor of the story line. This aids their recall of the story. On the other hand, a different orienting task, such as reordering sentences, has no effect on story recall because readers of a story pay sufficient attention to the relational information between sentences, even without the reordering task. These relations are reversed for descriptive texts. The reordering task helps recall by focusing the reader's attention on otherwise neglected order information, but the missing letters task has no effect because readers of essays are quite careful about the details anyway. Thus, simply placing obstacles in the path of readers to force them to expend extra effort does not benefit their learning. Instead, positive effects can be expected only if the extra processing they engage in is appropriate to the task.

If the effort is appropriate to the task, however, engaging the reader in active processing can be quite helpful. We have seen this for learning from text in the experiments previously discussed. This is also the case for sentence memory. There is a curvilinear relation between the strength of a causal connection between two statements and the memory strength of their connection measured by cued recall, indicating that neither too weak nor too strong links are elaborated as successfully as intermediate links (e.g. Myers, Shinjo, & Duffy, 1987; van den Broek, 1990). Analogous results have been reported by Battig (1979) for paired-associate learning, who reported better retention when the learning was made more difficult through intratask interference. There is also a literature on skill acquisition (Schmidt & Bjork, 1992) which shows that making the learning process too smooth is counterproductive. Learners acquiring a new skill must have the opportunity to face difficulties and learn to repair mistakes. Novice skiers certainly do not learn anything positive when their friends take them down an expert slope without preparation, but neither do they make much progress when they spend all their time on the bunny hill.

Using texts with coherence gaps to stimulate deeper processing in readers is but one technique that can be employed to stimulate reader activity. It is not an easy technique to use, as we have seen, for its effectiveness depends on the match between the nature of the gaps in the text and the reader's background knowledge, which is not easily established. Furthermore, other instructional or experimental manipulations may override it, as was shown by E. Kintsch and W. Kintsch (1995). In this study we used the same texts again as in McNamara et al. (1996) but asked readers to comment on their understanding as they read each sentence. Thus, we forced readers to be active processors and did not allow high-knowledge readers to assume superficial processing strategies. Under these conditions, the interaction between prior knowledge and text coherence disappeared, and the high-coherence text was as good as or better than the low-coherence text for all readers. However, when no experimenter (or teacher) is available to ensure that the student processes the text deeply, letting the student read a challenging text rather than one too readily comprehended might still be a useful technique to ensure reader activity.

Mannes and Kintsch (1987) have reported a study that is similar in spirit to the experiments discussed here. In their study, readers were given an advance organizer that either fit perfectly with the target text and hence made it easy to read, or that structurally mismatched the target text so that the readers had to engage in some cognitive effort to relate the advance information and the target text. The target text was a rather long article from a popular science publication about the industrial use of microbes. Because our students knew very little about microbes beforehand, we prepared an advance organizer that told them everything they needed to know about them. We prepared two forms of this advance organizer that differed in the order in which the material was presented but, as much as possible, not in the content of the material. In one case, the general information about microbes occurred in exactly the same order as it was presented in the target text. We called this the congruent advance organizer. In the other version, the material was presented as in the encyclopedia article that we had used as our source. This organization was incongruent with the text.

Subjects studied either form of the advanced organizer and took a short test on it. They then read the target text, which required a certain amount of knowledge about the properties of microbes. After reading the text, they were tested on what they remembered from it and what they had learned. The data shown in Figure 9.15 are representative for the results of this study. We observed a dissociation between measures of text memory (correct verifications of old sentences in Figure 9.15) and measures of learning (correct verifications of inference sentences in Figure 9.15). When the advance organizer and the content of the text were structurally congruent, subjects readily understood the text and remembered it better than when

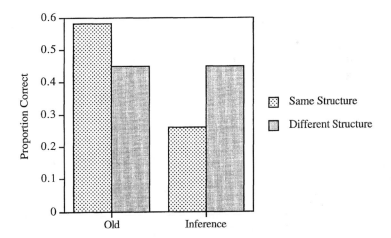

Figure 9.15   Proportion correct responses on a sentence verification task for old sentences and inferences when the structure of an advance organizer and a text were congruent (Same Structure) or incongruent (Different Structure). After Mannes and Kintsch (1987).

the advance information and the text were organized differently. The formation of a textbase was presumably facilitated because the macrostructure they had formed for the advance organizer provided a fitting schema for the text itself. When this was not the case, the textbase was not as perfect, and behavioral measures depending primarily on the textbase were lower. However, their situation model was enhanced because in understanding the target text, they had to retrieve and integrate information from the advance organizer that had presented the information in a different context. Therefore, a richer, more interrelated network was constructed, which later helped the readers with inference questions and problem solving (see also Mannes, 1994).

Making comprehension difficult for students is an effective technique to foster learning but only up to a point. If we make comprehension so difficult that students cannot succeed, nothing positive is achieved. E. Kintsch (1990) showed this very nicely in a study comparing the ability of sixth-grade students, tenth-grade students, and college students to summarize a text. The text was a descriptive, comparing two countries on a variety of dimensions. In one version, the text had a well-ordered and clearly signaled macrostructure; in a second version, the content was the same but was presented in a disorganized, though locally coherent way. Figure 9.16 shows some of the results of this study. An ideal summary should consist entirely or mostly of sentences corresponding to macropropositions expressed in the text or inferred. By that standard, sixth-grade students write pretty poor summaries, though the quality of the summaries improves considerably with age. The important point is not this general improvement, however, but the interaction between the age of the students and the quality of the text they read. The college students actually wrote better summaries when they received the poorly organized text, paralleling the findings of some of the other studies reviewed here. For the sixth-graders, however, the poorly organized text was too difficult, such that they performed only about half as well with the poorly organized text as with the well-organized text.

Thus, there is evidence now from a number of studies from our laboratory as well as elsewhere that increasing the difficulty of the learning phase can have beneficial effects. Moreover, these studies are not limited to learning from text but involve other kinds of learning situations as well. Task difficulty can stimulate active processing, with the result that a more elaborate, better integrated situation model will be constructed. As we

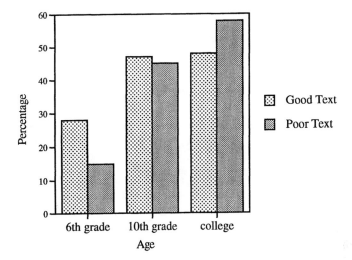

Figure 9.16   The percentage of statements in the subjects' summaries that correspond to macropropositions as a function of age for the good and poor text. After E. Kintsch (1990).

have seen, this statement must be carefully qualified. The student must have the necessary skills and knowledge to successfully engage in the required activity, and the activity must be task relevant.

9.7 Matching students with instructional texts

Studies like McNamara et al. (1996) and Voss and Silfies (1996) show how important it is to provide a learner with the right text, not too easy and not too hard. But how can that be done? To perform a theoretical analysis with the CI model of both the student and the text as was done in section 9.4 is clearly impractical. Of course, good teachers and friendly librarians who know their students and their books do so intuitively all time, and often quite successfully. Our goal is to individualize learning, yet teachers cannot always be there to help, nor can they know everything that is available, and large electronic databases just don't come with a friendly librarian.

Kintsch (1994c) has hypothesized the existence of "zones of learnability," in analogy with Vygotsky's "zones of proximal development" (Vygotsky, 1986). If a student's knowledge overlaps too much with an instructional text, there is simply not enough for the student to learn from that text. If there is no overlap, or almost no overlap, there can be no learning either: The necessary hooks in the students' knowledge, onto which the new information must be hung, are missing.

One way to determine whether a particular text falls within a student's zone of learnability is to represent both the student's knowledge and the text as vectors in the semantic space constructed by LSA and determine how far apart they are (see section 3.3 on LSA). Wolfe, Schreiner, Rehder, Laham, Foltz, Landauer, and Kintsch (in press) have investigated the potential of this idea.

Wolfe and his co-workers used the heart as their knowledge domain. They first assessed what average college students knew about the functioning of the heart and then developed a 40-point questionnaire to test for this knowledge. This questionnaire was used both as a measure of the students' background knowledge and, after instruction, as a measure of their learning. Specifically, if a student scored x points before instruction and y points after, the proportion of improvement was used as a measure of learning:

$$\text{learn}_{\text{quest}} = (y - x)/(40 - x)$$

Another, independent measure of the students' knowledge and learning was obtained by having each student write a 250-word essay on the functioning of the heart, both before and after instruction. These essays were graded by professional graders at the Educational Testing Service, and a second learning measure, $\text{learn}_{\text{essay}}$, was computed, based on the proportion of improvement between the grades on the before and after essays. The length of the essays was constrained to avoid the difficulty of comparing the content of essays of different lengths.

Students (the usual college sophomores) were randomly assigned to one of four instructional conditions. Actually, the instruction the students received was minimal; they were allowed to study a four-page text on the functioning of the heart for 20 minutes. One cannot expect much knowledge change from such instruction, but we hoped that the different effectiveness of the four texts we used would become apparent nevertheless. One of the texts (Text A) was from a junior-high textbook; we assumed it would be easy for everyone and perhaps too easy for some of the students. Texts B and C were from college level texts, with Text C being the harder one in our informal judgment. We assumed that these two texts would be approximately appropriate for the majority of our subjects. The fourth text, Text D, was from a medical journal and was definitely too hard for most or all of our subjects. All four texts were concerned with the functioning of the heart, and although their contents were by no means identical in detail, they were all intended to describe, at rather different levels of sophistication, how the heart functions. We wanted to find out how well prior knowledge predicts what students learned from these texts and whether we could use LSA for these predictions.

Latent semantic analysis was used in two ways: to represent the four instructional texts as vectors in the semantic space, and to represent the essays each student wrote before as well as after instruction as vectors in the same space. A new semantic space was constructed for this purpose that dealt specifically with knowledge about the heart. Thirty-six articles of an encyclopedia that dealt with the heart were used to construct this space. A comparison of the cosines among the four text vectors confirmed our intuitions that the texts were ordered from easiest to most difficult in the order A < B < C < D. In each case, the cosine between nearer texts were higher than the cosines between more distant texts.

Student scores on the two measures of knowledge, the questionnaire and the essay, were well correlated, $r = .74$. Furthermore, if we assume that Text B and C are standard texts, in the sense that their content is what college sophomores should know about the heart, the cosine between a subject's pretest essay and one of these texts provides another knowledge measure – how distant is that student's essay from where it should be in the LSA space? The fact that this third, LSA-derived measure of prior knowledge also correlated quite highly with either the question-based or the essay-based knowledge measures shows that we are dealing with a rather orderly data set and that LSA may be the right measuring stick for our purposes. Specifically, the correlation between the cosine for a student's pretest essay and Text C and scores on the questionnaire and essay grades were r = .64 and .69, respectively.

The main questions of interest were, however, whether prior knowledge predicted learning and whether there was any evidence for a non-monotonic relationship, as implied by the hypothesis of the zones of learnability. According to that hypothesis, the relationship between prior knowledge and learning should depend on the difficulty of the text. Specifically, students should not learn much from the too-easy Text A unless they really know nothing about the heart; nor should they learn much from the too-hard Text D unless they already know a lot.

We have a restricted range problem in this study, however. All our college sophomores knew a little bit about the heart, but there were very few really high-knowledge people, so we really did not have a text that was too easy. We therefore ran a fifth group of subjects, a group of medical school students, who were given the easy Text A to study. The results are shown in Figure 9.17. Figure 9.17 shows the mean improvement in learn$_{quest}$ and learn$_{essay}$ as a function of the average cosine between the texts that students read and their pretest essays. Including the medical students in Figure 9.17 clearly brings out the hypothesized nonmonotonic relationship between prior knowledge and amount learned. It is particularly noteworthy that two very different methods of measuring learning – by questionnaire and by essay grades – yielded comparable results.

According to Figure 9.17, a great deal can be gained by assigning students the right text for learning. We could easily have doubled the learning scores for the college students who read Text D, as well as improved

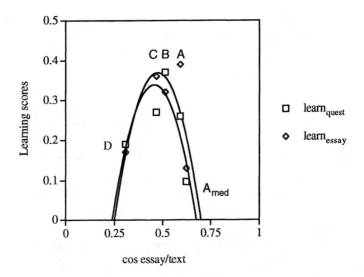

Figure 9.17   Mean learning scores as assessed by questionnaire and essay grades as a function of mean essay-to-text cosine scores for the four experimental groups (Texts D, C, B, A) and a group of medical school students (A$_{med}$). After Wolfe et al. (in press.)

the scores of students who read Text A, simply by giving them either of the other two texts! Wolfe et al. (in press) made some calculations that suggest that by assigning individual students to texts on the basis of their background knowledge, learning scores could have been improved by more than 50%. Even if in practice these calculations turn out to be optimistic, such a potential can hardly be ignored.

The complex interaction between learning, text characteristics, and background knowledge certainly deserves more research. However, Wolfe et al. (in press; see also Rehder, Schreiner, Wolfe, Laham, Landauer, & Kintsch, in press, for a more detailed analysis of the LSA measures that can be used to predict learning) have shown one thing quite clearly: LSA predicts learning about as well as the more cumbersome empirical measures (essays have to be graded, questionnaires require careful design), thus giving us a powerful research tool and perhaps even a practical tool that could be used to match students with the texts they could most profit from.

9.8 Educational implications

Learning from text, like all learning, involves the construction or modification of situation models. Hence, the first educational implication of the work discussed here is that if we are interested in learning, we must make sure that our measures are sensitive to learning – that is, they must reflect properties of the situation model rather than merely the textbase. Such measures are inference questions and problem-solving tasks, and, at least for laboratory studies, keyword sorting and cued association tasks. Recognition and fact questions, in contrast, may merely reflect understanding at the level of the textbase. Recall and summarization are intermediate in this respect because reproductive recall can be quite good even in the absence of an appropriate situation model, whereas the reconstructive component of recall can be more indicative of the nature of the learner's situation model. In the studies we have reviewed, textbase and situation model measures frequently gave different results. Failure to distinguish between measures of learning and measures of memory invites theoretical confusion and cannot produce educationally satisfactory results. Many educators have stressed the dangers of superficial understanding and the need for engaging students in deeper understanding. I hope that by tying the commonsense terms *deep* and *superficial understanding* into the theory of comprehension, and in particular to the concepts of textbase and situation model, I have been able to clarify the nature of these concepts and to sharpen their meaning.

The emphasis in this chapter has been on the formation of situation models that are well integrated with the learner's prior knowledge. If this integration is not achieved and if the information acquired remains accessible only via the episodic text memory, two problems arise. First, such information represents inert knowledge, in the sense that although it is possible to retrieve it as part of an episodic memory structure, it cannot be retrieved when it is needed for the performance of new tasks, for by the principle of encoding specificity, memory traces can be retrieved only via retrieval cues that were encoded when the traces were formed. Second, memory structures not linked to a person's base of knowledge and experiences are rapidly forgotten, because the only effective retrieval cues, which often change quickly, are of a temporal and contextual nature.

If situation models with rich and stable links to prior knowledge are the goal, how is such a result best achieved? The answer depends on conditions. First, it is necessary that the reader/learner be able to form a coherent mental representation of the text. This is a necessary but not sufficient condition for learning. A well-written text, in which the local coherence relations are marked syntactically and lexically, and in which the macrostructure is well organized and clearly signaled, usually guarantees this result. A poorly organized text with coherence gaps may still be understandable but only if the learner can rely on background knowledge that enables him or her to overcome the deficiencies of the text.

Nevertheless, a coherent text representation is not sufficient for learning; it must be linked to prior knowledge in as many ways as possible. The only way to encode such links with prior knowledge during reading is for the reader to use prior knowledge in building a situation model. Here the limitations of a well-written text become apparent. If a reader has no background at all to link with a new text, a hospitable text may result in text memory in the sense we have discussed but not in learning. To learn something new we must have some hooks in long-term memory to hang it on.

The fact that a reader has available appropriate background knowledge does not in itself guarantee learning, for the knowledge must be used in the processes of understanding. Otherwise, no links will be generated between it and the new text. As we have seen, this is not always the case.

Readers with appropriate knowledge do not always bother to employ that knowledge for learning. Readers also tend to take the path of least resistance, and if they have the feeling that they are easily understanding the text they read, they may not bother to activate their knowledge and form the links between it and the text that alone guarantee learning. Hence, there exists an instructional need to stimulate reader activity.

In some of our experiments, we encouraged readers to be active by giving them a less than perfect text. Because this text had both local and global coherence gaps, readers could not understand it without using their knowledge. High-knowledge readers, therefore, brought their knowledge to bear on the interpretation of the text and became successful learners. The same readers could also have done so when they read a well-written, explicit, and coherent text, but they did not feel the need to do so.

There are many other ways to make readers active learners. Students who have their own learning goals, who own their questions and are not merely responding passively to what they perceive as arbitrary and irrelevant teacher demands, tend to be active learners who are not satisfied with superficial understanding. Dewey (1897), for this reason, demanded long ago that all learning should be incidental, part of a meaningful activity in which the student engages. Many current instructional programs have adopted this strategy (e.g., Bereiter & Scardamalia, 1989). Others have devised specific teaching strategies that ensure the active participation of the learner, such as the reciprocal teaching method of Brown and Palincsar (1989), or that are specifically suited for learning from text, the *questioning-the-author* method used by Beck, McKeown, Worthy, Sandora, and Kucan (1996). There are many ways to engage the reader. The research discussed here shows why we need them and what we want to achieve by using them.

A main theme of this chapter has been the need to distinguish between memory for a text and learning from a text. It is possible to reproduce a text from memory without being able to use it for any other purpose; the information provided by the text remains inert knowledge. Only if the episodic text memory is intimately intertwined with the reader's long-term memory structure will it be accessible in novel situations, become a part of the reader's active knowledge. For school learning, for instance, it does not make much difference whether the student can reproduce the textbook from memory. What is important is that the information in the book become integrated with the student's prior knowledge. For a long time, studies of text comprehension did not provide information on the factors that determine the success or failure of this integration process. We could tell anyone who wanted to know how to make a text more memorable and easier to comprehend, but that was not an answer that was of much use. Authors of textbooks, training programs, instructional manuals, and the like are not concerned with text memory, but they want to get a certain body of information across to the student. Until a few years ago, we really had very little to offer such people.

The research results reviewed in this chapter clearly show that this situation has greatly improved; we have learned a lot about learning from text in recent years. It is not a simple story, but the primary factors in learning from text are reasonably clear at this point. A major determinant of learning from text is background knowledge. To learn effectively, we need hooks in prior knowledge, long-term memory, or personal experience on which to hang the information to be learned. Learning is most successful when such hooks are plentiful and when there is a clear relation between the hooks and the learning material so that the student hangs things on the right hooks.

Although the existence of such hooks in prior knowledge is a necessary condition for learning, it is not a sufficient condition. It is not enough that a hook in long-term memory is available – it also must be used. Hence, the importance of making learners active, intentional agents rather than passive vessels into which information is poured at will. It is clear that if learners have an adequate background, they will perform better if they take an active role in their learning – making inferences, filling gaps, generating macrostructures, elaborating, and the like. It has also been shown that at least in some cases learners with an adequate background knowledge will perform below their capabilities if they do not assume such an active role. How does one create an active learner? We have used here for the most part the somewhat counterintuitive technique of providing the learner with a poorly written text, a text that lacks coherence, thereby forcing the learner to fill in the gaps in the text. Further research will be needed to determine more closely the boundary conditions for the effectiveness of this strategy or of the other strategies designed to induce active learning that have been used successfully in recent years in text research. Even now, however, this is an area of research that seems ready for the step from the laboratory to practice.

10

Word problems

People spend a great deal of time reading, some much more than others. The amount of time spent in leisure reading, according to one study (Guthrie & Greaney, 1991), is 63 minutes per day, 39 minutes for newspapers and 24 minutes for books. These times are medians of highly skewed distributions and they are probably underestimates because a substantial part of leisure reading is secondary to some other activity (cooking, planning a vacation, waiting in a doctor's office) and hence is underreported. In addition, the median estimated time people spend in occupational reading amounts to another 61 minutes (much more for professional workers). Once again, it is hard to get accurate reports, because so much of occupational reading is embedded in another activity. Scanning a production schedule tends not to be reported as reading.

It is clear from these numbers that reading takes a considerable portion of our time, even if we live outside a university and even if much of the reading we do occurs in the service of some other activity. Comprehension, memory, and learning are the key concepts when we look at reading for its own sake for relaxation or acquiring knowledge. But we need to broaden our approach when looking at reading in the service of other goals, such as solving a mathematical problem or performing some action.

Word problems are popular in arithmetic and algebra classes, as well as in physics and engineering courses, because they lend an air of realism and authenticity to the drill that is necessary for the acquisition of formal skills. Most students profess to hate them and find them confusing. They know the math but not whether to add or subtract or what to multiply with what. Teachers are challenged to make their students understand what they are doing, instead of applying rules mechanically.

To the psychologist, word problems provide some wonderful research opportunities. Not only are they texts, so that one can recall and summarize them just like stories, but one can also observe the student's problem solving and the eventual answer. What the student remembers and what the student does are related in informative ways and mutually constrain each other. Thus, a richer set of experimental observations can be obtained than in other text research.

10.1 Word arithmetic problems

Word problems play a significant role in the teaching of arithmetic in schools all over the world. They are used very differently, however, in different countries. An illuminating comparison of Soviet and U.S. elementary mathematics textbooks for grades 1 to 3 was reported by Stigler, Fuson, Ham, and Kim (1986). In the books that they analyzed, the Soviet texts contained somewhat more word problems than did the U.S. texts, but this difference was minor compared with the striking differences in the nature of the word problems and how they were presented. Across the different types of word problems (e.g., Table 10.1 on page 335) the Soviet texts maintained an approximately even distribution. Each type of word problem was represented equally often, and problem types were mixed up and interspersed among numerical problems, so that most pages contained at least some word problems. In contrast, the American texts focused on a few problem types. A single Compare problem and two kinds of Change problems are used almost exclusively; among the Combine problems, the missing-whole version is three to ten times as frequent as the missing-part version. That is, most of the word problems found in U.S. texts are the ones that U.S. children find easiest. Furthermore, problems of the same type tend to be blocked, and word problems are generally segregated from the rest of the material into special problem-solving sections at the end of chapters.

Most efforts to study how children learn to solve word arithmetic problems have focused on the formal aspects of the problem. Thus, the first models of word arithmetic problem solving by Riley, Greeno, and Heller (1983) and Briars and Larkin (1984) had no explicit language-processing component and instead dealt with only the problem representations the children constructed, the inferences they made, and the counting operations they used. However, the language used to express a problem makes a difference. A well-known example of how important the language can be has been provided by Hudson (1983). Only 39% of Hudson's first-grade students were able to solve the following problem:

(1)   Joe has 8 sticks.
      He has 5 more sticks than Tom has.
      How many sticks does Tom have?

However, the arithmetically identical problem

(2)   There were 8 birds and 5 worms.
      How many birds did not get a worm?

was solved by 79% of the children. Nevertheless, focusing first on the formal properties of word problems was a good research strategy. Once the formalisms were understood, problem-solving models could be merged with text comprehension models to yield complete theories of word problem solving. Thus, the Riley et al. (1983) theory of arithmetic problem solving was combined with the van Dijk and Kintsch (1983) text comprehension model by Kintsch and Greeno (1985).

10.1.1 Schemas for solving word arithmetic problems

Kintsch and Greeno (1985) argued that word problem solving involves a text understanding phase that yields the kind of mental representation needed by the second problem-solving phase to compute an answer. Many texts have a conventional structure that readers know and use to organize their mental representation of the text. Thus, stories are organized by the story schema and legal briefs by an argumentation schema. Word problems have their own schemas that have to be learned in school, recognized as relevant when the problem is being read, and used as an

organizational basis for the text. The schemas are the structures identified and described by Riley et al. (1983): the Transfer schema, the Part-
Whole schema, and the More(Less)-Than schema in their various versions. They are all based on the notion of a set. A set is a schema, too, a
frame with slots to be filled by particular quantities and objects:

SET
object:<count noun>
quantity:<number, some, many>
specification: <owner, location, time>
role:<start, transfer, result;
   superset, subset;
   large-set, small-set, difference-set>

Thus, the sentence *Joe had 5 marbles* yields a set with *Joe* as the owner, *5*
as the quantity, and *past* as specification. Its role depends on the problem
context. For example, it might be the start-set of a Transfer problem (*He
gave away 3 marbles. How many marbles does he have now?*), or the subset
of a Combine problem (*Jack had 3 marbles. How many do they have altogether?*), or the large set of a Compare problem (*He had 2 more marbles
than Jack. How many marbles did Jack have?*)

   Riley, Greeno, and Heller (1983) classified word arithmetic problems
into 14 types in three main classes, as shown in the following list:

Table 10.1. *Types of word problems*

Change	Combine	Compare
Result unknown	*Superset unknown*	*Difference unknown*
1. Joe had 3 marbles. Then Tom gave him 5 more marbles. How many marbles does Joe have now?	1. Joe has 3 marbles. Tom has 5 marbles. How many marbles do they have altogether?	1. Joe has 8 marbles. Tom has 5 marbles. How many marbles does Joe have more than Tom?
2. Joe had 8 marbles. Then he gave 5 marbles to Tom. How many marbles does Joe have now?		2. Joe has 8 marbles. Tom has 5 marbles. How many marbles does Tom have less than Joe?

(cont.)

Table 10.1. *Types of word problems*   (*cont.*)

Change	Combine	Compare
Change unknown	*Subset unknown*	*Compared quantity unknown*
3. Joe had 3 marbles. Then Tom gave him some marbles. Now Joe has 8 marbles. How many marbles did Tom give him?	2. Joe and Tom have 8 marbles altogether. Joe has 3 marbles. How many marbles does Tom have?	3. Joe has 3 marbles. Tom has 5 more marbles than Joe. How many marbles does Tom have?
4. Joe had 8 marbles. Then he gave some marbles to Tom. Now he has 3 marbles. How many marbles did he give to Tom?		4. Joe has 8 marbles. Tom has 5 marbles less than Joe. How many marbles does Tom have?
State unknown		*Referent unknown*
5. Joe had some marbles. Then Tom gave him 5 more marbles. Now Joe has 8 marbles. How many marbles did Joe have in the beginning?		5. Joe has 8 marbles. He has 5 more marbles than Tom. How many marbles does Tom have?
6. Joe had some marbles. Then he gave 5 marbles to Tom. Now Joe has 3 marbles. How many marbles did Joe have in the beginning?		6. Joe has 3 marbles. He has 5 marbles less than Tom. How many marbles does Tom have?

Source: After Riley, Greeno, and Heller (1983).

These are the kinds of problems children are given in kindergarten to third grade. They differ greatly in difficulty, with most children being able to solve the easiest types of problems, such as Change-1 or Combine-1, whereas only a small minority of American school children can solve correctly the more unusual and more difficult problems, such as Compare-3.

The Kintsch and Greeno (1985) model understands these problems by creating various sets from the information supplied by the text and using one of its higher-order schemas to interrelate these sets. Every time the model encounters a noun phrase with a quantifier it creates a set and attempts to fill as many slots of the set schema with information from the text as possible. It then uses semantic information in the text to select one of its higher-order schemas. A phrase containing *more-than*, for instance, cues the Compare schema, and a transfer verb (*give, take, lose,* etc.) cues the Transfer schema. If one child has so many *cars* and the other so many *dolls* and the question asks for the number of *toys, toys* is the superset and cues the appropriate schema.

Consider how the model understands and solves a Change-3 problem:

(3) John had 3 marbles.
   Then Tom gave him some more marbles.
   Now Joe has 8 marbles.
   How many marbles did Tom give him?

- The *3 marbles* in the first sentence provide the cue for making a set S_1 of *3 marbles*, with owner *Joe* in the *past*, role unknown.
- Similarly, a second set is formed on the basis of the next sentence, the objects being *marbles*, quantity *some*, and specification that *Joe* is the owner, at a *later time*. Furthermore, *give* cues the Transfer schema, with the result that S_1 can be assigned the role of *start-set* and S_2 the role of *transfer-set*. An expectation is created for the missing *result-set*.
- It is filled by S_3, which is created on the basis of the third sentence: *8 marbles*, owned by *Joe now*, the *result* of the transfer process.
- The final sentence merely asks to calculate the as yet unspecified quantity of S_2. This is done by using a counting procedure called Add-On, as is typical for first-grade students.

A More-Than schema is used to solve a Compare-5 problem:

(4)   Joe has 8 marbles.
      He has 5 more marbles than Tom.
      How many marbles does Tom have?

- S_1: objects: marbles
        quantity: 8
        specification: owner Joe
        role: unknown
- S_2: objects: marbles
        quantity: 5
        specification: owner Joe
        role: difference-set

S_1 is assigned the role of large-set; a request is made for a small-set.

- S_3: objects: marbles
        quantity: ?
        specification: owner Tom
        role: small-set

The solution procedure in this case is complex; first-graders do not appear to have a solution strategy for this type of problem. Therefore, they convert the More-Than schema into a Part-Whole schema with S_1 as the superset, S_2 as a subset, and S_3 as the goal set for solution by a procedure called Separate-From. (These procedures are modeled after empirical work by Carpenter and Moser, 1983.)

The Kintsch and Greeno (1985) model can be thought of as a production system with smart rules. It differs in that respect from the CI model, because it uses cues in the text to select the right schema to organize a problem. Because only three schemas are needed for children's word problems, this poses no insurmountable difficulties. I discuss below, however, the CI version of the model proposed in Kintsch (1988), which explores contradictory hypotheses about the role of sets in parallel and uses an integration process to select the one that fits a problem best.

Computer simulations based on the Kintsch and Greeno (1985) model were constructed by Fletcher (1985), Dellarosa (1986), and Cummins et al. (1988). These simulations serve several purposes. First, they show that the model actually works as originally conceived. All 18 problem types are solved successfully by the simulation, as well as a number of richer story problems described in Cummins et al. (1988). Second, these simulations were able to account reasonably well for the observed problem difficulty in terms of the nature and number of the operations the simulations had to perform. Difficult problems tend to make greater processing demands and require less familiar operations and schemas (e.g., the More-Than schema is less familiar to kindergarten to third-grade children than the Transfer schema is). Most interesting, however, is the ability of the simulation to account for the kinds of errors the children make in solving these problems. The way it does so provides some real insight into why word problems are so hard.

10.1.2 Error simulation

What is it that children learn when they solve word arithmetic problems? According to the logicomathematical development view, which has its roots in the work of Piaget, children learn to solve certain kinds of problems by acquiring the conceptual knowledge necessary for these problems. This is the view taken by, among others, Riley et al. (1983) and Briars and Larkin (1984). Riley et al. (1983), for instance, hypothesize that the problem solving of good students involves complete schemas such as those we have described, whereas poor problem solvers work with impoverished schemas that represent individual sets but not the relations among the sets.

Alternatively, one might hypothesize that the children have the necessary formal knowledge but that certain difficult problems employ linguistic forms that are unfamiliar to the children. This linguistic development view contrasts with the logicomathematical hypothesis because it places the source of difficulty not in the children's deficient conceptual structures but in their lack of linguistic knowledge. The child may have an adequate understanding of the Part-Whole schema, for example, but might not know how to map a phrase like *How many more Xs than Ys?* onto that schema.

Cummins et al. (1988) have shown that one can decide among these competing hypotheses by considering the way errors occur in the simulation and comparing these errors to the ones children make. The trick is to lesion the simulation, to take out certain processing components or pieces of knowledge, and see how it behaves. If a lesion makes no difference, the piece obviously was superfluous in the first place. If a lesion leads to a catastrophic breakdown, we know that the piece in question is vital because catastrophic breakdowns do not (or only very rarely) occur in our data set. The children always do something and say something, though it might not be what the problem demands. Indeed, the children in one of Cummins's experiments produced errors on 45% of all trials, but most of these errors were systematic – only 8% of the trials yielded uninterpretable errors. Thus, we should examine the kinds of errors the children make and determine what we have to do to our simulation so that it produces such errors.

It typically happens that when a child is unable to solve a problem, he or she solves a simpler problem that is within the child's abilities. The evidence for this claim lies in the systematic correspondences that we observed between the children's recall of a word problem and their solution behavior. What they were doing did not resemble random errors – there clearly was method in their errors!

Interestingly, the major types of systematic errors that we found in our data can be reproduced by the simulation by means of certain kinds of lesions. The simulation contains two separate sources of knowledge: linguistic and world knowledge that allows it to understand a word arithmetic problem, and mathematical knowledge that is necessary for the solution of the problem. Any lesions in the mathematical knowledge – that is, primarily the notion of what a set is, the higher-order schemas relating sets, and the counting strategies children use – produce catastrophic failures in our simulation. The system breaks down or produces a weird result. That is not what the children do. However, some lesions of the linguistic knowledge that is used in the simulation produce precisely the kind of errors that were observed in the children. The difficulty seems to be in certain key words and phrases that are either unfamiliar to the children from their everyday experience or that are used in a special restricted way in word arithmetic problems. The data are described in detail in Cummins et al. (1988); I present here only a few typical examples for illustration.

Combine-2 problems are surprisingly difficult for first-graders. Errors occurred on 32% of all trials. The most frequent error was that the children turned the (difficult) Combine-2 problem into an (easy) Combine-1 problem. As an example, consider the following:

(5)   Mark and Sally have 7 trucks altogether.
      Mark has 2 trucks.
      How many trucks does Sally have?

The correct propositional parse for the first line is

HAVE[AND[MARK,SALLY], SEVEN[TRUCKS]].

The problem for the children is the interpretation of the *and-altogether*. As DeCorte, Verschaffel, and DeWinn (1985) have shown, children tend to substitute *each* for *and-altogether*. If we lesion the simulation so that it no longer knows the correct meaning of *and-altogether*, it parses the first line of the problem as

HAVE[MARK, SEVEN[TRUCKS]] & HAVE[SALLY,
SEVEN[TRUCKS]]

As a consequence, the system will create 2 sets of 7 trucks – one for Sally and one for Mark. The quantity of trucks in Mark's set gets updated to 2 by the second sentence, and the problem becomes a superset problem. In answer to the question, the simulation uses its "Already-know-the-answer" strategy and responds with 7.

   Real children make this sort of error 45% of the time. The children also recall the problem as a Combine-1 problem:

(6)   Sally has 7 trucks.
      Mark has 2 trucks.
      How many trucks do Mark and Sally have?

This type of misrecall occurs on 74% of the trials on which the children made a superset error, whereas it was rare when other types of errors occurred, and it did not occur at all when the problem was solved correctly. Figure 10.1 shows the recall data, including a control group of subjects who read the problem but did not solve it.

   Compare-5 problems were also a difficult problem type for our subjects. Errors occurred in our data again on 32% of all trials; when an error occurred, either the difference set was given as the answer (32%), or the two numbers in the problem were added (44%). The simulation yields

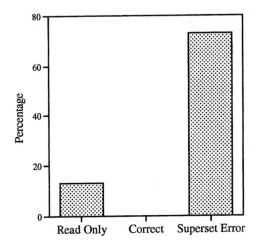

Figure 10.1   Misrecall of subset problems as a superset problem.

both of these error types if we lesion a key piece of its linguistic knowl-edge. *Have-more-than* requires a complex linguistic construction, involv-ing three sets: a large-set, a small-set, and a difference-set. If it is simply parsed as *more-than,* the simulation makes the same errors that the chil-dren do:

(7)   Joe has 8 sticks.
       He has 5 more sticks than Tom.
       How many sticks does Tom have?

The correct parsing of the second line is

       HAVE-MORE-THAN[JOE, TOM, FIVE[STICKS]].

With the lesion, the model parses this line as

       MORE-THAN[[EIGHT[STICKS],FIVE[STICKS]]
                   └ OF-JOE   └OF-TOM

This incorrect parsing does not yield a well-structured problem, but nei-ther the children nor the simulation is at a loss. The children use one of their default strategies to come up with a reasonable answer. Two of these default strategies apply: the "Already-know-the-answer" strategy yields the difference set error – *Tom has 5 sticks.* The "Addition" strategy based on the keyword *more* yields the addition error – *Tom has 13 sticks.* These two errors in fact accounted for 76% of all errors the children made. Furthermore, the way the children recalled the problem correlated highly with the way they solved it. If they made an addition error, the most frequent recall pattern was

(8) Joe has 8 sticks.
      Tom has 5 more sticks.
      How many sticks do they have?

Figure 10.2 shows the frequency with which this pattern of recall was observed for Compare-5 problems when subjects made an addition error, when they solved the problem correctly, and when they only read the problem without solving it in a control condition.

The subjects' tendency to simplify problems and solve the simplified problem rather than the original one does not always result in errors. For instance, the second line of the Compare-5 problem exemplified in (7) is rather clumsily worded. The real structure of the problem is expressed much better by *Tom has 5 sticks fewer than Joe.* Here the *fewer* directly keys subtraction, and the owner of the set is kept in subject position. The

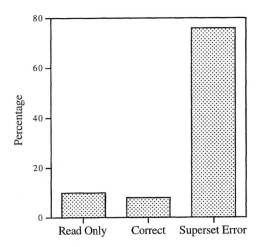

Figure 10.2   Misrecall of a compare problem as an addition problem.

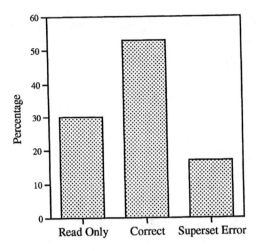

Figure 10.3   Misrecall of a Compare-5 problem as a Compare-4 problem.

structure of the problem remains the same, however, by this transformation; it is simply better formulated because in effect a Compare-5 problem is turned into the easier Compare-4 type. As Figure 10.3 shows, this kind of structure transformation occurs quite frequently when the problem is solved correctly and even when it is only read without attempting a solution, whereas it is rare when an error occurs.

Problem solving and problem recall are intimately intertwined in these data. Recall is reconstructive; the subject recalls what he or she did – not necessarily what was on the page. This does not look like a language-processing module impervious to outside influences à la Fodor and Chomsky. How the problem is solved depends on how the problem language is understood and, correspondingly, how it is recalled depends on how it was solved. The same structures are the bases for both language understanding and problem solving.

If the Cummins et al. (1988) simulation was missing certain pieces of linguistic knowledge, it succeeded in reproducing the most frequent error patterns that we observed in our first- and second-grade corpus. If it lacked mathematical knowledge, it did not produce the kinds of errors the children made. Therefore, the considerable difference that exists in the children's' ability to solve word and equivalent numerical problems appears to be due mostly to linguistic factors. Certain words and phrases that play an important role in word problems are not part of the children's everyday vocabulary, and their meaning and use must be learned, or relearned, specifically in school.

Data that further support these conclusions have been reported by Stern (1993a) and Cummins (1991). Cummins also showed that by suitably rewording word problems to avoid common linguistic ambiguities, performance on word problems can be significantly improved.

This is not to say that mathematical knowledge plays no role. On the contrary, it plays a crucial role; neither the simulation nor the students get anywhere without it. Rather, what makes word arithmetic problems especially difficult is the lack of language skills that would allow the child to represent correctly certain relationships among sets. Indeed, numerical competence is much more strongly related to the ability to solve word problems than is verbal intelligence in a large-scale longitudinal study reported in Stern (1993b). For instance, in a causal path analysis, verbal intelligence in grade 3 was related to different types of word problem solving in grade 4 with coefficients varying between .16 and .24. On the other hand, numerical competence in grade 2 showed a much stronger relation to word problem solving in grade 4, with coefficients between .31 and .41. The sine qua non of word problem solving is certainly numerical competence, but it is not the only factor and by itself is no guarantee of success in word problem solving. The linguistic factors discussed here matter, too. Furthermore, the rather low correlations between verbal ability and word problem solving observed by Stern (1993b) may be slightly misleading because the linguistic skills that matter in this respect are specific to mathematics and may not be adequately assessed by a general verbal intelligence test.

10.1.3 Situation models

Word problems do not have to be as simple and impoverished as those studied above (and those used in most American schools). Cummins et al. (1988, experiment 2), in addition to simulating the standard problems also worked with a set of sixteen complex story problems. Formally, these problems could be reduced to one of the standard types, but they were presented in the context of a little story with a familiar, everyday scenario, with real goals and motivations for the actors. The simulation that was developed was also given the new problem set to solve. Apart from telling it the meanings of several new words, the simulation was not changed at all. Nevertheless, it managed to solve thirteen of the complex problems correctly. It also accounted quite well for the kinds of errors children made in solving these problems when the simulation's linguistic knowledge was degraded. Degrading its mathematical knowledge, in contrast, yielded errors quite unlike those the children made. The simulation failed to solve three of the problems. The reason for this failure was the same in each case: It did not have enough linguistic or general world knowledge to understand the situation described in the story. In one case, for instance, it failed to connect a reference to *some pencils* a boy gave his sister with a later reference *the 5 pencils he gave her*. In another case, it did not know that *trade* implies a switch of ownership.

What we see here is the central importance of situational understanding in word problem solving. The reader must have a correct and complete situation model of the various actions, objects, and events described in a story problem. In the textually simplest arithmetic problem, this amounts to little more than learning how to use correctly a few key words and phrases. As problem texts get richer, however, all kinds of linguistic and world knowledge may be required for the construction of an adequate situation model. Familiarity with the overall domain becomes very important, as we have already seen from the example of Hudson (1983). Stern and Lehrndorfer (1992) provide some nice experimental demonstrations that problems of a certain type can be solved by children at a certain age when the problems are embedded in familiar contexts, but not otherwise.

Reusser (1989) has stressed most emphatically the importance of situation models in word problem solving. Reusser developed a simulation model that extends the Cummins et al. (1988) model by building in an explicit situation model. This was a significant innovation in the evolution of such models. In the past, theorists of word problem solving attempted to go directly from the text to the equation (and instructors stressing key-word strategies followed suit). Kintsch and Greeno (1985) and Cummins et al. (1988) presented a more complex model in which text understanding is interwoven with the construction of a mathematical problem representation (in terms of sets and their interrelations), from which equations and calculation procedures are derived. Reusser (1989) emphasizes the importance of another layer of representation intermediate between the textbase and the mathematization of the problem: the situation model that specifies actors, actions, states, and events in the problem in terms of everyday concepts. It is necessary to constrain the formal problem model; if the situation model is incorrect because of some linguistic ambiguity or because of an unfamiliar domain, it is unlikely that a correct problem model will be constructed.

The inclusion of a situation model allows Reusser's simulation to solve complex story problems. It also has proved to be a rich source of pedagogic implications, both for teaching word arithmetic (e.g., Staub & Reusser, 1995; Reusser, 1993) and in our own work on word algebra problem solving, which is described in the next section.

10.1.4 The CI model for word problem solving

The Kintsch and Greeno (1985) theory and the simulations based upon it (Cummins et al., 1988; Reusser, 1989) are top-down schema theories. Problems are understood because cues in the text lead to the activation of an appropriate arithmetic schema around which the text is organized and on which solution procedures can be based. If the right schema is activated, the problem will be solved correctly. This model has the same difficulties as all top-down schema theories, in that the cues that tell a student which arithmetic schema is needed may be subtle, complex, multiple, unreliable, and even contradictory. Instead of jumping to perhaps premature conclusions and committing oneself to a single hypothesis about the nature of a word problem, it might be better to consider all the evidence for several alternatives in parallel in the context of the story as a whole. That is what the CI architecture is designed to do, and Kintsch (1988) has shown that it is quite possible to embed the Kintsch and Greeno theory within the CI framework.

Which version of the theory is the better one, however? As we have just seen, quite a bit of productive work could be done with the top-down version. Nevertheless, there are reasons to prefer the CI architecture in this case, too. If one just looks at the end result, both versions of the theory achieve identical outcomes. They differ in the way a schema is selected. In the earlier version, the organizing schema is selected on the basis of a cue or cues in the text, which then controls the rest of the process in a top-down fashion. In the CI version, evidence for various alternative schemas is collected in parallel, and the schema that best satisfies the multiple constraints of a problem eventually wins out. The fact that there are multiple or even contradictory cues is easily incorporated in the CI version of the theory. Thus, experimental evidence that during the course of reading a word problem subjects consider more than one alternative, and that they combine multiple cues, would support the CI version of the theory and contradict or at least require a revision and elaboration of the single-schema version.

Such evidence has been obtained in an experiment by Lewis, reported in Kintsch and Lewis (1993). Lewis asked subjects to make a choice between two alternative hypotheses about a problem, addition or subtraction, at several query points during reading the problem. Thus, the time course of hypothesis formation could be recorded. The problems she used contained two cues, the overall structure of the problem and a keyword favoring either addition or subtraction.

Prototypical problems used by Lewis – four versions of Compare problems from Table 10.1 – are shown in Table 10.2. The keywords in the example in Table 10.2 are *taller* and *shorter*. *Taller* is associated with *more* and hence with addition; *shorter* is associated with *less* and hence with subtraction. Lewis used 16 problems of this kind with different keyword pairs, such as fast-slow or hot-cold. The force of these keywords was either consistent with the nature of the problem, or inconsistent. Linguistically, the two comparative terms are not equivalent. *Taller* is the default term, which can be used without particular connotations, as in *How tall is Jeff? Smaller* is the marked member of the pair. Its use is not

Table 10.2.   *Problem types used by Lewis*

	Consistent	Inconsistent
Add	Tom is 175 cm tall.	Tom is 175 cm tall.
	Jeff is 12 cm taller than Tom.	He is 12 cm shorter than Jeff.
	How tall is Jeff?	How tall is Jeff?
Subtract	Tom is 175 cm tall.	Tom is 175 cm tall.
	Jeff is 12 cm shorter than Tom.	He is 12 cm taller than Jeff.
	How tall is Jeff?	How tall is Jeff?

neutral. *How small is Jeff?* implies that Jeff is small. One would therefore expect that unmarked comparative terms would influence the course of hypothesis formation little or not at all; marked terms, however, should have a stronger effect, because normally speakers use such terms only if they have something special in mind.

Lewis's data for 144 college students are shown in Figures 10.4 and 10.5 for addition and subtraction problems, respectively. These figures show the percentage with which subjects chose the correct hypothesis about the appropriate mathematical operation at three query points located at the end of each of the three sentences of the word problems. Logically, subjects should guess randomly after the first sentence and should respond correctly at the end of the second sentence. The final question is logically redundant. The keyword should be disregarded, and hence the consistent and inconsistent problem version should be equivalent. This is not what happened. Performance was imperfect after the second sentence and generally improved after the third sentence. When the keyword was consistent with the problem structure, the correct hypothesis was chosen earlier and with a higher final accuracy. Inconsistent keywords depressed both the rate and asymptote of performance. There was a significant interaction between consistency and markedness. Linguistically marked com-

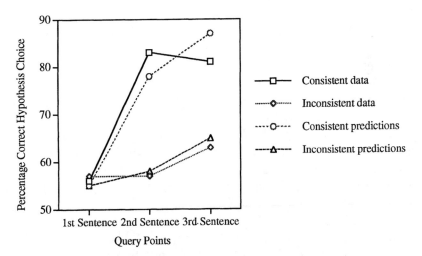

Figure 10.4 Percentage correct hypothesis choice for addition problems at three query points.

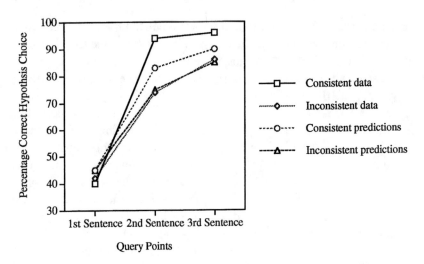

Figure 10.5   Percentage correct hypothesis choice for subtraction problems at three query points.

parison terms dramatically interfered with performance on the addition problems, whereas the unmarked term had a lesser, though still significant effect on the subtraction problems. Furthermore, guessing after the initial sentence showed a distinct bias in favor of addition, presumably because of the prevalence of addition problems in U.S. schools.

To simulate these results, we assume that there are two procedures, ADD and SUBTRACT, that will be chosen with probabilities according to the ratio rule,

$$\Pr(\text{ADD}) = \frac{s(\text{ADD})}{s(\text{ADD}) + s(\text{SUBTRACT})}$$

where $s(\text{ADD})$ and $s(\text{SUBTRACT})$ are the strength values of these procedures determined by the spreading activation mechanism of the CI model. The strengths of these procedures depend on how much support they receive from their associated schemas, ADD-SCHEMA and SUB-SCHEMA, as well as from the *more-* or *less-* keywords. The schemas in turn are supported by the text. Text propositions favoring either the ADD-SCHEMA or the SUB-SCHEMA are linked to the respective schema nodes. Text propositions, such as those derived from the first sentence of these problems, which do not indicate the problem structure, are linked equally to both hypotheses, although more weakly (Figures 10.6a, 10.6b, and 10.6c).

Figures 10.6a, 10.6b, and 10.6c provide a processing trace of the model for the inconsistent addition problem. The parameter values used were estimated by informal exploration to maximize the goodness of fit of the model to the data in Figures 10.4 and 10.5. Specifically, links among text propositions and and links among schemas and procedures were assigned a value of 1. Links between text propositions and the schema they supported were given a value of .8. Neutral propositions were linked to both schemas with a value of .4. Marked key words were linked directly to the procedure with a value of .4. All other links were zero. Each node was linked to itself with a value of 1, except for the ADD procedure, which was assigned a value of 1.2, which is the model's way of accounting for the observed response bias in favor of addition. Intuitively, these parameter estimates seem reasonable in this problem context.

The first sentence, shown in Figure 10.6a, expresses the proposition TALL[TOM] with the modifier 175CM. These nodes are linked to both schemas, which in turn are linked to their corresponding procedures. The network settles with the activation values shown. The probability of choosing the correct hypothesis (ADD) at this query point is .58/(.58 + .47) = .55; that is, the model starts out with a modest addition bias.

The second sentence, in Figure 10.6b, adds another proposition with a modifier,

SHORTER[TOM,JEFF]
|____ 12CM

which unequivocally specifies the problem as an addition problem; these propositions are therefore linked to the ADD-SCHEMA only. However, the key word *shorter* suggests subtraction and is therefore linked to the SUBTRACT procedure. The activation values that result from the settling of the network are also shown. SHORTER[TOM,JEFF] becomes the strongest proposition, which seems right intuitively. The probability of choosing the correct procedure becomes .42/(.42 + .31) = .58, thus barely increasing over the prior value. This is comparable to the results observed for inconsistent addition problems.

Figure 10.6c shows the final proposition – [HOW[TALL[JEFF]]] –

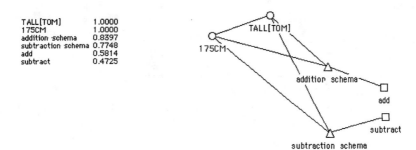

TALL[TOM]	1.0000
175CM	1.0000
addition schema	0.8397
subtraction schema	0.7748
add	0.5814
subtract	0.4725

"Tom is 175 cm tall."

(a)

TALL[TOM]	0.8493
175CM	0.5603
SHORTER[TOM,JEFF]	1.0000
12CM	0.7184
addition schema	0.9603
subtraction schema	0.3562
add	0.4244
subtract	0.3087

"He is 12 cm taller than Jeff."

(b)

Figure 10.6   A processing trace for an inconsistent addition problem at three query points. Final activation values of the nodes are shown next to each graph.

which further strengthens the add procedure (it supports the ADD-SCHEMA in the same way as the previous sentence) but succeeds in lifting the probability of choosing the correct procedure to only .65. This far from perfect performance level attests to the strong interference produced by the marked keyword and corresponds to the actual performance of Lewis's subjects.

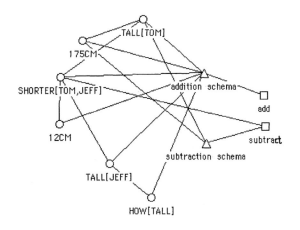

TALL[TOM]	0.5975
175CM	0.3608
SHORTER[TOM,JEFF]	0.9432
12CM	0.5837
TALL[JEFF]	0.7579
HOW[TALL]	0.5212
addition schema	1.0000
subtraction schema	0.1937
add	0.3587
subtract	0.1920

"How tall is Jeff?"

(c)

Figure 10.6 (*cont.*).

Figures 10.4 and 10.5 show the predictions for all four problem types (Add, Subtract, Consistent, & Inconsistent) used in the Lewis experiment. It is obvious that the predictions agree rather well with the data. Indeed, a chi square goodness of fit test yields a nonsignificant value, χ^2 (9) = 18.75, which is quite impressive considering (1) that each of the 12 data points was based on 576 observations so that the goodness of fit test is very sensitive, and (2) that we have estimated only three parameters.

The success of the CI model in accounting for these data does not mean that alternative models are wrong. However, it is worth noting that time course predictions for the formation of hypotheses could be obtained with the CI model without any additional assumptions, just by running the model sentence by sentence. Also, key word effects and bias parameters could be incorporated in a natural way. That is not to say that alternative models could not be similarly elaborated, although for single-schema, top-down control models some rather arbitrary assumptions would be needed to account for the time course data as well as the key-word effects.

What intellectual gain has been achieved by modeling these data? If one wants to know about the time course of hypothesis formation, key-word effects, or response biases, one merely has to look at the data to find out. The simulation does not tell us anything about these matters that the data did not already reveal. The primary value of the simulation is that it allows us to understand the particular results of this study within a broad, overarching framework that ties together many different observations about language understanding and problem solving. It lets us see these results as pieces of a much larger puzzle, as systematic observations related to a host of others.

There may also be some more immediate gain. As Kintsch and Lewis (1993) have suggested, if we want to find out about inconsistency effects in Change problems, we would have to run another expensive experiment. Or we can boldly calculate. According to our simulation, the following problem should have a solution probability of .88.

(9)   Tom has 12 marbles.
       Jeff gives Tom 3 more.
       How many . . .?

If the problem is reformulated with an inconsistent marked term: *Tom has 12 marbles. He takes away 3 marbles from Jeff,* the probability of a correct solution ought to drop to about .63. Thus, we don't have to do a new experiment for every new problem – we can use the model to simulate outcomes. How successful such an engineering approach would be remains to be seen, but it certainly should be tried.

10.1.5 The emergence of schemas

The CI model for word arithmetic problem solving as formulated in Kintsch (1988) and Kintsch and Lewis (1993) differs from the earlier generation of models primarily in that the CI model considers alternative schemas in parallel as candidates for forming a problem model. In contrast, in Kintsch and Greeno (1985) and Cummins et al. (1988) smart rules were employed to select the right schema in the first place. The CI model undoubtedly represents progress over the earlier formulation, but it is not the end of the story. Arithmetic problem schemas must be learned, whereas Kintsch (1988) assumes that the children already have full-fledged schemas for arithmetic that need only to be applied correctly. Stern (1993b) has shown that this is by no means the case and that acquiring the right kind of arithmetic problem schemas is a major facet of learning to solve word problems. I sketch here Stern's findings and outline what the next generation model for word problem solving should look like. It incorporates the work discussed so far but turns further away from the abstract schema concept and toward the notion of situated cognition.

The Kintsch (1988) formulation corresponds to the performance of children who have had a great deal of experience with these particular word problems. However, a schema-based problem model is the end product of learning to solve word problems in school; it does not characterize the way children learn to solve these problems. Stern (1993b) showed convincingly that children in the early elementary school years do not have an abstract schema that they use to form problem models in the way we have surmised. Instead, their knowledge is more accurately characterized as a set of concrete, situation-bound principles about arithmetic that allow them to solve many problems and out of which abstract general schemas will eventually be constructed.

Stern's data come from an eight-year longitudinal study that assessed the cognitive and social development of a large group of school children in Munich, Germany – the LOGIK project of Weinert and Schneider (in press). Two observations from this study form the core of Stern's argument. First, in a large number of cases, students can provide the correct answer to a word problem but are unable to explain how they arrived at their answer. Specifically, they are unable to write a correct equation for their solution. This happens to all students, both high and low achievers, and for all kinds of problems, as long as the problem is challenging for a particular student. The student is able to figure out the problem by what he or she knows about numbers and arithmetic operations, taking into account the situational constraints imposed by the problem, but without being able to form a metalinguistically explicit problem model. Figure 10.7 shows some representative results. Percentage of errors, correct solutions with equation, and correct solutions without equation are shown for a three-year period for the following problem:

(10) Three children are celebrating a birthday.
      Mother bought 10 apple tarts.
      Each child eats 2 apple tarts.
      How many tarts will be left over?

This problem can be understood in terms of concrete operations and can be solved correctly without forming an abstract problem model. Across three years of schooling, the percentage of errors is approximately halved,

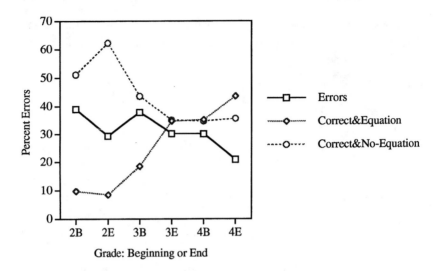

Figure 10.7   The percentage error, percentage correct solutions with correct equation, and percentage of correct solutions without correct equation for the "apple tart" problem in grades 2, 3, and 4. After Stern (1993b).

but the proportion of correctly solved problems for which no equation or an incorrect equation was given remained around 35%.

The second observation that, according to Stern, indicates that children do not have fully developed abstract arithmetic schemas is based on an analysis of children's attempted solutions of various types of problems. If solving a certain problem is evidence that the student has formed the correct problem model for this type of problem, then the student should also be able to solve other problems requiring the same problem model. This is often not the case. As an example, consider a student who successfully solves

(11) Fred had 4 balls.
      He has 3 more balls than Elly.
      How many balls does Elly have?

and

(12) Tom has 7 balls.
      Jane has 11 balls.
      How many balls have they altogether?

According to Stern's argument, the first problem provides evidence that the student has a Compare schema for unknown referents; the second provides evidence that the student has a Combine schema. The student therefore should be able to solve

(13) Jan has 7 rabbits.
He has 4 more rabbits than Mike.
How many rabbits do Jan and Mike have together?

In this problem the Compare schema must be used first to determine how many rabbits Mike has, but that is not specifically asked for. About one third of the children in the two grades where all these problems were tested solved the first two problems correctly but could not solve the third problem. (The reverse, that the third problem was solved correctly but errors were made on either of the first two, was very rarely observed, indicating that we are not dealing here with random variability but with a true asymmetry.)

Problem models, therefore, are not derived from metalinguistically available schemas, except at a very late stage of schooling. Stern (1993b) discusses some evidence that suggests such schemas are in fact the end result of learning how to solve word problems.

Stern also points out that the assumption that children use arithmetic schemas to solve word problems is somewhat inconsistent with the essence of the CI models. In other applications of the model, schemas are not treated as full-fledged structures, ready to be retrieved and used, but as emergent structures that are put together in the context of a particular task from smaller knowledge units. In the case of word arithmetic problem solving, the knowledge units used to construct problem models are the arithmetic principles as they are learned in concrete task contexts by the child. Only later will schemas be abstracted from these principles. One principle will come to be associated with another one, thus eventually becoming a unit and a schema. But while the children are learning to solve word problems, their knowledge is less orderly, less abstract, and more situated. For instance, commutativity may be contextually restricted to numbers below 20; the possibility of reformulating *more* statements by *less* statements may be realized in some contexts but not others; the term *more than* may be understood in the context of an action but not in the context of a static comparison. Instead of a few powerful schemas, children appear to have a lot of disjointed, situationally restricted knowledge. So far, no one has systematically analyzed what these bits and pieces are and how they are interrelated. Once this is done, a simulation within the framework of the CI model could be constructed to account more accurately for the learning that children engage in when they solve word problems. The Kintsch (1988) formulation might be the final, most sophisticated version of a sequence of models characterized by increasingly general and more powerful arithmetic schemas, but starting with quite restricted and context-bound knowledge structures. This would be by no means an idle exercise but would have considerable theoretical and practical interest. It would be a good environment in which to study how schemas emerge, and it could be used to explore various instructional scenarios. Instructors and tutors can no longer assume that their students merely need to apply their arithmetic schemas in solving word problems; they need to be concerned how these schemas emerge in the first place.

10.2 Word algebra problems

There are some good reasons why one should study word algebra problems. The domain of algebra is so much richer and more complex than that of arithmetic, and hence the texts of word problems are longer and more interesting, placing greater demands on a model of discourse comprehension. Furthermore, the central issues in algebra word problem solving appear to be the same as in the arithmetic domain. In particular, the importance of situation models in algebra word problem solving is at least as high as in arithmetic word problem solving. In a pioneering study, using extensive protocol analyses, Hall, Kibler, Wenger, and Truxaw (1989) have shown that competent college students reason within the situational context of a story problem to identify the quantitative constraints required for a solution. They use the text to build, elaborate, and verify a situation model from which they derive their solution. A variety of reasoning strategies are used by students to develop these situation models, which are by no means restricted to the algebraically relevant aspects of a problem. Integrating the dual representations of a problem at the situational and mathematical level appears to be the central aspect of competence according to Hall and his co-workers, as indeed it was for children working on arithmetic word problems.

10.2.1 Algebraic schemas

The basic components of a model of word algebra problem solving might therefore be quite similar to those of our model for arithmetic word problem solving. However, the very richness and complexity of the algebra domain that attracted us in the first place might seem to make this approach impossible. We had to deal with only a few arithmetic schemas – those used by first-graders discussed earlier, the Part-Whole schema, which subsumes these at a more advanced stage of development, plus a few more primitive versions characteristic of earlier levels of development, as described by Riley et al. (1983). But how many algebra schemas are there? Mayer (1981) compiled a list of 1,097 problem types from current algebra texts. How can we deal with such complexity?

It turns out that a complete simulation of algebra word problem solving is indeed impossible. It is not the complexity of algebra that is the decisive obstacle, but linguistic considerations. The algebra is really quite straightforward. No more than a few schemas are needed to solve the vast majority of problems, plus some knowledge of other domains such as geometry, physics, statistics, and so on. Thus, a relatively small number of algebraic schemas can do all the work that is needed for the construction of the necessary formal problem models. The difficulty is in the construction of the situation model, without which the student cannot get to the right problem model. The demands on the construction of situation models in college and high-school algebra problems are open-ended, employing all kinds of linguistic and general world knowledge that might be needed for that purpose. For the arithmetic simulation of Cummins et al. (1988), the general knowledge that had to be given to the simulation was quite limited. If a new concept was encountered in a problem that was not already known to the simulation, it asked the experimenter, and the experimenter could give simple answers: *steal* is like *take away, deer* and *pencil* are countable objects; *cars* and *trains* belong to the superset *vehicle; cars* and *dolls* to the superset *toys; yellow* is a modifier. The simulation needs to know no more. This strategy does not work for algebra word problems. One really must know what words mean, what their implications are, how various objects move in the world, what their shapes are, and so on, endlessly. As we have regretted in other places in this book, there is no knowledge base that contains all that information in a form that could be used by a simulation program.

The only way one could build a simulation of word algebra problem solving would be to restrict the domain radically, say to a blocks world, so that the simulation could know everything there is to know in that domain. Further restrictions would have to be placed on the form of the linguistic input. This did not seem an attractive alternative to us. We decided, therefore, in favor of a hand simulation in which the problem of general world knowledge is avoided by using our own intuitions as required. There is a great deal this approach cannot deliver in comparison with a real simulation, but some useful implications can still be gathered from it.

10.2.2 A model for word algebra problems

The model we have constructed is described in Nathan, Kintsch, and Young (1992). It is a direct development from the models for arithmetic, in particular Reusser (1989), because the interplay between the situation model and the problem model is central to it. A major innovation is the algebraic schemas on which the more than 1,000 problem types of algebra are based. Four Rate schemas are needed to deal with the largest class of algebra problems, rate problems, which I describe presently. Another class of problems involves physics, geometry, and schemas from other domains. This is essentially an open class. Examples are Newton's second law (the sum of all forces for a system in equilibrium must be zero); Ohm's law; the Pythagorean theorem; and the formulas for the area and circumference of a circle and other geometric shapes. Finally, there is a third class of word algebra problems – number problems – which are not schema based but must be constructed from the text directly without the use of a schema. We focus here on rate problems.

The four Rate schemas are all of the same form,

$$\text{Unit}_1 = \text{rate-of-Unit}_1\text{-per-Unit}_2 \times \text{Unit}_2$$

The units may be amount per time (a boat travels 4 km per hour), cost per unit (a pound of almonds costs \$5.99), portion to total cost (7% of the cost of a car), and amount to amount (5% acid in 3 gallons of solution). These Rate schemas are the building blocks of algebraic problem models. The story text usually specifies one or two of the members of a schema (Unit_1, Unit_2, rate). If only one member is missing, it can be computed from the formula. Algebra problems usually require the instantiation of more than one schema, together with the relation between them. Thus, we might have two kinds of nuts with different costs, and mix the two according to certain specifications, requiring three cost-per-unit schemas. To construct a problem model, the problem solver must (1) pick the right schema, which can be done on the basis of textual cues, just as in the case of the arithmetic schemas; (2) specify as many elements for each schema as the text allows; and (3) find or infer from the text the relationships among the schemas used. Once a problem model has been constructed, an equation for the problem can be found by constraint propagation within the problem model.

The working of the model is best illustrated by an example. Figure 10.8 shows a common distance-rate-time problem. Its textbase contains three propositions. The time slot of the first proposition is unspecified, but the reader must assume some initial point in time to build a situation model. Both planes leave from the same place but at different times and at different speeds. At some point in time, they will have covered the same distance and the second plane will overtake the first. It is easiest to think of the model that students construct for this situation as an animation: Two planes start from the same place on the some route and continue until they meet. The rather clumsy two-dimensional graph in Figure 10.8 is merely a substitute for this scene. The actual situation model represents directly what happens in the real world.

Nathan et al. (1992) used some simple graphical conventions to construct a problem model. Every Rate schema is represented by a vertical arrangement of three circles, the two units, and the rate that relates them. Quantitative values from the problem text that specify either a unit or a rate can be written inside the appropriate circles. Thus, the schema from Plane 1 consists of a time slot and a distance slot, both unspecified because nothing was said about either in the problem, and a rate, which the problem identified as 200 miles per hour. This particular schema was selected from all algebraic schemas the reader knows on the basis of such keywords as distance, rate, time, and moving objects. A second schema is similarly constructed for Plane 2.

To complete the problem model, the student must find out what information the text provides that specifies the relation between the two Rate schemas that have been constructed. First, there is a relation between the flying times of the two airplanes: one leaves 3 hours after the other. To

Text:
A plane leaves Denver and travels east at 200 miles per hour. Three hours later, a second plane leaves Denver on a parallel course and travels east at 350 miles per hour. How long will the second plane take to overtake the first plane?

Textbase:

LEAVE[PLANE1,DENVER]   LEAVE[PLANE2,DENVER]   OVERTAKE[P1,P2]
    rate: 200MPH   rate: 350MPH
    direction: EAST   direction: EAST
                time:3 H LATER   time: ?
                loc: PARALLEL COURSE

Situation Model:

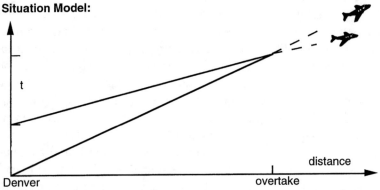

Problem Model:

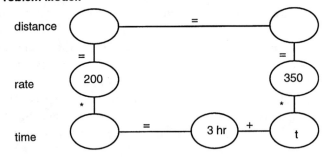

Equation: $200(t+3) = 350t$

Figure 10.8   A word algebra problem: the text, textbase, situation model, problem model, and equation.

enter this information correctly into the problem model, the student must realize that this means that the flying time of Plane 1 equals the flying time of Plane 2 plus the 3 hours. The other piece of information needed is not explicit and must be inferred on the basis of the student's world knowledge: If the planes start from the same place and fly along the same route, they will have covered the same distance at the point at which the faster one overtakes the slower plane. Students have a great deal of experience with races between various kinds of vehicles and are quite familiar with this situation. Therefore, this knowledge is available, but it must be activated at this point and used to complete the problem model.

An equation is easily derived from the problem model. The unknown in the problem is the time t that the second plane needs to overtake the first. This can be entered in the problem schema as shown. Next, $t + 3$ can be computed as the travel time for Plane 1. Finally, the distances traveled by each plane can be expressed as the product of time multiplied by speed, and set equal, resulting in the equation shown in Figure 10.8. The equation can then be solved as in any numerical problem.

This is indeed a complex model for solving a simple problem! Similar problem models can be constructed for all rate problems and, with some obvious extensions, also physics and geometry problems. But is this complexity necessary for these rather simple problems? First, algebra word problems are not simple for most people and most students. Second, there is some evidence that the model presented here is by no means unnecessarily complex. What we lack and cannot have for the reasons we have discussed is a full simulation of the model and direct empirical tests of it, as in the case of word arithmetic problems. (The subtlety of inferring *equal distance* from *overtake* is a good example of the kind of general world knowledge that is necessary for these problems that we do not know how to represent in a knowledge base.) We can argue for the present model on three grounds.

First, the components of the model are directly motivated by our research on word arithmetic problems. We had to introduce a situation model and problem model representation between the textbase and equation to understand how people solve word arithmetic problems. It would be surprising if we could do with less in the case of word algebra. Second, in their study of word algebra problem solving, Hall et al. (1989) obtained strong empirical evidence that good students engage in extensive reasoning at the level of the situation model and that the major difficulty they

have is in coordinating their formal model with their situational understanding. Finally, Nathan et al. (1992) and Nathan (1991) have collected
some experimental evidence that supports the psychological reality of the
structures and processes assumed here. For this research they adopted
the strategy of developing an algebra word problem tutor from the principles about word problem solving that have been discussed here.

10.2.3 The ANIMATE tutor for solving word algebra problems

Intelligent tutoring is based on the premise that the system solves a problem in a way that simulates what human experts do. The system also has
a model of the student and is able to interpret the student's behavior in
terms of that model and of its own understanding of the problem. Hence,
it can diagnose errors and take remedial steps. Because we cannot simulate human word algebra problem solving, this approach is not open to us.

However, suppose the model described here is essentially correct. If
that were the case, what instructional implications would it have? What
are the difficult steps in solving word algebra problems where students
might need help? Because reading is not problematic for college students,
they are perfectly capable of forming a textbase. Also, because our initial
goal is to bring their performance on word problems up to their level of
performance on numerical problems, we will not bother helping them
with the equations. Furthermore, we know that college students have no
trouble understanding the situations described in algebra word problems.
There are some exceptions, especially in the areas of statistics and probability, and we have also encountered some rather fuzzy notions about the
concept of "interest." However, these exceptions are neglected here. In
general, students do not need help constructing situation models from
the simple contexts depicted in word problems. They do need help with
the formation of the problem model, because they often skip this stage
and jump to equations without a clear understanding of the problem
structure. Thus, we must force them to build explicit problem models,
and we must provide them with the means to do so. Some students and
experts successfully use notes and graphs for this purpose, but in general
students do not have available a systematic, easy system for designing
problem models. Nathan et al. (1992) decided to teach students the
graphic system we used to represent problem models in our theory as a
systematic way to construct such models while attempting to solve them.

This has proven to be quite feasible. With minimal instruction, students learn to use this way of representing a problem and most find it useful. Good students sometimes prefer not to be bothered because they have their own ways of doing these things, but average or poor students are often able to gain insights by using this simple representational scheme that they have been unable to obtain in years of traditional instruction.

However, students are even more in need of help with another difficulty in word algebra problem solving. It is not enough to give students a means to build formal problem models. They must be able to tell whether they have built the right one, the one that corresponds to their situation model.

Problem models are a necessary step in problem solving because we are unable to compute the solution of a problem directly in our situation model. This is not the case for all problems. Children need not compute symbolically a problem like $9 = 7 + 2$, for they have the answer available directly. We need not formalize the problem of how to make coffee with an unfamiliar coffee machine, for we can solve the puzzle by responding directly to the pot's affordances (Larkin, 1989). Many problems, however, cannot be solved without recourse to some formal computational system. Building a highway bridge and solving differential equations are some examples. Algebra word problems generally are in that class, too. We have a perfectly good situation model for the problem in Figure 10.7, but it will not help us to find a solution. For that, we need to reformulate the problem mathematically. In using mathematics, however, there is the danger of losing the correspondence between the mathematical formulation of the problem and its real-world structure (Greeno, 1989; Kintsch, 1991). Situation model and problem model must match. At all levels of education in science and engineering this match is often difficult to ensure and is frequently not achieved. The difficulty is not the formal system per se, nor is it situational understanding per se; it lies in the correspondence between the formalization and the situation.

This is a notoriously difficult issue in engineering or software design. But eventually the real world gives the formalist some feedback as to the adequacy of the formalization: Bridges last for centuries, or they collapse; the software is perfect but does not do what the customer imagined it would. Experienced algebra word problem solvers provide their own feedback by checking their answers for reasonableness against their situation model. That is exactly where students need help; otherwise they come up with negative values for the length of a board and similar absurdities (Paige & Simon, 1966). Because algebra students cannot operate in the real world and receive feedback from it, the next best thing is to supply them with a substitute world in the form of an animation that acts out what is implied by the problem model they have constructed. Thus, in the case of the problem in Figure 10.8, the animation would show Plane 1 leaving; after a delay, Plane 2 leaves at a greater speed. After some time, t it overtakes the first plane and the animation stops. On the other hand, if the student makes an error and constructs a problem model in which the slow plane leaves after the fast plane, this is exactly what happens in the simulation, and the student invariably realizes the error. Similarly, if the student forgets to specify the distances the planes travel, they will simply go on flying, even after one overtakes the other. The student notices that something is wrong, and now has a chance to figure out what.

Nathan et al. (1992) have built such a tutor, called ANIMATE. It is not an intelligent tutor, because the system does not understand the problem at all. It merely executes an animation as instructed by the student's problem model (it paints fences, mixes solutions, stacks up piles of money, or lets objects move). If the right thing happens, the student realizes that the solution is correct. If the wrong thing happens, the student must figure out how to correct it. If nothing happens because the simulation was not given enough information to execute anything, the student knows that one or more pieces are missing from his formal model and can try to complete it.

Figure 10.9 provides a graphical description of word problem solving. Both problem-relevant information and situation-relevant information are extracted from the problem text, forming potentially isolated problem representations that must be coordinated. This link is what the ANIMATE tutor focuses on. ANIMATE has two components, Network, which is a system that allows problem models to be constructed according to the graphical conventions we have sketched, and the Animation, which runs whatever Network tells it to. The purpose of ANIMATE is to enable the student with the two links in the figure labeled *Is it right?* and *What went wrong?* by making explicit the correspondence between the problem model (in Network) and the situation model (the Animation).

ANIMATE works quite well. Although it has never received a field test in a classroom study, it has passed a number of laboratory tests with good grades (Nathan et al., 1992). Nathan showed that with only minimal

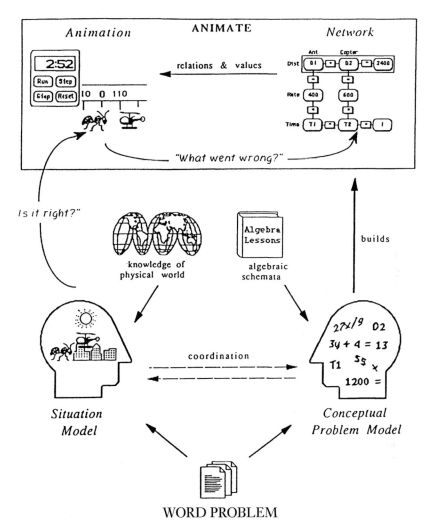

Figure 10.9   The role of the ANIMATE tutor in helping students to solve world algebra problems. From Nathan et al. (1992).

training on ANIMATE, students outperformed suitable control groups who worked on new word problems without the system. The various components of ANIMATE were tested separately in this study, which clearly established the significant role of the animation. For instance, in a pre- and posttraining comparison, students who were trained with Network only, without the animation, showed an improvement of 30%, whereas students who were trained with the whole system, including the animation, improved by 57.5%. For comparison, a conventionally instructed control group improved by 9%. Such results are impressive if one remembers that these students had many years of conventional training and were exposed to the ANIMATE environment for only a single brief session.

Nathan (1991) performed an extensive protocol study of a small group of students using ANIMATE with Work, Mixture, and Investment problems as well as Motion problems. He gave his subjects a pre- and posttest of comparable difficulty, so that their improvement as a function of training with the ANIMATE system could be accurately determined. ANIMATE was by no means equally effective for everyone. The two subjects who scored highest on the pretest performed very well on the posttest. A second group of three subjects performed almost equally well on the posttest, in spite of error scores in excess of 50% on the pretest. The two remaining subjects scored poorly on the posttest, although for one of these subjects that was a great improvement over the pretest, where he got almost nothing right. Nathan also gave the subjects in this study an impossible problem (a problem that had no solution). Only the three middle subjects who showed the greatest improvement from pre- to posttest recognized that this was an impossible problem. It is not surprising that the two poor subjects failed to do so, but the two subjects who were very good from the beginning also did not recognize that the problem was not well specified. Even though they knew how to solve these problems, their procedures were mechanical rather than based on understanding.

The protocols Nathan collected suggest that ANIMATE did not provide enough help for the two poorest subjects, who were lost and reduced to making random adjustments to the animation. These learners needed more guidance than ANIMATE could give them. If they had been given more elementary problems to solve, they could perhaps have made better use of ANIMATE and learned successfully. The two subjects who already knew how to solve these problems also did not learn much. They relied on what they knew and failed to use ANIMATE to deepen their understanding. If they had been given more challenging problems, they might have found more use for ANIMATE and learned to engage in situational reasoning in the process. For the other three subjects, ANIMATE seemed just right. The problems were difficult for them but not too difficult, and the kind of support ANIMATE provided enabled them to solve these problems and learn a great deal in the process. My hunch is not that this style of tutoring does not work with poor students or with very good students. Rather, in order to learn students must receive problems that are adjusted to their level of skill: problems they cannot quite solve on their own but which they can just manage with the scaffolding provided by the tutor.

It is unfortunate that ANIMATE was never used in a real educational environment. As it is, it is impossible to judge its value as a classroom tool. But from a theoretical perspective, the kind of work that has been done with ANIMATE has proven to be quite interesting. Discourse comprehension theory can be used for the analysis of word problem solving, and such an analysis allows us to significantly expand and elaborate the theory.

> How people understand and solve word problems in algebra or arithmetic is of particular interest for the theory of text comprehension because for these kinds of tasks comprehension does not merely result in the formation of a mental representation that is to be tested or evaluated later by some indirect measure; instead, comprehension directly results in an action. Thus, the empirical data constrain the simulations of mental processing more tightly. In addition to the usual predictions about comprehensibility and memory, the model can also predict whether a solution will be correct or what sort of error might occur. The simulations of how children solve word arithmetic problems first focused on the arithmetic, then on the language, and then more and more on the child's understanding of the situation and the mathematization of that understanding. Much the same thing can be said about college students solving algebra problems. The crucial step is always the formalization of the student's situational understanding in terms of a mathematical problem model. What is achieved by the simulations that were developed and tested here is to spell

out the components involved in this formalization: the mathematical concepts and operations themselves, the informal situational understanding, and the knowledge of the linguistic conventions used in word problems. All three can be sources of errors and difficulties for a student that can be studied and understood by tracing their sources in a simulation. We cannot observe directly the students' thinking, but we can simulate it, manipulate conditions in the simulation, and try to reproduce behavior that we see in our students. Thus, we can understand what students are faced with and help them more effectively when needed.

11

Beyond text

The model for word problem solving that was developed in the previous chapter can provide a framework for a broad range of related comprehension tasks whenever a verbal instruction – a text or an oral communication – must be understood in the context of a particular task and situation to guide the actions of the comprehender. In the previous chapter the action required was to calculate a numerical answer to a mathematical word problem; the text was used to construct a situation model and a corresponding problem model. The formal problem model provided the mathematization of the problem, which made it possible to employ the tools of arithmetic or algebra for the solution of the problem. An analogous situation is encountered in many other tasks, in particular tasks that require the use of a computer for the solution of a problem. Instead of a mathematical problem model, we are dealing in this case with a formal system model. To use the computer, the situational understanding of a task must be reformulated into what we have called a system model (Fischer, Henninger, & Redmiles, 1991).

The formal specification of a computing task in terms of a system model is analogous to the formulation of a word problem in terms of a mathematical problem model. It requires a situational understanding of the task at hand, as well as a knowledge of the formal constraints of the computer system that must be respected in generating the system model. The required situational understanding can be more complex than in the case of word problems. In a word problem the question (usually) specifies precisely the goal of the computation. When people perform tasks on a computer system, an explicit specification of the goal state is not necessarily available. The goal of the action is frequently specified only in general, situational terms and must first be translated into system terms.

For instance, suppose my goal is to send a certain manuscript to a colleague. In system terms, this might mean that I want a file containing this manuscript to be available to my colleague at her computer. Alternatively, in a different system, it might mean that I print out the manuscript and mail it to her. Thus, the formulation of a sufficiently precise goal schema in system terms may in itself be nontrivial – for instance, if a user has an inadequate understanding of the system characteristics.

A goal schema, formulated within a particular system model, guides action through the mechanism of pattern completion. The term pattern completion or redintegration – *Komplexergänzung* – was introduced by Selz (1922; see also the discussion in Kintsch, 1974). The basic notion is that, given a portion of some pattern, the whole pattern completes itself. Thus, in action planning an action goal anticipates the outcome of the action and thereby guides the action toward that outcome. In the following sections, I show how this kind of pattern completion process functions to allow experienced users to perform routine computing tasks.

11.1 Action planning

Action planning on the basis of verbal instructions can be understood within the framework of the construction–integration model. The kinds of actions considered here are routine tasks in familiar situations – in particular, computing tasks. The tasks concerned are not so simple that they are entirely scripted, that is, require merely a fixed action sequence. But neither are they so complex that they require intentional, active search and problem solving. They are the kind of task that experts spend much of their time with. They are performed semiautomatically, with little conscious effort, on a regular basis, but always in somewhat different ways, because the situational context and the task requirements are complex and conflicting and never quite the same. Specifically, in Mannes and Kintsch (1991) we studied routine computing tasks involving file maintenance and editing as well as using the mail system.

11.1.1 Routine actions

We started by observing how experienced computer users perform such tasks while providing concurrent think-aloud protocols. Our subjects knew immediately what to do in response to the instructions we gave them and provided rich verbal protocols. These protocols were propositionalized and formed the core of the knowledge for our computer simulation. In addition, this knowledge base was augmented in three ways:

1. Six other experienced computer users were shown each of the propositions generated in the concurrent verbal protocols and asked to provide a free association – the first thing that came to mind. These subjects were not told anything about our purposes, so that the associations they produced (such as as *post office* and *stamp* in response to *mail*) were frequently irrelevant to the computer context.
2. For all propositions that stated a request (e.g., to enter mail, edit a file), a second proposition was added that stated what the outcome of the action would be if the request were acted on. This information was sometimes generated spontaneously in the protocols or the free association task, but because it was crucial for our purposes we had to make sure that it was available for every request.
3. We added a few action plans that were needed to perform the tasks we were concerned with that were not generated spontaneously by our subjects.

Three types of nodes in the long-term memory network were thus generated: *general knowledge about computers* (e.g., to use the mail, you must be at the mail-level, not the system-level), *general knowledge about the tasks* to be done (e.g., to write a letter to someone, you need an address), and specific action plans called *plan elements,* which are the commands needed to execute the task.[1] Plan elements are formally propositions, like all other elements in the network. They take three arguments: a *plan name* (e.g., REPLY to a message), a *set of conditions* that must exist in the world for this plan element to be executable (e.g., a message must exist in order to reply to it), and a *set of outcomes* of the execution of the plan elements (e.g., the sender of the message receives the reply). Figure 11.1 shows an example of a plan element, and the following are some examples of plan–element names (out of a total of 26 used in the simulation). A question mark indicates an unbound variable.

(EDIT FILE?)

---

1 Plan elements are analogous to productions in ACT* (Anderson, 1983).

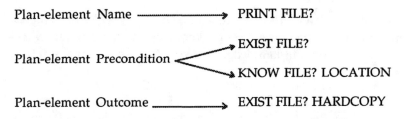

Plan-element Name ────────────→ PRINT FILE?

Plan-element Precondition ──────→ EXIST FILE?

──→ KNOW FILE? LOCATION

Plan-element Outcome ──────────→ EXIST FILE? HARDCOPY

Figure 11.1   A sample plan element for printing a file.

(PASTE TEXT? FILE?)
(FIND FILE?)
(PRINT FILE?)
(SEND FILE? MAIL)
(SEND FILE? SYSTEM)
(COPY MESSAGE)
(RENAME FILE? FILE^NEWNAME)

The nodes thus generated were connected via argument overlap, forming an 81 × 81 long-term memory matrix that was fixed and did not change during the course of a simulation. This long-term memory network was then used in generating dynamically a task network in working memory when the system was instructed to perform some particular task.

Generating the task network involved the following sequence of steps:

1. The instruction was propositionalized, yielding two types of propositions: REQUESTS to do something (e.g., "print the file called 'letter'" → (REQUEST ((PRINT FILE^LETTER))), and INTHEWORLD propositions describing the task environment (e.g., "there is a file called 'Letter' in the world" → (EXIST(FILE^LETTER INTHEWORLD))).

2. For every REQUEST proposition, the anticipated OUTCOME of that request was retrieved from long-term memory and added to the task net. Thus, for the request to print the file "letter" the outcome (EXIST (FILE^LETTER HARDCOPY)) was included.

3. Every REQUEST, INTHEWORLD, and OUTCOME proposition in the task network served as a retrieval cue to sample *n* propositions from the long-term memory network. Thus, the task network was enriched by related information from long-term memory. For large values of *n*, the

system used practically everything it knew that was related to the task at hand; for small values of *n*, on the other hand, the system might sometimes fail to use critical information it knew about but did not sample on a particular occasion, leading it to make an error (see section 11.3 for further discussion of this aspect of the model).

4. All plan elements in long-term memory were bound to existing objects in the world and added to the proposition list. Thus, if two files are mentioned in the instructions, two copies of all plan elements with the variable FILE?, one bound to each INTHEWORLD file, were generated.

5. The next step was to link the nodes that had been generated in working memory into a network:

- Positive links were established on the basis of argument overlap. This assures, for instance, that a (REQUEST SEND X) is linked to all plan elements with the name SEND, or that (OUTCOME Y) is linked to all elements that have the outcome Y.
- Inhibitory links were established (1) between a requested outcome Z and a plan element that had outcome ~Z; (2) between a plan element that had precondition X and a plan element that had the outcome ~X; and (3) between an INTHEWORLD proposition and a plan element that has the same INTHEWORLD proposition as its outcome; thus, (KNOW (FILE^LETTER LOCATION INTHEWORLD)) inhibits the plan element (FIND (FILE^LETTER)).

Figure 11.2 illustrates how inhibitory links function in this system. They allow a requested outcome to inhibit incompatible plans; they allow each plan element to protect its preconditions; and they deactivate plan elements that are no longer necessary because their outcomes already exist INTHEWORLD.

Thus, a task network was constructed from two sources: (1) the instructions given to the system, which included information about the state of the world, and (2) what the system knew about the task and itself.

The task network thus constructed was then integrated by spreading activation around until the activation pattern stabilized. This pattern indicates what the system wants to do: which plan elements are strongly activated, which are less activated, which are altogether deactivated.

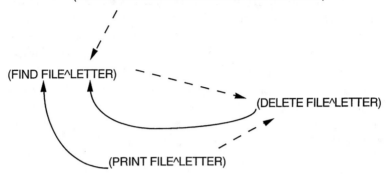

Figure 11.2   Excitatory (solid lines) and inhibitory (broken lines) relations among plan elements and INTHEWORLD propositions.

However, it is usually not possible to carry out the action one wants to do most, because the preconditions for that action might not be met by the existing INTHEWORLD environment. Thus, we cannot send a letter without first writing it, entering the mail system, and so on. We therefore introduced a distinction between *can-do* and *want-to nodes.*

Accordingly, all computations were done in the network of want-to nodes, but the can-do nodes determined what action was taken. Each want-to node activated a corresponding can-do node in proportion to its own strength. However, can-do nodes were inhibited if their preconditions did not exist INTHEWORLD. Thus, although the system wants most strongly to send a letter, it cannot do so because there is no letter. It therefore executes the most highly activated can-do plan element. As we shall see, this tends to be an action that produces the missing preconditions and starts a chain of intermediary actions that change the state of the world step by step and eventually result in the execution of the desired final action.

Mannes and Kintsch (1991) give a formal and detailed description of how task networks are constructed and integrated and describe a computer program called NETWORK that performs these operations. I must refer the reader to this original paper for the details of how this system works and focus here instead on the major conceptual issues involved. The details of such a program are, of course, all important, but they are available elsewhere, which allows me to discuss the theoretically significant points at a more general level.

First, we work through a very simple task: "Include an address you know in a letter that is in a file." This text, translated into propositional form, becomes the core of the task net: There exists a text called "letter" in a file called "letter," as well as a known text called "address," and a request to include the address in the "letter" file. Next, the system searches its long-term memory for the outcome of the request to include a text in a file. It retrieves the outcome proposition (IN TEXT ^ ADDRESS FILE^LETTER) and adds it to the task net. Then, each of the propositions already generated is used to retrieve further information from long-term memory, resulting in the inclusion of another set of propositions in the task network. In this particular case, however, these enrichment propositions play no role whatever, so we can neglect them. Finally, the variables in the 26 plan elements in long-term memory are bound to the objects existing INTHEWORLD, yielding 33 bound plan elements for the task net. Note that all plan elements containing the variable TEXT? will be duplicated in this process, the variable being bound once to TEXT ^ LETTER and once to TEXT ^ ADDDRESS.

The task network thus constructed was a 78×78 matrix. The following link strengths were used: links based on argument overlap were assigned a value of .4, whereas positive links based on causal relations (as in Figure 11.2), as well as request and outcome links, were emphasized by assigning them a higher value (.7). Inhibitory links were set at -10 to assure their effectiveness in a network consisting mainly of positive links. These link strengths were obtained on the basis of informal trial-and-error explorations for a workable parameter set (which remained unchanged for all simulations that were performed).

The task network was now ready for integrating. The activation values for the four most highly activated plan elements after the first integration cycle are illustrated in Figure 11.3 (complete results are in the original paper). The system wants most strongly to paste the address into the letter or to type it, but because the preconditions for these actions are not met INTHEWORLD, only the want-to but not the can-do nodes are activated. The most strongly activated can-do node is FIND^LETTER. Hence, this action is performed, and the outcome of this action – the location of the "letter" file is now known – is added to the list of INTHE-WORLD propositions.

Thus, a new, changed task net is obtained, which is now integrated in turn. As shown in Figure 11.3, after the second integration cycle, the sys-

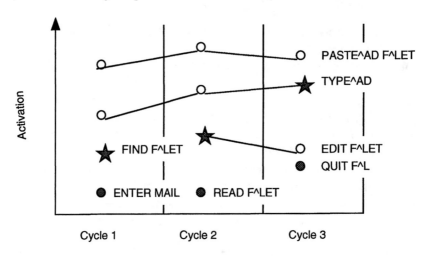

Figure 11.3   Relative activation values for selected plan elements on the first three cycles of the "Include" task. AD abbreviates ADDRESS and LET abbreviates LETTER. Want-to nodes are shown as open circles, can-do nodes are shown as filled circles. A star indicates the action taken on each cycle.

tem still wants most strongly to paste in the address or type it, but cannot do so. The strongest can-do node now is EDIT FILE^LETTER. This action is executed, it once again changes the state of the world – the file "letter" is now in a buffer, ready for typing – and another processing cycle begins. This time TYPE TEXT^ADDRESS can actually be performed; it generates the outcome (IN TEXT^ADDRESS FILE^LETTER), which completes the pattern established by the original request. As a final step (not shown in Figure 11.3), the system exits the newly created FILE^LETTER/ADDRESS.

We have here an example of situated cognition. The system does not plan ahead by setting up a search space and finding a goal path by means-end analysis or some other heuristic. Instead, it looks at the situation, comprehends it in terms of its goals, figures out what it wants to do, and does what it can do, thereby creating a new situation. It then comprehends the changed situation and acts again, producing another change in its world. In the example just described, each of these changes was a step in the right direction, eventually allowing the system to reach its goal. There is no guarantee that this would have been the case, but in an orderly world about which the system has sufficient knowledge, that is exactly what should happen.

This action without planning, but responding in a goal-directed manner to an ever changing situation, has considerable intuitive appeal. Consider what happens when I decide to leave the building: I do not plan to open the door, go out in the hallway, turn right, descend the stairs, and so on. Instead, I simply respond to the open door by walking through it, respond to being in the hallway by walking toward the stairs, and so on. Such routine tasks are different from real problem solving. For example, when I design an experiment, I do try to think of all the possibilities in advance and plan very far ahead. Not all thinking consists in understanding situations in terms of particular goals. More complex, intentional problem-solving processes certainly are required in many cases, but not all planning is problem solving, and much that we have treated in cognitive science as problem solving might be better understood within a comprehension paradigm.

Mannes and Kintsch (1991) work through several more illustrative tasks in their paper. One is a version of the notorious conflicting subgoal task: "Print and delete the file." To handle the sequencing in this task is not trivial for most AI programs and may require special mechanisms. NETWORK solves the task without problems. The spreading activation process favors PRINT over DELETE because of the causal chaining built into the plan elements (Figure 11.2). PRINT inhibits DELETE because it would destroy a precondition necessary for printing, but not vice versa.

NETWORK also handles more complex, two-step tasks, such as "Revise a manuscript you are working on with a colleague by removing a paragraph, and then send the revised manuscript to that person." Quite a few steps are involved in executing these instructions, all in the proper sequence. There is much that could go wrong, therefore, but NETWORK manages not to lose its way.

I have already commented on one characteristic of NETWORK, namely, that it does not plan ahead, but responds to each situation as well as it can in a goal-directed way. Another aspect of NETWORK worth noting is that it is nondeterministic. In generating a task net, it does not include all information it has available in long-term memory but only a random sample – whatever the current propositions in working memory are able to retrieve. This means that it has different information available on different trials with the same task, and hence it may take a different course of action. If by accident a crucial piece of information is missing (has not been sampled from long-term memory), it may fail at a task that it could do otherwise (see section 11.1.3 for further discussion) or perform it in a different way. That, of course, happens to people, too. Mannes and Kintsch (1991) asked one of their subjects, an experienced computer user who had just performed one of the tasks we had given him in a rather clumsy, inelegant way, why he had not chosen a more optimal solution. He immediately understood the optimal solution but commented that he just had not thought of it. Because of its random sampling mechanism, NETWORK also might "not think" of a possible solution path.

We, the theorists, have built into NETWORK all the knowledge it has. Thus, NETWORK does not address the question of how knowledge is acquired; yet once constructed, NETWORK can learn from experience. Mannes and Kintsch (1991) reported some initial observations of how such a system could learn from its own experience by remembering particular cases it had worked on. Case-based reasoning is a large and important topic in cognitive science, and our explorations with NETWORK are certainly not the last word on this topic, but they are worth noting here because of the extreme simplicity of our approach. We simply add a node that encodes a few essential features of a case NETWORK had already solved to its long-term memory network. If retrieved when NETWORK works on a new case (e.g., because there is some overlap between the current task and the prior task), this case node participates in the integration process as part of the task network, often playing a major role in redirecting the activation flow.

To illustrate how NETWORK reasons with cases, Mannes and Kintsch describe how NETWORK solved the "Revise manuscript" task after having previously worked on three related tasks. For each prior task, we created a memory node consisting of the most strongly activated arguments of the nonplan-element propositions in the network, plus the names of the plan elements involved in performing the task. Thus, for the "Include" task shown in Figure 11.3, the arguments FILE^LETTER, TEXT^ADDRESS, and so on would be included, together with the plan elements that were actually executed (FIND, EDIT, TYPE, EXIT). Given a new problem involving a FILE^LETTER, this case memory might be retrieved from long-term memory and strengthen the plan elements associated with it. If the two tasks are sufficiently similar, this might be a good thing: Relevant plan elements would be strengthened, and irrelevant, potentially interfering elements would be weakened, leading to a quicker solution of the problem. On the other hand, case memory can equally well interfere with the solution of new problems – for instance, if the new task requires some entirely different action involving FILE^LETTER. Both positive and negative effects of case memory are well demonstrated, and it remains to be seen whether NETWORK can simulate these results in detail.

Considerable work needs to be done on case-based reasoning in NETWORK. For instance, just what information, and how much, does a case memory contain? Do we need a special forgetting mechanism (a more recently performed task probably has a stronger influence than one done a long time ago)? Thus, there are many open questions at this point, but they seem worth studying, for NETWORK has some potential advantages over other case-based reasoning systems. It requires neither a special selection mechanism nor special evaluation procedures nor analogical reasoning. All we need is to add properly defined memory nodes to our network – the retrieval and integration mechanisms are already there. It would be interesting to see how far such a simple-minded model can be pushed.

11.1.2 Novices and experts

Expert–novice differences have received much attention in the literature on skill acquisition (Chi, Feltovich, & Glaser, 1981; Larkin, 1983). Experts not only know more than novices; they perform tasks in a qualitatively different way, seemingly unaffected by the resource and working memory demands that are such a burden for novices and intermediates (Ericsson & Charness, 1994). Doane and her colleagues (Doane, Kintsch, & Polson, 1989; Doane et al., 1992) have investigated this phenomenon within the context of the construction–integration model. The skill that they examined is particularly interesting and challenging: UNIX command production.

It is widely known that UNIX is an extremely powerful and useful programming language but very difficult to master. Authors such as Norman (1981) have pointed to the arcane command names employed in UNIX as one source of this difficulty, but as we show later, this is no more than a minor problem among many more serious ones that UNIX poses for its users.

Doane, Pellegrino, and Klatzky (1990) observed UNIX users of various levels of experience, some of them over extended periods: novices (average experience with UNIX 8 months), intermediates (average experience 2 years) and experts (5 years' experience). All subjects had taken classes in the advanced features of UNIX and were active users of UNIX. Thus, even the novices in this study were by no means inexperienced. Subjects were given brief verbal instructions to produce legal UNIX commands, using as few keystrokes as possible. There were three types of tasks: single commands (e.g., "display a file"), multiple commands (e.g., "arrange the contents of a file alphabetically," "display the file names of the current directory"), and composite commands (e.g., "sort the contents of a file alphabetically and print the first ten elements"). Composite commands are thus little custom-made programs to perform specific tasks and made up of elementary command sequences using special UNIX facilities such as pipes or redirection symbols.

Doane et al. (1990) made a number of interesting observations. Both novice and intermediate users knew the elements of UNIX; that is, they could successfully execute the single and multiple commands, but they could not put these elements together to form composite commands. The novices failed entirely at this task, and the intermediates often found nonoptimal solutions by using unnecessarily complex redirection methods rather than directly piping the output of one command into the next one. Only the experts could effectively use the input-output (I/O) redirection facilities of UNIX – one of its central and most powerful design features!

Doane et al. (1989) simulated these results in a system called UNICOM, which was modeled after the NETWORK system described in the previous section. A knowledge base for UNICOM was constructed on the basis of the empirical results of Doane et al. (1990). It consisted of general, declarative knowledge and plan elements (procedural knowledge or productions). General knowledge contained both specific information about the syntax of UNIX commands and the I/O redirection syntax, as well as more abstract conceptual knowledge about commands and redirection in UNIX. The plan elements were formally equivalent to those in NETWORK (Figure 11.1): a name, preconditions, and outcomes. As in

Figure 11.2, each plan element activated those plan elements that generate its preconditions and inhibited those elements that interfere with its preconditions. Thus, the model is designed so that the interconnections among plan elements represent the user's knowledge about causal relationships within the UNIX operating system.

The verbal instructions were again propositionalized into REQUEST, OUTCOME, and INTHEWORLD propositions, as in the previous section. UNICOM integrated these instructions together with its knowledge and responded by performing the most activated among its plan elements whose preconditions were met, as was described in the previous section for NETWORK. In this way, the system performs correctly all the tasks used in the Doane et al. (1990) experiment. Thus, it simulates the behavior of the expert subjects in that study, roughly speaking, for even experts sometimes make errors.

To simulate the behavior of the intermediate and novice subjects, we (Doane et al., 1989) lesioned the knowledge base of UNICOM. We took out all the knowledge, general and specific, about redirecting input and output of commands to simulate the novice subjects. To simulate the intermediate subjects, we gave the system knowledge about redirection in general and information about the use of redirection symbols, but we deleted more advanced features, such as knowledge about the use of pipes. With these lesioned knowledge bases, UNICOM reproduced the major features of the Doane, Pellegrino, Klatzky data. The system correctly performed single and multiple commands, unless knowledge about a specific command was deleted, but it was unable to perform composite tasks. It failed completely in the novice version and succeeded only occasionally, and without finding an optimal solution, in performing a composite command in the intermediate version.

We also were able to simulate the performance of particular users. Our strategy was to give UNICOM all the knowledge a specific user had employed in solving the task. This knowledge was determined from the explicit evidence the user had provided in a verbal report. We then ran UNICOM with this knowledge base on the problems that we had previously given to the subject and noted whether or not UNICOM's behavior matched that of the subject. If we had everything right – the theory as well as the knowledge – the behavior of the subject and our simulation should match closely.

For instance, one of our tasks was "Display the first 10 elements of the file 'eggplant,' sorted alphabetically." The correct command is **ls/sort/head** (where / is a pipe, **ls** means list, **sort** means alphabetize and **head** limits the action to the top 10 elements). A novice subject we studied had shown evidence that he knew the command **ls**, but not **sort** and **head**. With this kind of knowledge, both the novice and the system failed at the task, both entering "unknown" as their response. Two years later, the subject, now an intermediate, entered **ls** as his only response. As we assessed his knowledge base, we found that he now also knew the command **sort**. Given this addition to its knowledge base, UNICOM matched this behavior. Although the **ls** command was available on the first test, it was not differently activated. On the second test, however, **ls** became more strongly activated. Because the outcome of **ls** is an unmet precondition of **sort**, additional activation was generated by the **sort** command. For both the user and UNICOM, then, knowing only **ls** resulted in no response, whereas knowing both **ls** and **sort** resulted in the response **ls**. Thus, if UNICOM is given the same knowledge that individual subjects appear to have at different levels of skill, UNICOM will perform the same way the subjects did.

We further investigated expert–novice differences in a study of prompt comprehension (Doane et al., 1992). In that study we gave subjects difficult UNIX tasks to perform, while providing them with various types of prompts as needed. The fact that quite different prompts were helpful to novices and experts reveals qualitative differences that exist in the programming skills of novices and experts.

In Figure 11.4 a sample task is shown together with a series of help prompts that were shown to the subjects whenever they made an error. The prompts were shown one at a time in a fixed order, regardless of the nature of the error. There were four types of prompts. Some prompts, such as P2, provide specific command syntax knowledge. On the other hand, P3 merely provides general conceptual information rather than a specific command syntax. Other prompts are merely reminders, reminding the user of information already made available in earlier prompts (P5, for example). Finally, P6 provides order information. If the user is unable to solve the problem with all these prompts, the correct solution is revealed in the last prompt.

Naturally, experts outperformed novices and intermediates, but there was a clear difference in the kind of prompts experts and novices found most useful, as shown in Figure 11.5. Novices needed a lot of specific

Task Description

> Format the text in ATT2 using the -ms macro package and
> store the formatted version in ATT1

Prompts

Prompt 1   You will need to use the
following command
One that will format the contents
of a file using the -ms macro package

Prompt 2   You will need to use this
command

nroff -ms   will format the contents
of a file using the -ms macro package

Prompt 3   You will need to use a
special symbol that redirects command
output to a file

Prompt 4   You will need to use the
arrow symbol " ≥" that redirects output
from a command to a file

Prompt 5   You will need to use the
arrow symbol " ≥" and the command
nroff -ms

Prompt 6   You'll need to use an
nroff -ms   on ATT2 (which will output
the formatted contents of ATT2), and
you'll need to redirect this output as
input to ATT1

Prompt 7   You will need to use
exactly the following command
elements (though not necessarily
in this order):
≥, nroff -ms

Prompt 8   You'll need to use the
command nroff -ms   followed by the
arrow symbol " ≥"

Prompt 9   The correct production is
nroff -ms ATT2>ATT1
Please enter this production now

Figure 11.4   Example of task description and prompts for the problem
"nroff – ms ATT2>ATT1." From Doane et al. (1992).

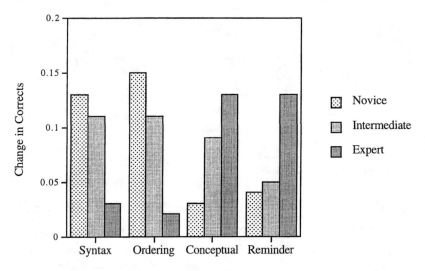

Figure 11.5   Changes in percentage correct after four types of prompts for novice, intermediate, and expert UNIX users. After Doane et al. (1992).

information about command syntax and ordering. Experts profited little from this type of information, presumably because they knew it already; however, more general prompts – conceptual information and reminders – were most helpful in their case. This finding suggests that the errors made by experts have a different source than novice errors. Even though experts have the requisite knowledge, they may forget something, or it simply does not occur to them. Hence, a general reminder will nudge them back onto the right path. Does this mean that experts are simply being careless when they make an error? We investigate this interesting question further in the following section.

So far, the only difference between experts and novices that we have examined has to do with the amount of knowledge. However, real users have other problems, too; they may have misconceptions, and they may make errors because their working memory becomes overloaded. Doane et al. (1992) have not studied the misconceptions UNIX users have, nor have we simulated them as was done, for instance, in the *Buggy* system of Brown and vanLehn (1980). We did, however, obtain evidence for memory load problems in our study of prompt comprehension study. Memory losses may involve both item and order information. In our study, novices and intermediates left out five or six times as many items initially as experts (very few deletion errors were made by anyone after the third prompt). Loss of order information as indexed by substitution errors showed a similar pattern. Such errors were two to three times more frequent among novices and intermediates than among experts, and they continued to be a serious problem up to the sixth prompt, which first provided the order information the novices and intermediates were lacking. Thus, memory loss appeared to be a serious problem for the novices and intermediates, whereas the experts managed working memory much more successfully.

Novices and intermediates need help retrieving the elements that go into making a composite command, and they need help with ordering these commands. The task of command construction severely taxes their working memory, so that memory errors become a serious problem. This is just what one would expect from the UNICOM simulations reported earlier. The number of elements that go into the construction of a composite command, together with their ordering, imposes a significant burden on working memory. Furthermore, the user must also represent and maintain in working memory the invisible intermediate results of the process. Nowhere does UNIX tell the user what the outcome of the first computational step is or the input to the next step. The user must anticipate and remember such information without help from the system. Only experts with well-established retrieval structures are up to this task. Novices and intermediates not only lack knowledge; they can become confused even when they have it.

11.1.3 Simulation of errors

One puzzling fact about skilled performance is that even experts, who certainly know better, make errors. Indeed, error rates for experts are often surprisingly high. For instance, in the prompting study described in the previous section, experts made many fewer errors than intermediates and novices in producing composite UNIX commands, but their initial solution attempts were by no means always successful, with error rates varying for different problems between about 13% and 65%. Card, Moran, and Newell (1983) have studied a skilled user performing two tasks, manuscript editing and electronic circuit design editing. Errors were made on 37% of the editing operations. Most of these were detected during the generation of the command sequence, but 21% of the commands issued by this highly skilled user contained an error that had to be corrected later. Similarly, Hanson, Kraut, and Farber (1984) collected a large database from 16 experienced UNIX users performing document preparation and e-mail tasks. They observed an overall error rate of 10%, with a range for different commands from 3% to 50%. Why do experts make errors, and can simulations with the construction–integration model account for this phenomenon?

Kitajima and Polson (1995) have developed a simulation of a human–computer interaction task that suggests an answer to this puzzle. The sample task that they analyze involves the use of the popular graphics application, Cricket Graph. A user is given a set of data and instructed to produce a graph with certain characteristics. This is a much more complex problem than the routine tasks studied by Mannes and Kintsch (1991) or even the production of composite UNIX commands simulated by Doane et al. (1992). Nevertheless, Kitajima and Polson successfully simulated performance on this task with a model designed in much the same way as these simpler models. That is, they used a propositional representation for the various knowledge sources involved: the display the user is confronted with, the user's goals, the user's knowledge about graphs and computer systems, and finally the objects and actions involved (what we called the plan elements in Figure 11.1). A task network was constructed from these elements in much the same way as in Mannes and Kintsch (1991), and an integration process then selected the strongest action candidate for execution. This action changed the display in one way or another, which led to the selection of a new action, until the desired goal state was reached.

However, to achieve their goal, Kitajima and Polson had to elaborate this basic model in several ways. First, the practice of binding all objects in the environment to all possible actions had to be abandoned – there were simply too many possibilities, leading to a combinatorial explosion. Interviews with human users suggested that these users simply were not paying attention to most of these possibilities. Selective attention is of course something familiar to psychologists, and Kitajima and Polson found a ready way to incorporate such a mechanism into the CI model. First, the model does a construction–integration cycle with just the objects (e.g., menu items, whatever else there is on the screen) in view and the task goals to decide which objects to pay attention to. Then, in a second construction–integration cycle, it selects an appropriate action, restricting its attention to the objects selected in the first cycle. On the basis of the initial integration process, the model focuses specifically on three candidate objects, constructs action–object pairs for these objects, and then goes through another integration cycle to select the strongest action–object pair from this set. Thus, the model did not have to consider all possible actions at each step, only those involving the objects it was currently paying attention to.[2]

Kitajima and Polson's first and by no means trivial result was that this system actually could draw the graph it was supposed to. This is a complex task, involving several subtasks and subgoals, and it is of some interest to note that a comprehension-based planner is still able to find its way through such a complex task. It was not at all clear that problem-solving tasks of this complexity could be simulated within the CI framework. Kitajima and Polson's work thus further obscures the border between comprehension processes and problem solving and suggests that the domain of the comprehension paradigm may be wider than anyone suspected.

Even more important than the mere fact that it is possible to simulate such complex problem-solving behavior with a comprehension model are some of the implications of this simulation. Each action cycle in the Kitajima and Polson (1995) model has two parts: an attention cycle and an action selection cycle. The attention cycle must focus on the right objects for a correct action to occur, but what basis do we have for making this selection? Activation spreads from the task goal and anticipated outcome to the objects on the screen in proportion to their relatedness to the task goal and outcome. Sometimes this relatedness is established because relevant knowledge of the user is sampled in the elaboration phase, thus providing a link between a screen object and the task goal even if no obvious and external relation exists. But often there is an obvious relationship between goals and screen objects, because screen objects tend to be labeled in ways that indicate their goal relevance. Thus, if a user wants to delete an object, there might be a screen object labeled "delete" or "erase"; if something needs to be copied, the user will look for "copy" or "duplicate," or some similar term. Labels often, but not always, indicate the action to

2   The details of this simulation are described in Kitajima and Polson (1995).

which an object is relevant. The Kitajima and Polson model strongly relies on such labels. If the labels do not indicate which objects are relevant, the model might still make a correct decision if it has a great deal of knowledge about the task at hand and if it uses that knowledge, but for the most part it will be lost. So are human users. Novices rely heavily on a label-following strategy, failing when that strategy fails. Experts are more flexible and often can figure things out on the basis of their knowledge and experience, but even experts do better when they can follow the labels.

Figure 11.6 shows data on Cricket Graph users from a dissertation by Franzke (1994). On the first trial, novice users of Cricket Graph are able to act quickly if the action is labeled in the same way as in the instructions or by means of a synonym. The action time increases sharply when an inference is required, that is, when there is no menu item that is linked to the instruction either directly or by a synonym. Action times are even longer when no verbal link exists at all (e.g., to change an axis in a graph you must double click on it in Cricket Graph – even longtime Macintosh users have a hard time figuring this out!). On a second trial, the time dif-

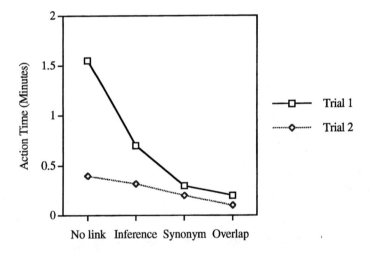

Figure 11.6   Time required for using the Cricket Graph software for actions that are labeled in the same way as the instruction, actions that are labeled with a synonym, actions that are labeled in such a way that the user must make an inference, and actions that are not labeled at all. The data are for the first and second trial of novice users. After Franzke (1994).

ferences are greatly reduced, but they are still apparent. Indeed, some recent unpublished data of Polson show that even experts are faster when they can rely on the label-following strategy than when they cannot. Thus, the label-following strategy appears to be the choice of novices in a wide variety of situations and remains important even when a user has become familiar with an application. The Kitajima and Polson (1995) model correctly implies the importance of this label-following strategy in human–computer interaction because labels play an often crucial role in directing attention to the task-relevant objects on the screen in the integration cycle that precedes the actual action selection.

The other aspect of Kitajima and Polson's (1995) model that is of particular interest here is their error simulation. A simulation that can solve all the problems is not a good simulation of human behavior because humans, even experts, make errors. Kitajima and Polson found a natural way to account for these errors. One of the parameters of the model is the rate of sampling knowledge that is related to the current display, as in Mannes and Kintsch (1991). N_{sample} is the number of times each element in the representation that has been constructed is used to retrieve a related knowledge element, where the probability of sampling a particular knowledge element depends on the strength of its relationship to the cue, relative to all other elements. Kitajima and Polson ran 50 simulations each for values of N_{sample} between 4 and 20. Some of their results are shown in Figure 11.7, where the error rate for various component actions is shown as a function of how much long-term memory is retrieved. Although some actions are much more knowledge-dependent than others, it is clear that the sampling rate is a major determinant of success. If an item is allowed to retrieve no more than four associated knowledge elements from long-term memory, the error rates vary between 8% and 75%. When up to 20 elements can be sampled, the error rates drop to between 0% an d 15%. Thus, the model has a natural explanation for such errors. If users try hard to retrieve whatever knowledge they have, error rates will be low. But if users are sloppy and do not use the knowledge they have, large error rates will result.

The three simulations discussed here – routine actions by Mannes and Kintsch (1991), UNIX commands by Doane et al. (1992), and Cricket Graph by Kitajima and Polson (1995) – demonstrate that the CI model of comprehension can be extended beyond text comprehension. The same

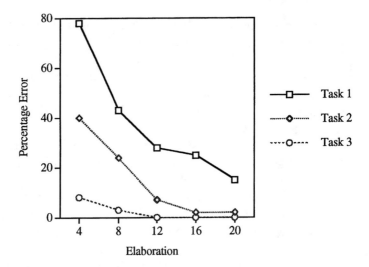

Figure 11.7   Predicted error rates for a difficult (Task 1), an intermediate (Task 2), and an easy task (Task 3) as a function of the amount of elaboration, the N_{sample} parameter in the model. After Kitajima and Polson (1995).

basic processes of bottom–up, relatively context-free construction followed by contextual integration can account for text comprehension as well as for at least some ways of comprehending a situation and taking action on that basis. Just where the limits of the CI model are in this respect is still an open question. It seems clear that there are limits and that more complex forms of planning and problem solving require the construction of problem spaces and goal hierarchies in the manner envisaged originally by Newell and Simon (1972). But at this point it certainly appears worthwhile to investigate other possible fields of inquiry that traditionally have not been considered in terms of comprehension, to try to delineate further the scope of the comprehension paradigm.

Where is the boundary between comprehension and problem solving? Action planning and decision making, at least in some cases, can be considered within the framework of comprehension theory. Just how successful the comprehension account of these phenomena will be in the long run remains to be seen, but we certainly have here a reversal from the days when text researchers were enjoined to look at text understanding as a process of problem solving. Instead, we can now look at planning and decision making as a comprehension process!

What are the essential, distinctive psychological assumptions about action planning that characterize the models presented in this chapter and differentiate them from alternative accounts? There is first the representation of knowledge as a network of propositions. Perhaps alternative forms of knowledge representation could also be made to work, but the work discussed in this chapter illustrates how smoothly the knowledge net representation chosen here meshes with the mechanisms of the construction–integration model. We also should note, however, that the knowledge net is no longer strictly an associative net, for the pattern of interconnections among plan elements reflects causal knowledge: plans that interfere with each other inhibit each other, plans that require each other activate each other.

The assumptions involved in the construction of the task net and its integration are in part dictated by external constraints that are not specific to the present model. Any model must somehow represent the instructions and the state of the world. The psychologically important assumptions concern the process of knowledge elaboration and variable binding. They are determined by the philosophy of dumb construction rules that is basic to the CI model: Knowledge elaboration is associative and context independent, and its depth is variable; variable binding, too, is promiscuous – every plan is bound to every object in sight. Thus, the construction processes in action planning are simple and context free, just as in the case of text comprehension. The system obtains its power via the integration process in both cases.

A few more noteworthy assumptions in this model of action planning need to be mentioned here. This is a planning model without planning in the strict sense. The model just comprehends a situation, takes an action that changes the situation, and responds to the situation again until a solution or a dead end is reached. There is no setting up of subgoals, no planning ahead; no memory for earlier actions is necessary, except for the external memory provided by the changed situation itself.

The distinction between want-to and can-do nodes is crucial.

The constraint satisfaction process must consider all potential actions, not just the ones currently possible. Reasoning must be general, but at the same time action is limited by the possible.

We also note that the extreme simplicity of the model, which was sufficient to model routine computing actions and UNIX command production, had to be abandoned in the more complex Cricket Graph domain. It was no longer feasible to bind all variables in the plan elements to all objects present; instead, a selection had to be made of those objects that were to be attended to in the light of the task at hand and the current display on the computer screen. This is clearly a gain in psychological accuracy, for selective attention is a ubiquitous phenomenon, but it comes at the cost of substantially complicating the model mechanisms.

11.2 Problem solving, decision, and judgment

In this and the following sections I discuss some possible extensions of the CI model to new areas. I have not really worked in these areas, and other than suggestions on how the CI theory might be applied there I have nothing to offer. The only solid research results I discuss have been obtained independently elsewhere (the work of Kunda & Thagard (1996) on impression formation), and I am merely pointing out the relationship of their work to the CI model. So why discuss these topics at all? Would not silence be more appropriate if one does not have anything definitive to offer? I think not. In the coming years, research on the topics treated here so superficially may yield the richest rewards and may perhaps transform cognitive science into a broader and richer discipline than it is now.

11.2.1 The role of comprehension in problem solving and decision making

Throughout these chapters I have insisted on a distinction between problem solving and comprehension. Comprehension is automatic, bottom-up, described by the mechanisms of the CI theory. Problem solving is a controlled, resource-demanding process involving the construction of problem spaces and specialized search strategies, as originally envisaged by Newell and Simon (1972).

Not everyone will want to follow me here. So let me try to explain and justify this distinction in a little more detail. Both comprehension and problem solving involve a construction phase and a solution phase. The main difference between them lies in the nature of the constructions involved in generating a mental representation. For comprehension, the CI theory claims, the construction phase is essentially guided by the textual (or other perceptual) input. Propositions are constructed more or less closely, mirroring the input sentences of a text sentence by sentence. This is a highly constrained process, at least for the ideal reader, because actual readers sometimes deviate in unpredictable ways from the text (not forming certain propositions invited by the text, or constructing propositions that do not accurately reflect the text, usually simplifying it). The next step in the construction process – knowledge elaboration – is less predictable, because memory retrieval is probabilistic. However, because we all live in the same world and therefore have similar knowledge structures and memories, even this phase is not totally unpredictable, at least for an ensemble of comprehenders. The construction operations themselves are typically highly practiced and demand few mental resources. This is the realm of long-term working memory, for mental representations that later will also serve as retrieval structures are being generated automatically and reliably.

A very different situation obtains for true problem-solving tasks. Typically, the input vastly underconstrains the construction of a problem representation. Instead of a text that almost dictates the kind of mental representation that will be constructed, the problem statement itself gives few hints as to what the problem space looks like. Conscious, complex, resource-demanding mental operations are required to set up a problem space. Because this can be done in many different ways, it is difficult or impossible to predict how a given individual will approach a problem. Often, the operators that must be used for the construction of the problem space are unfamiliar. The problem solver in this situation cannot rely on a few well-practiced, highly overlearned, automatic operations, and hence not on available retrieval structures in long-term working memory. Thus, the resource demands of problem solving are much greater than in comprehending a reasonably familiar text.

However, the boundaries between comprehension and problem solving are obscured when we are dealing with expert problem solvers, whose behavior is in some ways more like comprehension. Experts in some problem-solving domains rely on their long-term working memory in much the same way as text comprehenders do (Ericsson & Kintsch, 1995). The expert chess player, for instance, calculates moves almost as automatically as a text comprehender understands a sentence, generating a retrieval structure in the process that will support later memory retrieval.

The solution phase in problem solving and the integration phase in text comprehension are also different in nature. The CI theory claims that a spreading activation process is all that is needed for integrating the kind of networks constructed in text comprehension. Spreading activation almost certainly also plays a role in problem solving, but in addition a variety of more directed processes also play a role. In many cases a problem space is so huge that spreading activation processes become ineffective, and problem solvers must employ other solution strategies (such as the means–end analyses of Newell & Simon, 1972). As a consequence, a relatively simple theory (like the CI theory) may suffice to account for orderly, predictable comprehension, whereas the theory of problem solving (like SOAR, Newell, 1990) might need to be considerably more complex.

To indicate how problem solving might be analyzed within the CI theory, I briefly discuss two classic examples: the Tower of Hanoi as the prototype of a whole class of laboratory problem-solving tasks, and a decision task that illustrates the representativeness bias in decision making.

One of the most analyzed problem-solving tasks is the Tower of Hanoi: a board with three sticks and three (or more) disks, graduated in size with a hole in the center so that they can be placed on the sticks. Initially all three disks are on the first stick, as shown in Figure 11.8. The task is to move the three disks to the third stick 3, with two constraints: only the top disk of a pile of sticks can be moved, and a larger disk can never be

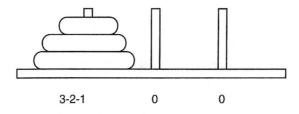

3-2-1   0   0

Figure 11.8   Initial state of the Tower of Hanoi problem and formal notation.

placed on top of a smaller disk. With just three disks it is not a difficult problem, and most people solve it after some fumbling.

The strategies people use in solving the Tower of Hanoi problem have been analyzed and documented by Kotovsky, Hayes, and Simon (1985). Typically, novices initially adopt a simple difference-reduction strategy, which proves ineffective. They then shift to a means-end strategy in which subgoals are created (e.g., "clear everything off the largest disk, so it can be moved"). Once they adopt the right subgoals, they solve the problem quickly.

Now consider how one could solve the Tower of Hanoi task by relying strictly on comprehension processes, that is, by constructing a network representing this task and using spreading activation to integrate this network.

We first need a more compact notation, which I have already introduced in Figure 11.8: (3–2–1, 0, 0) means that the largest disk 3, the medium disk 2, and the smallest disk 1 are all on the first stick, and that no disks are on the second and third sticks; (3, 2–1, 0) means that the largest disk is on the first stick and the other two disks are on the second stick; (3, 1–2, 0) is not a permissible state, because the medium disk 2 cannot be placed on top of the small disk 1.

Thus, the anticipated goal state is (0, 0, 3–2–1) – all disks on the third stick. The task for the comprehender is to construct a network of moves that link the initial state with this anticipated goal state. The minimum such network is shown in Figure 11.9. The initial state is labeled WORLD. There are two possible moves from here, labeled DO: move disk 1 either to stick 2 or stick 3. Which is the right one? We need to construct a path linking the given state of the problem in the world with the anticipated outcome. [0, 2–1, 3] is the first state that links up with the anticipated goal state: Disk 3 is in the right place. If the network shown in Figure 11.9 is integrated, the resulting activation values for the two competing moves – first disk to stick 2 or 3 – clearly favor the correct move, and hence a decision that starts the solution process off on the right path can be made.

But note that in order to link up the current state of the world and the outcome state, a large and complex network had to be constructed, including nine intervening nodes! This may not look like much compared with the networks we are familiar with from analyses of text comprehen-

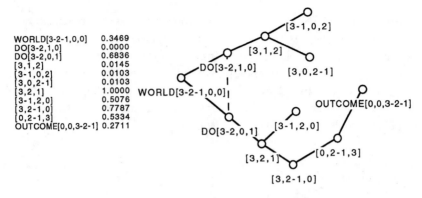

Figure 11.9   State network for the Tower of Hanoi – initial state. The activation values of the nodes after integration are shown in the left part of the figure.

sion, but there is a crucial difference. In text comprehension, readers can rely on well-practiced, automated encoding strategies and their long-term working memory, which makes it possible for them to handle large networks. Here, the task is unfamiliar and the construction rules must be laboriously applied, resulting in excessive demands on working memory.

This little *Gedankenexperiment* suggests that the Tower of Hanoi, even in this simple three-disk version, involves more than mere comprehension and requires something else, namely, the problem-solving strategies Kotovsky et al. (1985) observed in their subjects. Here is a problem beyond the CI theory. However, imagine a problem formally equivalent to the Tower of Hanoi but that does not involve the movement of meaningless disks according to arbitrary rules. Imagine instead a problem in medical diagnosis and that we are dealing with an expert diagnostician. The links in this case between the DO nodes and the anticipated OUTCOME node might be retrieval structures in long-term working memory. What is a difficult task for the subject in the laboratory might be trivial for the expert in her or his domain. The CI theory might possibly describe the expert's behavior, even if it cannot deal with the laboratory problem. There are boundaries between comprehension and problem solving, but to determine just where they lie will require further research.

The second illustration to be discussed here is different, in that it is clearly a problem within the scope of the comprehension theory. It concerns a striking but common error in decision making that Tversky and Kahneman (1983) have labeled the *representativeness bias:* Subjects judge that a conjunction of two sets is more probable than one of the sets involved if the other set is highly representative. This is a clear violation of probability theory, for P(A), P(B) $\leq$ P[A^B] for all sets A and B. Concretely, if subjects are given the text

(1)   Linda is 31 years old, single, outspoken, and very bright. She majored in philosophy. In college, she was involved in several social issues, including the environment, the peace campaign, and the antinuclear campaign.

and are asked to judge which of the following two statements is more probable:

(2)   Linda is a bank teller.
(3)   Linda is a bank teller and is active in the feminist movement.

they frequently select the second statement, in violation of the axioms of probability theory.

Pennington and Hastie (1993) have argued that decision makers do not always base their decisions on a complete rational analysis of the situation but often represent a situation as a story, favoring the decision that fits best into the story context that they have constructed. That is, they form a mental representation at the narrative level, rather than at an abstract, formal level. The CI theory allows us to model both of these alternatives. First, let us assume that a subject in a decision experiment represents the Linda text as a narrative. That is, the subject treats the Linda text just as any other story. The question of interest is how well the test sentences (2) and (3) will fit into the subject's story representation. Intuitively, BANK TELLER is going to be connected weakly to some of the nodes of the Linda text, as shown in Figure 11.10, whereas the links between the text propositions and BANK TELLER & FEMINIST ought to be stronger.

To estimate these link strengths objectively, latent semantic analysis can be used. In the encyclopedia space, the cosines between sentence (2) and the three sentences of (1) are .04, .02, and .04, respectively. The cosines between sentence (3) and the three text sentences are .09, .06, and .11, respectively. These cosine values can be used as link strengths in the network shown in Figure 11.10. Multiplying by 10 puts them on a scale

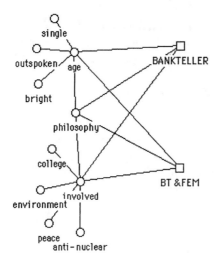

Figure 11.10   Network corresponding to a story representation of text (1) linked to the test statements (2) and (3) with link strengths estimates obtained from LSA.

comparable to the link values between text propositions, which are set to 1. With these values, the spreading activation process yields final activation values of .31 for BANK TELLER and .75 for BANK TELLER & FEMINIST. Hence, the model predicts that the more highly activated BANK TELLER & FEMINIST should be the preferred response.

Does this little exercise in modeling a classical result tell us anything worthwhile, or is it just that – a little exercise? I think it has significant implications that ought to be explored. We might not need a representativeness bias in order to understand the Linda results. If a subject represents the text as a story and the decision is based on activation values in that representation, Tversky and Kahneman's result follows. However, a subject with an elementary knowledge of probability theory may form a higher-level, abstract, formal representation, as shown in Figure 11.11. This representation includes the same net as before, with the same link strengths estimated from LSA, but in addition there is another part of the net that brings to bear the subject's knowledge of probability theory as it applies to this situation. I have indicated the general knowledge of probability theory in terms of relations among the sets A and B and a the-

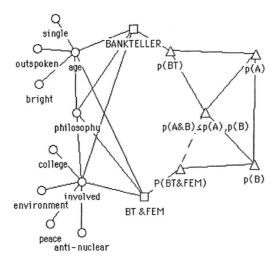

Figure 11.11   Network corresponding to a story representation of text (1) as well as a probability theory representation linked to the test statements (2) and (3) with link strengths estimates obtained from LSA.

orem from probability theory, P(A&B) ≤ P(A),P(B), which the decision maker must know. Set A is linked to BANKTELLER, (BT), and set B is linked to BANKTELLER & FEMINIST, (BT&FEM). The general theorem supports the hypothesis that p(BT) is greater but contradicts the hypothesis that p(BT&FEM) is greater. As a result, BT receives an activation value of .34, but BT&FEM receives only .01. Therefore, a correct response will be made.

If a decision maker represents the problem formally (which requires not only a knowledge of probability theory but also that an encoding strategy must be used to ensure that this knowledge will actually be applied), a "correct" response will be made. If only a narrative-level representation is used instead, a response will be made that is incorrect in the formal sense but consistent with the story representation: From what we know about Linda, she surely looks like a feminist, even though she has a job as a bank teller.

The CI model thus allows us to reanalyze and reinterpret a classical example from the literature on decision making. But obviously, analyzing a single example is by no means the same as proposing a new theory of decision making. Furthermore, our reanalysis is not even original, because others have advocated this general approach before, and what has been added here is merely the technical framework of the CI model. Cheng and Holyoak (1985), for instance, have distinguished between formal and informal decision schemas in a manner compatible with our analysis. More specifically, Pennington and Hastie (1993) have shown that the informal decision schema often used to make decisions by jurors is the story schema: Jurors try to make a coherent story out of what they are told. Our analysis of the Linda story merely shows that the CI architecture provides a convenient framework for modeling such story-based decision making. More generally, Hammond (1996) has argued for a distinction between intuitive and formal decision procedures. The CI model, especially in combination with LSA, which permits us to use reasonably accurate and objective estimates of the semantic relations upon which intuitive decisions are based, may provide a suitable framework to formalize ideas that have been proposed within the field of decision making and to relate these ideas to other comprehension phenomena that have hitherto been regarded as separate and distinct.

That this is not an idle speculation but a real possibility is nicely illustrated by the model of impression formation that has recently been proposed by Kunda and Thagard (1996). I describe their work in detail and show how it can be translated into the CI framework because it is such a good example of theorizing in this vein in this field.

11.2.2 Impression formation

How do people judge how friendly, or aggressive, or clever someone is whom they have just met? Much depends on how this particular person looks and acts, but it has long been known that the stereotypes people hold about the social class of the person modify and shape their impression about the character of a person. Everyone has certain beliefs about how sex, age, race, or profession are related to traits and behaviors, and these expectations combine with what we actually perceive to determine our impression. Social psychologists have compiled a huge empirical literature on these topics, and a number of alternative theoretical viewpoints have been developed over the years. My purpose is not to review this literature or to evaluate the theories but to suggest that the CI model provides a novel framework to view the phenomena of impression formation and to relate them to other comprehension processes. Recently Kunda and Thagard (1996) have proposed a parallel constraint satisfaction theory to account for many interesting findings in the field of impression formation. Their proposal is closely related to the CI model. Like the CI model, it demonstrates how this type of theory can account for a rich and complex research area. Because impression formation is not usually thought of in the same terms as text comprehension, I sketch Kunda and Thagard's proposal in some detail and show how it is related to the CI model. Both models provide similar accounts of how perceptual data and information about stereotypes from long-term memory become merged in impression formation.

Kunda and Thagard (1996) represent a person or event as a network of interrelated nodes, much as a text is represented in the CI model. The nodes are in part based on perception, but there are also knowledge elaborations – the perceiver's beliefs, stereotypes, and prejudices. Actually, Kunda and Thagard's model is not a construction–integration theory, because it does not deal with the construction of the network at all. The perceptual factors that determine the saliency of various aspects of a person's appearance or action – what makes people pay attention to particular aspects and not others – as well as the belief structures and retrieval processes that determine the knowledge elaborations that the perceiver contributes to the perceptual network, are assumed as given. Kunda and Thagard's theory is concerned with the integration process that generates a holistic impression out of these disparate and usually contradictory elements. The authors can rely on a rich and well-tested experimental literature to help them to identify the salient aspects of a particular problem and to set up a plausible network for it. Once such a network has been generated, they integrate this network, using a mathematical algorithm that is closely related to the one used here. To show just how closely related it is, I describe a few of their examples, using their networks but employing the integration mechanism of the CI model instead of the one they use. The results are qualitatively, though not numerically, identical with the ones reported in Kunda and Thagard (1996).

The heart of their paper is a discussion of twelve phenomena concerning impression formation that have been studied extensively in the social psychology literature. They discuss the rich but often confusing empirical evidence concerning each one of these phenomena and then show how a simple and straightforward analysis in terms of a constraint satisfaction network provides a satisfactory account for each phenomenon. Further-more, the account they provide is consistent across the twelve phenom-ena they discuss. Thus, they develop an elegant and comprehensive the-ory of impression formation.

It is not my purpose either to describe this theory in detail or to evalu-ate it against alternative conceptions. Rather, my point is to demonstrate its close resemblance to the CI model in order to show how these phe-nomena, too, can be interpreted within the comprehension paradigm of cognition. Thus, I take the first four impression formation phenomena analyzed by Kunda and Thagard to illustrate their model, without, how-ever, discussing the empirical evidence motivating the networks they set up or the controversies surrounding this evidence.

Phenomenon 1: Stereotypes color the meaning of behavior. The same ambiguous action performed by different people will be interpreted dif-ferently, depending on stereotypes about the social class to which the actor belongs. For instance, if a black man shoves someone, the act will be perceived as more aggressive than when a white man shoves someone. Kunda and Thagard (1996) conceptualize the situation as shown in Fig-ure 11.12. Suppose it has been observed that a black man pushes some-one. In addition, there are the two competing interpretation – that at the shove was friendly or aggressive – plus the stereotype that links the nodes *black* and *aggressive*. With all node and link strengths set to 1 or –1 for the inhibitory links, the integration process yields the results shown in Fig-ure 11.12: The shove is clearly interpreted as violent rather than jovial. If a white man is doing the shoving, and the observer does not think of *white* as *aggressive*, the interpretation of the shove remains ambiguous, as shown in Figure 11.13.

Phenomenon 2: Stereotypes color the meaning of traits. What a trait like *aggressive* means depends on who is being characterized by that trait. Lawyers and construction workers are perceived as being about equally aggressive, but there is a difference between the refined aggression of the lawyers and the crude aggression of the construction workers. The net-works that Kunda and Thagard (1996) set up are shown in Figures 11.14 and 11.15. *Aggressive* is linked to *punch* and *argue;* however, in the context of *lawyer,* the *punch* node is inhibited by the *upper-middle-class* node char-

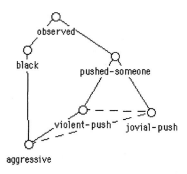

observed	1.0000
black	0.9988
pushed-someone	0.9998
aggressive	0.9978
violent-push	0.9984
jovial-push	0.0000

Figure 11.12   Stereotypes affect the meaning of behavior. *Violent push* is strongly activated by the stereotype that *blacks are aggressive.* Inhibitory links are indicated by dashed lines.

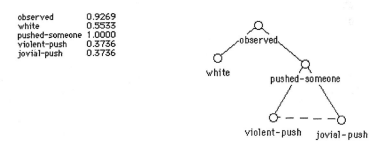

observed	0.9269
white	0.5533
pushed-someone	1.0000
violent-push	0.3736
jovial-push	0.3736

Figure 11.13   In the absence of a stereotype, an ambiguous act remains ambiguous. *Violent-push* and *jovial-push* are both weakly but equally activated.

acteristic of lawyers, and the *argue* node is supported by the *verbal* node also characteristic of lawyers. In contrast, *construction workers* are characterized by the nodes *working class* and *unrefined,* both of which support *punch* and are unrelated to *argue.* The results are displayed in Figures 11.14 and 11.15. Aggressive lawyers argue rather than punch. Aggressive construction workers argue just as much, but even more likely, they punch.

Phenomenon 3: Individuating information can determine which of a stereotype's subtypes is used. Suppose that an observer has a more differentiated stereotype about blacks than in the first example discussed. The *blacks are*

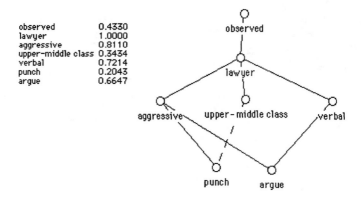

observed	0.4330
lawyer	1.0000
aggressive	0.8110
upper-middle class	0.3434
verbal	0.7214
punch	0.2043
argue	0.6647

Figure 11.14   Stereotypes influence the meaning of a trait. *Argue* is more activated than *punch* as characteristics of *aggressive* in the context of *lawyer.*

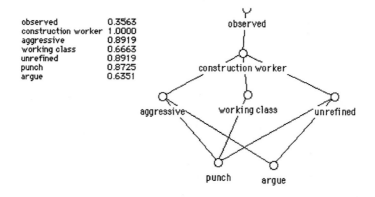

observed	0.3563
construction worker	1.0000
aggressive	0.8919
working class	0.6663
unrefined	0.8919
punch	0.8725
argue	0.6351

Figure 11.15   Stereotypes influence the meaning of a trait. *Punch* is more activated than *argue* as characteristics of *aggressive* in the context of *construction worker.*

aggressive stereotype is now reserved for *ghetto-blacks,* and there is now another (weaker) subtype of *black-businessman,* which is not linked to aggression. Being well dressed is the observable characteristic of a black businessman in this scenario. Kunda and Thagard (1996) thus arrive at the network shown in Figure 11.16, where heavy lines have been assigned a value of 2 to reflect their greater strength. With this more differentiated stereotype, observing a well-dressed black will not activate the *aggressive*

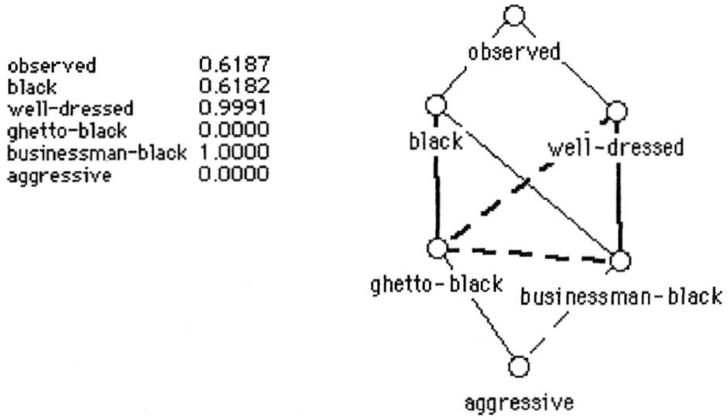

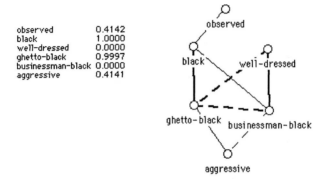

```
observed              0.6187
black                 0.6182
well-dressed          0.9991
ghetto-black          0.0000
businessman-black     1.0000
aggressive            0.0000
```

Figure 11.16   Subtypes of stereotypes and individuating information. A well-dressed black is perceived as a businessman.

```
observed              0.4142
black                 1.0000
well-dressed          0.0000
ghetto-black          0.9997
businessman-black     0.0000
aggressive            0.4141
```

Figure 11.17   Subtypes of stereotypes and individuating information. If *well-dressed* is not observed, a black is perceived as an aggressive ghetto black.

node. On the other hand, in the same network, if a black is observed who is not well dressed, *aggressive* will become activated, as shown in Figure 11.17.

Phenomenon 4: Stereotypes typically do not affect trait ratings in the presence of unambiguous diagnostic information. Although stereotypes can color perceptions, they typically do not override it. Thus, if there is strong unambiguous evidence that is perceptually available, stereotypes have little or no effect. If it is clearly seen that a person punches another adult, that act will be interpreted as aggressive, whether the person is a house-wife, who normally isn't expected to act that way, or a construction worker, for whom punching someone is more expected. The calculations according to the CI model are shown in Figures 11.18 and 11.19.

The examples described here cannot do justice to Kunda and Tha-gard's (1996) interesting paper. By reworking them with the formalism of the CI model, I do not intend to claim that one formalism is better than another but merely to demonstrate that this important area of research in social psychology can be brought within the scope of a general model of comprehension. Impression formation is thus seen as having much

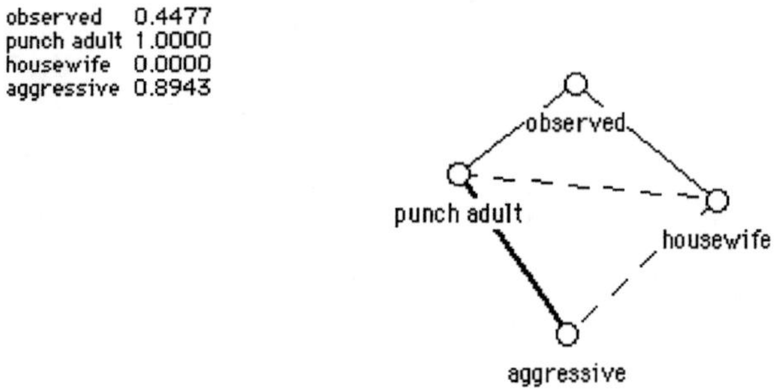

```
observed    0.4477
punch adult 1.0000
housewife   0.0000
aggressive  0.8943
```

Figure 11.18   Unambiguous diagnostic information overrides the stereotype. A housewife's punching someone is interpreted as aggressive.

```
observed             0.5700
punch adult          1.0000
construction worker  0.7850
aggressive           0.8891
```

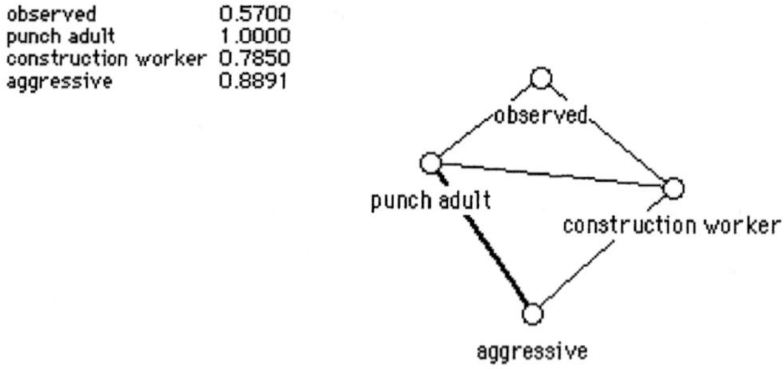

Figure 11.19   Unambiguous diagnostic information overrides the stereotype. A construction worker's punching someone is no more aggressive than a housewife's punching someone.

in common with text comprehension. In both cases there is a bottom-up, data-driven construction process that yields a complex network in which many factors are combined – important and unimportant ones, mutually supportive and mutually contradictory ones, input data as well as knowledge elaborations. Integrating this network yields a new, coherent whole – an impression, or a text representation.

11.3 The representation of the self in working memory

The CI model focuses on the integration of knowledge and memory and on texts or other nontextual sources in the process of comprehending a text or situation. It deals with the environment to be comprehended and the long-term memory that enables a person to comprehend it. The linkage between environment and long-term memory is effected in working memory, as described by Ericsson and Kintsch (1995).

Long-term memory is conceptualized as a huge network the nodes of which represent cognitive elements – knowledge, experience, beliefs. A minute part of this network is activated, available in working memory, and a larger part is connected by retrieval structures to the contents of working memory and is directly retrievable on demand, thus forming a long-term working memory.

Suppose we admit to this network not only cognitive elements but also noncognitive elements, such as emotions and body states. There is nothing very revolutionary about this proposal because it has already been argued (in chapter 3 and elsewhere) that the cognitive elements of the network, such as propositions, are not defined by their content or structure – that is merely a crutch for the theorist – but by their position in the network. Hence, adding noncognitive nodes that define and mutually constrain each other, in the same way that propositions do, seems like a natural extension of the original framework.

What I have in mind with noncognitive nodes are brain states that represent information about one's own body. Part of our network is already made up of brain states that represent sensations and perceptions from the environment. In addition, we now also include feelings about the body. Damasio (1994) has made some useful suggestions about how this might work. According to Damasio, the brain represents the state of the body by means of *somatic markers*. Certain parts of the brain (the amygdala and prefrontal cortices) are involved in the control of the state of the body, effecting changes in adjustments in the body. The body signals these state changes back to other parts of the brain (the somatosensory cortex), where these signals may be attended to and become conscious. Moreover, it is not necessary for the body actually to assume a particular state. The amygdala and prefrontal cortex may influence the somatosensory cortex directly, so that it acts as if the body were in a particular state.

Suppose that working memory contains, in addition to the cognitive nodes that comprise short-term memory or consciousness, a set of somatic markers that we experience as general body feelings. Introspectively, this appears plausible. These somatic markers in working memory can serve as cues that, via retrieval structures, can readily retrieve all kinds of information about one's own body. Thus, although I am not conscious now of the position of a my right foot, this information is directly available. People certainly have had the years of practice necessary to acquire the retrieval structures that provide access to information about their own body.

If somatic markers are always present in working memory, we must then modify our view of what is involved in perception. Traditionally, we think of perception as representing the environment, enriched by the perceiver's prior knowledge and beliefs. But if somatic markers are an important part of working memory, body feelings become parts of the perceptual experience, just as knowledge and beliefs do. Damasio (1994) has pointed out that perception consists of more than simply receiving sensory information. When I look out the window of my study on the scene below, I see the city nestled in the trees, the flat curve of the horizon, and the sky above speckled with afternoon clouds. I move my head as the eyes scan the horizon, the familiar view makes me feel good, and I stretch my legs and take a deep breath. All of this contributes to the perception, not just the visual image. When I recreate the image later, traces of my movements, the way I sat in my chair, and the somatic reactions that occurred in the first place are regenerated with it. I experience a little of that good feeling that went with the original perception. Cognition does not occur in a vacuum or in a disembodied mind but in a perceiving, feeling, acting body. The image is reconstructed in the brain, and its content includes the reactions of the body that occurred in response to the original scene – not just what happened on the retina, but bodily reactions in the widest sense, motor as well as visceral. It is my perception and my memory image because its content is not only visual but also includes a variety of somatic reactions of my body.

What we would gain from adding somatic markers as nodes to our network is the possibility of formulating an account of emotions, attention, and motivation, as I suggest later. First, however, this would be a way of representing the self in working memory.

The arena in which cognition takes place is working memory, alias short-term memory, alias focus of attention, alias consciousness. The whole model of cognition as it has been constructed here is based on the contents and operations in working memory, but a moment's consideration shows that we have omitted rather a lot from our working memory. Take the typical reader as modeled by the CI model: Working memory contains a dynamically changing stream of about seven (atomic) propositions. But there must be more than that. There is an awareness of the physical environment, especially of changes in it. There is an awareness not only of the goal set for this particular reading task but also of multiple other goals. There is the constant background feeling of one's body – its position, tone, and feeling. There is the self that is reading.

The self is important, for we know quite well from experience, observation, as well as experiment, that everything self-related is special for an organism and receives favored treatment. Yet experimental psychologists and most cognitive scientists have refused to deal with the self concept. In part, this refusal has been based on the prevalent view of the self, which they rightly find unsatisfactory: that the self, in one way or another, is some sort of homunculus that does the experiencing. However, thinking about cognition in terms of shifting patterns of activation in a large network suggests a more plausible alternative: that the self does not exist but is continuously reconstructed as the activated part of the network.

The self nodes consist of some highly and more or less permanently activated nodes in our long-term memory, including our name, the persons closest too us, our occupation, and other significant items. These personal memory nodes would always be activated, though with some fluctuations. The memories that make up my self are probably not entirely the same when I am at home with my family and when I am speaking at a professional meeting. Moreover, such essentially propositional nodes are not the only ones that constitute the self. There is another group of nodes in the network representing the body that is part of the self.

I am not only my memories but also my body. These nodes may represent limbs and muscles, the position of the body in space, visceral information, as well as the chemical or hormonal balance or imbalance of the body. I make no attempt either to list or describe all that might be involved but only point to the existence and significance of this part of our being, which I lump together as the somatic nodes in the network. Not all these somatic nodes are so strongly or permanently activated. Our body sense depends on context: whether I am sitting in my chair or climbing a mountain, whether I am hungry or satiated, excited or drowsy. But at any time, there is a group of somatic nodes that is sufficiently activated and that, together with the memory nodes, constitute my self – or more precisely, that is how the CI theory could model the self.

The two groups of self nodes form a single, tightly interrelated cluster. In consequence, perception is not just a sensory event but also has an inherent somatic component. Another way of saying this is that perception is not only a cognitive process but also an emotional process. We react to the world not only with our sense organs but also with gut-level feelings. The things that excite us, please us, scare us are the ones most closely linked to the somatic level. Our most central memories are the ones most intimately linked to our body.

All this is clearly speculation. Furthermore, at this point these speculations are not sufficiently well formulated to be empirically testable. However, some support for notions like the ones advanced here exists.

Damasio (1994) has provided evidence from neuroscience for his theory of somatic markers. He specifically points to the importance of body reactions for cognition. Feelings about the body – real or vicarious – become conditioned to certain perceptions and actions and thus become crucial to the cognitive processes involved in planning and decision making. Actions and perceptions that are tied to good body feelings are favored over others, and those tied to negative feelings are avoided, thus directly influencing planning and decision making. The search of problem spaces and the rational calculation of outcomes is cut short in this way, allowing a person to act without becoming lost in thought and planning. Damasio reiterates here a point made by Simon (1969) that, far from being irrelevant by-products of decision making, emotions are crucial for resource management in a system with limited capacity, such as human working memory.

There is another line of evidence from cognitive science that appears to require an explicit account of the self. Many observations about language and language use have been amassed by such writers as Lakoff (1987) and Glenberg (1997) to show that language expresses relationships with reference to the human body and that we interpret language by means of our body schema. Through the experience with our own bodies we acquire a number of schemas, such as the container schema, the part-whole schema, or the source-path-goal schema. These body schemas are transferred to language and the world. We understand the world in terms of these schemas, and language has evolved around the use of them. We know what a container is because of our direct experience with our body. It has an inside, an outside, and a boundary, and we can map our understanding of these relationships, which is extralinguistic and experiential, on the world by means of metaphorical language. We understand *Mary felt trapped in her marriage and wanted to get out* by assigning to *marriage* the role of the *container*. In *John and Mary are splitting up*, we map *marriage* into the part-whole schema instead (examples from Lakoff, 1987). We understand the world with reference to our own body experience and action; when language evolved, it reflected this bodily basis of understanding.

A working memory in which somatic nodes are continuously active may provide a mechanism for the explanation of the linguistic phenomena described by Lakoff (1987). All spatial perception occurs in the context of activated somatic nodes that represent the position and state of our body. Thus, from the very beginning, spatial information about the world is linked to our own body. For instance, the concept *more* is acquired in a spatial context, as an increase in quantity along the verticality dimension, which is given directly in our bodily experience. Once acquired in this context, the use of the word *more* is extended metaphorically to nonspatial contexts, resulting in the *more is up, less is down* metaphor. Language is embodied because it is linked to the representations of our own body in working memory – in its daily use, in its acquisition by the individual, and in its cultural evolution.

11.3.1 Evaluative and motivational functions of self-representation

If a model of working memory can be formulated that includes self nodes in the manner envisaged here, it might be possible to broaden the scope of comprehension theory to include a number of phenomena that we know are important but that we heretofore have had no way of dealing with systematically within a cognitive framework. Most relevant for discourse comprehension is the ubiquitous finding that self-relevant, emotional material has a special status in comprehension and memory. More generally, however, we may have a way for dealing with attention, motivation, and emotion.

Emotional factors in comprehension. Given that the self is an undifferentiated whole but a complex structure, one ought to distinguish, at a minimum, between nodes with positive and negative valences, GOOD and BAD self-nodes. Propositions in a text (or events in the environment, in general) are not only self-relevant to varying degrees but may be self-relevant in a positive or negative sense, giving rise to positive or negative emotions. It has often been pointed out that when people read a text, their emotional responses may be more important and salient than the propositional content of the text (for example, Miall, 1989; Oatley, 1992).

I illustrate this point with an example from the literature on decision biases, continuing the argument introduced in section 11.2.1 that some of the well-documented decision biases can be understood as comprehension problems. If readers construct a text representation at the narrative level only and base their decisions on the activation values that various decision-relevant propositions achieve in this representation, it is easy to see why certain decision errors occur. If, on the other hand, readers construct an abstract representation, applying schemas appropriate to the domain (e.g., probability theory in the example we have discussed), they will arrive at the formally correct answer. This also holds in a context where emotions play a central role. Consider the following decision problem first used by Tversky and Kahneman (1983).

(2)   Imagine that the United States is preparing for the outbreak of an unusual Asian disease that is expected to kill 600 people. Two alternative programs to combat the disease have been proposed. Assume that the exact scientific estimates of the consequences of the programs are as follows:

   If Program A is adopted, 200 people will be saved,

   If Program B is adopted, there is a one-third probability that 600 people will be saved and a two-thirds probability that no people will be saved.
   Which of the two programs would you favor?

People overwhelmingly prefer Program A (72%). Why? The classical answer is that people's subjective utility function is negatively accelerated, so when they compute the utility of the two choices, saving 600 lives is weighted less than three times as highly as saving 200 lives. The CI theory suggests a different answer. People may not compute utilities at all. Instead, Program A will become more activated because it is linked only to positive self-nodes, whereas Program B will be less activated because it is risky and hence inhibited by negative self-nodes. Specifically, if we let S1, S2, and S3 stand for the first three sentences of (2), we obtain the network shown in Figure 11.20, in which GOOD and BAD are self-nodes with their activation values clamped. GOOD is connected with a strength of 1 to saving 600 people and a strength of .5 to saving 200 people (reflecting the negatively accelerated subjective utility function), and BAD is connected with a value of −1 to saving none. All other links have a value of 1, except for the mutually exclusive decision alternatives, which have a negative link. Integrating this network yields an activation value of .57 for Program A (save-200) and .19 for Program B (save-600-or-none).

Tversky and Kahneman also showed that if the alternatives in (2) are reworded as

(3) If Program A is adopted, 400 people will die.
     If Program B is adopted, there is a one-third probability nobody will die and a two-thirds probability that 600 people will die.

Program B is now preferred over Program A (78% vs. 22%). The CI theory readily predicts this switch, as Figure 11.21 shows. The negative

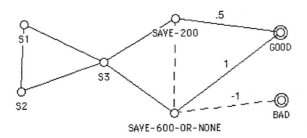

Figure 11.20

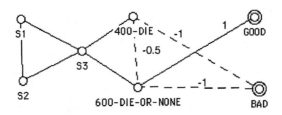

Figure 11.21

wording produces inhibition from the BAD node (.5 for 400 dying, 1 for 600 dying), whereas the GOOD node is connected to only none-dying. Integrating this new network yields much lower activation values for both choices, but their relative strength is now reversed: Program A has zero activation value, whereas Program B is favored with an activation value of .05. I am not aware of any data showing that negatively worded choice-pairs in planning decisions are less activated than positively worded choices, but that is a prediction of this kind of model.

Note that there is nothing in the CI model as such that yields these predictions. Rather, they are a consequence of the assumption we made about the nature of the mental representation that is being constructed. If people employ a nonanalytical comprehension strategy, treating the text just like a story, they will make these "errors" in judgment. However, if they take a more analytic approach and construct an abstract representation, employing their knowledge of probability theory, both decision alternatives will be equally strong (*exp-value* abbreviates the proposition *expected value equals 200*) (see Figure 11.22).

In this case, both save-200 and save-600-or-none receive activation values of .41. Thus, it is not a question whether people have "decision biases" but, rather, how they approach the decision problem. If they treat it as an everyday comprehension problem, their choices will be quite different than if they employ an analytic strategy, representing the information provided by the text in terms of the appropriate probability schema. Some decision makers cannot use this strategy because they do not have the necessary knowledge of probability theory and hence are unable to construct a representation at this level. Tversky and Kahneman's point is that many decision makers who have the right schema still make errors.

Thus, by formally incorporating into the CI model the self-relevance of textual information, in both a positive and negative way, some inter-

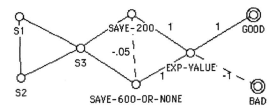

Figure 11.22

esting and important empirical phenomena may be accounted for within the framework of the theory.

Attention and motivation. If we admit self-nodes into working memory, representations of the environment that are linked to these self-nodes will receive an extra boost in activation. That is, they will more likely be attended to than environmental stimuli without such links. A tight cluster of self-nodes in working memory to which some of the propositional nodes are linked will modulate the pattern of activation in such a way that self-linked nodes become more strongly activated. Hence, self-relevant nodes will also obtain a greater long-term memory strength. The likelihood that they will attain enough strength to become conscious increases, as does the likelihood that these nodes will be retrieved from memory at a later time. Indeed, the relatively stable self-nodes could play a significant role as retrieval cues in the process of retrieving other episodic or semantic memories.

The self-nodes, being permanently activated, thus can serve as energizers in working memory, activating other nodes in working memory that they are linked to. If the nodes being activated by the self are representations of environmental stimuli, we talk about attention (leaving aside the question whether there are sources of attention other than self-relevance). If the nodes being activated by the self are plans and action schemas, we talk about motivation (leaving aside the possibility that motivation need not always be tied to specific goals). Thus, although the view of working memory explored here may not provide a complete account of attention and motivation, it might be a useful way to model some aspects of attention and motivation.

Consider three hypothetical plan nodes in working memory. Plan A is closely linked to the self; it is associated with pleasant emotions and good body states and is positively linked to higher-order plans. Plan B is only distantly related to the self by some chain of other nodes in long-term memory. Finally, let Plan C be associated with negative emotional states. Plan A, because it is linked to highly and permanently activated self-nodes, will stay continuously activated, at least at a high enough level that it could control action under appropriate conditions. Plan B will be much harder to activate, even if appropriate conditions exist, and Plan C will be inhibited. It might be possible in this way to build a system that is motivated, in that it will spontaneously tend to act in certain ways and avoid acting in other ways.

Consciousness. Plan A does not need to be conscious, however, and neither do the self-nodes themselves, in spite of their high levels of activation. The equation of short-term memory/focus-of-attention with consciousness is no longer permissible in the expanded model of working memory. Consciousness requires not only a high level of activation in working memory but also an appropriate form of encoding. Just where the boundaries must be placed is a question that cannot be discussed here, but in terms of the hierarchy of mental representations described in chapter 2, a sufficiently high level might have to be reached before the contents of working memory could become conscious. Thus, even a highly activated procedural representation may not be conscious, whereas representations at the linguistic or abstract level would be more likely to be conscious. Many plans are vague, represented at a level that is not readily accessible to consciousness. They may be strong and very much part of our self, but represented at a subsymbolic, sublinguistic, unconscious level. Whether such an approach to consciousness would have sufficient explanatory power to be worth pursuing remains to be explored, however.

Interest. Representing the self in working memory may also provide us with a new way of looking at what kinds of things people find interesting. I have speculated in Kintsch (1980) that there are two forms of interest. Some things are inherently interesting, like sex and violence. Anything that has to do with the self, in fact, is in that category. According to the extended working memory model, these interests are represented by nodes in the network that are directly and perhaps multiply linked to the cluster of self-nodes. Hence, they will be more attended to, better remembered, and judged to be more interesting than nodes without such direct links. The other class of interesting things are those that are neither too familiar nor too strange – objects of intermediate novelty (Berlyne, 1960). Those are the things that arouse our curiosity, without necessarily being linked to our own self. This form of interest seems rather different in its psychological origin than the intrinsic interest based on links to the self. "Interest," like so many other psychological concepts, is a folk concept, and perhaps scientific theory will have to separate what language has put together. James (1969) thought so for emotions, which he claimed were a heterogeneous class of phenomena lumped together by our language. In the CI theory, it may be possible to treat emotion as a unitary phenomenon after all – in much the same way as James wanted to, namely, as perceptions of bodily states.

11.3.2 Cognition and emotion

In the expanded model of working memory that I have proposed, I have suggested that attention be treated as links to the self and motivation as attention to plan nodes. Consider the network of self-nodes again. One can think of it as a representation of our own state, body, and mind. It is a dynamic representation, continually changing and continually being reconstructed. The representation of the body includes information about the biochemical state of the brain, the state of the viscera, and current information about the musculoskeletal frame. The body not only furnishes a place for our thoughts but contributes content, too (Damasio, 1994). Much of this representation is at a level not accessible to consciousness, yielding phenomenologically a vague background feeling of the body. When new representations about the world or the body are being constructed in working memory as a consequence of the ongoing perception and action of the organism, these may or may not match the existing self-representation. Such mismatches are perceived as emotions or feelings.

A crucial role in these mismatches is played by the plans and goals currently active in working memory. An active goal is a node in the self-net, and if representations are constructed in working memory that conflict with this goal, an emotion is experienced. These mismatching representations may be based on perceptions, but they also may be purely mental in origin. Because mental representations, in contrast to body representations, tend to involve higher levels (language, abstract thought), they would be more likely to be conscious. Different types of emotions are experienced because of the contents of the representations that produce a mismatch.

The idea that emotions arise out of a mismatch between a representation constructed from an experience and our self-representation is found in Damasio (1994), Oatley and Johnson-Laird (1987), and Oatley (1992), among others. It seems quite possible to incorporate it into a network model of cognition and emotion such as the extended working-memory model sketched here. Working out the details of such a model and testing its empirical adequacy must remain as a challenge at this time. However, there are a few topics in the field of cognition and emotion that have been thoroughly investigated to which the ideas sketched here are clearly relevant.

There is first the mood dependence of memory. In general, memories acquired in one emotional state are best retrieved when one is again in the same emotional state, though the evidence for this claim is neither strong nor unequivocal (Bower, 1981). The expanded working-memory model can in principle account for this result as follows. If a memory node is linked to self-nodes of a particular emotional tone, the reinstatement of that emotional tone can only facilitate the retrieval of that memory, though it may not be sufficient by itself. It is interesting that the strongest evidence for the mood dependence of memory comes from studies of autobiographical memory (Eich, Macauley, & Ryan, 1994), where one would expect links to self-nodes to be most relevant.

Although mood may bias memory retrieval, a retrieved memory may affect mood by the same mechanism. A depressive person may encode an experience by linking it with negative emotional nodes. If the experience is reinstated, it will tend to activate these negative emotions. Thus, depression may feed on itself in a vicious feedback cycle (Baddeley, 1989). The expanded working-memory model may eventually help us to better understand this process.

Another phenomenon that has been extensively researched is the emotional distinctiveness of memories. Certain memories – flashbulb memories (Neisser & Harsch, 1993) – are associated with very strong emotional responses. Recall is particularly vivid for such memories. Actually flashbulb memories are not notably accurate; it is just that people have great confidence in them (Weaver, 1993). Consider two memories, both poorly encoded and fragmentary, one linked to a very strong, emotional self-node, the other only weakly linked to the self. Suppose that upon retrieval of these fragmentary nodes, both memories may be reconstructed more or less faithfully. However, the first reconstruction will be highly activated because of its strong emotional links, whereas the second will be only weakly activated. Confidence in the first memory would be high and confidence in the second would be low, though both could be equally accurate or inaccurate. An explanation of flashbulb memories along these lines, as suggested by the expanded working-memory model, might be possible.

Cognition and emotion and cognition and motivation are research topics for the future. I have not much to say about these topics at present, except that they are important and should no longer be neglected. I can do no more here than sketch a possible path that might lead to a serious investigation of these phenomena in the future, a path that is consistent with the framework for cognition developed here.

11.4 Outlook

How good a paradigm is comprehension for the study of cognition? More precisely, how good a paradigm is the model of comprehension that was developed in these pages, the construction–integration architecture? Whether or not the extension beyond cognition that was tentatively explored in the previous section can be realized is of secondary importance. The primary question concerns the adequacy of the construction–integration framework as a paradigm for cognition proper.

In my not entirely unbiased view the evidence appears rather positive and the outlook promising. First, the model does well in its core area, text comprehension. Second, extensions to related cognitive phenomena that do not, or do not only, involve text comprehension have been successful and more appear feasible. Third, we are beginning to see the limitations of the comprehension paradigm; once we know what is lacking, we can try to supply the missing components of the theory, or, better, attempt to coordinate the CI theory with other approaches that complement it in just the right way.

The field of text comprehension includes most of the central topics of cognition. Compare the topics discussed in chapters 5 through 10 of the present volume with the outline of a typical textbook of cognitive psychology. Most of the traditional topics of cognitive psychology come up for discussion in the context of research on text comprehension. Word identification, lexical access, priming studies, inference, spatial cognition, and imagery are represented. Psycholinguistic topics such as sentence parsing, anaphora resolution, and metaphor have been discussed. Memory issues are central to text research: working memory, the theory of long-term working memory (which in fact has been developed in part within the context of discourse processing), free recall, cued recall, and recognition, as well as sentence verification. Problem solving appears in the research on word arithmetic problems, as well as in the work on action planning. Skill acquisition is treated in the context of reading skills. Learning, a topic often neglected in the past by cognitive psychologists, has become a major concern in text research. Thus, one can more or less match the major topics of a cognitive psychology text with the chapters of the present book. Some topics are underrepresented, especially the general area of perception and attention. This reflects more an idiosyncrasy of the present approach to text research rather than a necessary limitation – in fact, these topics are central in theories of reading, which focus more on the decoding end of the process than on the comprehension end, as was done here. A few topics considered here are not usually found in cognitive psychology texts, such as the research on macrostructures, which is text specific. But on the whole one can truthfully say that text research faithfully mirrors the concerns of cognitive psychology in general. Therefore, to say that the CI model accounts well for the phenomena discussed here is a strong claim.

Although the scope of the theory presented here is broad, some limitations must be acknowledged. Some topics that one would expect in a book on discourse comprehension are neglected here. The decoding aspects of reading have already been mentioned. Another major omission is the whole area of conversation with its fascinating interplay of pragmatic and cognitive factors. Of course, there is no reason in principle why the present approach could not be extended in either direction.

The present chapter has been concerned with another issue: trying to extend the CI theory beyond the text or discourse domain. To some extent, this appears feasible. The CI model has brought useful insights in the area of skill acquisition, elucidating the kinds of qualitative differences that characterize expert versus novice performance. In the hands of Kitajima and Polson (1995) (section 11.1.3), this kind of theorizing has proved to be capable of dealing with complex problem-solving tasks and is beginning to have practical implications for training. The CI models have enabled us to explore the boundaries between automatic comprehension and strategic problem-solving processes, even accounting for how biases and emotions may influence comprehension. There are many situations in which we comprehend our environment in much the same way as we comprehend a text. That is, we construct bottom–up, crude, local interpretations that are then integrated via a constraint satisfaction process. However, the effectiveness of such processes in complex situations is limited; successful problem solving requires more than that on occasion.

The qualifying phrase *on occasion* in the previous sentence is important. Although bottom–up construction rules in combination with an integration process are not sufficient to account for all of cognition, they account for a great deal. At some point we need something like impasse recognition and impasse resolution procedures that are more powerful than the mechanisms described by the CI theory. What I find surprising and significant is how far cognitive theories get without such analytic mechanisms.

Traditionally, cognitive scientists, psychologists, but especially linguists and philosophers, have thought of cognition (thinking) in terms of powerful, analytic procedures, modeled more or less closely after the example of logic. Alternatively, we can look at cognition in a very different way, in terms of separate levels of representation and distinctive processes operating on these levels. That is the approach of the CI theory.

The basis of cognition may be an associative system, constructed from a person's experience with the world. Latent semantic analysis (LSA) can be a model for such a system, with the crucial difference that LSA learns from the dependencies among printed words only, whereas people learn by interacting with the world and other people, including but not restricted to reading. Dimension reduction may play a role in enabling us to generalize from experience, just as for LSA. Many tasks are performed on the basis of this system alone, or partly on the basis of this system, even tasks that at first glance would seem to require more analytic processing, as is suggested by our successful use of LSA in a variety of situations.

The CI theory adds to this associative basis a powerful computational device, the constraint–satisfaction mechanism via spreading activation. The cognitive operations postulated by the CI theory dominate at the level of linguistic representations, the narrative-linguistic level of chapter 2. This is the level at which the comprehension paradigm is most appropriate. Initial processes deal with associative relations of different strengths and responses based directly on these relations. The comprehension mechanism is a way of forming contextually sensitive constructions from this associative basis.

Human cognition encapsulates different levels of representation, from direct representations that are not dependent on language to the level of abstract, analytic thought that are the traditional focus of problem-solving theories in cognitive science. Thus, human cognition employs other, more complex, more analytic computations than can be achieved by spreading activation networks. It is not my goal here to specify what these are, or how they interface with the mechanisms described by the CI theory. However, a complete theory of cognition has to account for interactions among at least these three levels of processing and representation: the associative, the linguistic, and the abstract symbolic.

References

Albrecht, J. E., O'Brien, E. J., Mason, R. A., & Myers, J. L. (1995). The role of perspective in the accessibility of goals during reading. *Journal of Experimental Psychology: Learning, Memory, and Cognition, 21,* 364–72.

Albrecht, J. E., & Myers, J. L. (1995). The role of context in accessing distant information during reading. *Journal of Experimental Psychology: Learning, Memory, and Cognition, 21,* 1459–68.

Albrecht, J. E., & O'Brien, E. J. (1991). Effects of centrality on retrieval of text-based concepts. *Journal of Experimental Psychology: Learning, Memory, and Cognition, 17,* 932–9.

(1993). Updating a mental model: Maintaining both global and local coherence. *Journal of Experimental Psychology: Learning, Memory, and Cognition, 19,* 1061–70.

(1995). Goal processing and the maintenance of global coherence. In R. F. Lorch & E. J. O'Brien (Eds.), *Sources of coherence in reading* (pp. 263–78). Hillsdale, NJ: Erlbaum.

Altmann, G. T. M., & Steedman, M. (1988). Interaction with context during human sentence processing. *Cognition, 30,* 191–238.

Anderson, A., Garrod, S., & Sanford, A. J. (1983). The accessibility of pronominal antecedents as a function of episode shift in narrative text. *Quarterly Journal of Experimental Psychology, 35,* 427–40.

Anderson, J. R. (1978). Arguments concerning representations for mental imagery. *Psychological Review, 85,* 249–77.

(1983). *The architecture of cognition.* Cambridge, MA: Harvard University Press.

(1990). *The adaptive character of thought.* Hillsdale, NJ: Erlbaum.

(1993). *Rules of the mind.* Hillsdale, NJ: Erlbaum.

Anderson, J. R., & Bower, G. H. (1972). *Human associative memory.* Washington, DC: Winston.

Anderson, R. C., & Ortony, A. (1975). On putting apples into bottles – a problem of polysemy. *Cognitive Psychology, 7,* 167–80.

Baddeley, A. D. (1986). *Working memory.* New York: Oxford University Press.
(1989). The psychology of remembering and forgetting. In T. Butler (Ed.),
Memory: History, culture, and mind. London: Basil Blackwell.

Baddeley, A. D., Papagno, C., & Valla, G. (1988). When long-term learning
depends on short-term storage. *Journal of Memory and Language, 27,*
586–96.

Baddeley, A. D., & Wilson, B. (1988). Comprehension and working memory: A
single-case neuropsychological study. *Journal of Memory and Language, 27,*
479–98.

Barclay, J. R., Bransford, J. D., Franks, J. J., McCarrell, N. S., & Nitsch, K.
(1974). Comprehension and semantic flexibility. *Journal of Verbal Learning
and Verbal Behavior, 13,* 471–81.

Barr, A., & Feigenbaum, E. A. (1982). *The handbook of artificial intelligence.* Los
Altos, CA: William Kaufman.

Barsalou, L. W. (1993). Flexibility, structure, and linguistic vagary in concepts:
Manifestations of a compositional system of perceptual symbols. In A. C.
Collins, S. E. Gathercole, & M. A. Conway (Eds.), *Theories of memories.*
London: Erlbaum.

Barshi, I. (1997). Message length and misunderstandings in aviation communication: Linguistic properties and cognitive constraints. Ph.D. dissertation.
Boulder: University of Colorado.

Bartlett, F. C. (1932). *Remembering.* Cambridge, UK: Cambridge University
Press.

Bateson, G. (1972). *Steps to an ecology of mind.* New York: Ballantine.

Battig, W. F. (1979). The flexibility of human memory. In L. S. Cermak &
F. I. M. Craik (Eds.), *Levels of processing in human memory* (pp. 23–44).
Hillsdale, NJ: Erlbaum.

Beck, I. L., McKeown, M. G., Sinatra, G. M., & Loxterman, J. A. (1991). Revising social studies texts from a text-processing perspective: Evidence of
improved comprehensibility. *Reading Research Quarterly, 27,* 251–76.

Beck, I. L., McKeown, M. G., Worthy, J., Sandora, C., & Kucan L. (1996).
Questioning the author: A yearlong classroom implementation to engage
students with text. *Elementary School Journal, 96,* 385–414.

Bereiter, C., & Scardamalia, M. (1989). Intentional learning as a goal of instruction. In L. B. Resnick (Ed.), *Knowing, learning, and instruction* (pp. 361–92).
Hillsdale, NJ: Erlbaum.

Berlyne, D. E. (1960). *Conflict, arousal, and curiosity.* New York: McGraw-Hill.

Beyer, R. (1990) *Psychologische Analyse kognitiver Prozesse bei der Textverar-
beitung.* Berlin: Habilitationsschrift, Humboldt Universität.

Bierwisch, M. (1969). On certain problems of semantic representation. *Foundations of Language, 5,* 153–84.

Bisanz, G. L., Das, J. P., Varnhagen, C. K., & Henderson, H. K. (1992). Structure and components of reading times and recall for sentences in narratives: Exploring changes with age and reading ability. *Journal of Educational Psychology, 84,* 102–14.

Bisanz, G. L., LaPorte, R. E., Vesonder, G. T., & Voss, J. F. (1978). Contextual prerequisites for understanding: Some investigations of comprehension and recall. *Journal of Verbal Learning and Verbal Behavior, 17,* 337–57.

Bousfield, W. A., & Sedgwick, C. H. (1944). The analysis of sequences of restricted associative responses. *Journal of General Psychology, 30,* 149–65.

Bovair, S., & Kieras, D. E. (1985). A guide to propositional analysis for research on technical prose. In B. K. Britton & J. B. Black (Eds.), *Understanding expository text* (pp. 315–62). Hillsdale, NJ: Erlbaum.

Bower, G. H. (1981). Mood and memory. *American Psychologist, 36,* 129–48.

Bower, G. H., Black, J. B., & Turner, T. J. (1979). Scripts in memory for text. *Cognitive Psychology, 11,* 177–220.

Bransford, J. D., Barclay, J. R., & Franks, J. J. (1972). Sentence memory: A constructive versus interpretive approach. *Cognitive Psychology, 3,* 193–209.

Bransford, J. D., & Franks, J. J. (1971). The abstraction of linguistic ideas. *Cognitive Psychology, 2,* 331–50.

Bransford, J. D., & Johnson, M. K. (1972). Contextual prerequisites for understanding: Some investigations of comprehension and recall. *Journal of Verbal Learning and Verbal Behavior, 11,* 717–26.

Briars, D. J., & Larkin, J. H. (1984). An integrated model of skill in solving elementary word problems. *Cognition and Instruction, 1,* 245–96.

Britton, B. K., & Eisenhart, F. J. (1993). Expertise, text coherence, and constraint satisfaction: Effects on harmony and settling rate. In *Proceedings of the Cognitive Science Society* (pp. 266–71). Hillsdale, NJ: Erlbaum.

Britton, B. K., & Gulgoz, S. (1991). Using Kintsch's model to improve instructional text: Effects of inference calls on recall and cognitive structures. *Journal of Educational Psychology, 83,* 329–45.

Broadbent, D. E. (1975). The magic number seven after fifteen years. In A. Kennedy & A. Wilkes (Eds.), *Studies in long-term memory* (pp. 3–18). London: Wiley.

Brown, A. L., & Palincsar, A. S. (1989). Guided, cooperative learning and individual knowledge acquisition. In L. B. Resnick (Ed.), *Knowing, learning, and instruction.* Hillsdale, NJ: Erlbaum.

Brown, J. S., & VanLehn, K. (1980). Repair theory: A generative theory of bugs in procedural skills. *Cognitive Science, 4,* 379–426.

Bruner, J. S. (1986). *Actual minds, possible worlds.* Cambridge, MA: Harvard University Press.

Cacciari, C., & Glucksberg, S. (1994). Understanding figurative language. In

M. A. Gernsbacher (Eds.), *Handbook of psycholinguistics* (pp. 447–78). San Diego: Academic Press.

Cantor, J., & Engle, R. W. (1993). Working memory capacity as long-term memory activation: An individual difference approach. *Journal of Experimental Psychology: Learning, Memory, and Cognition, 19,* 1101–14.

Cantor, J., Engle, R. W., & Hamilton, G. (1991). Short-term memory, working memory, and verbal abilities: How do they relate? *Intelligence, 15,* 229–46.

Card, S. K., Moran, T. P., & Newell, A. (1983). *The psychology of human-computer interaction.* Hillsdale, NJ: Erlbaum.

Carpenter, P. A., & Just, M. A. (1977). Reading comprehension as the eyes see it. In M. A. Just & P. A. Carpenter (Eds.), *Cognitive processes in comprehension.* Hillsdale, NJ: Erlbaum.

Carpenter, T. P., & Moser, J. M. (1983). The acquisition of addition and subtraction concepts. In R. Lesh & M. Landau (Eds.), *Acquisition of mathematical concepts and processes* (pp. 7–44). Hillsdale, NJ: Erlbaum.

Chafe, W. L. (1974). Language and consciousness. *Language, 58,* 111–33.

Chandrasekaran, B., & Narayanan, N. H. (1990). Integrating imagery and visual representations. In *The Twelfth Annual Conference of the Cognitive Science Society* (pp. 670–7). Hillsdale, NJ: Erlbaum.

Charniak, E. (1993). *Statistical language analysis.* Cambridge, MA: MIT Press.

Chase, W. G., & Ericsson, K. A. (1982). Skill and working memory. In G. H. Bower (Eds.), *The psychology of learning and motivation.* New York: Academic Press.

Cheng, P. W., & Holyoak, K. J. (1985). Pragmatic reasoning schemas. *Cognitive Psychology, 17,* 391–416.

Chi, M. T. H. (1976). Short-term memory limitations in children: Capacity of processing deficits? *Memory & Cognition, 4,* 545–80.

Chi, M. T. H., Feltovich, P. J., & Glaser, R. (1981). Categorization and representation of physics problems by experts and novices. *Cognitive Science, 5,* 121–52.

Chomsky, N. (1966). *Cartesian linguistics.* New York: Harper.

Clark, H. H., & Marshall, C. R. (1981). Definite reference and mutual knowledge. In A. K. Joshi, B. Webster, & I. A. Sagg (Eds.), *Elements of discourse understanding.* Cambridge, UK: Cambridge University Press.

Clark, H. H., & Sengul, C. J. (1979). In search of referents for nouns and pronouns. *Memory & Cognition, 7,* 35–41.

Collins, A. M., & Quillian, M. R. (1969). Retrieval from semantic memory. *Journal of Verbal Learning and Verbal Behavior, 8,* 240–7.

Conrad, C. (1972). Cognitive economy in semantic memory. *Journal of Experimental Psychology, 92,* 149–54.

Cummins, D. D. (1991). Children's interpretations of arithmetic word problems. *Cognition and Instruction, 8,* 261–89.

Cummins, D. D., Kintsch, W., Reusser, K., & Weimer, R. (1988). The role of understanding in solving word problems. *Cognitive Psychology, 20,* 405–38.

Damasio, A. R. (1994). *Descartes' error: Emotion, reason, and the human brain.* New York: Putnams.

Daneman, M., & Carpenter, P. A. (1980). Individual differences in working memory and reading. *Journal of Verbal Learning and Verbal Behavior, 19,* 450–66.

DeCorte, E., Verschaffel, L., & DeWinn, L. (1985). The influence of rewording verbal problems on children's problem representation and solutions. *Journal of Educational Psychology, 77,* 460–70.

Deerwester, S., Dumais, S. T., Furnas, G. W., Landauer, T. K., & Harshman, R. (1990). Indexing by Latent Semantic Analysis. *Journal of the American Society for Information Science, 41,* 391–407.

Dell, G. S., McKoon, G., & Ratcliff, R. (1983). The activation of antecedent information during the processing of anaphoric reference in reading. *Journal of Verbal Learning and Verbal Behavior, 22,* 121–32.

Dellarosa, D. (1986). A computer simulation of children's arithmetic word problem solving. *Behavior Research Methods, Instruments, & Computers, 18,* 147–54.

Dewey, J. (1897). The University Elementary School: History and character. *University [of Chicago] Record, 2,* 72–75.

Doane, S. M., Kintsch, W., & Polson, P. G. (1989). Action planning: Producing UNIX commands. In *The Eleventh Annual Conference of the Cognitive Science Society* (pp. 458–65). Hillsdale, NJ: Erlbaum.

Doane, S. M., McNamara, D. S., Kintsch, W., Polson, P. G., & Clawson, D. (1992). Prompt comprehension in UNIX command production. *Memory, & Cognition, 20,* 327–43.

Doane, S. M., Pellegrino, J. W., & Klatzky, R. L. (1990). Expertise in a computer operating system: Conceptualization and performance. *Human–Computer Interaction, 5,* 267–304.

Donald, M. (1991). *Origins of the modern mind.* Cambridge, MA: Harvard University Press.

Ehrlich, K. (1980). Comprehension of pronouns. *Quarterly Journal of Experimental Psychology, 32,* 247–55.

Ehrlich, K., & Rayner, K. (1983). Pronoun assignment and semantic integration during reading: Eye-movements and immediacy of processing. *Journal of Verbal Learning and Verbal Behavior, 22,* 75–87.

Eich, E., Macauley, D., & Ryan, L. (1994). Mood dependent memory for events of the personal past. *Journal of Experimental Psychology: General, 123,* 201–15.

Ericsson, K. A. (1985). Memory skill. *Canadian Journal of Psychology, 39,* 188–231.

Ericsson, K. A., & Charness, N. (1994). Expert performance: Its structure and acquisition. *American Psychologist, 49*, 727–47.

Ericsson, K. A., & Chase, W. G. (1982). Exceptional memory. *American Scientist, 70*, 607–15.

Ericsson, K. A., & Kintsch, W. (1995). Long-term working memory. *Psychological Review, 102*, 211–45.

Ericsson, K. A., & Simon, H. A. (1993). *Protocol analysis: Verbal reports as data* (Rev. ed.). Cambridge, MA: MIT Press.

Estes, W. K. (1986). Array models for category learning. *Cognitive Psychology, 18*, 500–49.

(1995). A general theory of classification and memory applied to discourse processing. In W. A. Weaver, S. Mannes, & C. R. Fletcher (Eds.), *Discourse comprehension: Essays in honor of Walter Kintsch* (pp. 35–48). Hillsdale, NJ: Erlbaum.

Farnham-Diggory, S., & Gregg, L. (1975). Short-term memory function in young readers. *Journal of Experimental Child Psychology, 19*, 279–98.

Ferreira, F., & Clifton, C. (1986). The independence of syntactic processing. *Journal of Memory and Language, 25*, 348–68.

Ferstl, E. C. (1994a). The Construction-Integration Model: A framework for studying context effects in sentence processing. In *The Sixteenth Annual Conference of the Cognitive Science Society* (pp. 289–94). Hillsdale, NJ: Erlbaum.

(1994b) *Context effects in syntactic ambiguity resolution: The location of prepositional phrase attachment.* Ph.D. dissertation, University of Colorado.

Ferstl, E. C., & Kintsch, W. (in press). Learning from text: Structural knowledge assessment in the study of discourse comprehension. In S. R. Goldman & H. van Oostendorp (Eds.), *The construction of mental representations during reading.*

Fincher-Kiefer, R. H. (1993). The role of predictive inferences in situation model construction. *Discourse Processes, 16*, 99–124.

Fischer, B., & Glanzer, M. (1986). Short-term storage and the processing of cohesion during reading. *Quarterly Journal of Experimental Psychology, 38*, 431–60.

Fischer, G., Henninger, S., & Redmiles, D. (1991). Cognitive tools for locating and comprehending software objects for reuse. In *The Thirteenth International Conference on Software Engineering* (pp. 318–28). Austin, TX: ACM, IEEE.

Fletcher, C. R. (1981). Short-term memory processes in text comprehension. *Journal of Verbal Learning and Verbal Behavior, 20*, 264–74.

(1984). Markedness and topic continuity in discourse processing. *Journal of Verbal Learning and Verbal Behavior, 23*, 487–93.

(1985). Understanding and solving arithmetic word problems: A computer simulation. *Behavior Research Methods, Instruments, and Computers, 17,* 565–71.

Fletcher, C. R., & Bloom, C. P. (1988). Causal reasoning in the comprehension of simple narrative texts. *Journal of Memory and Language, 27,* 235–44.

Fodor, J. A. (1983). *The modularity of mind.* Cambridge, MA: MIT Press.

Foertsch, J., & Gernsbacher, M. A. (1994). In search of complete comprehension: Getting "Minimalists" to work. *Discourse Processes, 18,* 271–96.

Foltz, P. W. (1996). Latent Semantic Analysis for text-based research. *Behavior Research Methods, Instruments, & Computers, 28,* 197–202.

Forster, K. I. (1970). Visual perception on rapidly presented word sequences of varying complexity. *Perception and Psychophysics, 8,* 215–21.

Fox, B. A. (1987). *Discourse structure and anaphora.* New York: Cambridge University Press.

(1984). Anaphora in popular written English narratives. In R. S. Tomlin (Eds.), *Coherence and grounding in discourse.* Amsterdam: Benjamins.

Franzke, M. (1994) *Exploration, acquisition, and retention of skill with display-based systems.* Ph.D. Dissertation, University of Colorado.

Frederiksen, J. R. (1981). Sources of process interaction in reading. In A. M. Lesgold & C. A. Perfetti (Eds.), *Interactive processes in reading.* Hillsdale, NJ: Erlbaum.

Furnas, G. W. (1990). Formal models for imaginal deduction. In *The Twelfth Annual Conference of the Cognitive Science Society* (pp. 662–9). Hillsdale, NJ: Erlbaum.

Gallistel, C. R. (1990). *The organization of learning.* Cambridge, MA: MIT Press.

Garrod, S., Freudenthal, D., & Boyle, E. (1994). The role of different types of anaphor in the on-line resolution of sentences in a discourse. *Journal of Memory and Language, 33,* 38–68.

Garrod, S., O'Brien, E. J., Morris, R. K., & Rayner, K. (1990). Elaborative inferencing as an active or passive process. *Journal of Experimental Psychology: Learning, Memory, and Cognition, 16,* 250–7.

Garnham, A., Oakhill, J., & Johnson-Laird, P. N. (1982). Referential continuity and the coherence of discourse. *Cognition, 11,* 29–46.

Gernsbacher, M. A. (1989). Mechanisms that improve referential access. *Cognition, 32,* 99–156.

(1990). *Language comprehension as structure building.* Hillsdale, NJ: Erlbaum.

(1993). Less skilled readers have less efficient suppresion mechanisms. *Psychological Science, 4,* 294–8.

Gernsbacher, M. A., & Faust, M. E. (1991). The mechanism of suppresssion: A component of general comprehension. *Journal of Experimental Psychology: Learning, Memory, and Cognition., 17,* 245–62.

432 References

Gernsbacher, M. A., Varner, K. R., & Faust, M. E. (1990). Individual differences in general comprehension skills. *Journal of Experimental Psychology: Learning, Memory, and Cognition, 16,* 430–45.

Gibbs, R. W. (1994). Figurative thought and figurative language. In M. A. Gernsbacher (Ed.), *Handbook of psycholinguistics* (pp. 411–46). San Diego: Academic Press.

Gibson, J. J. (1977). The theory of affordances. In R. Shaw & J. Bransford (Eds.), *Perceiving, acting, and knowing: Toward an ecological psychology* (pp. 67–82). Hillsdale, NJ: Erlbaum.

Gillund, G., & Shiffrin, R. M. (1984). A retrieval model for both recognition and recall. *Psychological Review, 91,* 1–67.

Givón, T. (1983). *Topic continuity in discourse.* Amsterdam: Benjamins.

(1995). *Functionalism and grammar.* Amsterdam: Benjamins.

Glanzer, M., Dorfman, D., & Kaplan, B. (1981). Short-term storage in the processing of text. *Journal of Verbal Learning and Verbal Behavior, 20,* 656–70.

Glanzer, M., Fischer, B., & Dorfman, D. (1984). Short-term storage in reading. *Journal of Verbal Learning and Verbal Behavior, 23,* 467–86.

Glenberg, A. M. (1997). What memory is for. *Behavioral and Brain Sciences, 20,* 1–55.

Glenberg, A. M., Kruley, P., & Langston, W. E. (1994). Analogical processes in comprehension. In M. A. Gernsbacher (Ed)., *Handbook of Psycholinguistics* (pp. 609–40). San Diego, CA: Academic Press.

Glenberg, A. M., & Langston, W. E. (1992). Comprehension of illustrated text: Pictures help to build mental models. *Journal of Memory and Language, 31,* 129–51.

Glucksberg, S., Gildea, P., & Bookian, H. D. (1982). On understanding literal speech: Can people ignore metaphors? *Journal of Verbal Learning and Verbal Behavior, 21,* 85–98.

Goetz, E. T., Anderson, R. C., & Schallert, D. L. (1981). The representation of sentences in memory. *Journal of Verbal Learning and Verbal Behavior, 20,* 369–85.

Goldman, S. R., & Varma, S. (1995). CAPping the construction–integration model of discourse comprehension. In W. A. Weaver, S. Mannes, & C. R. Fletcher (Eds.), *Discourse understanding: Essays in honor of Walter Kintsch.* Hillsdale, NJ: Erlbaum.

Golden, R. M. (1997). Causal network analysis validation using synthetic recall protocols. *Behavior Research Methods, Instruments, & Computers, 29,* 15–24.

Gordon, P. C., & Scearce, K. A. (1995). Pronominalization and discourse coherence, discourse structure and pronoun interpretation. *Memory & Cognition, 23,* 313–23.

Graesser, A. C. (1981). *Prose comprehension beyond the word.* New York: Springer.

Graesser, A. C., Hoffmann, N. L., & Clark, L. F. (1980). Structural components of reading times. *Journal of Verbal Learning and Verbal Behavior, 19*, 131–51.

Graesser, A. C., & Kreuz, R. J. (1993). A theory of inference generation during text comprehension. *Discourse Processes, 16*, 145–60.

Graesser, A. C., Singer, M., & Trabasso, T. (1994). Constructing inferences during narrative text comprehension. *Psychological Review, 101*, 375–95.

Graesser, A. C., & Zwaan, R. A. (1995). Inference generation and the construction of situation models. In C. A. Weaver, S. Mannes, & C. R. Fletcher (Eds.), *Discourse comprehension: Essays in honor of Walter Kintsch* (pp. 117–39). Hillsdale, NJ: Erlbaum.

Graf, P., & Schacter, D. L. (1985). Implicit and explicit memory for new associations in normal and amnesic subjects. *Journal of Experimental Psychology: Learning, Memory and Cognition, 11*, 501–18.

Greene, S. B., Gerrig, R. J., McKoon, G., & Ratcliff, R. (1994). Unheralded pronouns and management by common ground. *Journal of Memory and Language, 33*, 511–26.

Greene, S. B., McKoon, G., & Ratcliff, R. (1992). Pronoun resolution and discourse models. *Journal of Experimental Psychology: Learning, Memory, and Cognition, 18*, 266–83.

Greeno, J. G. (1989). Situations, mental models, and generative knowledge. In D. Klahr & K. Kotovsky (Eds.), *Complex information processing* (pp. 285–318). Hillsdale, NJ: Erlbaum.

(1994). Gibson's affordances. *Psychological Review, 101*, 336–42.

(1995). Understanding concepts in activity. In C. A. Weaver, S. Mannes, & C. R. Fletcher (Eds.), *Discourse comprehension: Essays in honor of Walter Kintsch* (pp. 65–96). Hillsdale, NJ: Erlbaum.

Groen, G. J., & Patel, V. L. (1988). The relationship between comprehension and reasoning in medical expertise. In M. T. H. Chi, R. Glaser, & M. J. Farr (Eds.), *The nature of expertise* (pp. 287–310). Hillsdale, NJ: Erlbaum.

Grosz, B. J., & Sidner, C. (1986). Attention, intention, and the structure of discourse. *Computational Linguistics, 12*, 175–204.

Guindon, R., & Kintsch, W. (1984). Priming macropropositions: Evidence for the primacy of macropropositions in memory. *Journal of Verbal Learning and Verbal Behavior, 23*, 508–18.

Guthke, T. (1991). *Psychologische Untersuchungen zu Inferenzen beim Satz und Textverstehen*. Berlin: Ph.D. dissertation, Humboldt Universität.

Guthrie, J. T., & Greaney, V. (1991). Literacy acts. In R. Barr, M. L. Kamil, P. B. Mosenthal, & P. D. Pearson (Eds.), *Handbook of reading research* (pp. 68–96). New York: Longman.

Haberlandt, K., & Bingham, G. (1984). The effect of input direction on the processing of script statements. *Journal of Verbal Learning and Verbal Behavior, 23*, 162–77.

Haberlandt, K., & Graesser, A. C. (1989). Processing of new arguments at clause boundaries. *Memory & Cognition. 17*, 86–193.

Haberlandt, K., Graesser, A. C., Schneider, N. J., & Kiely, J. (1986) Effects of task and new arguments on word reading times. *Journal of Memory and Language, 25*, 314–22.

Haenggi, D., Kintsch, W., & Gernsbacher, M. A. (1995). Spatial situation models and text comprehension. *Discourse Processes, 19*, 173–200.

Hall, R., Kibler, D., Wenger, E., & Truxaw, C. (1989). Exploring the episodic structure of algebra story problem solving. *Cognition and Instruction, 6*, 223–83.

Hammond, K. R. (1996). *Human judgment and social policy: Irreducible uncertainty, inevitable errors, unavoidable injustice.* New York: Oxford University Press.

Hanson, S. J., Kraut, R. E., & Farber, J. M. (1984). Interface design and multivariate analysis of UNIX command use. *ACM Transactions on Office Information Systems, 2*, 42–57.

Henley, N. M. (1969). A psychological study of the semantics of animal terms. *Journal of Verbal Learning and Verbal Behavior, 8*, 176–84.

Hintzman, D. L. (1988). Judgments of frequency and recognition memory in a multiple-trace memory model. *Psychological Review, 95*, 528–51.

Hudson, T. (1983). Correspondences and numerical differences between disjoint sets. *Child Development, 54*, 84–90.

Hull, C. L. (1943). *Principles of behavior.* New York: Appleton-Century.

Hutchins, E. (1995). *Cognition in the wild.* Cambridge, MA: MIT Press.

Huttenlocher, J., & Burke, D. (1976). Why does memory span increase with age? *Journal of Verbal Learning and Verbal Behavior, 8*, 1–31.

James, W. (1969). What is emotion? In *William James: Collected essays and reviews.* New York: Russell and Russell. (Originally published in 1884.)

Jenkins, J. J. (1974). Remember that old theory of memory? Well, forget it! *American Psychologist, 29*, 785–95.

Johnson, C. S. (1967). Hierarchical clustering schemes. *Psychometrika, 32*, 241–54.

Johnson-Laird, P. N. (1983). *Mental models.* Cambridge, MA: Harvard University Press.

Johnson-Laird, P. N., Byrne, R. M. J., & Schaecken, W. (1992). Propositional reasoning by model. *Psychological Review, 99*, 418–39.

Jurafsky, D. (1996). A probabilistic model of lexical semantic access and disambiguation. *Cognitive Science, 20*, 177–94.

Just, M. A., & Carpenter, P. A. (1980). A theory of reading: From eye fixations to comprehension. *Psychological Review, 87*, 329–54.

(1987). The *psychology of reading and language to comprehension.* Boston: Allyn & Bacon.

(1992). A capacity theory of comprehension: Individual differences in working memory. *Psychological Review, 99,* 122–49.

Karmiloff-Smith, A. (1992). *Beyond modularity.* Cambridge, MA: MIT Press.

Katz, J. J., & Fodor, J. A. (1963). The structure of semantic theory. *Language, 39,* 170–210.

Kelly, M. C., & Rubin, D. C. (1988). Natural rhythmic patterns in English: Evidence from child counting-out rhymes. *Journal of Memory and Language, 27,* 718–40.

Kieras, D. E. (1980). Initial mention as a signal to thematic content in technical passages. *Memory & Cognition, 8,* 345–53.

Kimble, G. A. (1996). *Psychology: The hope of a science.* Cambridge, MA: MIT Press.

Kintsch, E. (1990). Macroprocesses and microprocesses in the development of summarization skill. *Cognition and Instruction, 7,* 161–95.

Kintsch, E., & Kintsch, W. (1995). Strategies to promote active learning from texts: Individual differences in background knowledge. *Swiss Journal of Psychology, 54,* 141–51.

Kintsch, W. (1966). Recognition learning as a function of the length of the retention interval and changes in the retention interval. *Journal of Mathematical Psychology, 3,* 412–33.

(1972). Notes on the structure of semantic memory. In E. Tulving & W. Donaldson (Eds.), *Organization and memory* (pp. 247–308). New York: Academic Press.

(1974). *The representation of meaning in memory.* Hillsdale, NJ: Erlbaum.

(1976). Memory for prose. In C. N. Cofer (Ed.), *The structure of human memory* (pp. 90–113). San Francisco: Freeman.

(1977a). *Memory and cognition.* New York: Wiley.

(1977b). On comprehending stories. In M. A. Just & P. Carpenter (Eds.), *Cognitive processes in comprehension* (pp. 33–61). Hillsdale, NJ: Erlbaum.

(1980). Learning from text, levels of comprehension, or: Why anyone would read a story anyway. *Poetics, 9,* 87–98.

(1985). Text processing: A psychological model. In T. A. van Dijk (Ed.), *Handbook of discourse analysis* (pp. 231–43). London: Academic Press.

(1987). Generating scripts from memory. In E. van der Meer & J. Hoffmann (Eds.), *Knowledge aided information processing* (pp. 61–80). Amsterdam: Elsevier.

(1988). The use of knowledge in discourse processing: A construction–integration model. *Psychological Review, 95,* 163–82.

(1989). The representation of knowledge and the use of knowledge in discourse comprehension. In R. Dietrich & C. F. Graumann (Eds.), *Language processing in social context* (pp. 185–209). Amsterdam: North Holland.

(1991). A theory of discourse comprehension: Implications for a tutor for word algebra problems. In M. Pope, R. J. Simmons, J. I. Pozo, & M. Carretero (Eds.), *Proceedings of the 1989 EARLI conference* (pp. 235–53). London: Pergamon Press.

(1992a). A cognitive architecture for comprehension. In H. L. Pick, P. vandenBroek, & D. C. Knill (Eds.), *The study of cognition: Conceptual and methodological issues* (pp. 143–64). Washington, DC: American Psychological Association.

(1992b). How readers construct situation models for stories: The role of syntactic cues and causal inferences. In A. F. Healy, S. M. Kosslyn, & R. M. Shiffrin (Eds.), *From learning processes to cognitive processes: Essays in honor of William K. Estes* (pp. 261–78). Hillsdale, NJ: Erlbaum.

(1993). Information accretion and reduction in text processing: Inferences. *Discourse Processes, 16,* 193–202.

(1994a). Discourse processes. In G. d'Ydewalle, P. Eelen, & P. Bertelson (Eds.), *International perspectives on psychological science. vol. 2: The state of the art* (pp. 135–55). Hillsdale, NJ: Erlbaum.

(1994b). Kognitionspsychologische Modelle des Textverstehens: Literarische Texte. In K. Reusser & M. Reusser (Eds.), *Verstehen* (pp. 39–54). Bern: Hans Huber.

(1994c). Learning from text. *American Psychologist, 49,* 294–303.

(1996). Lernen aus Texten. In J. Hoffmann & W. Kintsch (Eds.), *Lernen* (pp. 503–28). Göttingen: Hogrefe.

Kintsch, W., & Greene, E. (1978). The role of culture-specific schemata in the comprehension and recall of stories. *Discourse Processes, 1,* 1–13.

Kintsch, W., & Greeno, J. G. (1985). Understanding and solving word arithmetic problems. *Psychological Review, 92,* 109–29.

Kintsch, W., & Keenan, J. M. (1973). Reading rate and retention as a function of the number of propositions in the base structure of sentences. *Cognitive Psychology, 5,* 257–79.

Kintsch, W., & Kozminsky, E. (1977). Summarizing stories after reading and listening. *Journal of Educational Psychology, 69,* 491–9.

Kintsch, W., Kozminsky, E., Streby, W. J., McKoon, G., & Keenan, J. M. (1975). Comprehension and recall as a function of content variables. *Journal of Verbal Learning and Verbal Behavior, 14,* 196–214.

Kintsch, W., & Lewis, A. B. (1993). The time course of hypothesis formation in solving arithmetic word problems. In M. Denis & G. Sabah (Eds.), *Mode-*

les et concepts pour la science cognitive: Hommage a Jean-François Le Ny (pp. 11–23). Grenoble: Press Universitaires.

Kintsch, W., & Mannes, S. M. (1987). Generating scripts from memory. In E. van der Meer & J. Hoffmann (Eds.), *Knowledge-aided information processing* (pp. 61–80). Amsterdam: Elsevier Science Publishers.

Kintsch, W., & Mross, E. F. (1985). Context effects in word identification. *Journal of Memory and Language, 24,* 336–49.

Kintsch, W., & van Dijk, T. A. (1978). Towards a model of text comprehension and production. *Psychological Review, 85,* 363–94.

Kintsch, W., & Welsch, D. M. (1991). The construction–integration model: A framework for studying memory for text. In W. E. Hockley & S. Lewandowsky (Eds.), *Relating theory and data: Essays on human memory in honor of Bennett B. Murdock* (pp. 367–85). Hillsdale, NJ.: Erlbaum.

Kintsch, W., Welsch, D. M., Schmalhofer, F., & Zimny, S. (1990). Sentence memory: A theoretical analysis. *Journal of Memory and Language, 29,* 133–59.

Kintsch, W., & Witte, R. S. (1962). Concurrent conditioning of bar press and salivary responding. *Journal of Comparative and Physiological Psychology, 55,* 963–8.

Kintsch, W., & Yarborough, J. J. (1982). Role of rhetorical structure in text comprehension. *Journal of Educational Psychology. 74,* 828–34.

Kitajima, M., & Polson, P. G. (1995). A comprehension-based model of correct performance and errors in skilled, display-based human–computer interaction. *International Journal of Human–Computer Studies, 43,* 65–99.

Kohler, I. (1962). Experiments with goggles. *Scientific American* (May issue).

Kolodner, J. L. (1993). *Case-based reasoning.* Hillsdale, NJ: Erlbaum.

Kosslyn, S. M. (1980). *Image and mind.* Cambridge, MA: Harvard University Press.

(1994). *Image and brain.* Cambridge, MA: MIT Press.

Kotovsky, K., Hayes, J. R., & Simon, H. A. (1985). Why are some problems hard? Evidence from Tower of Hanoi. *Cognitive Psychology, 17,* 248–94.

Kunda, Z., & Thagard, P. (1996). Forming impressions from stereotypes, traits, and behaviors: A parallel constraint satisfaction theory. *Psychological Review, 103,* 284–308.

Lakoff, G. (1987). *Women, fire, and dangerous things.* Chicago: University of Chicago Press.

Landauer, T. K., & Dumais, S. T. (1997). A solution to Plato's problem: The Latent Semantic Analysis theory of acquisition, induction and representation of knowledge. *Psychological Review, 104,* 211–40.

Landauer, T. K., Foltz, P. W., & Laham, D. (in press). An introduction to Latent Semantic Analysis. *Discourse Processes.*

Larkin, J. H. (1989). Display-based problem solving. In D. Klahr & K. Kotovsky (Eds.), *Complex information processing* (pp. 319–432). Hillsdale, NJ: Erlbaum.

——— (1983). Expert and novice differences in solving physics word problems. In D. Gentner & A. L. Stevens (Eds.), *Mental models.* Hillsdale, NJ: Erlbaum.

Lave, J. (1988). *Cognition in practice: Mind, mathematics, culture in everyday life.* New York: Cambridge University Press.

Lehnert, W. G. (1981). Plot units and narrative summarization. *Cognitive Science, 4,* 293–332.

Leibowitz, H. W., & Post, R. B. (1982). The two modes of processing concept and some implications. In J. Beck (Ed.), *Organization and representation in perception* (pp. 343–64). Hillsdale, NJ: Erlbaum.

Lesgold, A. M., Roth, S. F., & Curtis, M. E. (1979). Foregrounding effects in discourse comprehension. *Journal of Verbal Learning and Verbal Behavior, 18,* 291–308.

Linde, C. (1979). Focus of attention and the choice of pronouns. In T. Givón (Ed.), *Syntax and semantics.* New York: Academic Press.

Long, D. L., & Golding, J. M. (1993). Superordinate goal inferences: Are they automatically generated during reading? *Discourse Processes. 16,* 55–73.

Long, D. L., Golding, J. M., & Graesser, A. C. (1992). A test of the on-line status of goal-related inferences. *Journal of Memory and Language, 31,* 634–47.

Long, D. L., Oppy, B. J., & Seely, M. R. (1994). Individual differences in the time course of differential processing. *Journal of Experimental Psychology: Learning, Memory, and Cognition, 20,* 1456–70.

Lorch, R. F., Lorch, E. P., & Inman, W. E. (1993). Effects of signalling topic structure on text recall. *Journal of Educational Psychology, 85,* 281–90.

Lorch, R. F., Lorch, E. P., & Mathews, P. D. (1985). On-line processing of the topic structure of a text. *Journal of Memory and Language, 24,* 350–62.

Lord, A. B. (1960). *The singer of tales.* Cambridge, MA: Harvard University Press.

Magliano, J. P., Baggett, W. B., Johnson, B. K., & Graesser, A. C. (1993). The time course of generating causal antecedent and causal consequence inferences. *Discourse Processes, 16,* 35–53.

Mandler, J. M., & Johnson, N. S. (1977). Remembrance of things parsed: Story structure and recall. *Cognitive Psychology, 9,* 111–51.

Mani, K., & Johnson-Laird, P. N. (1982). The mental representation of spatial descriptions. *Memory & Cognition, 10,* 181–7.

Mannes, S. M. (1994). Strategic processing of text. *Journal of Educational Psychology, 86,* 577–88.

Mannes, S. M., & Kintsch, W. (1987). Knowledge organization and text organization. *Cognition and Instruction, 4,* 91–115.

(1991). Planning routine computing tasks: Understanding what to do. *Cognitive Science, 15,* 305–42.

Marr, D. (1982). *Vision.* San Francisco: Freeman.

Masson, M. E. J., & Miller, J. A. (1983). Working memory and individual differences in comprehension and memory of text. *Journal of Educational Psychology, 75,* 314–18.

Mayer, R. E. (1981). Frequency norms and structural analysis of algebra story problems into families, categories, and templates. *Instructional Science, 10,* 135–75.

McClelland, J. L., & Rumelhart, D. E. (1986). *Parallel distributed processing.* Cambridge, MA: MIT Press.

McConkie, G. W., & Zola, D. (1981). Language constraints and the functional stimulus in reading. In A. M. Lesgold & C. A. Perfetti (Eds.), *Interactive processes in reading.* Hillsdale, NJ: Erlbaum.

McDaniel, M. A., Blischak, D., & Einstein, G. I. (1995). Understanding the special mnemonic characteristics of fairy tales. In I. C. A. Weaver, S. Mannes, & C. A. Fletcher (Eds.), *Discourse comprehension: Essays in honor of Walter Kintsch* (pp. 157–76). Hillsdale, NJ: Erlbaum.

McDonald, J. L., & MacWhinney, B. (1995). The time course of anaphora resolution: Effects of implicit verb causality and gender. *Journal of Memory and Language, 34,* 543–66.

McKeown, M. G., Beck, I. L., Sinatra, G. M., & Loxterman, J. A. (1992). The contribution of prior knowledge and coherent text to comprehension. *Reading Research Quarterly, 27,* 78–93.

McKoon, G., & Ratcliff, R. (1988). Contextually relevant aspects of meaning. *Journal of Experimental Psychology: Learning, Memory, and Cognition, 14,* 331–43.

(1992). Inference during reading. *Psychological Review, 99,* 440–66.

(1995). The minimalist hypothesis: Directions for research. In I. C. A. Weaver, S. Mannes, & C. R. Fletcher (Eds.), *Discourse comprehension: Essays in honor of Walter Kintsch* (pp. 97–116). Hillsdale, NJ: Erlbaum.

McNamara, D. S., & Kintsch, W. (1996). Learning from text: Effect of prior knowledge and text coherence. *Discourse Processes, 22,* 247–88.

McNamara, D. S., & Healy, A. F. (1995). A generation advantage for multiplication skill and nonword vocabulary acquisition. In A. F. Healy & L. E. Bourne (Eds.), *Learning and memory of knowledge and skills* (pp. 132–69). Newbury Park, CA: Sage.

McNamara, D. S., Kintsch, E., Songer, N. B., & Kintsch, W. (1996). Are good texts always better? Text coherence, background knowledge, and levels of understanding in learning from text. *Cognition and Instruction, 14,* 1–43.

McNamara, D. S., & Kintsch, W. (1996). Working memory in text comprehension: Interrupting difficult text. In *The Seventeenth Proceedings of the Cognitive Science Society*. Hillsdale, NJ: Erlbaum.

Meyer, B. J. F. (1975). *The organization of prose and its effect on memory*. Amsterdam: North Holland.

Meyer, D. E., & Schvaneveldt, R. W. (1971). Facilitation in recognizing pairs of words: Evidence of a dependence between retrieval operations. *Journal of Experimental Psychology, 90*, 227–34.

Miall, S. D. (1989). Beyond the schema given: Affective comprehension of literary narratives. *Cognition and Emotion, 3*, 55–78.

Miller, G. A. (1956). The magical number seven, plus or minus two: Some limits of our capacity for processing information. *Psychological Review, 63*, 81–97.

Miller, J. R., & Kintsch, W. (1980). Readability and recall for short passages: A theoretical analysis. *Journal of Experimental Psychology: Human Learning and Memory, 6*, 335–54.

Minsky, M. (1975). A framework for representing knowledge. In P. H. Winston (Ed.), *The psychology of computer vision*. New York: McGraw-Hill.

Mishkin, M., & Petri, H. L. (1984). Memories and habits: Some implications for the analysis of learning and retention. In L. R. Squire & N. Butters (Eds.), *Neuropsychology of memory* (pp. 287–96). New York: Guilford Press.

Miyake, A., Just, M. A., & Carpenter, P. A. (1994). Working memory constraints on the resolution of lexical ambiguity: Maintaining multiple interpretations in neutral contexts. *Journal of Memory and Language, 33*, 175–202.

Moravcsik, J. E., & Kintsch, W. (1993). Writing quality, reading skills, and domain knowledge as factors in text comprehension. *Canadian Journal of Experimental Psychology, 47*, 360–74.

Morrow, D. G., Greenspan, S. L., & Bower, G. H. (1987). Accessibility and situation models in narrative comprehension. *Journal of Memory and Language, 26*, 165–87.

Mross, E. F. (1989) *Macroprocessing in expository text comprehension*. Ph.D. dissertation, University of Colorado, Boulder.

Mross, E. F., & Roberts, J. (1992). *The construction–integration model: A program manual*. No. 92–14. University of Colorado, Institute of Cognitive Science.

Murdock, B. B., Jr. (1982). A theory for the storage and retrieval of items and associative information. *Psychological Review, 89*, 609–26.

(1993). TODAM2: A model for the storage and retrieval of item, associative, and serial order information. *Psychological Review, 100*, 187–203.

Murray, L., & Trevarthen, C. (1985). Emotional regulation of interactions between two-month-olds and their mothers. In T. M. Field & N. A. Fox (Eds.), *Social perception in infants* (pp. 177–97). Norwood, NJ: Ablex.

Myers, J. L., O'Brien, E. J., Albrecht, J. E., & Mason, R. A. (1994). Maintaining global coherence during reading. *Journal of Experimental Psychology: Learning, Memory, and Cognition, 20*, 876–86.

Myers, J. L., Shinjo, M., & Duffy, S. A. (1987). Degree of causal relatedness and memory. *Journal of Memory and Language, 26*, 453–65.

Nathan, M. J. (1991) *A tutor for word algebra problems*. Ph.D. dissertation, University of Colorado.

Nathan, M. J., Kintsch, W., & Young, E. (1992). A theory of word algebra problem comprehension and its implications for the design of learning environments. *Cognition and Instruction, 9*, 329–89.

Neisser, U. (1994). Multiple systems: A new approach to cognitive theory. *The European Journal of Cognitive Psychology, 6*, 225–42.

Neisser, U., & Harsch, N. (1993). Phantom flashbulbs: False recollections of hearing the news about Challenger. In E. Winograd & U. Neisser (Eds.), *Affect and accuracy in recall: Studies of flashbulb memory*. New York: Cambridge University Press.

Nelson, K. (1996). *Language in cognitive development: The emergence of the mediated mind*. New York: Cambridge University Press.

Newell, A. (1990). *Unified theories of cognition*. Cambridge, MA: Harvard University Press.

Newell, A., & Simon, H. A. (1972). *Human problem solving*. Englewood Cliffs, NJ: Prentice-Hall.

———— (1976). Computer science as empirical inquiry: Symbols and search. *Communications of the ACM, 19*, 113–26.

Noordman, L. G. M., & Vonk, W. (1992). Readers' knowledge and the control of inferences in reading. *Language and Cognitive Processes, 7*, 373–91.

Norman, D. A. (1981). The trouble with UNIX. *Datamation*, 139–50.

Oatley, K. (1992). *Best laid schemes: The psychology of emotion*. New York: Cambridge University Press.

Oatley, K., & Johnson-Laird, P. N. (1987). Toward a cognitive theory of emotion. *Cognition and Emotion, 1*, 29–50.

O'Brien, E. J. (1995). Automatic components of discourse comprehension. In R. F. Lorch & E. J. O'Brien (Eds.), *Sources of coherence in reading* (pp. 159–76). Hillsdale, NJ: Erlbaum.

O'Brien, E. J., & Albrecht, J. E. (1991). The role of context in accessing antecedents in text. *Journal of Experimental Psychology: Learning, Memory, and Cognition, 17*, 94–102.

O'Brien, E. J., Shank, D. M., Myers, J. L., & Rayner, K. (1988). Elaborative inferences during reading: Do they occur on-line? *Journal of Experimental Psychology: Learning, Memory, and Cognition, 14*, 410–20.

Olson, J. R., & Biolsi, K. J. (1991). Techniques for representing expert knowledge. In K. A. Ericsson & J. Smith (Eds.), *Toward a general theory of expertise* (pp. 240–85). Cambridge, UK: Cambridge University Press.

Omanson, R. C. (1982). The relation between centrality and story category variation. *Journal of Verbal Learning and Verbal Behavior, 21,* 326–37.

Otero, J., & Kintsch, W. (1992). Failures to detect contradictions in text: What readers believe vs. what they read. *Psychological Science, 3,* 229–34.

Paige, J. M., & Simon, H. A. (1966). Cognitive processes in solving algebra word problems. In B. Kleinmuntz (Ed.), *Problem solving.* New York: Wiley.

Patel, V. L., Arocha, J. F., & Kaufman, D. R. (1994). Diagnostic reasoning and medical expertise. In D. L. Medin (Ed.), *The psychology of learning and motivation* (pp. 187–252). San Diego: Academic Press.

Pearlmutter, N. J., & MacDonald, M. C. (1995). Individual differences and probabilistic constraints in syntactic ambiguity resolution. *Journal of Memory and Language, 34,* 521–42.

Pennington, N., & Hastie, R. (1993). Explanation-based decision making: Effects of memory structure on judgment. *Journal of Experimental Psychology: Learning, Memory, and Cognition., 14,* 521–33.

Perfetti, C. A. (1985). *Reading Ability.* New York: Oxford University Press.

(1993). Why inferences might be restricted. *Discourse Processes. 16,* 181–92.

Perfetti, C. A., & Britt, M. A. (1995). Where do propositions come from? In C. A. Weaver, S. Mannes, & C. R. Fletcher (Eds.), *Discourse comprehension: Essays in honor of Walter Kintsch* pp. (11–34). Hillsdale, NJ: Erlbaum.

Perrig, W., & Kintsch, W. (1985). Propositional and situational representations of text. *Journal of Memory and Language, 24,* 503–18.

Posner, M. I., & McCandliss, B. D. (1993). Converging methods for investigating lexical access. *Psychological Science, 4,* 305–09.

Potter, M. C. (1983). Representational buffers: The eye–mind hypothesis in picture perception, reading, and visual search. In K. Rayner (Ed.), *Eye movements in reading: Perceptual and language processes* (pp. 413–37). New York: Academic Press.

Poulsen, D., Kintsch, E., Kintsch, W., & Premack, D. (1979). Children's comprehension and memory for stories. *Journal of Experimental Child Psychology, 28,* 379–403.

Pylyshyn, Z. W. (1981). The imagery debate: Analogue media versus tacit knowledge. *Psychological Review, 88,* 16–45.

(1984). *Computation and cognition.* Cambridge, MA: MIT Press.

Raajmakers, J. G., & Shiffrin, R. M. (1981). Search of associative memory. *Psychological Review, 88,* 93–34.

Ratcliff, R., & McKoon, G. (1978). Priming in item recognition: Evidence for the propositional structure of sentences. *Journal of Verbal Learning and Verbal Behavior, 17,* 403–18.

Rayner, K., Pacht, J. M., & Duffy, S. A. (1994). Effects of prior encounter and global discourse bias on the processing of lexically ambiguous words: Evidence from eye fixations. *Journal of Memory and Language, 33,* 527–44.

Recht, D. R., & Leslie, L. (1988). Effect of prior knowledge on good and poor readers. *Journal of Educational Psychology, 80,* 16–20.

Reder, L. M. (1982). Plausibility judgments versus fact retrieval: Alternative strategies for sentence verification. *Psychological Review, 89,* 250–80.

(1987). Strategy selection in question answering. *Cognitive Psychology, 19,* 90–38.

Rehder, R., Schreiner, M. E., Wolfe, M. B. W., Laham, D., Landauer, T. K., & Kintsch, W. (in press). Using Latent Semantic Analysis to assess knowledge: Some technical considerations. *Discourse Processes.*

Reusser, K. (1989). From text to situation to equation: Cognitive simulation of understanding and solving mathematical word problems. In H. Mandl, E. DeCorte, N. Bennett, & H. F. Friedrich (Eds.), *Learning and instruction* (pp. 477–98). Oxford: Pergamon Press.

(1993). Tutoring systems and pedagogical theory. In S. Lajoie & S. Derry (Eds.), *Computers as cognitive tools* (pp. 143–77). Hillsdale, NJ: Erlbaum.

Richman, H. B., Staszewski, J. J., & Simon, H. A. (1995). Simulation of expert memory using EPAM IV. *Psychological Review. 102,* 305–30.

Riley, M. S., Greeno, J. G., & Heller, J. H. (1983). Development of children's problem solving ability in arithmetic. In H. P. Ginsburg (Ed.), *The development of mathematical thinking* (pp. 153–96). New York: Academic Press.

Rips, L. J. (1994). *The psychology of proof: Deductive reasoning in human thinking.* Cambridge, MA: MIT Press.

Rizzo, N. D. (1939). Studies in visual and auditory memory span with specific reference to reading disability. *Journal of Experimental Education, 8,* 208–44.

Rodenhausen, H. (1992). Mathematical aspects of Kintsch's model of discourse comprehension. *Psychological Review, 99,* 547–49.

Rosch, E., & Mervis, C. B. (1975). Family resemblance studies in the internal structure of of categories. *Cognitive Psychology, 7,* 573–605.

Rubin, D. C. (1988). Learning poetic language. In F. S. Kessel (Ed.), *The development of language and language researchers: Essays in honor of Roger Brown* (pp. 339–51). Hillsdale, NJ: Erlbaum.

Rumelhart, D. E., & McClelland, J. L. (Ed.). (1986). *Parallel distributed processing.* Cambridge, MA: MIT Press.

Sanford, A. J., & Garrod, S. C. (1981). *Understanding written language.* London: Wiley.

Sanford, A. J., Moar, K., & Garrod, S. (1988). Proper names as controllers of discourse focus. *Language and Speech, 31,* 43–56.

Santa, J. L. (1977). Spatial transformations of words and pictures. *Journal of Experimental Psychology: Human Learning and Memory, 3*, 418–27.

Schank, R. C. (1982). *Dynamic memory.* Cambridge, UK: Cambridge University Press.

Schank, R. C., & Abelson, R. P. (1977). *Scripts, plans, goals, and understanding.* Hillsdale, NJ: Erlbaum.

Schmalhofer, F. (1986). Verlaufscharakteristiken des Informationsabruf beim Wiedererkennen und Verifizieren von Säitzen. *Zeitschrift für Experimentelle und Angewandte Psychologie, 33*, 133–49.

Schmidt, H. G., & Boshuizen, H. P. A. (1993). On the origin of intermediate effects in clinical case recall. *Memory & Cognition, 21*, 338–51.

Schmidt, R. A., & Bjork, R. A. (1992). New conceptualizations of practice: Common principles in three paradigms suggest new concepts for training. *Psychological Science, 3*, 207–17.

Schneider, W., Körkel, J., & Weinert, F. E. (1989). Domain-specific knowledge and memory performance: A comparison of high- and low-aptitude children. *Journal of Educational Psychology, 81*, 306–12.

Schönpflug, W., & Esser, K. B. (1995). Memory and its Graeculi: Metamemory and control in extended memory systems. In C. A. Weaver, S. Mannes, & C. R. Fletcher (Eds.), *Discourse comprehension: Essays in honor of Walter Kintsch* (pp. 245–56). Hillsdale, NJ: Erlbaum.

Schvaneveldt, R. W. (Ed.). (1990). *Pathfinder associative networks: Studies in knowledge organization.* Norwood, NJ: Ablex.

Schwanenflugel, P. J., & C. R. White (1991). The influence of paragraph information on the processing of upcoming words. *Reading Research Quarterly, 26*, 160–77.

Selz, O. (1922). *Zur Psychologie des Denkens und Irrtums.* Bonn: Cohen.

Shepard, R. N. (1967). Recognition memory for words, sentences, and pictures. *Journal of Experimental Psychology, 62*, 302–9.

Shepard, R. N., & Metzler, J. (1971). Mental rotation of three-dimensional objects. *Science, 171*, 701–3.

Shepard, R. N., & Teghtsoonian, M. (1961). Retention of information under conditions approaching a steady state. *Journal of Experimental Psychology, 62*, 302–9.

Simon, H. A. (1969) *The sciences of the artificial.* Cambridge, MA: MIT Press.
  (1995). The information-processing theory of mind. *American Psychologist, 50*, 507–8.

Singer, M. (1982). Comparing memory for natural and laboratory reading. *Journal of Experimental Psychology: General, 111*, 331–47.

Singer, M., Graesser, A. C., & Trabasso, T. (1994). Minimal or global inference during reading. *Journal of Memory and Language, 33*, 421–41.

Singer, M., & Kintsch, W. (in preparation). *Recognition memory for sentences.*

Singer, M., & Ritchot, K. F. M. (1996). The role of working memory capacity and knowledge access in text inference processing. *Memory & Cognition, 24*, 733–43.

Skinner, B. F. (1938). *The behavior of organisms.* New York: Appleton-Century-Crofts.

Smith, E. E., & Medin, D. L. (1981). *Categories and concepts.* Cambridge, MA: Harvard University Press.

Smith, E. E., Shoben, E. J., & Rips, L. J. (1974). Structure and process in semantic memory: A feature model for semantic decision. *Psychological Review, 81*, 214–41.

Smolensky, P. (1986). Information processing in dynamical systems: Foundations of harmony theory. In D. F. Rumelhart & J. L. McClelland (Eds.), *Parallel distributed processes.* Cambridge, MA: MIT Press.

Spence, K. W. (1956). *Behavior theory and conditioning.* New Haven, CT: Yale University Press.

Squire, L. R. (1992). Memory and the hippocampus: A synthesis of findings with rats, monkeys, and humans. *Psychological Review, 99*, 195–231.

Squire, L. R., & Knowlton, B. (1995). Learning about categories in the absence of memory. *Proceedings of the National Academy of Sciences, 92*, 12470.

Squire, L. R., Knowlton, B., & Musen, G. (1993). The structure and organization of memory. *Annual Review of Psychology, 44*, 453–95.

Stanners, R. F., Price, J. M., & Painton, S. (1982). Interrelationships among text elements in fictional prose. *Applied Psycholinguistics. 3*, 95–107.

Stanovich, K. E. (1980). Toward an interactive-compensatory model of individual differences in reading fluency. *Reading Research Quarterly, 16*, 32–1.

Staub, F. C., & Reusser, K. (1995). The role of presentational structures in understanding and solving mathematical word problems. In C. A. Weaver, S. Mannes, & C. R. Fletcher (Eds.), *Discourse comprehension: Essays in honor of Walter Kintsch* (pp. 285–306). Hillsdale, NJ: Erlbaum.

Steinhart, D. J. (1996) *Resolving lexical ambiguity: Does context play a role?* MA thesis, University of Colorado.

Stern, E. (1993a). What makes certain arithmetic word problems involving comparison of sets so difficult for children? *Journal of Educational Psychology, 85*, 7–23.

(1993b). Die Entwicklung des mathematischen Verständnisses im Kindesalter. Habilitationsschrift, Universität München.

Stern, E., & Lehrndorfer, A. (1992). The role of situational context in solving word problems. *Cognitive Development, 7*, 259–68.

Sternberg, S. (1969). Memory scanning: Mental processes revealed by reaction time experiments. *American Scientist, 57*, 421–57.

Stigler, J. W., Fuson, K. C., Ham, M., & Kim, M. S. (1986). An analysis of addition and subtraction word problems in American and Soviet elementary mathematics textbooks. *Cognition and Instruction, 3,* 153–71.

Suchman, L. A. (1987). *Plans and situated actions: The problem of human–machine communication.* Norwood, NJ: Ablex.

Swinney, D. A. (1979). Lexical access during sentence comprehension: (Re)consideration of context effects. *Journal of Verbal Learning and Verbal Behavior, 18,* 645–59.

Tapiero, I., & Denhière, G. (1995). Simulating recall and recognition using Kintsch's Construction–Integration model. In C. A. Weaver, S. Mannes, & C. R. Fletcher (Eds.), *Discourse comprehension: Essays in honor of Walter Kintsch* (pp. 211–32). Hillsdale, NJ: Erlbaum.

Taraban, R., & McClelland, J. L. (1988). Constituent attachment and thematic role assignment in sentence processing: Influence of content-based expectations. *Journal of Memory and Language, 27,* 597–632.

Taylor, H. A., & Tversky, B. (1992). Spatial models derived from survey and route descriptions. *Journal of Memory and Learning, 31,* 261–92.

Thomson, D. M. (1972). Context effects in recognition memory. *Journal of Verbal Learning and Verbal Behavior, 11,* 497–511.

Till, R. E., Mross, E. F., & Kintsch, W. (1988). Time course of priming for associate and inference words in a discourse context. *Memory & Cognition, 16,* 283–98.

Tolman, E. C. (1932). *Purposive behavior in animals and men.* New York: Century.

Trabasso, T., & van den Broek, P. (1985). Causal thinking and the representation of narrative events. *Journal of Memory and Language, 24,* 612–30.

Trabasso, T., & Suh, S. (1993). Understanding text: Achieving explanatory coherence through on-line inferences and mental operations in working memory. *Discourse Processes, 16,* 3–34.

Tulving, E., & Thomson, D. M. (1973). Encoding specificity and retrieval processes in episodic memory. *Psychological Review, 80,* 352–73.

Tversky, A., & Kahneman, D. (1983). Extensional and intuitive reasoning: The conjunction fallacy in probability judgment. *Psychological Review, 90,* 293–315.

Tyler, L. K., & Marslen-Wilson, W. D. (1982). Processing utterances in discourse contexts: On-line resolution of anaphors. *Journal of Semantics, 1,* 297–315.

Underwood, B. J., & Freund, J. S. (1968). Errors in recognition learning and retention. *Journal of Experimental Psychology, 78,* 55–63.

van Dijk, T. A. (1972). *Some aspects of text grammars.* The Hague: Mouton.
  (1980). *Macrostructures.* The Hague: Mouton.

van Dijk, T. A., & Kintsch, W. (1983). *Strategies of discourse comprehension.* New York: Academic Press.

van den Broek, P. (1990). Causal inferences in the comprehension of narrative texts. In A. C. Graesser, & G. H. Bower (Eds.), *Psychology of learning and motivation: Inferences and text comprehension* (pp. 175–94). San Diego: Academic Press.

van den Broek, P., Risden, K., Fletcher, C. R., & Thurlow, R. (1996). A "Landscape" view of reading: Fluctuating patterns of activation and the construction of a stable meaning. In B. K. Britton & A. C. Graesser (Eds.), *Models of understanding text* (pp. 165–88). Hillsdale, NJ: Erlbaum.

Varma, S., & Goldman, S. R. (1996). Resonance-based reinstatement of anaphoric antecedents. Paper presented at the Seventh Annual Winter Conference, Jackson Hole, WY.

Vonk, W., Hustinx, L. G. M. M., & Simons, W. H. G. (1992). The use of referential expressions in structuring discourse. *Language and Cognitive Processes. 7,* 301–33.

Voss, J. F., & Silfies, L. N. (1996). Learning from history texts: The interaction of knowledge and comprehension skill with text structure. *Cognition and Instruction, 14,* 45–68.

Vygotsky, L. S. (1986). *Thought and language.* Cambridge, MA: MIT Press.

Walker, C. H. (1987). Relative importance of domain knowledge and overall aptitude on acquisition of domain-related knowledge. *Cognition and Instruction, 4,* 25–42.

Walker, C. H., & Yekovich, F. R. (1984). Script-based inferences: Effects of text and knowledge variables on recognition memory. *Journal of Verbal Learning and Verbal Behavior, 23,* 357–70.

Walker, W. H., & Kintsch, W. (1985). Automatic and strategic aspects of knowledge retrieval. *Cognitive Science, 9,* 261–83.

Wallace, W. T., & Rubin, D. C. (1988). "The wreck of the old 97": A real event remembered in song. In U. Neisser & E. Winograd (Eds.), *Remembering reconsidered: Ecological and traditional approaches to the study of memory* (pp. 283–310). New York: Cambridge University Press.

Wanner, E. (1975). *On remembering, forgetting and understanding sentences.* The Hague: Mouton.

Weaver, C. A. (1993). Do you need a "flash" to form a flashbulb memory? *Journal of Experimental Psychology: General, 122,* 39–46.

Weinert, F. E., & Schneider, W. (Eds.). (in press). *Individual development from 3 to 12: Findings from the Munich Longitudinal Study.* Cambridge: Cambridge University Press.

Weisskranz, L., Warrington, E. K., Sanders, M. D., & Marshall, J. (1974). Visual capacity in the hemianopic field following restricted occipital ablation. *Brain, 97,* 709–28.

Wertheimer, M. (1945). *Productive thinking.* New York: Harper.

Whitney, P., Budd, D., Bramuci, R. S., & Crane, R. C. (1995). On babies, bathwater, and schemata: A reconsideration of top-down processes in comprehension. *Discourse Processes, 20,* 135–66.

Whitney, P., Ritchie, B. G., & Clark, M. B. (1991). Working memory capacity and the use of elaborative inferences in text comprehension. *Discourse Processes, 14,* 133–46.

Wisniewski, E. J. (1995). Prior knowledge and functionally relevant features in concept learning. *Journal of Experimental Psychology: Learning. Memory, and Cognition, 21,* 449–468.

Wolfe, M. B. W., & Kintsch, W. (in preparation). Story recall: Joining comprehension theory and memory theory.

Wolfe, M. B., Schreiner, M. E., Rehder, R., Laham, D., Foltz, P. W., Landauer, T. K., & Kintsch, W. (in press). Learning from text: Matching reader and text by Latent Semantic Analysis. *Discourse Processes.*

Yekovich, F. R., Walker, C. H., Ogle, L. T., & Thompson, M. A. (1990). The influence of domain knowledge on inferencing in low-aptitude individuals. In A. C. Graesser & G. H. Bower (Eds.), *The psychology of learning and motivation* (pp. 175–96). New York: Academic Press.

Zwaan, R. A., Langston, M. C., & Graesser, A. C. (1995). The construction of situation models in narrative comprehension: An event-indexing model. *Psychological Science, 6,* 292–97.

Zwaan, R. A., Magliano, J. P., & Graesser, A. C. (1995). Dimensions of situation model construction in narrative comprehension. *Journal of Experimental Psychology: Learning, Memory, and Cognition, 21,* 386–97.

Name Index

Abelson, R. P., 36, 37, 94
Aesop, 268
Albrecht, J. E., 175n, 181, 190, 194, 235
Altman, G. T. M., 172, 173
Anderson, A., 148
Anderson, J. R., 2, 6, 7, 42, 44, 45, 248, 373n
Anderson, R. C., 71, 135
Aristotle, 35–6

Baddeley, A. D., 125, 126, 127, 217, 239, 420
Baggett, W. B., 194, 198
Barclay, J. R., 78, 104f, 105, 135, 191, 192
Barr, A., 36
Barsalou, L. W., 30, 44, 79, 80
Barshi, I., 70
Bartlett, F. C., 29, 68, 94, 265
Bateson, G., 31
Battig, W. F., 320
Beck, I. L., 312, 329
Bereiter, C., 329
Berlyne, D. E., 419
Beyer, R., 308, 309f, 311, 313
Bierwisch, M., 37n

Bingham, G., 82
Biolsi, K. J., 295
Bisanz, G. L., 282–3, 285, 286, 297
Bjork, R. A., 320
Black, J. B., 37, 82
Blischak, D., 319
Bloom, C. P., 234
Bookian, H. D., 82
Boshuizen, H. P. A., 233
Bousfield, W. A., 83
Bovair, S., 55
Bower, G. H., 37, 82, 201, 202, 248, 420
Boyle, E., 148, 149, 152, 153, 154
Bramuci, R. S., 37
Bransford, J. D., 78, 104f, 105, 135, 191, 192, 244, 287, 291
Briars, D. J., 334
Britt, M. A., 60n
Britton, B. K., 169, 309, 310, 311, 313, 317
Broadbent, D. E., 217
Brown, A. L., 329
Brown, J. S., 386
Bruner, J. S., 27
Budd, D., 37

Burke, D., 238
Byrne, R. M. J., 192

Cacciari, C., 158
Cantor, J., 239, 240
Card, S. K., 387
Carpenter, P. A., 101, 124, 148,
    223, 238–9, 240, 241, 242,
    243, 283, 284
Carpenter, T. P., 338
Chafe, W. L., 148, 226
Chandrasekaren, B., 47
Charness, N., 381
Charniak, E., 174n
Chase, W. G., 212, 219
Chatfield, N., 278
Cheng, P. W., 402
Chi, M. T. H., 238, 381
Chomsky, N., 32n, 344
Clark, H. H., 148, 235
Clark, L. F., 282, 285
Clark, M. B., 244
Clawson, D., 97, 381, 384, 385f,
    386, 388, 391
Clifton, C., 173
Collins, A. M., 36, 75
Conrad, C., 36
Crane, R. C., 37
Cummins, D. D., xv, 54, 338,
    339, 340, 344, 345, 346,
    347, 354, 359
Curtis, M. E., 148

Damasio, A. R., 409, 410, 412,
    419, 420
Daneman, M., 238–9, 240
Das, J. P., 282–3, 285, 286
DeCorte, E., 341

Deerwester, S., 87
Dell, G. S., 145, 146
Dellarosa, D., 338
Denhière, G., 266
Descartes, R., 13
Dewey, J., 329
DeWinn, L., 341
Doane, S. M., xv, 97, 381, 382,
    383, 384, 386, 388, 391
Donald, M., 27, 28, 31
Dorfman, D., 222, 223t, 230, 234
Duffy, S. A., 129, 145, 320
Dumais, S. T., 87, 88, 89, 134

Eco, U., 157
Ehrlich, K., 148, 149
Eich, E., 420
Einstein, G. I., 319
Eisenhart, F. J., 169
Engle, R. W., 239, 240
Ericsson, K. A., xvi, 3, 76, 77,
    118, 190, 212, 213, 216,
    217, 218f, 219, 220f, 222,
    223, 231, 238, 239, 241,
    244, 245, 381, 396, 409
Esser, K. B., 29
Estes, W. K., 35, 90

Farber, J. M., 388
Farnham-Diggory, S., 238
Faust, M. E., 284
Feigenbaum, E. A., 36
Feltovich, P. J., 381
Ferreira, F., 173
Ferstl, E. C., xvi, 101, 168, 170,
    171, 172, 173, 174, 297,
    299f, 300, 301, 302
Fincher-Kiefer, R. H., 199

Fischer, B., 222
Fischer, G., xv, 107, 371
Fletcher, C. R., xv, 148, 156,
    179, 180, 198, 199, 234, 338
Fodor, J. A., 34, 128, 344
Foertsch, J., 193
Foltz, P. W., 87, 88, 89, 90, 324,
    326f, 327
Forster, K. I., 72
Fox, B. A., 156, 179
Franks, J. J., 78, 104f, 105, 135,
    191, 192, 291
Franzke, M., xvi, 390
Frederiksen, J. R., 283
Freudenthal, D., 148, 149, 152,
    153, 154
Freund, J. S., 248
Furnas, G. W., 45, 87
Fuson, K. C., 333

Gallistel, C. R., 20, 21
Garnham, A., 148
Garrod, S., 148, 149, 152, 153,
    154, 156, 194
Gernsbacher, M. A., 144, 147,
    169n, 193, 201, 202f, 203f,
    204, 223, 284
Gerrig, R. J., 148, 156, 226
Gibbs, R. W., 157, 161
Gibson, J. J., 21, 23, 29
Gildea, P., 82
Gillund, G., 35, 235, 249, 253,
    254, 256, 257, 261, 267,
    268, 273, 274, 275, 276
Givón, T., 68, 156, 226
Glanzer, M., 222, 223t, 230, 231,
    234
Glaser, R., 381

Glenberg, A. M., 44, 198, 413
Glucksberg, S., 82, 158
Goetz, E. T., 71
Golden, R. M., 268
Golding, J. M., 194
Goldman, S. R., 99, 235
Gordon, P. C., 148
Graesser, A. C., 193, 194, 198,
    282, 285
Graf, P., 25
Greaney, V., 332
Greene, E., 68
Greene, S. B., 148, 156, 226
Greeno, J. G., xv, 23, 24, 29, 334,
    335–6t, 335, 337, 338, 339,
    346, 347, 354, 359, 365
Greenspan, S. L., 201, 202
Gregg, L., 238
Groen, G. L., 233
Grosz, B. J., 156
Guindon, R., 174, 175, 176n
Gulgoz, S., 309, 310, 311, 313,
    317
Guthke, T., 189
Guthrie, J. T., 332

Haberlandt, K., 82, 285
Haenggi, D., 201, 202f, 203f, 204
Hall, R., 358, 363
Ham, M., 333
Hamilton, G., 239
Hammond, K. R., 402
Hanson, S. J., 388
Harsch, N., 420
Harshman, R., 87
Hastie, R., 399, 402
Hayes, B., 247
Hayes, J. R., 397, 398

Healy, A. F., 319
Heller, J. H., 334, 335–6t, 335, 339, 359
Henderson, H. K., 282–3, 285, 286
Henley, N. M., 297
Henninger, S., 107, 371
Hintzman, D. L., 35, 249, 253
Hoffman, N. L., 282, 285
Holyoak, K. J., 402
Homer, 212
Hudson, T., 334, 346
Hull, C. L., 20
Hustinx, L. G. M. M., 180
Hutchins, E., 31
Huttenlocher, J., 238

Inman, W. E., 179

James, W., 419
Jenkins, J. J., 216
Johnson, B. K., 194, 198
Johnson, C. S., 298
Johnson, M. K., 244, 287
Johnson, N. S., 211
Johnson–Laird, P. N., 118, 148, 192, 198, 420
Jurafsky, D., 174n
Just, M. A., 101, 124, 148, 223, 239, 240, 241, 242, 243, 283, 284

Kahneman, D., 399, 400, 414, 415, 416
Kaplan, B., 223, 230, 234
Karmiloff-Smith, A., 27, 30
Katz, J. J., 34
Keenan, J. M., 72, 197, 221, 229, 285

Kelly, M. C., 207, 208
Kibler, D., 358, 363
Kiely, J., 285
Kieras, D. E., 55, 174
Kim, M. S., 333
Kimble, G. A., 20
Kintsch, E., xv, xvi, 50, 68, 207, 309f, 311, 313, 315f, 316f, 318, 320, 322, 323
Kintsch, W., 20, 34n, 37, 38, 39, 46, 49, 54, 60n, 61, 67, 68, 69–70, 72, 76, 77, 78, 81, 83, 84f, 85, 95, 96, 97, 101, 102, 104f, 105, 106, 107, 108, 118, 130, 131, 132, 133, 134, 136, 142, 158, 168, 174, 175, 176n, 177, 181, 183, 189, 190, 197, 199, 200, 201, 202f, 203f, 204, 213, 216, 217, 218f, 219, 220f, 221, 222, 223, 228, 229, 230, 231, 234, 238, 239, 241, 244, 245, 248, 251, 252f, 253f, 264, 265, 266, 274, 275, 276, 278, 285, 286, 287, 288f, 289f, 292, 293, 294f, 297, 299, 300, 301, 302, 303f, 306f, 310, 311, 313, 315f, 316f, 317, 318, 319f, 320, 321f, 323, 324, 326f, 327, 335, 337, 338, 339, 340, 344, 345, 346, 347, 348, 354, 355, 358, 359, 360, 361, 364, 365, 366, 367f, 372, 376, 379, 380, 381, 382, 383, 384, 385f, 386, 388, 391, 396, 409, 418

Kitajima, M., 97, 388, 389, 390, 391, 392f, 422
Klatzky, R. L., 382, 383
Knowlton, B., 25, 26
Kohler, I., 22
Kolodner, J. L., 211
Körkel, J., 287
Kosslyn, S. M., 44, 45
Kotovsky, K., 397, 398
Kozminsky, E., 174, 221, 285
Kraut, R. E., 388
Kreuz, R. J., 193
Kruley, P., 198
Kucan, L., 329
Kunda, Z., 394, 402, 403, 404, 406, 408

Laham, D., 87, 88, 90, 324, 326f, 327
Lakoff, G., 43, 157, 413
Landauer, T. K., xv, xvi, 87, 88, 89, 90, 134, 324, 326f, 327
Langston, M. C., 198
Langston, W. E., 198
LaPorte, R. E., 297
Larkin, J. H., 31, 334, 339, 365, 381
Lave, J., 23
Lehnert, W. G., 211
Lehrndorfer, A., 346
Leibniz, G. W. F., 32
Leibowitz, H. W., 24
Lesgold, A. M., 148
Leslie, L., 287
Lewis, A. B., 348, 349, 352, 353, 354
Lewis, C., xv
Linde, C., 179

Long, D. L., 132, 194, 198, 232, 284, 285, 286
Lorch, E. P., 176, 179
Lorch, R. F., 176, 179
Lord, A. B., 212
Loxterman, J. A., 312

McCandliss, B. D., 126, 127
McCarrell, N. S., 78, 135
Macauley, D., 420
McClelland, J. L., 35, 170, 171
McConkie, G. W., 283
McDaniel, M. A., 319
McDonald, J. L., 148
MacDonald, M. C., 242
McKeown, M. G., 312, 329
McKoon, G., 73, 78, 145, 146, 148, 156, 174, 193, 221, 226, 285
McNamara, D. S., xv, 97, 230, 309f, 311, 313, 315f, 316f, 317, 318, 319, 320, 323, 381, 384, 385f, 386, 388, 391
MacWhinney, B., 148
Magliano, J. P., 194, 198
Mandler, J. M., 211
Mani, K., 198
Mannes, S. M., xv, 37, 83, 84f, 85, 97, 320, 321f, 322, 372, 376, 379, 380, 388, 391
Marr, D., 5
Marshall, C. R., 235
Marshall, J., 24
Marslen-Wilson, W. D., 148
Mason, R. A., 181, 190, 194, 235
Masson, M. E. J., 239
Mathews, P. D., 176, 179
Mayer, R. E., 359

Medin, D. L., 34, 35
Mervis, C. B., 35
Metzler, J., 44
Meyer, B. J. F., 222
Meyer, D. E., 36
Miall, S. D., 414
Miller, G. A., 217
Miller, J. A., 239
Miller, J. R., 264, 266, 310
Minsky, M., 36
Mishkin, M., 25
Miyake, A., xvi, 243
Moar, K., 148
Moran, T. P., 387
Moravcsik, J. E., xv, 104f, 105,
    287, 288f, 289f, 291
Morris, R. K., 194
Morrow, D. G., 201, 202
Moser, J. M., 338
Mross, E. F., xv, 100, 101, 130,
    131, 132, 133, 134, 139n,
    177–8, 179, 198, 228, 254,
    286
Murdock, B. B., Jr., 35, 249, 253
Murray, L., 22
Musen, G., 25
Musil, R., 205
Myers, J. L., 181, 190, 194, 235,
    238, 320

Narayanan, N. H., 47
Nathan, M. J., xv, 107, 360, 361,
    364, 366, 367f, 368
Neisser, U., 21, 22, 29, 420
Nelson, K., 27
Newell, A., 1, 2, 6, 7, 29, 42, 123,
    216, 387, 392, 394, 396
Nitsch, K., 78, 135

Noordman, L. G. M., 195–6, 197
Norman, D. A., 381

Oakill, J., 148
Oatley, K., 414, 420
O'Brien, E. J., 175n, 181, 190,
    194, 235
Ogle, L. T., 289
Olson, J. R., 295
Omanson, R. C., 286
Oppy, B. J., 132, 198, 232, 284,
    285, 286
Ortony, A., 135
Otero, J., xv, 181, 183

Pacht, J. M., 129, 145
Paige, J. M., 366
Painton, S., 297
Palinscar, A. S., 329
Papagno, C., 127
Patel, V. L., 233
Pearlmutter, N. J., 242
Pellegrino, J. W., 382, 383
Pennington, N., 399, 402
Perfetti, C. A., 60n, 199, 282,
    283
Perrig, W., xv, 199, 200, 201
Petri, H. L., 25
Polson, P. G., xv, xvi, 97, 381,
    382, 383, 384, 385f, 386,
    388, 389, 390, 391, 392f, 422
Posner, M. I., 126, 127
Post, R. B., 24
Potter, M. C., 124, 125, 126
Poulsen, D., 68
Premack, D., 68
Price, J. M., 297
Pylyshyn, Z. W., 6, 45

Quillian, M. R., 36, 75

Raajmakers, J. G., 85, 97
Ratcliff, R., 73, 78, 145, 146,
    148, 156, 174, 193, 226
Rayner, K., 129, 145, 148, 194
Recht, D. R., 287
Reder, L. M., 252
Redmiles, D., 107, 371
Rehder, R., 324, 326f, 327
Reusser, K., xv, 54, 338, 339,
    340, 344, 345, 346, 347,
    354, 359, 360
Richman, H. B., 235
Riley, M. S., 334, 335, 335–6t,
    335, 339, 359
Rips, L. J., 34, 192
Risden, K., 198, 199
Ritchie, B. G., 244
Ritchot, K. F. M., 244
Rizzo, N. D., 238
Roberts, J., 100, 139n, 254
Rodenhausen, H., 99
Rosch, E., 35
Roth, S. F., 148
Rubin, D. C., 207, 208, 212
Rumelhart, D. E., 35
Ryan, L., 420

Sandburg, C., 159
Sanders, M. D., 24
Sandora, C., 329
Sanford, A. J., 148, 156
Santa, J. L., 44
Scardamalia, M., 329
Scearce, K. A., 148
Schacter, D. L., 25
Schaecken, W., 192

Schallert, D. L., 71
Schank, R. C., 36, 37, 82, 94
Schmalhofer, F., xv, 251, 252,
    253f
Schmidt, H. G., 233
Schmidt, R. A., 320
Schneider, N. J., 285
Schneider, W., 287, 355
Schönpflug, W., 29
Schreiner, M. E., xvi, 324, 326f,
    327
Schvaneveldt, R. W., 36, 298
Schwanenflugel, P.J., 136, 137t,
    139, 142, 144
Sedgwick, C. H., 83
Seely, M. R., 132, 198, 232, 284,
    285, 286
Selz, O., 94, 372
Sengul, C. J., 148
Shakespeare, W., 206
Shank, D. M., 194, 211
Shepard, R. N., 44, 247
Shiffrin, R. M., 35, 85, 97, 235,
    249, 253, 254, 256, 257,
    261, 267, 268, 273, 274,
    275, 276
Shinjo, M., 320
Shoben, E. J., 34
Sidner, C., 156
Silfies, L. N., 288, 290, 323
Simon, H. A., 2, 3, 29, 31, 235,
    366, 392, 394, 396, 397,
    398, 412
Simons, W. H. G., 180
Sinatra, G. M., 312
Singer, M., 193, 216, 244, 251,
    264
Skinner, B. F., 20

Smith, E. E., 34, 35
Smolensky, P., 169
Songer, N. B., 309f, 311, 313,
   315f, 316f, 318, 320, 323
Spence, K. W., 20
Squire, L. R., 25, 26
Stanners, R. F., 297
Stanovich, K. E., 283
Staszewski, J. J., 235
Staub, F. C., 347
Steedman, M., 172, 173
Steinhart, D. J., xvi, 133, 134,
   135
Stern, E., 345, 346, 354, 355,
   356, 357
Sternberg, S., 219
Stigler, J. W., 333
Streby, W. J., 221, 285
Suchman, L. A., 23
Suh, S., 194, 198
Swinney, D. A., 127, 128, 129,
   131

Tapiero, I., xv, 266
Taraban, R., 170, 171
Taylor, H. A., 201
Tegthsoonian, M., 248
Thagard, P., 394, 402, 403, 404,
   406, 408
Thompson, M. A., 289
Thomson, D. M., 248, 250
Thurlow, R., 198, 199
Till, R. E., 101, 131, 132, 133,
   134, 198, 228, 286
Tolman, E. C., 20
Trabasso, T., 193, 194, 198, 270,
   285, 286
Trevarthen, C., 22

Truxaw, C., 358, 363
Tulving, E., 250
Turner, T. J., 37, 82
Tversky, A., 399, 400, 414, 415,
   416
Tversky, B., 201
Tyler, L. K., 148

Underwood, B. J., 248

Valla, G., 127
van den Broek, P., xvi, 198, 199,
   270, 285, 286, 320
van Dijk, T. A., 37n, 38, 39, 49,
   50, 66, 67, 68, 69–70, 95,
   102, 118, 174, 184, 216,
   223, 234, 264, 265, 278, 334
VanLehn, K., 386
Varma, S., xvi, 99, 235
Varner, K. R., 284
Varnhagen, C. K., 282–3, 285,
   286
Verschaffel, L., 341
Vesonder, G. T., 297
von Humboldt, W., 32
Vonk, W., 180, 195–6, 197
Voss, J. F., 288, 290, 297, 323
Vygotsky, L. S., 323

Walker, C. H., 251, 254, 287, 289
Walker, W. H., 83, 274, 299
Wallace, W. T., 212
Wanner, E., 70
Warrington, E. K., 24
Weaver, C. A., xv, 420
Weimer, R., 54, 338, 339, 340,
   344, 345, 346, 347, 354, 359
Weinert, F. E., 287, 355

Weisskranz, L., 24
Welsch, D. M., 78, 95, 251, 252f, 253f
Wenger, E., 358, 363
Wertheimer, M., 290
White, C. R., 136, 137t, 139, 142, 144
Whitney, P., 37, 244
Wilhelm, G., 32
Wilson, B., 127
Wisniewski, E. J., 35
Witte, R. S., 20

Wolfe, M. B., xvi, 275, 276, 324, 326f, 327
Worthy, J., 329

Yarborough, J. J., 68
Yekovich, F. R., 251, 254, 289
Young, E., 107, 360, 361, 364, 366, 367f

Zimny, S., xvi, 251, 252f, 253f
Zola, D., 283
Zwann, R. A., 198

Subject Index

abstract representation, 18
action planning
  graphics application, 387–92
  routine computing, 372–81
  UNIX, 381–7
affordance, 23
algebra word problems, 358–64
  ANIMATE tutor, 364–9
anaphora, 144–57
architecture of cognition, 5–7
arithmetic word problems
  errors, 339–45
  schema, 337–8, 354–8
  situation models, 347
  types, 335–6
associative nets, 35

behaviorism, 20
buffer, memory
  intermediate stores, 124–8
  short-term memory in read-
    ing, 34–5

cognitive development, 27–9
coherence
  levels, 39
  matrix, 98, 103

role in learning from text,
  307–13
concepts, 74
consciousness, 418
construction–integration model
  story comprehension, 268–73
  word arithmetic problems,
    347–54
contradictions in text, 93–103,
  181–4
cycles of processing in comprehension, 101

decision making, 399–402,
  414–17
declarative memory, 25
direct and indirect representation, 20
discourse focus, 154

emergent structures, 82–6,
  354–8
emotion, 22, 419–21
encapsulated meaning, 42–4
episodic memory
  in text comprehension, 224–6
episodic representation, 17

errors
  in arithmetic word problems,
    339–45
  in skilled performance, 387–92

feature, 34, 41
frame, 36, 41
free recall, 117
  simulation of story recall,
    268–77
  of text, 264–80

habit system, 24, 27
homographs, 128–36

imagery, 18, 30, 44–7, 108–11
implicit memory, 25
impression formation, 402–9
inferences, 97
  classification, 188–92
  in discourse, 193–97
  in learning from text, 307,
    313–23
  time course, 198, 229
information processing theory,
  6–7
interest, 418–9
interrupting reading, 222–3,
  230–1

knowledge activation, 97
  in text comprehension,
    227–34
knowledge net, 74

latent semantic analysis, 86–91
  decision making, 399–402,
    414–17
  essay grading, 325

macrostructures, 184–8
matching students and texts,
  323–7
metaphor comprehension,
  158–65
retrieval structures, 235–8
summaries, 277–80
word meanings, 130–44
learning from text
  active processing, 313–23,
    329
  advance organizer, 321–23
  domain knowledge, 313–23
  matching students and texts,
    323–7
  measurement, 295–302
  vs. memory for text, 290–3
  simulation, 293–5, 302–7
levels of representation, 49
  in sentence recognition,
    251–3, 258–64
literary texts, 205–6
  comprehension strategies,
    211–13

macrostructure, 50, 64–9, 181–4
  formation, 174–7
  as LSA vectors, 184–8
  signaling, 177–80
  topic shift, 179–80
meaning
  of paragraphs, 185–7
  of words, 77, 123–4, 130–6
mental representation
  embedding of levels, 30
  redescription, 30
  role of culture, 31
  role of environment, 31
  types, 15, 16

metaphor, 157–65
microstructure, 50, 54, 292
motivation, 413–18

narrative representation, 18
novice and expert planning,
    381–7

parsing of sentences in the
    CI-model, 168–74
perceptual representation, 21
predicate-argument schema, 37
priming, 73, 130–44
problem model, 107, 337–8,
    339–45
problem solving, 394–8
procedural representation, 17
production rule, 42, 373
proposition
    atomic, 37, 273
    complex, 38, 273
    psychological reality, 69–73
propositional networks, 37
propositionalizing text, 54–60
propositional representations
    of knowledge, 73–82
    of text, 32, 33, 49–54

reading skills
    decoding, 282–3
    domain knowledge, 287–90,
        328
    language skills, 283–7
reading span, 239
recognition memory
    importance effects, 253–7
    levels of representation,
        258–64

sentence recognition, 251–3
    for text, 247–64
reconstructive recall, 265,
    288–90
retrieval structure, 76, 224–34
    modeled by LSA, 345–8
rhetorical schemas, 68

schema, 36, 41, 82–6, 94
    in word problems, 337–8,
        354–8, 360–4
script, 36, 41, 82–6, 111–18
self
    representation of, 409–13
semantic memory, 30
semantic nets, 36, 41, 75
situated cognition, 23, 378
situation model, 49, 103–7,
    108–18
    in arithmetic word problems,
        345–7
    in literary texts, 209–11
    spatial situation models,
        199–204
skilled memory, 217–21
summaries, 118, 277–80
system model, 107, 371

textbase, 49, 103–7, 232, 290

versification, 206–9

working memory, 126, 215–21
    long-term working memory,
        219–21
    representation of self, 409–13

zone of learnability, 323–7